Coleridge's Notebooks

Coleridge's Notebooks

A Selection

Edited by
SEAMUS PERRY

OXFORD
UNIVERSITY PRESS
Great Clarendon Street, Oxford, OX2 6DP
Oxford University Press is a department of the University of Oxford.
It furthers the University's objective of excellence in research, scholarship,
and education by publishing worldwide in
Oxford New York
Auckland Bangkok Buenos Aires Cape Town Chennai
Dar es Salaam Delhi Hong Kong Istanbul Karachi Kolkata
Kuala Lumpur Madrid Melbourne Mexico City Mumbai Nairobi
São Paulo Shanghai Singapore Taipei Tokyo Toronto
and an associated company in Berlin
Oxford is a registered trade mark of Oxford University Press
in the UK and certain other countries
Published in the United States
by Oxford University Press Inc., New York

First published 2002

British Library Cataloguing in Publication Data
Data available
Library of Congress Cataloging in Publication Data
Data available
ISBN 0-19-871201-4
1 3 5 7 9 10 8 6 4 2
Typeset in Caslon
by Regent Typesetting, London
Printed in Great Britain
on acid-free paper by
T.J. International Ltd,
Padstow, Cornwall

Contents

Preface

I should first express my thanks to Mrs Joan Coleridge for her kind encouragement at an early stage of this selected edition. My principal indebtedness is to the British Library, which holds the manuscripts from which these entries have been transcribed: my thanks to the staff of the manuscript reading room, who have been unfailingly helpful and efficient. I am also most grateful for permission to consult the photocopies of many of the notebooks held by Jesus College, Cambridge, and thank especially Dr Frances Willmoth for her great assistance. Anyone working on Coleridge owes an immense debt to the extraordinary scholarship of the late Kathleen Coburn, editor of *The Notebooks of Samuel Taylor Coleridge* and general editor of the Bollingen *Collected Works of Samuel Taylor Coleridge*, as well as to the individual editors in that remarkable enterprise, and to the late E. L. Griggs, editor of Coleridge's letters. My own debt will be clear from the pages of commentary below. I wish to thank my colleagues in the Department of English Literature at Glasgow for their characteristic generosity with advice and scholarship, and especially Robert Cummings. The study-weekends and biennial conference held by the Friends of Coleridge never fail to rouse Coleridgean spirits; my students at the Bread Loaf Graduate School of English, held at Lincoln College, Oxford, annually confirmed me in my enthusiasm; and Lucy Newlyn, Nicholas Roe, and Jane Stabler kindly encouraged me along in-between. At Oxford University Press, Sophie Goldsworthy, Fiona Kinnear, and, especially, Frances Whistler have, at different stages, looked after the book with more than exemplary care and terrific patience; and I am most grateful to my copy-editor, Jackie Pritchard. Pauline Perry made my visits to London possible and then comfortable. I am much indebted to Nicola Trott for help of all sorts, as ever.

Coleridge's words are his own, but my share of the book I dedicate with admiration and affection to Nick and Jane.

S. P.

Glasgow, December 2001

Introduction

1. Coleridge and the Notebook

Samuel Taylor Coleridge (1772–1834) is one of the most remarkable writers and thinkers in one of English Literature's most remarkable periods; and his Notebook is one of its masterpieces—perhaps the unacknowledged prose masterpiece of the age. It is well known to Coleridge scholars, of course, who refer to it habitually; and it has always had some noble champions outside the Coleridgean establishment (Geoffrey Grigson was a great admirer). But, on the whole, it has remained an undiscovered treasure to the general reader, the lover of poetry, and even the non-specialist student. Which is a great pity: for it is an astonishing and eminently readable document, a work, by turns, of philosophical profundity, descriptive beauty, verbal brilliance, and human comedy (and sometimes tragicomedy; and sometimes tragedy). The Notebook was an almost-lifelong companion; and at times—for though a gregarious man, he was often quite alone—it was Coleridge's only associate, to which he entrusted his most private thoughts. 'Since I left you', he wrote to Wordsworth in 1812, as they sought to patch up their catastrophic falling-out of eighteen months before, 'my Pocket books have been my only full Confidants' (*CL* iii. 408); and four years before that, he had addressed the 'dear Book! Sole Confidant of a breaking Heart' (*CN* iii. 3325): its pages record one of the most protracted, and most deeply plumbed, acts of what Coleridge himself called (in an early version of 'Frost at Midnight') 'the self-watching subtilizing mind'—in another phrase, 'the flux and reflux of the mind in all its subtlest thoughts and feelings' (*CPW* i. 241 n.; *BL* ii. 21).

What sort of mind was it? No other great English poet has been, at once, so intent and omnivorous an intellectual, so predisposed to cross the apparently firm boundaries between discrete kinds of thought; and the full diverse range of his mind is best on show here. One of the most abiding insistences of his thinking life was the virtue of bringing various things, even things opposite, into coincidence or reconciliation: 'Extremes Meet' was his favourite proverb. He considered the poet's imagination to be one venue for the unified meeting of diverse things: as he writes in *Biographia Literaria*, the imagination 'reveals itself in the balance or reconciliation of opposite or discordant qualities' (*BL* ii. 16);

and the Christian philosopher's mind, instinct with 'that ultimate end of human Thought, and human Feeling, Unity', was another such place. His capacity to be so stirred by the paradoxical aspiration to find '"the reconciliation of '*the many*' with '*the one*'—of a *plurality with unity*["]' (*SWF* i. 278) derives in large part, you suspect, because it describes so encompassingly his own central experience. He was drawn throughout his career by the idea of a single great work—be it an epic poem or an immense treatise upon the Logos—which would work an effect of colossal reconciliation upon the many diverse elements of his thought; but he became notorious for abandoning his works in a fragmentary state (like 'Kubla Khan' and 'Christabel') or publishing them in an undisguisedly provisional or incomplete form (*Biographia* has several chapters missing) or not managing to write them at all (no author has promised—to himself, to friends, to publishers, to the public—so many unwritten works). The problem stopping him stemmed not from any particular lack of staying power or humble organizational capacity, but rather (in John Beer's words) 'from the nature of the elements he was trying to reconcile':[1] the elements were so diverse, his commitment to their synthesis so intimidatingly strong.

Journalism, an occasional and impermanent form, enablingly slackened his self-imposed expectations;[2] the circumstances of marginalia, letters, conversation, all worked similarly. But it was the Notebook, in its unplanned, unfolding, various existence, which allowed his multiform genius its natural outlet. His professed ultimate 'end', that vast and inclusive 'Unity', inspires the Notebook's tremendous drive for inclusiveness (nothing is irrelevant, for everything must find a place somewhere); but the Notebook's moment-to-moment life testifies to quite a different sort of truth: not unity and encompassing synthesis at all, but his mind's immense and multiple activity, in all its unmeeting extremes.[3] His response to Kantian philosophy stands here next to exquisite accounts of the sun setting in Borrowdale, his remarkable dream analysis beside his responses to politics, close readings of poems and high-spirited etymological speculations next to jokes and puns and stories and Irish bulls, breathlessly immediate accounts of climbing the Cumbrian mountains

[1] John Beer, *Romantic Influences: Contemporary—Victorian—Modern* (Basingstoke, 1993), 17.

[2] See Zachary Leader, 'Coleridge and the Uses of Journalism', in Jeremy Treglown and Bridget Bennett (eds.), *Grub Street and the Ivory Tower: Literary Journalism and Literary Scholarship from Fielding to the Internet* (Oxford, 1998), 22–40.

[3] I try to describe the special Coleridgean place of the Notebook as a genre in my *Coleridge and the Uses of Division* (Oxford, 1999), 31.

next to delightful (and delighted) observations of his children growing up, and desperate outpourings of love-forsaken grief. The sometimes forbidding compulsions of his metaphysics appear here, literally, mingled with the events of his often fraught personal life—a proximity which implies an important truth about Coleridge: 'My philosophical opinions are blended with, or deduced from, my feelings', he once told a correspondent, '& this, I think, peculiarizes my style of Writing' (*CL* i. 279). When he announces to himself, 'Seem to have made up my mind to write my metaphysical works, as *my Life*, & *in* my Life—intermixed with all the other events / or history of the mind & fortunes of S.T. Coleridge', critics often catch a first glimpse of *Biographia Literaria*, his philosophical autobiography; we could equally see it as an inadvertent description of the Notebook too.

He can write at times with an analogical turn for aphorism that one might almost take for a Wittgenstein ('To *think* of a thing is different from to *perceive it*, as "to walk" is from "to feel the ground under you"'); sometimes with a haunting directness and intimacy ('As I have been falling to sleep, the thought of you has come upon so strongly, that I have opened my eyes as if to look at you —'); or, again, in a voice of rueful self-portraiture ('I lay too many Eggs in the hot Sands of this Wilderness, the World! with Ostrich Carelessness, & Ostrich Oblivion'). Sometimes, he writes vividly about the ancient philosophical problems that preoccupied him, transforming them into a wholly personal idiom:

Poem on Spirit – or on Spinoza – I would make a pilgrimage to the Deserts of Arabia to find the man who could make [me] understand how the *one can be many*! Eternal universal mystery! It seems as if it were impossible; yet it *is* – & it is every where! –

And there are many other voices, including eerie (sometimes funny) reportings of his dream life, on which he bestows an unprecedented attentiveness:

Ghost of a mountain / the forms seizing my body, as I passed, became realities – I, a Ghost, till I had reconquered my Substance /

There are too, as we would expect, some fine passages of literary criticism and poetic comment, often anticipating in more immediate and vigorous language the insights that would find a more formal and often abstract expression in his published works:

Idly talk they who speak of Poets as mere Indulgers of Fancy, Imagination, Superstition, &c – They are the Bridlers by Delight, the Purifiers, they that combine them with *reason* & order, the true Protoplasts, Gods of Love who tame the Chaos.

As Kathleen Coburn has written, the Notebook allows us 'to catch one of the great minds in human history in its wide ranges of introspection, observation, and analysis, looking at what interests him, and following his eye where his attention and imagination direct *him*'.[4] And in that mixture of 'introspection' with 'observation', our idea of Coleridge is importantly enriched. For while he was, to be sure, the intensely inward and abstracted metaphysician which his age admired (or deplored), there was also a quite different aspect to him: no one, as Humphry House once remarked, is more natively equipped to detect 'bye-ways beauty', not even Gerard Manley Hopkins—whose own *Notebooks*, which House edited, are one of the few rivals to Coleridge's (*CHH* 48). Geoffrey Grigson once anthologized some entries from Coleridge's Notebook under the title 'Things Seen';[5] and nicely so, for Coleridge, our most abstract poet-metaphysician, is also one of our greatest laureates of 'things', and no thing is self-evidently unworthy of 'a Poet intensely watching' (*CM* i. 612):

What a beautiful Thing urine is, in a Pot, brown yellow, transpicuous, the Image, diamond shaped of the Candle in it, especially, as it now appeared, I having emptied the Snuffers into it, & the Snuff floating about, & painting all-shaped Shadows on the Bottom.

Natural description could find delight in less outlandish subjects too: he was always stirred by the flight of birds; and no one has written better in English about the appearance of the sea. His accounts of walking in the hills of the Lake District and in the Trossachs are unparalleled, vivid present-tense accounts of moving through a landscape; in more subdued mood, he is one of our greatest writers about sunlight, about light effects on water, about moonlit scenery. No valley can have enjoyed such loving notice as Borrowdale in the first few years of the nineteenth century.

Critics like Hazlitt saw (and many critics continue to see) Coleridge lost in the immaterialities of consciousness, and in misty philosophies of consciousness; but the Notebook shows how one-sided a caricature that always was. As Thomas McFarland excellently says, '[t]he notebooks record the collisions of a hugely developed sense of inner reality with a hugely developed sense of outer reality, with neither sense giving ground' (*CPT* 111): he is describing the raw material of Coleridge's long thinking

[4] Kathleen Coburn, *The Self Conscious Imagination* . . . (1974), 3.
[5] Geoffrey Grigson (ed.), *The Romantics* (1942), 146.

life (though we might find as much collusion as collision); and it is here in the Notebook, that it stands revealed in its fullest Coleridgean range.

2. Publishing the Notebook

I have been referring to 'the Notebook'; but in fact there are some seventy individual volumes, of very different sizes and put to diverse sorts of purpose. The majority of them are now in the British Library in London: it is from these that I have drawn my selection. The other major holding is in the Library of Victoria College, University of Toronto; and there are smaller collections in the Berg Collection of the New York Public Library and the Huntington Library, San Marino, California. (For details, the reader should consult *CN*.)

The earliest entries, from the 'Gutch' book, are jottings in a poet's workbook, dating from the later 1790s, Coleridge's most fertile poetic period. Some notebooks are sturdy and well-bound in leather; others small pocket-books which came with a pencil. He kept some of the notebooks as desk books, copying into them, in ink, entries he had first scribbled, in pencil, in pocket-books balanced on his knee as he travelled in a coach or leant against a rock as he caught his breath at the top of a mountain, gazing about him and writing down what he saw. As the series of notebooks progresses, the entries tend to become more polished—as though he were leaving fragments ready for his disciples posthumously to publish, or to gather into attempted syntheses of their own. Coleridge seems often to have referred to the Notebook while writing, or dictating, his works: they frequently contain the first version of sentiments and arguments which he would later publish in more formal style, and sometimes he would lift passages in their entirety.

Snippets of material from the Notebook first appeared publicly in *Omniana, or Horae Otiosiores* ('About Everything, or Leisure Hours'), co-authored with Southey, and published by Longman in 1812. *Omniana* begins the tradition of making the Notebook public, which is in large part a family tradition. When, after Coleridge's death, his nephew (and son-in-law) Henry Nelson Coleridge collected the *Literary Remains* (4 vols., 1836–9), he reprinted the *Omniana* contributions in the first volume, along with some material from the Notebook, and entitled the whole section 'Omniana 1809–1816'; he had also included some likely Notebook fragments among the entries in his edition of Coleridge's *Table Talk* (1835). The devoted James Gillman, Coleridge's physician-guardian for the last two decades of his life, quoted a little from the Notebook in the first (and, as it turned out, only) volume of his *Life of Coleridge* (1838), and evidently planned to utilize more in the second volume: transcriptions existed at one stage. Some excerpts describing Coleridge's walking tours were used by E. H. Coleridge to annotate his two-volume *Letters of Samuel Taylor Coleridge* in 1895.

The first major gathering of material from the Notebook was E. H. Coleridge's *Anima Poetae: From the Unpublished Note-books of Samuel Taylor Coleridge* (1895). E. H. Coleridge improved his great-uncle's text rather more than modern practice might prefer, adding words unannounced and tweaking sentences into better shape; and the volume is without much annotation of any kind, which must have limited the choice of material included. He was also very discreet about Coleridge's unhappy love-life and his opium addiction. But his remains an immensely useful and fresh anthology; and for many years, and for many great Coleridgeans, this little book was the nearest it was possible to be to the Notebook itself. Bits and pieces re-edited from manuscript appeared in Kathleen Coburn's thoughtful selection of Coleridge's prose, *Inquiring Spirit* (1951); and then, finally, the work received the full publication it deserved when Coburn's immense edition began to appear in 1957—at which point, it is not too much to say, the study of Coleridge changed its character for ever (and for good). At the time of writing, the great edition has reached its fourth volume and 1826; and its final instalment, eagerly awaited, is being expertly guided to completion by Anthony John Harding. (There is an engaging account of how Coburn discovered and came to edit the *Notebooks* in her memoir *In Pursuit of Coleridge* [1977].[6]) Further fragments from still-unpublished notebooks have appeared in several monographs; an important if small gathering appears in H. J. Jackson's *Oxford Authors* Coleridge (1985).

3. This Selection

The diversity and range that make the Notebook so rewarding have also proved the greatest obstacle to its wider appreciation. The Coburn edition will finally conclude its task in five thick volumes of scrupulous transcriptions, accompanied by five enormous volumes of explanatory notes: it is one of the unquestionable triumphs of modern scholarship; but it is, perhaps, not the easiest book in which a novice might begin

[6] Readers of Coburn's account should also read John Beer's review: *Times Literary Supplement* (13 January 1978), 22; and see Coburn's letter of 10 February.

reading. The present selected edition (drawn entirely from material held in the British Library) obviously entertains no ambitions to rival Coburn's, to which (of course) it is much indebted. For one thing, no selection, by definition, can replicate one of the most important aspects of the Notebook: its spacious sense of lifelong development.

The intentions of this volume, more modestly, are much the same as those E. H. Coleridge stated in his preface to *Anima Poetae*:

> The aim of the present work, however imperfectly accomplished, has been to present in a compendious shape a collection of unpublished aphorisms and sentences, and at the same time to enable the reader to form some estimate of those strange self-communings to which Coleridge devoted so much of his intellectual energies, and by means of which he hoped to pass through the mists and shadows of words and thoughts to a steadier contemplation, to the apprehension if not the comprehension of the mysteries of Truth and Being. (*AP*, pp. xiii–xiv)

That is to say, I aim to offer the reader a selection of entries from the Notebook which implies its range: Coleridge watching the landscape, recollecting dreams, repeating jokes, and crying out about Sara Hutchinson, as well as Coleridge the theorist of imagination, the antagonist of Lockean empiricism, and the close reader of Shakespeare. I hope I have managed to include most of the widely noticed passages which the secondary literature about Coleridge often discusses; and some less familiar ones too. Throughout, I have tried to keep in mind which entries were likely to be of most interest to the general reader, to admirers of Coleridge's poetry and of romantic poetry more generally, and to the literary student. I have chosen not to feature in great number those entries that deal with the more abstruse reaches of Coleridge's theologico-philosophical speculations (although I have kept in some of the kind). I do not think the subject uninteresting or unimportant, needless to say; but I suppose its importance is vivid to relatively few readers; my expertise would be stretched by annotating Coleridge's later theological speculations even more severely than usual; and, anyway, the book was long enough. To much the same end, I made my cut-off date 1820 (or thereabouts): the first entries come from 1794 or 1795, so the whole selection covers a round quarter-century. (E. H. Coleridge ended his *Anima Poetae* in 1828, after which, he said in his preface, the notebooks become 'devoted for the most part to a commentary on the Old and New Testament, to theological controversy, and to metaphysical disquisition' (p. xiv); but even his selection skips through its last nine years lightly.)

I have arranged the entries in chronological order (as best I can); and I have tried to keep a thread of biographical entries running through the book, to convey some sense of the shape of Coleridge's life. I have divided the book into chapters, each terminated by important epochs in the story. Chapter 1 covers the period of Coleridge's radical youth in Bristol; his most productive time as a poet (he was writing 'Frost at Midnight', 'Kubla Khan', 'The Ancient Mariner', and the first part of 'Christabel', among others); and the most intense time of partnership with Wordsworth. Chapter 2 begins with the trip to Germany with the Wordsworths in 1798; the return to England; his discovery of the Lakes, and his fateful meeting with Sara Hutchinson; his move to Keswick; and the tour of Scotland with the Wordsworths. Chapter 3 follows him to Malta, in search of better health, and accompanies him on his travels in Italy. At the beginning of Chapter 4, he is back in England, meditating his journal *The Friend*; his marriage has fallen apart irredeemably, exacerbated by his depression and (inseparable from that) his opium addiction; and the relationship with Wordsworth is worsening; the chapter closes with his arrival in London in 1810, devastated to learn that Wordsworth had 'no hope' of him. Chapter 5 sees him established as a lecturer in London, then transplanted back to the West Country, writing *Biographia*. A brief Coda leaves him at the beginning of his new life in the Gillmans' house in Highgate, about to embark on a career as Christian Sage.

4. Further Reading

The Notebook features prominently in almost all Coleridgean criticism published since *Anima Poetae*, but it has yet to receive the full critical account it deserves as a work in its own right. Much the best single essay remains Kathleen Coburn's short but suggestive book *The Self Conscious Imagination: A Study of the Coleridge Notebooks* (1974). There are some typically suggestive pages in Thomas McFarland's *Coleridge and the Pantheist Tradition* (Oxford, 1969); William Ruddick writes finely about some of the walking entries in '"As much Diversity as the Heart that Trembles": Coleridge's Notes on the Lakeland Fells', in Richard Gravil, Lucy Newlyn, and Nicholas Roe (eds.), *Coleridge's Imagination: Essays in Memory of Pete Laver* (Cambridge, 1985), 88–101; and Raimonda Modiano has some good pages on the Notebook landscapes and seascapes in *Coleridge and the Concept of Nature* (Basingstoke, 1985), 8–26. Jane Stabler offers a brief but discriminating introduction in her *Burke to Byron, Barbauld to Baillie 1790–1830* (Basingstoke, 2002), 203–5.

Abbreviations

1. Works

Place of publication is London, unless specified otherwise. Quotations from the Bible are from the King James version; Milton is quoted from *The Poems of John Milton*, ed. John Carey and Alastair Fowler, 2nd edn. (1980); Plato from *The Collected Dialogues of Plato including the letters*, ed. Edith Hamilton and Huntington Cairns (1961; repr., Princeton, 1989); Pope from *The Poems of Alexander Pope*, ed. John Butt (1963); Scott from Sir Walter Scott, *Selected Poems*, ed. Thomas Crawford (Oxford, 1972); and Shakespeare from *The Riverside Shakespeare*, ed. G. Blakemore Evans *et al.* (Boston, 1974).

(*a*) Works by Coleridge

The *Collected Works* and the *Notebooks* are (with the exception of volume one of the *Notebooks*, published by Pantheon Books), published in Princeton by Princeton University Press; and published in London by Routledge (formerly Routledge and Kegan Paul).

AP — *Anima Poetae: From the Unpublished Notebooks of Samuel Taylor Coleridge*, ed. E. H. Coleridge (1895).

AR — *Aids to Reflection* (*Collected Works* ix), ed. John Beer (1993).

BL — *Biographia Literaria or Biographical Sketches of my Literary Life and Opinions* (*Collected Works* vii), ed. James Engell and W. Jackson Bate (2 vols.; 1983).

CL — *The Collected Letters of Samuel Taylor Coleridge*, ed. Earl Leslie Griggs (6 vols.; Oxford, 1956–71).

CM — (*a*) *Marginalia*, vols. 1–2 (*Collected Works* xii. 1–2), ed. George Whalley (1980–4); (*b*) *Marginalia,* vols. 3–5 (*Collected Works* xii. 3–5), ed. H. J. Jackson and George Whalley (1992–2000).

CN — (*a*) *The Notebooks of Samuel Taylor Coleridge*, i–iii, ed. Kathleen Coburn (each in two parts; 1957–73); (*b*) *The Notebooks of Samuel Taylor Coleridge*, iv, ed. Kathleen Coburn and Merton Christensen (in two parts; 1990). I occasionally make reference to the prefatory pages of the 'Notes' volume of each double-set: pages in volume i are abbreviated as '*CN* i (n.)', etc.

CPW *The Complete Poetical Works of Samuel Taylor Coleridge [. . .]*, ed. Ernest Hartley Coleridge (2 vols.; Oxford, 1912). Continuously paginated.

DCP *The Poetical Works of Samuel Taylor Coleridge*, ed. James Dykes Campbell (1893).

EOT *Essays on his Times* (*Collected Works* iii), ed. David V. Erdman (3 vols.; 1969).

F *The Friend* (*Collected Works* iv), ed. Barbara E. Rooke (2 vols.; 1969).

J The photocopies of Coleridge's notebooks in the Old Library, Jesus College, Cambridge.

L *Logic* (*Collected Works* xiii), ed. J. R. de J. Jackson (1981).

LL *Lectures 1808–1819 On Literature* (*Collected Works* v), ed. R. A. Foakes (2 vols.; 1987).

LPR *Lectures 1795 On Politics and Religion* (*Collected Works* i), ed. Lewis Patton and Peter Mann (1971).

LR *The Literary Remains of Samuel Taylor Coleridge*, ed. Henry Nelson Coleridge (4 vols.; 1836–9).

LS *Lay Sermons* (*Collected Works* vi), ed. R. J. White (1972).

MS Coleridge's notebooks, in the British Library (as detailed in the Census of Manuscripts, p. xxvi).

PL *Lectures 1818–19 On the History of Philosophy* (*Collected Works* viii. 1–2), ed. J. R. de J. Jackson (2 vols.; 2000). Continuously paginated.

SWF *Shorter Works and Fragments* (*Collected Works* xi), ed. H. J. Jackson and J. R. de J. Jackson (2 vols.; 1995). Continuously paginated.

TT *Table Talk Recorded by Henry Nelson Coleridge (and John Taylor Coleridge)* (*Collected Works* xiv), ed. Carl Woodring (2 vols.; 1990).

W *The Watchman* (*Collected Works* ii); ed. Lewis Patton (1970).

(*b*) Other Works

CHH Humphry House, *Coleridge* (1953).

CMI Donald Sultana, *Samuel Taylor Coleridge in Malta and Italy* (Oxford, 1969).

CPT Thomas McFarland, *Coleridge and the Pantheist Tradition* (Oxford, 1969)

CV J. B. Beer, *Coleridge the Visionary* (1959).

DWJ *The Journals of Dorothy Wordsworth*, ed. Ernest de Selincourt (2 vols.; 1941).

GLC James Gillman, *The Life of Samuel Taylor Coleridge* (only 1 vol. published; 1838).

HCR Henry Crabb Robinson, *On Books and their Writers*, ed. Edith J. Morley (3 vols.; 1938). Continuously paginated.

IR *Samuel Taylor Coleridge: Interviews and Recollections*, ed. Seamus Perry (Basingstoke, 2000).

LambL *The Letters of Charles and Mary Anne Lamb*, ed. Edwin W. Marrs (3 vols. published to date; Ithaca, NY, 1975–).

Prel. William Wordsworth, *The Prelude 1799, 1805, 1850 [. . .]*, ed. Jonathan Wordsworth, M. H. Abrams, and Stephen Gill (New York, 1979). Quotations are identified by text (*1799* or *1805*).

RX John Livingston Lowes, *The Road to Xanadu: A Study in the Ways of the Imagination*, 2nd edn. ([1930]).

WB George Whalley, 'The Bristol Library Borrowings of Southey and Coleridge, 1793–8', *Library*, 3rd series, 4 (1950), 114–32.

WEY *The Letters of William and Dorothy Wordsworth: The Early Years, 1787–1805*, ed. Ernest de Selincourt, rev. Chester L. Shaver (Oxford, 1967).

WPrW *The Prose Works of William Wordsworth*, ed. W. J. B. Owen and Jane Worthington Smyser (3 vols.; Oxford, 1974).

WPW *The Poetical Works of William Wordsworth*, ed. Ernest de Selincourt and Helen Darbishire; 2nd edn., rev. Helen Darbishire (5 vols.; Oxford, 1952–9).

2. People

CL Charles Lamb (1775–1834), essayist and poet, and fellow Christ's Hospital schoolboy; one of STC's longest-lasting and most sympathetic friends.

DC Derwent Coleridge (1800–83), STC's second surviving child.

DW Dorothy Wordsworth (1771–1855), a vital element in the Wordsworth–Coleridge collaboration: 'a woman indeed!' thought STC—'her eye watchful in minutest observation of nature—and her taste a perfect electrometer' (*CL* i. 330–1).

HC David Hartley Coleridge (1796–1849), STC's first child.

JC Joseph Cottle (1770–1835), minor poet, the publisher of STC's early volumes, and his unreliable memoirist in *Early Recollect-*

ions, Chiefly Relating to the Late Samuel Taylor Coleridge, during his Long Residence in Bristol (1837).

RS Robert Southey (1774–1843), poet (later Poet Laureate) and historian. STC first met him in 1794, in Oxford, on the way to Wales for a walking tour: they fell into league as Pantisocrats, and (in that cause) each married a Fricker sister, STC under pressure from Southey. Later, the Southeys and the Coleridges lived together in Greta Hall, RS eventually assuming 'Vice-fathership' for the Coleridge children (*CL* ii. 1062), once STC had finally separated from his wife.

SC Sara(h) Coleridge (1770–1845), née Fricker: Sara was STC's re-spelling. They married in October 1795.

SH Sara Hutchinson (1775–1835), also Asra, *Ασρα*, *ΣΑΡΑ*, and other code-names in the Notebook. She was WW's sister-in-law, and a member of the Wordsworth household. She was the object of STC's most intense feeling for more than a decade after their first meeting in 1799; she worked with STC on his periodical *The Friend*.

STC Samuel Taylor Coleridge (1772–1834).

TP Thomas Poole (1765–1837), an affluent tanner, and an important friend to STC in Nether Stowey—'the man in whom *first* and in whom alone, I had felt an *anchor!*' (*CL* i. 491).

WH William Hazlitt (1778–1830), prominent essayist and journalist: an enthusiastic young admirer of STC, and subsequently one of his most vociferous opponents.

WW William Wordsworth (1770–1850), 'the great Poet of our Age' (*AR* 404). STC first met him in Bristol in 1795, but their most intense collaboration did not begin until 1797, STC living in Nether Stowey and the Wordsworths at Alfoxden Park, a few miles away, during which time they collaborated in *Lyrical Ballads* (1798; 1800). Coleridge is the addressee of WW's autobiographical poem, posthumously published as *The Prelude*; WW is the central figure in STC's most important work of literary criticism-cum-biography, *Biographia Literaria*.

Textual Note

1. The Text

My aim has been, above all, to produce a text that presents as few obstacles to the reader as may be. Coleridge was often writing quickly: words were left out or abbreviated or crushed into edges of pages. I have occasionally added a word or a mark of punctuation (in square brackets) when I thought it eased the intended sense, and I have completed Coleridge's contractions (also using square brackets)—although I have left his contracted forms of proper nouns and normal shortenings, like 'e.g.' and 'Mem.'. In the rare cases where the contents of my square brackets actually *replace* what Coleridge wrote (such as when I am upgrading a letter from his lower-case to a capital, at the beginning of a sentence) I have said so in the Commentary. Words are missing or incomplete, sometimes, because the manuscript has deteriorated: some of the pencil, for instance, must always have been pretty dim, and has become increasingly faint; and I have recorded in the Commentary when my square brackets supply letters lost through such deterioration. (The British Library supplies small pieces of white card to save the paper from finger-tips; but even the most assiduous and dextrous reader cannot prevent some unmediated contact.) Coleridge himself sometimes uses square brackets, to mark parentheses, and I distinguish his use from mine in the Commentary: there is little chance of getting us confused anyway. (I have left Coleridge's square brackets in their original form—unlike *CN*—to make sense of a joke in entry 416.)

Where I am doubtful about a word, I have represented it thus: '[?Coleridge]'; and where I cannot make it out at all thus: '[?]'. (In both sorts of case, I have recorded the efforts of more successful previous editors in the Commentary.) Coleridge's punctuation is idiosyncratic and spontaneous: Coburn's edition rationalizes an immense array of scratches, dots, blots, lines, and squiggles into the orthographic tidiness of the dash, ' – ', and the back slash or solidus, ' / '. (This last is one of Coleridge's favourite pieces of Notebook orthography—and should not be confused with the modern printers' convention for a line-break.) Coburn's practice perhaps creates a slightly misleading sense of the Notebook's orderliness: what are really very similar dots of ink find themselves diversely recorded in *CN* as stops, commas, dashes, and slashes, as particular context seems to require. I have made *some* attempt to register Coleridge's erratic practice, using a variety of dash lengths, and I have tried not to formalize the entries too far from the layout of Coleridge's manuscript page; but the representation cannot hope to be very rigorous: what constitutes a long dash or a short one, a squiggle or a solidus, is often imponderable; and whether or not Coleridge's lineation or indenting is significant is often a very nice decision.

I have silently brought 'Dr', 'Mr', and so forth into conformity; I have instituted single inverted commas (' ') as quotation marks throughout; and I have silently tidied Coleridge's apostrophes, umlauts, and accents: these often float in very approximate relation to the letters they supposedly attend, but it seems unduly off-putting to record their places as determined by a ruler. I have also rationalized Coleridge's oddly various forms of 'o'clock'. Coleridge's underlinings are represented by *italics*; his double-underlinings by *italics underlined*; and his (rare) triple-underlinings by *italics double-underlined*. Ellipses, marked '. . .', are mine, unless acknowledged Coleridge's in the Commentary.

I have not (unlike Coburn) reproduced Coleridge's deletions. Where an addition appears to have been made at much the same time as the original entry (a single word, as it might be, added by Coleridge on a first re-reading, to make better grammatical order of a passage), I have incorporated it without notice in the text; where the addition is obviously much later, or where its incorporation would knock the sentence in question too badly out of grammatical shape, I have reserved it for the Commentary.

2. The Commentary

The Commentary cites (in the headings to each of my notes) the place of the entry in Coleridge's manuscript; the number of the entry in Coburn's edition; any other appearances the entry has made in print (in, for example, *Anima Poetae*); and, finally, the date of the entry, as it may best be ascertained. For the citation of the source, I have given Notebook number (as allocated by anonymous early readers of the manuscripts, as used by *CN*, and as detailed in the British Library manuscript catalogue); the page number (as paginated by the British Library), recto or verso (v); and, prefixed by the symbol §, the number of the entry on that page (numbering the entries on each page from the first *new* entry, and not counting the continuation of an entry from the page before). Numbering the entries on the *page* like this seems likely to be more useful than citing the number of entries in each *book* (as given by Coburn). The British Library manuscripts have been released on microfilm, and may one day perhaps be digitized (few works would gain more from the editorial flexibility of such technology): I hope my style of reference will make comparison with such reproductions relatively straightforward. I should say, there is often some dispute about where an entry ends or begins, and I have not always found myself agreeing with Coburn; however, since her apportioning of the Notebook into discrete entries will undoubtedly remain the standard, I have accepted it when numbering a page's contents. (In a small number of cases, where I have included a passage corresponding to an excerpt from within a note as printed by Coburn, my entry obviously has no § number, and I have given only the number of the page.)

Dating the entries is sometimes very easy (when Coleridge has dated them himself); sometimes imponderable. I have made my best guesses, and when entirely stumped have leant on Coburn's superior guesswork: such dates are gratefully signalled with a '(*CN*)'. The early entries, and many of the entries after 1808, are very hard to be specific about, and the reader should not place too much weight on my ordering of material from these periods without consulting Coburn's scrupulously informative notes. This is especially true of items from the Gutch Notebook, where the order can only be very approximate.

As said above, I have not recorded deletions, nor which words are subsequent additions, in the main body of the text; but where the change in question seemed significant, I have mentioned in the Commentary what has been crossed out or written over or scratched through by Coleridge, and what has been added.

I have also recorded in the Commentary a small number of textual variants: those occurring between my text and the manuscript (*MS*), where I have deviated from Coleridge for reasons of clarity (I hope without distorting his sense); and those occurring between my text and Coburn's text (*CN*), the standard edition. I have been extremely wary to differ from so surely proven an expertise: no one can ever have known Coleridge's handwriting better than Coburn. Returning to the manuscript after consulting her edition, I have on several occasions abandoned my bright reading, finding her transcription had resolved the difficulty in a much cleverer and more elegant way. Nevertheless, in a number of cases, I have risked differing, and I should record them in case readers want to make up their own minds. Divergences from the manuscript are recorded thus:

Coleridge : Coleridge's *MS.*

and divergences from the Coburn edition, thus

Coleridge : Coleridge's *CN.*

(A divergence from *MS* is usually, needless to say, the same divergence from *CN* too.) Where it seemed helpful, in those cases where it was possible, I have also enclosed in brackets the reading of another edition, thus:

Coleridge : Coleridge's *CN.* (Coleridge *AP.*)

Where I have supplied words which damage to the manuscript has now rendered (to my eyes) difficult or wholly illegible, and a previous editor has been able to discern something, I have made a note of the earlier reading, thus:

[? Coleridge] : Coleridge *AP, CN.*
[?] : Coleridge *AP, CN.*

I have not, I should emphasize, included *all* divergences from Coburn in my notes: deciding whether a 'c' is a capital or not, whether a phrase reads 'Birth day' or 'Birthday', or whether a scratch of ink is a depressed hyphen or an ascendant comma is really not a scientific pursuit; and registering my differences would be pointlessly fussy. Coleridge's capital 'N's and 'A's are often (not always) more or less large-scale versions of the lower-case letters, which complicates matters; and it is not obvious anyway what significance attaches to often apparently random capitalization in the private space of a notebook entry.

In addition to such textual matters, the Commentary seeks to explain the more obscure allusions, to tease free the tangles of Coleridge's more reckless prose, and to make some cross-references to his other writings. In the early pages especially, scraps from a poet's workshop, some kind of contextual help is essential; many of the later entries, when the idiom has become a little more formal, can practically stand on their own. I have also included, here and there, some recommendations for further reading: these are not intended to constitute a comprehensive guide to the Coleridgean topics in question, nor even to list the most comprehensive treatment of those subjects; but simply to nominate some pieces of scholarship to which the reader might usefully turn next. Further recommendations may be found in Nicola Trott's contribution to Michael O'Neill (ed.), *Literature of the Romantic Period: A Bibliographical Guide* (Oxford, 1998), which lists the most important secondary works; and readers anxious for yet more should consult the excellent Richard Haven and Walter B. Crawford and Ann M. Crawford (eds.), *Samuel Taylor Coleridge: An Annotated Bibliography of Criticism and Scholarship, 1793–1975* (3 vols.; Boston, 1976–96).

Census of Manuscripts

The manuscripts from which the present selection has been drawn are all held in the British Library, London.

Notebook	*Description*	*British Library catalogue number*
Gutch[1]	(ff. i + 89)	MS Add. 27901
2	(ff. iii+33)	MS Add. 47497
3	(ff. vii+45)	MS Add. 47498
4	(ff. iii+58)	MS Add. 47500
5	(ff. ii+62)	MS Add. 47501
5½	(ff. iv+65)	MS Add. 47502
6	(ff. iv+50)	MS Add. 47503
7	(ff. iv+75)	MS Add. 47504
8	(ff. iv+58)	MS Add. 47505
9	(ff. ii+58)	MS Add. 47506
10	(ff. iv+52)	MS Add. 47507
11	(ff. iii+54)	MS Add. 47508
12	(ff. iv+56)	MS Add. 47509
13	(ff. iii+53)	MS Add. 47510
14	(ff. iv+49)	MS Add. 47511
15	(ff. iii+126)	MS Add. 47512
16	(ff. vi+131)	MS Add. 47513
17	(ff. iii+166)	MS Add. 47514
18	(ff. iii+176)	MS Add. 47515
20	(ff. iv+45)	MS Add. 47517
21	(ff. iii+136)	MS Add. 47518
21½	(ff. iii+73)	MS Add. 47519
22	(ff. iii+95)	MS Add. 47520
24	(ff. iii+60)	MS Add. 47522
25	(ff. iii+141)	MS Add. 47523
28	(ff. iii+92)	MS Add. 47526

[1] The Gutch Notebook, separately acquired by the Library, has been more thoroughly rebound than the other notebooks, and its original appearance is difficult to deduce.

ONE

THE WEST COUNTRY 1794–1798

1 Moon at present uninhabited owing to its little or no atmosphere but may in Time – An atheistic Romance might be formed – a Theistic one too. – Mem! —

2 Little Daisy – very late Spring. March – Quid si vivat? – Do all things in Faith. Never pluck a flower again! – Mem.

3 Optimism – by having no will but the will of Heaven, we call in Omnipotence to fight our battles! —

4 This is the true Sublime of Man!
this the meridian Majesty of our Nature!

5 What (Burke's book) repugnant feelings did it excite? I shuddered while I praised it – a web wrought with admirable beauty from a black bag of Poison!

6 Real Pain can alone cure us of imaginary ills! We feel a thousand miseries till we are lucky enough to feel Misery.

7 What we *must* do, let us love to do. It is a noble Chemistry, that turns Necessity into Pleasure!

8 Poetry, like schoolboys, by too frequent & severe correction, may be cowed into Dullness! —

9 — peculiar, not far-fetched – natural, but not obvious; delicate, not affected; dignified, not swelling; fiery, but not mad; rich in Imagery, but not loaded with it – in short, a union of harmony, and good sense; of pers[p]icuity, and conciseness[.] Thought is the *body* of such an Ode, Enthusiasm the Soul, and Imagination the Drapery! —

10 Upas Tree – a poem – or article. Mem.

11 Protoplast –

12 People starved into War – over an enlisting place in Bristol a quarter of Lamb and piece of Beef hung up —

13 Wandering Jew – a romance.

14 A Robber concealed over a room and hearing the noise of mirth & dancing – his Reflections / — —

15 Shivers in nakedness

16 The Whale followed by *Waves* – I would glide down the rivulet of quiet Life, a Trout! ——

17 — Bad means for a good end – I cannot conceive that there can be any road to Heaven through Hell —

18 My Clock here (patting his guts) chime[s] twelve —

19 Leaves already on the walk scattered —

20 Poetry without egotism comparatively uninteresting —
Mem. Write an Ode to *Meat & Drink*

21 When a man is attempting to describe another's character, he may be right or he may be wrong – but in one thing he will always succeed, in describing himself[.] If he express simple approbation, he praises from a consciousness of possession – If he approve with admiration, from a consciousness of deficiency[.] A. Ay! he is a *sober* man. – B. Ah Sir! what a 5
blessing is sobriety. N.B. A is a man conscious of sobriety who egotizes in tuism – B is one, who feeling the ill effects of a contrary habit[,] with blameless envy contemplates sobriety – – A. Yes! he is a warm man[,] a moneyed fellow – you may rely on him. B. Yes! Yes! Sir! No wonder! he has the blessing of being well in the world. 10

After the first violence of recentment when the heart is dephlogisticated —

To introduce this reflection in defence of plaintive egotism – and to examine all the charges against it – and from what feelings they proceed.

22 (Pantis[ocracy].) Themes to debauch Boys' minds
on the miseries of rich men & comforts of Poverty.

23 The poor and the rich in this resemble each other – they are usually unloving of their children – n.b. explain why.

24 Unitarian – travelling from Orthodoxy to Atheism – why? &c.

25 Property intended to secure to every man the produce of his Toil – as at present instituted, operates directly contrarywise to this. *Nota bene.*

26 Poetry – excites us to artificial feelings – makes us callous to real ones.

27 God no distance knows
All of the whole possessing. —

28 Our Constitution to some like Cheese – rotten parts they like the best.

29 Love and the wish of Poets when their tongue
Would teach to other bosoms what so charms
Their own.

Akenside.

30 Not to bring too horrid things like Gloucester's eyes on the stage [–] reprobate this notion – hysterical Humanité

31 Art of Printing diffused greater knowledge than Christianity – ?? –

32 Reviews –, a kind of establishment.

33 Dr Darwin's Poetry, a succession of Landscapes or Paintings – it arrests the attention too often, and so prevents the rapidity necessary to pathos – it makes the great little.
— seems to have written his poem as Painters who of beautiful Objects take Studies. 5

34 Millen[n]ium, an History of, as brought about by progression in natural philosophy – particularly, meteorology or science of airs & winds – Quære – Might not a Commentary on the Revelations be written from late philosophical discoveries –?.

35 as difficult
as to separate two dew-drops
blended together on a bosom
of a new-blown Rose.

36 a belly of most majestic periphery!

37 as prolix as the tale of some wretch at the gallows who had expected a Reprieve – tale to his confessor

38 Doctrine of necessity rendered not dangerous by the Imagination which contemplates immediate not remote effects — hence Vice always hateful & altho' equally [? monotonous] as Virtue

39 *My Works*

- Imitations of the Modern Latin Poets with an Essay Biog[raphical] & Crit[ical] on the Rest[oration] of Lit[erature] – 2 vol. Octavo.
- Answer to the System of Nature – Oct[avo].
- The Origin of Evil, an Epic Poem. 5
- Essay on Bowles
- Strictures on Godwin, Paley &c &c –
- Pantisocracy, or a practical Essay on the abolition of Indiv[id]ual Property.
- Carthon an Opera 10
- Poems.
- Edition of Collins & Gray with a preliminary Dissertation
- A Liturgy
- A Tragedy
- On the different Sects of Religion & Infidelity. – philosophical analysis of their Effects on mind & manners – . 15

40 Six Gallons of Water -
Twelve pounds of Sugar
Half a pound of Ginger
Eighteen Lemons.

Ginger to be sliced – Lemons to be peeled – The Sugar & Water to be boiled together, & the Scum – viz – the Monarchical part[–]must go to Pot – and out of the Pot – *Then* put in the Ginger with the Peels of the Lemons, and let the whole be boiled together gently for half an hour – When cold, put in the Lemon juice strained &c — then let the Sum total be put in the Barrel with three spoonfuls of Yeast – let it work three Days (Sundays Excepted –) and then put in a Gallon Barrel – Close up the Barrel – Nota bene – you may do it legally the habeas corpus act being suspended – let it remain a fortnight then bottle it. – The Wine not to be used even in warm weather till three Weeks after Bottling – in Winter not till after a month.— 15

41 Very fond of Vegetables, particularly Bacon & Peas. Bacon & Broad Beans. –

42 Mem. To reduce to a regular form the Swedenborgian's Reveries.

43 Mem. – To remember to examine into the Laws upon Wrecks as at present existing

44 Poem in one Book in the manner of Dante on the excursion of Thor –

45 1 An Essay on Tobit.
2 On the art of prolonging Life – by getting up in a morning.
3. On Marriage – in opposition to French Principles.
4. Jacob Behmen.
5 Life of John Henderson. 5
6 Ode to a Looking Glass.
7 Burnet's de montibus in English Blank Verse.
8 Escapes from Misery, a Poem –
Halo round the Candle – Sigh visible
9. Cavern – candle – 10
10 Life of David – a Sermon.
11. Wild Poem on Maniac – *Εραστ[ου] Γαληρος. ἀτ.*
12. Ode on St Withold.
13. Crotchets, by S.T. Coleridge —
14. Edition of Akenside 15
15 Of Collins and Gray –
16 Hymns to the Sun, the Moon, and the Elements – six hymns. —
In one of them to introduce a dissection of Atheism – particularly the Godwinian System of Pride —
Proud of what? an outcast of blind Nature ruled by a fatal Necessity – 20
Slave of an ideot Nature! – × ‡
17 Letters to Godwin
18 Randolp[h] consecrating D[uke]. of York's banners —
19 Ode to Southey
× Deprœliantiûm e carcere nubium &c 25
20 Egomist, a metaphysical Rhapsody —
21. Berkley's Maxims –
Vol. II 345.
‡ In the last Hymn a sublime enumeration of all the charms or Tremendities of Nature – then a bold avowal of Berkley's 30 System !!!!.
Ode to a Moth – against accumulation.
22 Adventures of *Christian*, the mutineer. ——
23 Military anecdotes – (N.B. promised to be Sergeants.[)]
24 History of Phrases – Ex. gr. The King must have men. 35

25 Hymn to Dr Darwin – in the manner of the Orphics.
26 Address to the Clergy against the Two Bills –
27 Satire addressed to a young Man who intended to study medicine at Edingburgh –

46 A Reader of Milton must be always on his Duty: he is surrounded with sense; it rises in every line; every word is to the purpose. There are no lazy intervals: all has been considered and demands & merits observation.

If this be called obscurity, let it be remembered [']tis such a one as is complaisant to the Reader – : not that vicious obscurity, which proceeds 5 from a muddled head &c –

47 stood up beautiful before God —

48 Nature
Wrote Rascal on his face by chalcographic art

49 Our quaint metaphysical opinions in an hour of anguish like playthings by the bedside of a child deadly sick.

50 Dreams sometimes useful by giving to the well-grounded *fears* & *hopes* of the understanding the *feelings* of vivid sense.

51 Love transforms the souls into a conformity with the object loved —

52 The prayers of [the] enthusiast a pious drunkenness, a spiritual concupiscence, presumptuous self-idolatry –

53 Made my heart tender thro' the power of Love – my mind preserved watchful & *inward*

54 Such fierce vivacity as fires the eye
Of Genius fancy-craz'd –

55 like a mighty Giantess,
Seized in sore travail & prodigious birth
Sick Nature struggled: long & strange her pangs,
Her groans were horrible; but o! most fair –
The Twins, she bore – *Equality* & *Peace*! 5

56 In the Essay on Berkley to speak of Sir Isaac Newton & other material theists – Aristotle, Metaphys[ics]. Lib I. Chapter IV.267 of Tom IV

57 In a distempered dream things & forms in themselves common & harmless inflict a terror of anguish. —

58 At Genoa the word, Liberty, is engraved on the chains of the galley-slaves, & the doors of Prisons. —

59 Hymns [–] Moon
In a cave in the mountains of Cashmere an Image of Ice, which makes its appearance thus – two days before the new *moon* there appears a bubble of Ice, which increases in size every day till the 15th day, at which it is an ell or more in height: then as the moon decreases, the Image does also till it vanishes. 5
Read the whole 107th page of Maurice's Indostan —

60 An ideot whose whole amusement consisted in looking at, & talking to a clock – which he supposed to be alive – / the Clock was removed – / he supposed that it had walked off – & he went away to seek it – – was absent nine days – at last, they found [him], almost famished in a field. – He asked where it was buried – for he was sure it was dead – / he was brought 5 home & the clock [put] in its place – his Joy – &c. He used to put part of every thing, he liked, into the clock-case.

61 The swallows interweaving there
Mid the paired sea-mews,
at distance wildly-wailing. —
The brook runs over
Sea-weeds. — 5
Sabbath day – from the
Miller's mossy wheel
the waterdrops dripp'd
leisurely —
on the broad mountain[-top] 10
The neighing wild-colt races with the wind
O'er fern & heath flowers —
a long deep Lane
So overshadow'd, it might seem one bower—
The damp Clay banks were furr'd with mouldly moss 15
Broad-breasted Pollards, with broad-branching head.

62 — the prophetic soul
Of the wide world dreaming on things to come.
Shak[espeare's] sonnets.

Most true it is, that I have look'd on truth
Askance & strangely. 5
Id.

63 Behind the thin
Grey cloud that cover'd but not hid the sky
The round full moon look'd small.—

64 The subtle snow in every breeze rose curling from the Grove, like pillars of cottage smoke.

65 — Hartley fell down & hurt himself – I caught him up crying & screaming – & ran out of doors with him. – The Moon caught his eye – he ceased crying immediately – & his eyes & the tears in them, how they glittered in the Moonlight!

66 — Some wilderness-plot, green & fountainous & unviolated by Man.

67 A dunghill at a distance sometimes smells like musk, & a dead dog like elder-flowers. —

68 Plagiarists *suspicious* of being pilfer'd – as pick pockets are observed commonly to walk with their hands in their breeches-pockets.

69 The Infant playing with its Mother's Shadow —
Rocking its little sister's cradle & singing to her with inarticulate voice. —

70 The flat pink-colour'd stone painted over in jagged circles & strange parallelograms with the greenish black-spotted lichens. —

71 The Sun-shine lies on the cottage-wall
A shining thro' the snow –

72 The picture of a horse sprawling – you have got [it] the wrong way – [']tis a horse galloping

73 [']Twas not a mist, nor was it quite a cloud,
But it pass'd smoothly on towards the Sea
Smoothly & lightly betwixt Earth & Heaven.
So thin a cloud –
It scarce bedimm'd the Star that shone behind it. 5

And Hesper now
Paus'd on the welkin's blue & cloudless brink,
A golden circlet! while the Star of Jove,
That other lovely Star, high o'er my head
Shone whitely in the center of his Haze. 10

— one black-blue cloud
Stretched, like the heaven, o'er all the cope of Heaven

74 Doing nothing ends in being nothing. —

75 old, palsied, & toothless generalities —

76 Snails of intellect, who see only with their Feelers. –

77 The reed-roof'd Village, still bepatch'd with snow
Smok'd in the sun-thaw.

78 Infancy and Infants —

1 The first smile – what kind of *reason* it displays – – the first smile after sickness. —
2 Asleep with the polyanthus held fast in its hand, its bells drooping over the rosy face — 5
3. Stretching after the stars. —
4. Seen asleep by the light of glowworms.
5. Sports of infants – their incessant activity, the *means* being the end. – Nature how lovely a school-mistress – A blank-verse, moral poem – children at houses at Industry. — 10
6 Infant beholding its new born Sister.
7 Kissing itself in the looking-glass
8 The Lapland Infant, seeing the Sun.
9. An infant's prayer on its mother's Lap / mother directing a Baby's hand. Hartley's love to Papa – scrawls pothooks, & reads what he *meant* 15 by them. —
10 The infants of Kings & Nobles, – Princess unkissed & foully husbanded – & the infants of the very poor, especially in cities.
15. Poor Williams seeking his Mother, in love with her Picture – & having that vision of Beauty & filial affection, that the Virgin Mary may 20 be supposed to give.
11 The Souls of Infants, a vision – (vide Swedenborg —)
12. Some tales of an Infant.

16. Exhort a young man to despise wealth, & marry a beautiful woman – at all events marry for Love. — 25
13 Στοργη – the absurdity of the Darwinian System – Birds – Allegators.
14. The wisdom & graciousness of God in the infancy of the human species – its beauty, long continuance &c &c.
Children in the wind – hair floating, tossing, a miniature of the agitated Trees, below which they play'd – the elder whirling for joy, the one in 30 petticoats, a fat Baby, eddying half willingly, half by the force of the Gust – driven backward, struggling forward – both drunk with the pleasure, both shouting their hymn of Joy.

TWO

GERMANY, LONDON, THE LAKES 1798–1804

79 Tuesday Night [September] 18th, 1798.
Over what place does the Moon hang to your eye, my dearest Sara? To me it hangs over the left bank of the Elbe and a long trembling road of moonlight comes transversely / from the left bank, reaches the stern of our Vessel, & there it ends. – We have drop[ped] anchor in the middle of 5 this grand Stream, 35 miles from Cuxhaven. We arrived at Cuxhaven this morning at eleven o'clock, after an unusually fine passage of only 48 hours – / Chester was ill the Whole time – Wordsworth shockingly ill! – Miss Wordsworth worst of all – vomiting & groaning & crying the whole time! – And I the whole time as well as I ever was – neither sick or giddy. The 10 sea rolled rather high, but I found the motion pleasant to me. – At Cuxhaven the Captain agreed that he would take us up to Hamburgh for a guinea a piece – to which we assented – & shall be there, if no fogs intervene, tomorrow morning. – The Ocean is a noble thing by night – / the foam that dashes against the vessel, beautiful[.] White clouds of 15 Foam roaring & rushing, by the side of the Vessel with multitudes of stars of flame that danced and spar[k]led & went out amidst it – light skirmishes – / First sight of land a [ba]rren Island – the main land – low, [f]lat, dreary – with light-houses & Land-marks – scarce able to hold its head above water. / – [']Tis the mouth of the Elbe – could not see but one 20 shore / Cuxhaven – / can see both in clear weather —— banks neat, & flat, & quite artificial – – Steeple & windmill, & cottage, & wind mill & house & steeple & wind mill & wind mill, & neat house, & steeple – beautiful Island 40 miles from Cuxhaven —

80 Sep[tember] 19 – Sea gulls flying about the Fishermen's Boats. Women rowing the boats with hats of various materials in the shape of punch-bowls. – –

Sep[tember] 19 – Afternoon 4 o'clock. – arrive at the Custom House. While Wordsworth went to seek an Hotel, I dashed into the town to deliver my letters of recommendation – Von Axen embarrassed me by his high & solemn politeness as well as by the difficulty he found in understanding me. I left him abruptly / called on Remnant – not at home! – Called on Mr. Chatterley / an odd beast! He asked me drily if I would take a cup of Tea. – Yes! – An old woman poured into her hand out of the Tea Cannister what *I* thought a very small portion – Oh! Oh! Oh! (exclaimed Chatterley) and she returned part of it into the Tea Cannister. – The Emigrant's Servant came & guided me to Der Wilder Man – where after much difficulty lodgings had been procured – my bedroom looked into & commanded the market-place. / – –

81 Sept[ember] 20th. – Awaked by the distressful cries of poultry crowing & clucking in the market-place. – Reviewed my expenses from Yarmouth to Hamburgh —

. . .

82 Friday, Sept[ember] 21st . . .

– 4 o'clock. Went with Klopstock to his Brother's who lives ten minutes walk from the Gates – / much disappointed in his countenance – / saw no likeness to the Bust & no comprehensiveness in the Forehead – no massiveness in the countenance in general / no expression or peculiarity in the eyes – Toothless in the upper jaw – under jaw all black Teeth / – a very lively, kind, courteous Man, who talked with Wordsworth for an hour; but shewed no great depth in any thing. He thought Glover's blank Verse superior to Milton's – & knew nothing of the older German Poets, & talked a great deal of nonsense about the superior power of concentering meaning in the German Language. – Shewed us a superb Edition of his works now printing – two Volumes, containing his Odes, printed – price 40 Shillings the Volume – / dearer than the same sort of books in England – told us that his first Ode was 50 years older than his last. I looked at him / considered him as the venerable Father of German Poetry / as a good man & a Christian / 74 years old, & with legs monstrously swelled – yet active, & lively, & chearful, & communicative / & the Tears came into my eyes / & could I have made myself invisible & inaudible, I should have wept outright. ———

In the picture of Lessing, he has a Toupee Periwig, which enormously injured the effect of his Physiognomy. – Klopstock wore the same powdered &c – / it had an ugly look. – Honor to Poets & great men. You think of them as parts of Nature / & any thing of Trick & Fashion wounds you as if you were to see epaulettes dangling from an Orange Tree. — 25

83 Oct[ober] 10th – Saw the Town of Ratzeburgh completely beautiful – 20 minutes past 5 [–] sky [–] the western with light sandy clouds [–] the East blue – blue over Ratzeburg / A red light in complete harmony with the red Town, the fading Woods, & the reeds on the Skirts of the Lake, and of the Isthmus, yellow-red, a few boats on the lake with single 5 persons paddling them.

84 Severity of the Winter – the King'sfisher, its slow short flight permitting you to observe all its colours, almost as if it had been a flower. —

85 The elder Languages fitter for Poetry because they expressed only prominent ideas with clearness, others but darkly – Therefore the French wholly unfit for Poetry; because [all] is *clear* in their Language – i.e. – Feelings created by obscure ideas associate themselves with the one *clear* idea. When no criticism is pretended to, & the Mind in its simplicity 5 gives itself up to a Poem as to a work of nature, Poetry gives most pleasure when only generally & not perfectly understood. – It was so by me with Gray's Bard, & Collins' Odes – The Bard once intoxicated me; & now I read it without pleasure. From this cause it is that what *I* call metaphysical Poetry gives me so much delight. — 10

86 A Plain man that
& whenever he wanted
to be witty, lifted up his thigh,
and let a fart — / —

87 O[']er the bridge of Rocks in whose Interstices the Foam still lay of the yester night's Torrent

Lesley Cleve Sep[tember] 11

88 The moon in thrusting thro' a thin slip of white Cloud about half her own breadth pushed with contracted point, like the narrow part of the Egg – then recovered her shape above, and her under[-]half contracted [?in the cloud].

89 Of the harm that bad Poets do in stealing & making unnovel beautiful Images.

90 The aromatic Smell of the Poplars in the fall of the Leaf

91 Celebrate this pocket book – Begin with a Dedication to the Inventor

92 Aspens – Oct[ober] 25 – one a lovely light yellow – the other red, or rather *poppy*-color'd.

93 Injury Scotchmen have done our Language —

94 – Few moments in life so interesting as those of an affectionate reception from those who have heard of you yet are strangers to your person.

95 Grasmere is a most sublime Crag, of a violet colour, patched here & there with islands of Heath plant – & wrinkled & guttered most picturesquely – contrasts with the Hills on my Right, which tho' in form ridgy & precipitous, are yet smooth & green – We pass the Inn at Scale-Hill, leaving it to our right & to our Right is Lowes Water which we see – – 5
[']tis a sweet Country that we see before us, Somersetshire Hill[s] & many a neat scattered House with Trees round of the Estates Men. – The White Houses here beautiful – / & look at the River & its two-arched Bridges – – We have curved round the Hill – the Bridges, the Plain, & Lowes Water are at my Back – & before me – O God, what a scene – — 10
the foreground a sloping wood sloping down to the River & meadows, the serpent River beyond the River & the wood meadows terminated by Melbreak walled by the Melbreak — at the end of this wall a peep of the Crummock Water and in continuation of the Melbreak, after a break, but in the same line the snowy Ridges, which seem to curve round, but a huge 15
Gable-Crag starts up in the middle & fronts me – close by my left hand a rocky woody Hill, & behind it, half hidden by it, the violet crag of Grasmere / the woody Hill leaves only the Top Third of Grasmere visible. –

I climb up the woody Hill & here have gained the Crummock Water – 20
but have lost the violet Crag —

– we pass thro' the wood, road ascending – now I am between the woody Hill / & a stone wall with trees growing over it & see nothing else – & now the Whole violet Crag rises & fronts me – Then the waters near the upper end of Crummock the archipelago of tiniest Island, 7 in number – 25
Pleiads – & two near the opposite shore

Buttermere comes upon us, a fragment of it – the view enclosed by a huge Concave Semicircle —

96 I have come suddenly upon Ulswater, running straight on the opposite Bank, till the Placefell, that noble Promontory[,] runs into it, & gives it the winding of a majestic River / a little below Place-fell a large Slice of calm silver – above this a bright ruffledness, or atomic sportiveness – motes in the sun? – Vortices of flies? – how shall I express the Banks – 5 waters all fused Silver, that House too! its slates rainwet silver in the sun, & its shadows running down in the water like a column – the Woods on the right shadowy with Sunshine, and in front of me the sloping hollow of sunpatched Fields, sloping up into Hills so playful / the playful Hills so going away in snow-streaked savage black mountain! – / 10

But I have omitted the two island Rocks in the Lake – & the colors of the Lake all changed! the one scarce-visible in the shadow-coloured Slip now bordered by the melted Silver – the other nearer to me, likewise in the glossy Shadow, but far removed from the Dazzle & quite conspicuous – the Sun, it being just past noon, hangs over the Lake – clouded so that any 15 but a weak eye might gaze on it – the clouds being in part bright white, part dusky Rain-clouds, with islets of blue Sky ——

How the scene changes – What tongues of Light shoot out from the Banks! —

We [visited] the water fall – too much water & no where ground low 20 enough to view it from / the chasm is very fine – & violet-coloured Beeches & Hawthorns quite Trees, red & purple with fruits, as if the berries were flowers – / the higher part of the water, the two streams running // athwart each other is original but where the Wheel-part is broken, it spreads into a muslin apron, & the whole water fall looks like a 25 long-waisted Lady-Giantess slipping down on her Back [–] but on the bridge where you see only the Wheel, it is very fine / it circumvolves, with a complete half-wheel

We gain the road that runs close by the Lake – the Lake so full, as in some parts to leave only the inner rim – curve round over a Bridge, fine Trees 30 between us & the Lake, thro' whose branches we glimpse the bare knobby Cliff opposite, & the Shadow of it so soft in the water –

and now I have gained the upper end of the first Reach, & look down to the other end, (towards Pooley) comprehending a long majestic Parallelogram[;] but when I stand so as to take in part of the 2nd Reach the 35 whole appears a semicircle enfolding in its two arms the convex semicircle of the bare knobby crag – but I turn my Back to the Lake / & what a Cliff / . . .

97 Sunday Morning left our bad Inn, & went down the lake by the opposite shore – the hoar-frost on the ground, the lake calm & would have been mirrorlike but that it had been *breathed* on by the mist – & that shapely White Cloud, the Day-moon, hung over the snowy mountain opposite to us — . / We passed the first *Great* Promontory, & What a scene! Where I stand, on the shore is a triangular Bay, taking in the whole of the water view – on the other shore is a straight deep wall of [?] / & one third of the bare mountains stands out from behind it – the top of the wall only in the sun – the rest black – & now it is all one deep wall of white vapour, save that black streaks shaped like strange creatures, seem to move in it & down it, in opposite direction to the motion of the great Body! – & over the forks of the Cliff behind, in shape so like a cloud, the Sun sent cutting it his thousand silky Hairs of amber & green Light – – I step two paces, and have lost the glory, but the edge has exactly the soft richness of the silver edge of a cloud behind which the Sun is travelling! —

The fog has now closed over the Lake, & we wander in darkness, save that the mist is here & there prettily color'd by the wither'd fern, over which it hovers —

98 If I begin a poem of Spinoza thus it should begin /

I would make a pilgrimage to the burning sands of Arabia, or &c &c[,] to find the Man who could explain to me [how] there can be *oneness*, there being infinite Perceptions – yet there must be a *one*ness, not an intense Union but an Absolute Unity, for &c —

99 Original? Yes! [']Tis implied in the very idea of a Monster

100 Wednesday, Nov[ember] 20th, Scotch Corner, where I was obliged for the swelling in my left foot to use a very warm Foot-bath. I found perpetually that the first Plunge into very warm Water produces precisely the same sensation, as a Plunge into exceedingly cold Water would.

101 N.B. to write a History of Levellers –

102 The long Entrancement of a True-love's Kiss.

103 Nov[ember] 29. Evening – The unmoveableness of all things thro' which so many men moved – harsh contrast! – Compared too with the universal motion of things in Nature.

104 Mackintosh intertrudes, not introduces his beauties. [N]othing grows out of his Main argument but much is shoved between / each digression occasions a move backward to find the road again – like a [si]ck man he recoils after every aff[?liction. The] Serpent by which the ancients emblem'd the Inventive faculty appears to me in its mode of motion most 5 exactly to emblem a writer of Genius. He varies his course yet still glides onwards – all lines of motion [are] his – all beautiful, & all propulsive –

Circular base of rising folds
that tower'd Fold above
fold a surging maze, 10
his Head Crested aloft,
and Carbuncle his eyes
With burnish'd Neck of
verdant Gold, erect Amidst
the circling spires that on the 15
Grass Floted Redundant —
So varied he & of his
tortuous train Curls many a
wanton wreath; yet still
he proceeds & is proceeding. — 20

105 Sunday – Dec[ember] 21, 1799, Hartley said – When I'm a man, I'll get a Ladder, & get up to the Sky, & pick out the Stars, & give them to Anny Sealy – I'll pick 'em out with a knife —

106 To have a continued Dream, representing visually & audibly all Milton's Paradise Lost.

107 Shakespere makes ignorant men describe Character

108 A great Vice is *metaphysical Solution* in Poetry

109 The varyingness of Lakes – Ulswater – Clarkson — in London lose your way from sameness – in country can't find it for variety

110 a cracked Looking-glass – such is man's mind – Spinoza

111 slanting pillars of misty light moved along under the Sun hid by clouds.

112 Leaves of Trees upturned by the stirring wind in twilight – an image for paleness from affright.

113 Two drunken men, arm in arm, the one imagining himself sober, the other acknowledging himself drunk, the former *acting* the other's leader & care-taker. June 2. 1800

114 Ladies reading Gilpin's &c while passing by the very places instead of looking at the places.

115 Poor fellow at a distance [–] idle? in this hay time when wages are so high? Come near – thin, pale, can scarce speak – or throw out his fishing rod.

116 An eminently beautiful Object is Fern, on a hill side, scattered thick but growing single – and all shaking themselves in the wind –

117 A Child scolding a flower in the words in which he had himself been scolded & whipt, is *poetry* / past passion with pleasure —

118 September 1 – the beards of Thistle & dandelions flying above the lonely mountains like life & I saw them thro' the Trees skimming the lake like Swallows —

119 Sunday Night ½ past 10, Septemb[er] 14. 1800 – a boy born / Bracy?

120 The most melancholy time after the death of a Friend, or Child[,] is when you first awake after your first Sleep / when the dizziness, heat, & drunkenness of Grief is gone / and the pang of hollowness is first felt.

121 Sept[ember] 27. 1800 – The child being very ill was baptized by the name of Derwent – The Child hour after hour made a noise exactly like the Creeking of a door which is being shut very slowly to prevent its creeking.

122 Sept[ember] 29. 1800 – after a most tremendous storm of Hail / the lower Half of the lake bright silver / over it & intercepting Borrodale a *thick palpable Blue* up to the moon / save that at the very top of the blue the clouds rolled lead-coloured – small detachments of these clouds running in thick flakes near the moon, & drinking its light in amber & white. – 5
The Moon in a clear azure sky – the Mountains seen indeed, and only seen – I never saw aught so sublime!

123 Princes by not moving away appear to advance / as the Moon to the Clouds.

124 Moonlight with no Moon visible – Brandel how & all the Mountains on the side of the Castle black [–] but the Castle & that high mountain on its right, in short, all Borrodale, in a white Shroud.

125 Learning without philosophy a *Cyclops*.

126 He knew not what to do – Something, he felt, must be done – he rose, drew his writing-desk suddenly before him – sate down, took the pen – & found that he knew not what to do. Octob[er] 30. 1800

127 Derwent laughed at six weeks old – the first thing he appeared to take notice of was the Trees bending &c in the strong wind – this too at 6 weeks.

128 Nov[ember] 18 – Derwent had tears in his eyes when he cried – Miss W. touched his face with her cold hands —
Hart[ley] seemed to learn to [?talk] by touching his mother

129 Friday Night, Nov[ember] 28, 1800, or rather Saturday Morning / a most frightful Dream of a Woman whose features were blended with darkness catching hold of my right eye & attempting to pull it out – I caught hold of her arm fast – a horrid feel – Wordsworth cried out aloud to me hearing [my] scream – heard his cry [&] thought it cruel he did not come / but did not wake till his cry was repeated a third time – the Woman's name Ebn Ebn Thalud – When I awoke, my right eyelid swelled –

130 Sat[urday] Nov[ember] 29 / Rydale looked more lovely than Grasmere – its fantastic variety being counteracted & counterpoised by the uniformity of the Snow every where — the sameness of Grasmere Sombrous

131 one of those thoughtful men whose plate of pudding often swims before their eyes while they are eating

132

upon a sunny Holiday
When the Bells were ringing merrily
I looked from my window
On the dazzling Lake that twinkled
Thro' the dancing Leaves of
The Trees on the Margin

133 He received a letter, knew from whom it came, determined not to read it – yet still his Heart burned, beat and was heavy – / at length he put it out of his pocket, and felt himself easier by that very act —

134 Luther – a hero[,] one fettered indeed with prejudices; but with those very fetters he would knock out the Brains of a modern Fort Esprit.

135 Children in making new words always do it analogously – explain this. –

136 Hotheaded men confuse, your cool-headed Gentry jumble, the man of warm feelings only produces order & true connections – in what a jumble M. & H. write – every third paragraph beginning with – 'Let us now return' or 'We come now to the consideration of such a thing['] – i.e. what *I said* I *would* come to in the Contents prefixed to the Chapter. — 5

137 The thin scattered rain-clouds were scudding along the Sky, above them with a visible interspace the crescent Moon hung, and partook not of the motion – her own hazy Light fill'd up the concave as if it had been painted & the colors had run. – Dec[ember] 19. 1800.

138 He to whom all things are one, who draweth all things to one, and seeth all things in one, may enjoy true peace & rest of Spirit. –

Jerome Taylor's Via Pacis.

139 To *think* of a thing is different from to *perceive it*, as 'to walk' is from [']to feel the ground under you['] – perhaps in the same way too – namely, a succession of perceptions accompanied by a sense of *nisus* & purpose.

140 Space – is it merely another word for the perception of a capability of additional magnitude – or does this very perception presuppose the idea of Space? – The latter is Kant's opinion.

141 Empirics are boastful, & Egotists[,] often because they introduce real or apparent novelty, which excites great opposition – personal opposition creates re-action (which is[,] of course, a consciousness of power) associated with the *person* reacting. Paracelsus was a boaster, it is true – so were the French Jacobins – & Wolff, tho' not a boaster, was persecuted into a 5 habit of Egotism in his philosophical writings. – So Dr John Brown – Milton, in his prose works – &c – and those in similar circumstances who from prudence abstain from Egotism in their writings, are still Egotists among their friends. / It would be unnatural effort not to be so / & Egotism in such cases is by no means offensive to a kind & discerning 10 man.

Some flatter themselves that they abhor egotism – & do not suffer it to appear prima facie either in their writings or conversation: however much & however personally they or their opinions have been opposed. – What now? – Observe, watch those men – – their habits of feeling & thinking 15 are made up of *contempt*, which is the concentrated Vinegar of Egotism, it is Lætitia mixta cum odio / a notion of the weakness of another conjoined with a notion of our own comparative strength, tho' that weakness is still strong enough to be *troublesome* to us tho' not formidable.

142 It seems to elucidate the Theory of Language, Hartley, just able to speak a few words, making a fire-place of stones, with stones for fire. / four stones – fire-place — two stones – fire / arbitrary symbols in Imagination / Hartley walked remarkably soon / & *therefore* learnt to talk rem[arkably] late.

5

143 Anti-optimism. Praised be our maker, & to the honor of our nature is it, that we may truly call this an *inhuman* opinion. Man strives after Good. —

144 Materialists unwilling to admit the mysterious of our nature make it all mysterious – nothing mysterious in nerves, eyes, &c: but that nerves think &c!! – Stir up the sediment into the transparent water, & so make all opaque.

145 — and the deep power of Joy
We see into the *Life* of Things —

i.e. – By deep feeling we make our *Ideas dim* – & this is what we mean by our Life – ourselves. I think of the Wall – it is before me, a distinct Image – here I necessarily think of the *Idea* & the Thinking I as two distinct & opposite Things. Now let me think of *myself* – of the thinking Being – the Idea becomes dim whatever it be – so dim that I know not what it is – but the Feeling is deep & steady – and this I call *I* – identifying the Percipient & the Perceived. –

5

146 As we recede from anthropomorphitism we must go either to the Trinity or to Pantheism – The Fathers who were Unitarians, were Anthropomorphites.

147 March 17, 1801. Tuesday – Hartley looking out of my study window fixed his eyes steadily & for some time on the opposite prospect, & then said – Will yon Mountains *always* be? – I shewed him the whole magnificent Prospect in a Looking Glass, and held it up so that the whole was like a Canopy or Ceiling over his head, & he struggled to express himself concerning the Difference between the Thing & the Image almost with convulsive Effort. – I never before saw such an Abstract of *Thinking* as a pure act & energy, of *Thinking* as distinguished from *Thoughts*.

5

148 Sympathy the Poet alone can excite / any Dabbler in stories may excite Pity. – The more I think, the more I am convinced that Admiration is an *essential* element of poetical Delight —

149 [As] loose & easily opened as the connections between the Jokes round a large Table of eager Joke-tellers.

150 Mind, shipwrecked by storms of doubt, now mastless, rudderless, shattered, – pulling in the dead swell of a dark & windless Sea.

151 He is always doing
something else

152 A dull kind of Being not yet privileged with Life.

153 A thousand clouds in the sky, & not one which the Moon did not bless in its fringes – I could have with ease counted all the stars, had not mine eye been too lazy to roll round the heaven, & my mood too placid —

154 Monday, Sept[ember] 14. 1801. Northern Lights remarkably fine – chiefly a purple blue / in shooting pyramids – moved from over Bassenthwaite behind Skiddaw. – Derwent's Birth day – one year old. —

155 Endeavouring to make the infinitely beloved Darling understand all my knowle[d]ge I learn the art of making the abstrusest Truths intelligible; & interesting even to the unlearned.

156 I do not wish you to act from these truths – no! still & always act from your *Feelings.* – but only meditate often on these Truths, that some time or other they may become your Feelings.

157 October 19, 1801. – on the Greta over the Bridge by Mr Edmondson's Father in law, the Ashes, their leaves of that light yellow which Autumn gives them, cast a reflection on the River like a painter's sun shine.

158 Oct[ober] 20., 1801. My Birth day. The Snow fell on Skiddaw, & Grysdale Pike, &c for the first time.

159 Thursday Evening, ½ past 6. Oct[ober] 22, 1801. All the mountains black & tremendously obscure, except Swinside – which looks great [–] a light green wood growing on the other mountains – at this time I saw one after the other, nearly in the same place, two perfect Moon Rainbows – the one foot in the field below my garden, the other in the field nearest but two to 5 the Church – – It was grey-moonlight-mist-color. Friday Morning, Mary Hutchinson arrived.

160 Sunday, November 1. 1801. Hartley breeched – dancing to the jingling of the money – but eager & solemn Joy, not his usual whirl-about gladness – but solemn to & fro eager looks, as befitted the importance of the æra.

161 The state should be to the Religions under its Protection as a well-drawn Picture, equally eyeing all in the Room.

162 The ready way to make the mind grow awry is to lace it too tight —

163 As I have been falling to sleep, the Thought of you has come upon so strongly, that I have opened my eyes as if to look at you —

164 N.B. to make a detailed comparison in the manner of Jerome Taylor between the searching for the first Cause of a Thing & the seeking the fountains of the Nile – so many streams each with their junctions &c – &c – at last, it all comes to a name —

165 Something inherently mean in action. Even the creation of the universe disturbs my Idea of the Almighty's greatness – would do so, but that I conceive that Thought with him creates.

166 The great federal Republic of [the] Universe —

167 Bright Reflections in the Canals of the blue & green Vitriol Bottles in the Druggists's shops in London.
Mere plictri-plactri —

168 God. Wenn ein Gott ist, so ist ein Zweck, so sind unsre Zwecke diesem untergeordnet; so ist ein Zusammenhang, ein Ganzes, in welchem wir handeln; wir richten etwas das mit unserm Tode nicht verlohren geht.
2. Implies the real existence of Truth & Goodness – of course, gives a possibility & thereby a hope of our attaining both. Condorcet – & suffrages. 5
3. No being that comprehends the whole! – What a blot in Creation. [A]m I – & such animalcules as I – the wisest thing of all! & that there are even such as we, is mere chance! —
3. The connection of gratitude with God. – Power in uttermost distress by unexpected means! – The plan & the motive gives gratitude. — 10
4. Courage – That courage which the Sold[iers] derive from B. – B from God. – His general. —
5. You become an atheist from the content[ion] of Evil – & by atheism you would make the evil thousandfold. —— × 15
— Evils in the Universe Spots in the Sun / those very Spots discovered by Herschel to be the marks of the Heat & Cold of different Summers —
× 6. The unspeakable Comfort to a good man's mind – nay, even to a criminal [–] to be *understood* – to have some one that understands one – & who does not feel, that on earth no one does. The Hope of this – always 20
more or less disappointed, gives the *passion* to Friendship

169 No one can leap over his Shadow / Poets leap over Death

170 better to do nothing
than *nothings* —

171 The Snow-patch'd mountain
Top seen dimly thro' the
Cloud.

172 Feb[ruary] 14. 1802.
Drank at Bellows a glass of wine, & 2 pretty large Beakers of Punch – in high spirits – went to bed – a luminous cloud interposed between my Limbs & the sheet – wherever I drew a figure with my nail on my leg or thigh, the same *appeared* on my limb & all, the path of the nail a luminous 5 white, like phosphorus in oxygen, or the falls which we made in the water in Wales – When I press my Thigh a great luminous Mist of White burst out of the spectrum Thigh.

173 Christ – satis[faction] for our Sins by perfect Obedience & Sacrifice of himself on the Cross – i.e. *Ideal* redeems mankind —

174 The strongest argument for [Chri]stianity the weak Argument that do yet persuade so many to believe – i.e. it fits the human heart —

175 A River, so translucent as not to be seen – and yet murmuring – shadowy world – & these a Dream / Inchanted River /

176 The Larches in spring push out their separate bundles of Leaves first into green Brushes or Pencils, which soon then are only small tassels

177 The current in the river like another river = Genius amongst his fellow-men —

178 Can see nothing extraordinary in her – a Poem noting all the virtues of the mild & retired kind.

179 A Poem on the endeavor to emancipate the soul from day-dreams — note the different attempts & the vain ones —

180 Quiet stream, with all its eddies, & the moonlight playing on them, quiet as if they were Ideas in the divine mind anterior to the Creation /

181 Milton, a Monody in the metres of Samson's Choruses – only with more rhymes / – poetical influences [–] political – moral – Dr Johnson /

182 Poem on this night on Helvellin / William & Dorothy & Mary / – Sara & I —

183 April 20, 1802
Tuesday Evening, ½ after 7 / Cut out my name & Dorothy's over the S H at Sara's Rock —

184 The yellow Hammer sings like one working [on] steel, or the file in [a] Brazier's Shop.

185 N.B. The great importance of breeding up children *happy* to at least 15 or 16 illustrated in my always dreaming of Christ Hospital and when not quite well having all those uneasy feelings which I had at School / feelings of Easter Monday &c —

186 The Thrush
Gurgling, quavering, shooting forth long notes. Then with short emissions as if pushing up against a stream —

187 Talk not with scorn of Authors – it was the chattering of the Geese that saved the Capitol

188 Derwent extends the idea of Door so far that he not only [calls] the Lids of Boxes Doors, but even the Covers of Books / a year & 8 months /

189 The rocks and Stones put on a vital semblance; and Life itself thereby seemed to forego its restlessness, to anticipate in its own nature an infinite repose, and to become, as it were, compatible with Immoveability.
Kirkstone /

190 The trout leaping in the Sunshine spreads on the bottom of the River concentric Circles of Light

191 Half tipsy, all the Objects become more inter[?fused] by & diffused by Difference perceived & destr[?oyed] at the same time —

192 I descended from Sca fell and went backward from Wastdale to another Point, a great mountain of Stones, from a pound to 20 Ton / climbed up them, and am now lownded on the other side, with *Hollow Stones* beneath me, the frightfullest Cove, with huge Precipice Walls – caps Helvellin hollow / that Gap I saw in the Air was the Steeple, and one of the 5 Ennerd[ale] Fells – from the spot, that lownds me, I see Derwentwater plainly [–] O for a better & less hazy day – the Castle Crag, & the River – had the weather been tolerable I could have seen my own House / I saw the spot where it was. — The clouds came on fast – & yet I long to ascend Bowfell – I pass along Scafell Precipices, & came to one place where I 10 thought [I] could descend, & get upon the low Ridge that runs between

Sca Fell & Bowfell, & look down into the wild *savage, savage* Head of Eskdale / Good heavens! what a climb! dropping from Precipices and at last should have been crag fast but for the chasm – at last got on the ridge, but the Clouds came on lower & thicker, & I thought it best to defer 15 Bowfell, so came down walking over hollow ground, with the fountain Streams of the Esk rumbling & gurgling under my feet – when these come out, it is a tolerable sized Beck, & divides into two[.] I creep down beside that nearest Scafell – it runs at a huge chasm, its sides perpendicular of solid rock, in many places 50 high / the breadth never more than 15 / 20 in a storm this would be a famous Scene indeed / but O Scafell, thy enormous Precipices / — Just by the hollow Stones are two enormous Columns / I am no measurer – they were vaster than any that I have ever seen, & were each a stone Mountain / they could not be less than 250 yards high / for they reached halfway, or more, down into the vale / The 25 whole Head of Scafell, & its Bowfell & Eskdale Head & Side bare Stone, in many places more than perpendicular / Helvellin is not to be compared with it / Came to a waterfall, down a slope of Rock just 80 yards steep / not far from perpendicular / below this is a succession of Falls, some more sloping than other[s], to the number of 8 – nearly at the bottom of 30 the Hill, you may stand so as to command 5 of them / with looking in over above / of which the first of 80 yards fall, & the fourth, about 50, but more perpendicular, are the most noticeable / but in a storm and thro' & out of Clouds the whole must be the grandest thing in the country / Just lying before [me] as I write this, there [are] 1, 2, 3, 4 Objects, I 35 cannot distinguish whether Hovels, or Hovel-shaped Stones / I have, crossing three becks, & recrossing, reached them / they are all stones / the one nearest the Beck covered with weeds & tree-bushes, looked so very like a Hovel at a distance, that I had made up my mind that the others might be Stones but that this would be a Peat Hovel – I am resting my 40 book on one of its ledges, & it has really the shape of a Hovel – it is a rival of Bowder —

193 Parodies on new Poems are a Ridicule, on old ones a Compliment. —

194 Socinianism moonlight – Methodism a Stove! O for some Sun to unite heat & Light!

195 Defences & proofs ab extra of personal Identity well ridiculed in the song of the little old woman & her little dog – If it is not me, he'll bark & he'll rail – But if it is me, he will wag his little Tail. —

196 Of the harm done by bad Poets in trivializing beautiful expressions & images, & associating Disgust & indifference with the technical forms of Poetry.

197 Poems. – Ghost of a mountain / the forms seizing my body, as I passed, became realities – I, a Ghost, till I had reconquered my Substance /.

198 a company of children driving an hungry hard-skinned Ass out of a cornfield, the Ass cannot by such weaklings be driven so hard but he will feed as he goes.

199 all our notions husked in the phantasms of Place & Time, that still escape the finest sieve & most searching Winnow of our Reason & Abstraction. —

200 mother listening for the *sound* of a still-born Child – blind Arab list'ning in the Wilderness.

201 The stedfast rainbow in the fast-moving, hurrying, hail-mist! – what a congregation of Images & Feelings, of fantastic Permanence amidst the rapid Change of Tempest – quietness the Daughter of Storm —

202 I lay too many Eggs in the hot Sands of this Wilderness, the World! with Ostrich Carelessness & Ostrich Oblivion. The greater part, I trust, are trod underfoot, & smashed; but yet no small number crawl forth into Life, some to furnish Feathers for the Caps of others, & still more to plume the Shafts in the Quivers of my Enemies, of them that lie in wait 5
against my Soul.

203 October 3 – Night – My Dreams uncommonly illustrative of the non-existence of Surprize in sleep – I dreamt that I was asleep in the Cloysters at Christ[']s Hospital & had awoken with a pain in my hand from some corrosion / boys & nurses daughters peeping at me / on their implying that I was not in the School, I answered yes I am / I am only twenty – I 5
then recollected that I was thirty, & of course could not be in the School – & was perplexed – but not the least surprize[d] that I could fall into such an error / So I dreamt of Dorothy, William & Mary – & that Dorothy was altered in every feature, a fat, thick-limbed & rather red-haired – in short, no resemblance to her at all – and I said, if I did not *know* you to be 10
Dorothy, I never should *suppose* it / Why, says she – I have not a feature the same / & yet I was not surprized —

I was followed up & down by a frightful pale woman who, I thought, wanted to kiss me, & had the property of giving a shameful Disease by breathing in the face / 15

& again I dreamt that a figure of a woman of a gigantic Height, dim & indefinite & [?smokelike] appeared – & that I was forced to run up toward it – & then it changed to a stool – & then appeared again in another place – & again I went up in great fright – & it changed to some other common thing – yet I felt no surprize. 20

204 October, 1802. Hartley at Mr Clarkson's sent for a Candle – the *Seems* made him miserable – what do you mean, my Love! – The Seems – the Seems – what seems to be & is not – Men & faces & I do not [know] what, ugly, & sometimes pretty & then turn ugly, & they seem when my eyes are open, & worse when they are shut – & the Candle cures the *seems*. 5

205 Great Injury that has resulted from the supposed Incompatibility of one talent with another / Judgment with Imagination, & Taste – Good sense with strong feeling &c – if it be false, as assuredly it is, the opinion has deprived us of a test which every man might apply – Locke's Opinions of Blackmore, Hume of Milton & Shakespere, *&c* 5

206 The first sight of green fields with the numberless nodding gold cups, & the winding River with Alders on its bank affected me, coming out of a city confinement, with the sweetness & power of a sudden Strain of Music. —.

207 All animals have a sense of *joke* – Calfs with their Horns – Dogs biting – women abusing their infants

208 A Harmony so divine that a crash of discordant sound by accident did not at all affect the *aloofened* mind.

209 Every season Nature converts me from some unloving Heresy – & will make a *Catholic* of me at last / the *Pear*-trees in the lovely Vale of Teme / Sunday, Dec[ember] 19.

210 Body & soul, an utterly absolute mawwallop –

211 A man melancholy mad with the Ideal – his contemplation of human faces, all warped, & all detestably ugly

212 Take away from sounds &c the sense of outness – what a horrid disease every moment would become / the driving over a pavement &c – apply this to sympathy – & disclosure of Feeling —

213 Sara Coleridge, born ½ past six, Dec[ember] 23. 1802 on Thursday. – I returned to Keswick on Friday 24th – ariving ½ past 2 p.m.

214 Were I Achilles, I would have had my leg cut off to have got rid of my vulnerable Heel.

215 In Natural Objects we feel ourselves, or think of ourselves, *only by Likenesses* – among men too often by *Differences*. Hence the soothing love-kindling effect of rural Nature / the bad passions of human societies. – And why is Difference linked with Hatred?

216 Language & all *symbols* give *outness* to Thoughts / & this the philosophical essence & purpose of Language /

217 Memory carried on by the *fear* of forgetting / thus *writing a thing down rids* the mind of it. —

218 A kindhearted man obliged to give a refusal, or the like, that will give great pain, finds relief in doing it roughly & fiercely – explain this, & use it in Christabel /

219 Derwent (July 6th / 1803) to whom I was explaining what his senses were for – he had never once thought of connecting sight with his eyes, &c – I asked him what his Tongue was for & I told him / & to convince, held his Tongue / he was not at all affected – having been used to have his voluntary power controlled by others. Sometime after I asked him again / 5
he had forgotten – I bade him hold his Tongue and try to say, Papa – he did, & finding that he could not speak, he turned pale as death and in the reaction from fear flushed red, & gave me a blow in the face / 2 years & 10 months old, within 8 days.

220 Sunday, July 10th – Derwent fever-hot. The Day before he ran round & round in the kitchen so long that for the first time in his consciousness he became giddy – he turned pale with fright, & repeatedly cried – 'The Kissen is walking away from Derwent['] – pawing out his hands as if stopping it. 5

221 Tuesday Night, July 19, 1803 – Intensely hot day – left off a waistcoat, & for yarn wore silk stockings – about 9 o'clock had unpleasant chillinesses [–] heard a noise which I thought Derwent's in sleep – listened anxiously[,] found it was a Calf bellowing – instantly came on my mind [?that] night, I slept out at Ottery, & the Calf in the Field across the river whose 5
lowing had so deeply impressed me – Chill + Child + Calf-[?lowing] probably the rivers Greta and Otter.

222 Monday, Morning, 20 minutes after 11, August 15, 1803, W. and D. Wordsworth, and S.T. Coleridge left Keswick, in the Jaunting Car, for Scotland, up the steep Hill . . .

. . . angles & concave Scollops, is that of a pulpit, & Reading Desk, only suppose them solid instead of hollow / The Pulpit's Front is bare of water, 5 which pours down on each side of it in two streams of unequal legs – both [?whirl] but the short Leg more copiously, falling – the reading Desk cloathes it with a thin surplice of white water. Close by the rock which helps to form the recess on the left as you look up the Brook is a little quiet Spout – / What a self-same Thing a Waterfall if you like / if you look at it 10 stedfastly, what fits & starts & convulsive Twitches of Motion //

The Ash hanging in an inclined Plane, like a sloping Plank Bridge, across the Brook half a stone throw from the waterfall – / the Hayfield close on my right, on the Hill above me, its limestone wall by my [?] hand / –

Seat of limestone, in the limestone Bank of the Dell Brook, coming out 15 from the rock, like a thick Slate, or London Flag Stone / – above it some 4 or 5 feet a low ruined Garden wall, overgrown with gooseberry Trees, which formed a thick bushy *Shed* over the seat – & above these a double-blossomed Cherry Tree in its barren Pomp, stretching out beyond the Shed, & dropping its [?]ing Blossoms into the River / — at Hesket we 20 stayed at Young Husband's, the Sign of the Queen's Head where I was before – a striking & noble-looking Girl, with a flat face, but yet with large features & large eyes a noble one[.] Out of the little parlour window looking across the market place & over the market House, a group of Ashes, of which the hithermost hath its topmost Twig exactly like a Rook 25 or magpie perching on the topmost Twig. N.B. The manifest magnitude which this Twig attained by its assimilation to a familiar Form, the size of which had been exempted by its old acquaintance, Queen Imagination, from all changes of perspective.

The sanded stone floor with the spitting Pot full of Saw Dust, two 30 Pictures of young Master & Miss with their round Birds' Eyes & parlour Dress, he with a paroquet on his hand, horizontal, the other hand pushed forward just below it – she with a rose in her uplifted perpend[icular] hand, the other hand grasping it to support it in that Posture. The whole Room struck me as Cleanliness quarrelling with Tobacco Ghosts — 35

223 Butterfly let loose, how very high, how madly, how purposeless / it pushes the air under it & runs up the Stairs of Air. 2 Butterflies, an Image of the restless Fondness of two young Lovers. Goose – / would be a noble Bird if it did not remind us of the Swan = Wyndham :: Burke

224 [A]t Carlisle dined – at ½ past 8 in the evening arrived at Longtown, Graham Arms – left it, Wednesday 9 o'clock, 17 [August].

At Carlisle I alarmed the whole Court, Judges, Counsellors, Tipstaves, Jurymen, Witnesses, & Spectators by hallooing to Wordsworth who was in a window on the other side of the Hall – *Dinner!* 5

Walked on the wall – the divine pearly Whiteness of those rich fleecy Clouds, so deliciously shaded toward the top of their component fleecy parts – Think of this often

Then visited Hatfield, impelled by Miss Wordsworth – *vain*, a hypocrite — It is not by mere Thought, I can understand this man / 10

225 Monday Noon, Aug[ust] 22, left Hamiltoun for Glasgow, where we arrived at 4 o'clock, having seen Douglas Castle on the way – The Castle of massive red Free stone, surrounded with Rosebeds, Shrubs & Climbers indigenous & planted / over the Clyde – the more perfectly impressive Abbey of Ballantyre / 5

at Glasgow, the hurry & Crowd of People & of Carts marking a populous trading City, but no Coaches or Carriages! —

Here I stood beside an asthmatic Town-Cryer, a ludicrous Combination // a woman-Shaver, & a man with his lathered Chin most amorously Ogling her as she had him by the Nose. 10

At Glasgow I was most pleased by the two great Washing-Houses & Drying Grounds / – Four Square Cloysters, with an open Square, & the Cauldron in the Middle / each Woman pays a ½ny for her Tub & ½, sometimes in scarce times 1d[,] for a Tub of hot water / a penny to the Watcher / – so that the poorest person who can get Cloathes to wash may 15 earn their living, whereas in other cities those only can do it who can pay for Lodgings with Fire & Washing utensils, &c – I suppose there might be 120 women in each House / –

226 A perpetual repetition of Suspensions of the Habeas Corpus Act compared to a man who *always* kept an oil Skin Cover over his new Hat.—

227 Sat[urday] 27. Sund[ay] 28. Mond[ay] 29.
Sat[urday]. 27. We came to the Ferry House, where W. & D. took [the] boat – I declined it / lost my road, clambered among woods almost to the top of the Fells – but regained it in about a mile / – the road a most delightful one, all along by the Side of the Lake, now open, now inclosed, 5 now a broad road[,] now a brown pathway thro' a green Lane. / About 2 miles from the Ferry, the views of the Foot of the Loch begin to be highly interesting & the Lake itself always highly so from the multitude & fine Shape of its Bays — But here as I leaned against an ash Tree, I [?saw] such a visionary Scene! – One promontory from the Right ran down into 10 the Lake like a stretched out Arm bent downwards with a *bend* as if to support something, then a long Island midway the Lake / then from the Left another promontory much resembling the former, but varying in the Steepness of its Segments / Again from the Right a high Headland falling down steep & high as far as the Tower / & in the far distance & exact 15 Center of the View a small Sugar Loaf Hill – all these in exquisite Harmony, every ridge branch out[,] every intervening Distance softened by the rainy Air / – Still as I went on, the view varied & improved in distinctness / Promontories that could not be distinguished from Islands, Island mistaken for Promontory / – till I arrived at the Foot in the Heart 20 of the Trossacks / I exclaimed Galilæe, vicisti! – If the Lake of Keswick were to push up a mile into Borrodale, and interweave itself among the Mountains, & if those mountains were built up still more detachedly in a universal harmonious *Dislocation* of all its component Cliffs – those Cliffs all wooded – variously wooded / young wood chiefly from *stumps* of huge 25 Trees / weeping Birches surmounting steep Precipices, as large as the largest weeping Willows / But I must see it again! – I returned to the Ferryman's House – & soon after my Friends – & an Artist, Wil[?son] of Edinburgh. / we had a merry meal in the Hovel black & varnished & glistering with peat Smoak, the Fowls roosting in the Chimney amid the 30 cloud of Smoke / we slept in the Barn upon the Hay / My Friend & the Artist had a sort of Hay Bed with Blankets spread on the ground / but I preferred the Hay Rick, & was right / the Brook ran as if running under my Hay pillow! – Next morning we went in the Boat to the End of the Lake / & so on by the old Path by the Garrison to the Ferry House by 35 Loch Lomond / where now the Fall was in all *its fury* – & formed with the Ferry Cottage, & the sweet Highland Lass a nice picture / the Boat gone to the Preaching, & we stayed all day in the comfortless Hovel, comfortless, but the two little Lasses did every thing with *such* Sweetness, and one of them, 14, with such native Elegance / O she was a divine Creature! 40

The Sight of the Boat full of Highland Men & Women and Children, from the Preaching, exquisitely fine / we soon reached E. Tarbet – all the while had Rain. / Never, never let me forget that small Herd boy, in his Tartan Plaid, dim-seen on the hilly field, & long heard ere seen, a melancholy *Voice*, calling to his Cattle! / – nor the beautiful Harmony of the 45 Heath, the dancing Fern, & the ever-moving Birches – That of itself enough to make Scotland visitable, its fields of Heath [(] those not subject to yearly Burning [)] giving a sort of feeling of Shot silk and ribbon Finery – in the *apotheosis* of Finery. On Monday we went to Arrochar, formerly a Gentleman's House on Lake Long / the view of the 50 Cobler interesting no doubt, but I was disappointed with the place! – Here I left Wordsworth and D[orothy,] returned myself to E. Tarbet – slept there – & now Tuesday, Aug[ust] 30, 1803 – am to make my own way alone to Edingburgh –

228 The Rain drops on the Lake to an army of Spirits, or Faeries, on a wilderness of White Sand / Multitude & Joyance[,] motion or a moving /

229 My words & actions imaged on his mind, distorted & snaky as the Boatman's Oar reflected in the Lake / —

230 Among the Beauties of the Highlands in Aug[ust] & Sept[ember] let me not forget the Fumitory with its white flower on the Hovels & Barns / & the Potatoe fields with white Blossoms – appearing to my eye the loveliest & richest flower Gardens –

231 The Head of Glen Nevish how simple for a Painter / & in how many words & how laboriously – in what dim similitudes & slow & dragging Circumlocutions must I give it – so give it that they who knew the place best would least recognize it in my description / the whole reach forms an Oval / but a huge rocky Hill rising up from the river to the breast of the 5 Mountain chokes it up at the Top / above & beyond this the great wall of this segment of the oval makes 2 very deep segments, 2 inverted arches, and between one solid upright bridge of mountain / in the further Inverted Arch, appears from behind, almost about to fill up the arch a bleak Bridge of mountain, shorter, thicker, less a striding ridge than that 10 which intervenes between the 2 Segments / the mountain at my back, first falling *down*, then shoots off like a Fall that meets a rock half way, into a steep but not precipitous Hill, rough with loose stones & overgrown with Birches — So having mounted a little & seen that there was not probably any thing more to be noticed, I turned back – & now my mind being as it 15 were leisurely and of[f] the stretch – with what delight did I look at a

floatage of Shadows on the water, made by the wavelets of the Stream / with what delight that most exquisite net at the bottom – sandy + pebbly river, all whose loops are wires of sunshine / gold finer than silk / beside yon Stone the Breeze seems to have blown them into a Heap, a rich mass of light, light spreading from the loop holes into the interstices / – O we turn from novelties & rarities to old Delights & simple Beauty! – . . . 20

a moorland with 2 mute flocks of Sheep in sight, & one or two more in *sound*, *guarded round* by M[ountains] not walled, the M[ountains] are too separate & individual – before me, on my road to F[ort] Aug[ustus] it is indeed more of *one mass*, delved, rifted, channel'd, wrinkled, & with a dipping, leaping, tipsy outline / but behind me, & to my left as I turn to look behind, I count 29 great lines of Motion or direction, the 14, 15, 16 so semicircled & hollowed, that I might have made 30 out of the 3 / all ind[eed] subdivisible enough! Up to my right – as I now stand toward F[ort] William that distant 25 30

& their long ridge so variously segmented — Silly words I am vexed with you – a File of Sheep among Heath, perfecting Ribboning – It is an *intuition*.

The Moor now tossed up & about into Hills, & these Hills inclosed, with Corn, or Potatoes in Blossom. All this to my Left & a Lake beyond, & a peep of another, & 5 heads of mountains with a continuous ridge before them, close in the whole / — But what a joyous Sight of cows & calves, a lowing browsing multitude, with milking Lasses chattering Erse [–] church & 20 or more scattered Hovels on the Cultivated Hill, that climbs half way up the black mountain Brays of Lochabar. Between the Lake & the Peep of the Lake a mountain of very various, but all superficial & gentle segments, runs down in between almost as gently as a man would lie on a bed, so imperceptibly declining from an Horizontal Line into a Slope / – Those who hold it undignified to illustrate Nature by Art – how little would the truly dignified say so. – how else can we bring the forms of Nature within our voluntary Memory! – The first Business is to subjugate them to our Intellect & voluntary Memory – then comes their Dignity by Sensation of Magnitude, Forms & Passions connected therewith. . . . 35 40 45

232 Wherever her eye turned, gladness came, like spots of Sunshine on green Moorland Hills, creating a new field in the Waste / – spots of sunshine seen thro' floating mists, or thinning Showers –

233 Ode to Solitude, Nature, Liberty – the Solitude free & natural, the Nature unmanacled & solitary, the Liberty natural & solitary – / – I feel here, as if I were here to wander on the winds, a blessed Ghost, till my Beloved came to me / go back with her & seek my children

234 Ode to Music – the thought I lost was that perhaps Music bringing me back to primary Feelings did really make [?moral] regeneration.

235 my Love rested among the Heath, & the purple Heath flowers' Shadows played on her naked feet, between the silken Ligatures of her Sandals

236 There have been times when looking up beneath the shelt[e]ring Tree, I could Invest every leaf with Awe.

237 Seem to have made up my mind to write my metaphysical works, as *my Life*, & *in* my Life – intermixed with all the other events / or history of the mind & fortunes of S.T. Coleridge —

238 Inconsequence of my Character, [?whence] Things often repeated / received a Letter which I knew would contain interesting matter – not quite certain whether it would be affectionate or reproachful, mournful or happy – this I have kept in my pocket sometimes half a day, sometimes a whole day – have opened it at length, just looked at the end, seen it was kind or cheerful – then let it lie on my Desk, or put it up once more in my pocket & have walked about my garden or Study an hour or more, wasting the activity & flutter of feeling excited by the letter in planning compositions, [or] have sate & read a book of Kant & last of all read my Letter, my spirits tamed

239 Ay! them's the Chaps for I! – a Young Rider, long silent, making a dart at the Jellies on their first appearance.

240 Laughter of Parents & Grandames at little children's motions, is Laughter in its original state / a little convulsive motion to get rid of a pleasure rising into pain / – this worthy of further Thought / – Love – *Desire*.

241 Valley of Stones – & the three Ships in the Sun, the broad Sun / – Remember at Linton the Pilchard Merchant from Cornwall, who agreed that all the rest of the Catholic Religion would be abandoned / but they never would give up their Fast & Lent Days / no! never give up Cornish Pilchards!

242 Mix up Truth & Imagination, so that the Imag[ination] may spread its own indefiniteness over that which really happened, & Reality its sense of *substance* & *distinctness* to Imagination / For the Soother of Absence —

243 I am sincerely glad, that he has bidden farewell to all small Poems – & is devoting himself to his great work – grandly imprisoning while it deifies his Attention & Feelings within the sacred Circle & Temple Walls of great Objects & elevated Conceptions. – In those little poems his own corrections, coming *of necessity* so often, at the end of every 14, or 20 lines 5
– or whatever the poem might chance to be – wore him out – difference of opinion with his best friends irritated him & he wrote at times too much with a sectarian Spirit, in a sort of Bravado. – But now he is at the Helm of a noble Bark; now he sails right onward – it is all open Ocean, & a steady Breeze; and he drives before it, unfretted by short Tacks, reefing & 10
unreefing the Sails, hawling & disentangling the ropes. – His only Disease is the having been out of his Element – his return to it is Food to Famine, it is both the specific Remedy, & the condition of Health.

244 Never to lose an opportunity of reasoning against the head-dimming, heart-damping Principle of judging a work by its Defects, not its Beauties. *Every* work must have the former – we know it a priori – but every work has not the Latter / & he therefore, who discovers them, tells you something that you could not with certainty or even with probability 5
have anticipated. —

245 A curious & more than curious Fact that when the country does not benefit, it depraves. Hence the violent vindictive passions – & the outrageous & dark & wild cruelties [–] of many country folks. — Continual Sight of Human Faces & human Houses, as in China, emasculates & dwarfs — 5

246 Without Drawing I feel myself but half invested with Language – Music too is wanting to me. – But yet tho' one should unite Poetry, Draftsman's[-]ship & Music – the greater & perhaps nobler[,] certainly all the subtler parts of one's nature, must be *solitary* – Man exists herein to himself & to God alone / – yea, in how much only to God – how much 5
lies *below* his own Consciousness.

247 the sunny mist, the luminous gloom, of Plato. —

248 Poem on Spirit – or on Spinoza – I would make a pilgrimage to the Deserts of Arabia to find the man who could make [me] understand how the *one can be many*! Eternal universal mystery! It seems as if it were impossible; yet it *is* – & it is every where! – It is indeed a contradiction *in Terms*: and only in Terms! – It is the copresence of Feeling & Life, limitless by their very essence, with Form, by its very essence limited – determinate – definite. — 5

249 Slanting Pillars of Light, like Ladders up to Heaven, their base always a field of vivid green Sunshine / – This is Oct[ober] 19. 1803. Wed[nesday] Morn[ing] tomorrow my Birth Day, 31 years of age! – O me! my very heart dies! – This *year* has been one painful Dream / I have done nothing! – O for God's sake, let me whip & spur, so that Christmas may not pass 5 without some thing having been done / – at all events to finish The Men & the Times, & to collect them & all my Newspaper Essays into one Volume / to collect all my poems, finishing the Vision of the Maid of Orleans, & the Dark Ladié, & make a second Volume / & to finish Christabel. – I ought too, in common gratitude, to write out my two 10 Tours, for Sally Wedgwood /

Oct[ober] 19. 1803. The general Fast Day – and all hearts anxious concerning the Invasion. – A grey Day, windy – the vale, like a place in Faery, with the autumnal Colours, the orange, the red-brown, the crimson, the light yellow, the yet lingering green, Beeches & Birches, as they were 15 blossoming Fire & Gold! – & the Sun in slanting pillars, or illuminated small parcels of mist, or single spots of softest greyish Light, now racing, now slowly gliding, now stationary / – the mountains cloudy – the Lake has been a mirror so very clear, that the water became almost invisible – & now it rolls in white Breakers, like a Sea; & the wind snatches up the 20 water, & drifts it like Snow / – and now the Rain Storm pelts against my Study Window! — [O *Σαρα Σαρα* why am I] not happy! why have I not an unencumbered Heart! these beloved Books still before me, this noble Room, the very centre to which a whole world of beauty converges, the deep reservoir into which all these streams & currents of lovely Forms 25 flow – my own mind so populous[,] so active, so full of noble schemes, so capable of realizing them / this heart so loving, so filled with noble affections – O [*Ασρα* !] wherefore am I not happy! why for years have I not enjoyed one pure & sincere pleasure! – one full Joy! – one genuine Delight, that rings sharp to the Beat of the Finger! – ‡ all cracked, & dull 30 with base Alloy! – Di boni! mihi vim et virtutem / vel tu, [?], eheu! perdite amatio!

‡ But still have said to the poetic Feeling when it has awak'd in the Heart – go! – come tomorrow. –

a day of Storm / at dinner an explosion of Temper from the Sisters / – a dead Sleep after Dinner / – the Rhubarb had its usual enfeebling-narcotic effect / I slept again with dreams of sorrow & pain, tho' not of downright Fright & prostration / I was worsted but not conquered – in sorrows and in sadness & in sore & angry Struggles – but not trampled down / but this will all come again, if I do not take care. 35 40

Storm all night – the wind scourging & lashing the rain, with the pauses of self-wearying Violence that returns to its wild work as if maddened by the necessity of the Pause / I, half-dozing, list'ning to the same, not without solicitations of the poetic Feeling / for from ‡ I have written, Oct[ober] 20. 1803, on Thursday Morning, 40 minutes past 2 o'clock. 45

250 In the North every Brook, every Crag, almost every Field has a name / a proof of greater Independence & of a Society truer to Nature. —

251 Images. Shadow of the Tree in the ruffled water distinguishable from the Breeze on the water only by its stationariness. – In clear water over an uneven channel, as in the Greta behind my House, a huge *Boa* convolvulus – an enormous Adder / – at other times, the waving Sword of Fire of the Cherub over Paradise. — 5

Star (at Barnard Castle) bright, large, the only one, right over the Tower – now absolutely cresting it – & now as we came nearer, twinkling behind the motionless Fragment, a high wall *ruined* into a rude Obelisk.

Shootings of water [–] threads down the Slope of the huge green Stone. – varieties of this on the Clyde, in my Scotch Tour. 10

The *white rose* of Eddy-foam, where the stream ran into a scooped or scolloped hollow of the Rock in its channel – this Shape, an exact white rose, was for ever overpowered by the Stream rushing down in upon it, and still obstinate in resurrection it spread up into the Scallop, by fits & starts, *blossoming* in a moment into a full Flower. — Hung over the Bridge, & musing[,] considering how much of this Scene of endless variety in Identity was Nature's – how much the living organ's! What would it be if I had the eyes of a fly! – what if the blunt eye of a Brobdi[n]gnag! — 15

Black round Ink-spots from 5 to 18 in the decaying Leaf of the Sycamore. 20
A circular glade in a forest of Birch Trees, and in the center of the circle, a

stone standing upright, twice a tall man's Height – and by its side a stately Ash Tree umbrellaing it. —

A road on the breast of the mountain, all wooded save at the very Top where the sharp naked crag lorded it – this road seen only by a stream of white Cows, gleaming behind the Trees, in the Interspaces. — 25

A host of little winged Flies on the Snow mangled by the Hail Storm near the Top of Helvellin.

Nov[ember] 27th – a most interesting morning. 1799. Awoke from one [of] my painful Coach-Sleeps, in the Coach to London[.] It was a rich Orange Sky like that of a winter Evening save that the fleecy dark blue Clouds that rippled above it, shewed it to be Morning[–] these soon became of a glowing Brass Colour, brassy Fleeces, wool packs in shape / rising high up into the Sky. The Sun at length rose upon the flat Plain, like a Hill of Fire in the distance, rose wholly, & in the water that flooded part of the Flat a deep column of Light. – But as the Coach went on, a Hill rose and intercepted the Sun — and the Sun in a few minutes *rose* over it, a compleat 2nd rising, thro' other clouds and with a different Glory. Soon after this I saw Starlings in vast Flights, borne along like smoke, mist – like a body unindued with voluntary Power / – now it shaped itself into a circular area, inclined – now they formed a Square – now a Globe – now from complete orb into an Ellipse – then oblongated into a Balloon with the Car suspended, now a concave Semicircle; still expanding, or contracting, thinning or condensing, now glimmering and shivering, now thickening, deepening, blackening! 30 35 40 45

252 Friday Evening, Nov[ember] 29. The immoveableness of all Things thro' which so many men were moving – harsh contrast compared with the universal motion, the harmonious System of Motions, in the country & every where in Nature. – In this dim Light London appeared to me as a huge place of Sepulchres thro' which Hosts of Spirits were gliding — 5

253 Nothing affects me much at the moment it happens – it either stupifies me, and I perhaps look at a merry-make & dance the hay of Flies, or listen entirely to the loud Click of the great Clock / or I am simply indifferent, not without some sense of philosophic Self-complacency. – For a Thing at the moment is but a Thing of the moment / it must be taken up into the mind, diffuse itself thro' the whole multitude of Shapes & Thoughts, not one of which it leaves untinged – between w[hi]ch & it some new Thought is not engendered / this a work of Time / but the Body feels it quicken with me — 5

254 On St Herbert's Island I saw a large Spider with most beautiful legs floating in the air on his Back by a single Thread which he was spinning out, and still as he spun, heaving on the air, as if the air beneath were a pavement elastic to his Strokes / – from the Top of a very high Tree he had spun his Line, at length reached the Bottom, tied his Thread round a 5 piece of Grass & re-ascended, to spin another / a net to hang as a fisherman's Sea net hangs in the Sun & Wind, to dry. —

255 One excellent use of communication of Sorrows to a Friend is this: that in relating what ails us we ourselves first know exactly what the real grief is – & see it for itself, in its own form & limits — Unspoken grief is a misty medley, of which the real affliction only plays the first fiddle, blows the Horn, to a scattered mob of obscure feelings – &c. Perhaps, at certain 5 moments a single almost insignificant Sorrow may, by association, bring together all the little relicts of pain & discomfort, bodily & mental, that we have endured even from Infancy. —

256 Oct[ober] 21st. 1803. Friday Morning. – A drisling Rain. Heavy masses of shapeless Vapour upon the mountains [O the perpetual Forms of Borrodale!] yet it is no unbroken Tale of dull Sadness – slanting Pillars travel across the Lake, at long Intervals – the vaporous mass whitens, in large Stains of Light / on the Lakeward ridge of that huge arm chair, of 5 Lowdore, fell a gleam of softest Light, that brought out the rich hues of the late Autumn. The woody Castle Crag between me & Lowdore is a rich Flower-Garden of Colours, the brightest yellows with the deepest Crimsons and the infinite Shades of Brown & Green / the *infinite* diversity of which blends the whole – so that the brighter colours seem as *colors* 10 upon a ground, not colored Things.

Little wool-packs of white bright vapour rest on different summits & declivities – the vale is narrowed by the mist & cloud – yet thro' the wall of mist you can see into a bason of sunny Light in Borrodale – the Birds are singing in the tender Rain as if it were the Rain of April, & the decaying 15 Foliage were Flowers & Blossoms. The pillar of Smoke from the Chimney rises up in the Mist, & is just distinguishable from it; & the Mountain Forms in the Gorge of Borrodale consubstantiate with the mist & cloud even as the pillared Smoke / a shade deeper, & a determinate Form. – Cleared up. the last thin Fleeces on the bathed Fells. 20

257 I have had some *Lights* lately respecting *Envy*. A. thought himself unkindly used by B. – he had exerted himself for B. with what warmth! honoring, praising B. beyond himself. – &c. &c – B. selfish – feeling all Fire respecting every Trifle of his own – quite backward to poor A. The *Up*, askance, pig Look, in the Boat &c[.] Soon after this A. felt distinctly 5 little ugly Touchlets of Pain & little Shrinkings Back at the Heart, at the report that B. had written a new Poem / an excellent one! – & he saw the faults of B & all that belonged to B. & detested himself dwelling upon them – &c. What was all this! – Evidently, the instinct of all fine minds to *totalize* – to make a *perfectly congruous whole* of every character – & a pain 10 at the being obliged to admit incongruities – This must be *plus'd* + by all the foregoing Pains which were self-referent, & by their combination introduce a selfish Brooding into this latter Pain — This is a very, very dim Sketch / but the *Fact* is stated. – Then, A. took himself to Task respecting *B.* – It is very true, that B. is not so zealous as he might be, in 15 some things – and over zealous for himself – But what is he on the whole? What compared with the mass of men? – It is astonishing how powerfully this Medicine acted – how instantly it effected a cure / one wakeful Hour's serious Analysis – – & the Light thrown upon the former Subject had a great Share in this – for one important part of the Process in the 20 growth of Envy is the Self-degradation (a painful, self-referent Feeling) consequent on the first consciousness of the pang – the Obscurity & Darkness of mind from ignorance of the Cause – dim notion that our nature is suddenly altered for the worse. &c &c. – Deeplier than ever do I see the necessity of understanding the whole complex mixed character of 25 our Friend – as well as our own / of frequently, in our kindest moods, reviewing it – intensifying our Love of the Good in it, & making up our mind to the Faulty – It would be a good Exercise to imagine & anticipate some painful Result of the faulty part of our Friend's character – fancy him acting thus & thus to you – when it would most wound you / then to 30 see how much of the wound might not be attributed to some lingering Selfishness in one's self – and at all events to fancy yourself forgiving it, passing it over, turning the attention forcibly to the valuable Parts of the character, & connecting a feeling of Respect & love with the *Person*, the visual Form – even during the manifestation of this unpleasant part of 35 the Character. Question is, whether I have not mistaken for Envy a very different Feeling. The same sort of Pain I have distinctly felt, at Mr. Pitt's being the Author of the Irish Union, deemed by me a great & wise measure / & introducing a subversion of my *Theory* of Pitt's Contemptibility. Yet it would be strange to say, I envied Mr. Pitt? – This 40

however is a mere Tenant of the understanding – not connected with my Person in any way. – Take this Feeling, namely, a Pain at the excellence of another, and add to it other pains purely personal – will it be Envy then? – But it is not Pain at the excellence of an other, but pain that that particular Person whom I had habitually despised, should have that excellence, 45 which if he really have, I must be forced to give him a share of my Esteem & Love —. This seems a Vice of personal Uncharitableness, not Envy. – I am by no means satisified with the analysis: & yet I think, that Envy might gradually rise out of this primary Pain of Incongruity / tho' it would be only a Sort of Envy – & no doubt different from Envy excited by the 50 possession of Excellence – the more of it, the more Envy —— let me re-enumerate. A had been dwelling on the faulty parts of B.'s character = L. These views of A's understanding were *just* on this point, only that they had been *exclusive*: occasioned by A. having been himself deeply wounded by B.'s selfishness. = M. – A. had been long, long idle owing 55 perhaps in part to his Idolatry of B. = N. 4. A. hears of some new Poems of B. – & feels Little painful Shrinking back at the Heart = O. – &, 5. a disposition to do something to surpass B. = P. — on the whole I suspect the Feeling to have been mere Resentment. —

258 Sunday, Oct[ober] 23rd. 1803. – To Grasmere yesterday, I returned today. O Thirlmere! – let me some how or other celebrate the world in thy mirror. – Conceive all possible varieties of Form, Fields, & Trees, and naked or ferny Crags – ravines, behaired with Birches – Cottages, smoking chimneys, dazzling *wet places* of small rock-precipices – dazzling 5 castle windows in the reflection – all these, within a divine outline in a mirror of 3 miles distinct vision! – and the distance closed in by the Reflection of Raven Crag, which at every bemisting of the mirror by gentle motion became a perfect vast Castle Tower, the corners rounded & pillar'd or fluted – / each corner ending in a round pillar, round save 10 that slice off by which it lies flat on & connects the two sides – all this in bright lightest yellow, yellow-green, green, crimson, and orange! – The single Birch Trees hung like Tresses of Sea Weed – the Cliffs like organ pipes! – and when a little Breath of Air spread a delicious Network over the Lake, all these colours seemed then to float on, like the reflection, of 15 the rising or setting Sun. – On Saturday, Oct[ober] 22nd, heard from T. Hutchinson that he had taken the Farm from Mr Hasle at Ulswater: & was to enter on it, with Sara next March —

259 Monday, Oct[ober] 24. 1803. I walked with Southey & Hazlitt thro' Borrodale into Watendlath, & so home to a late dinner. Of course it was to me a mere walk; for I must be alone, if either my Imagination or Heart are to be excited or enriched. Yet even so I worshipped with deep feeling the grand outline & perpetual Forms, that are the guardians of Borrodale, 5 & the presiding Majesty, yea, the very Soul of Keswick – The Birches were in all their Pride of gold & orange – the Lake was very full of Foam, the late great Flood having not yet wholly retired / I thought still more than before that if the Lake had pushed up into Borrodale, as far as the Bowder Stone, & if Borrodale were still better wooded, it would be 10 distinguished from the Trossachs chiefly by its continuity of massiveness – tho' there is one vast Crag to the left, as you go up Borrodale, complete Trossachs, all the dislocation & multitude of outjuttings & precipices – but this had only the *Tale* of woods no more! – On the whole, & as a whole, it is superior to the Trossachs, the view of the vale of Keswick 15 being so greatly superior to the Banks of Loch Ketterin, & the lovely round Vale of Borrodale with its exquisite combination of nigh & distant Mountains so incomparably finer than the vale & Lake Achry. – I ascended in a wrong place, but it led me to some glorious fantastic rocks – the mitre, the huge pyramid, & Peak Fantastic, with a lower Rock to the 20 Right of it, between which two in a narrow defile I went, having in this Toilsome Climb two most singular & noble views of the Lake & Vale of Keswick. — A whole flight of small Birds flung themselves down in a gale of wind into Borrodale like a *shoot* of Stones – each Bird seemed to dart onward by projection, & to descend by its own lifelessness & weight. – 25 What was the name of that most vivid of all vivid green mosses by the side of the falling water, as we clomb down into Watendlath! – that red moss, too? and that blood-red Fungus? – The Lake of Watendlath has hitherto always appeared of inferior impressiveness to me / it is so bare, & pondish, & swampy – the mountains at its head would be better in a 30 picture than they look in Nature – for the Forms & Combinations are fine, but they want something or other in colour, & distance[,] to make them *Satisfiers* – neither do the Crags on each side of us as we go by the River Side till we have passed the Bridge, impress me so deeply as they seem to have done many – but from the Bridge, & all the rest of the way 35 down to Baragh House – O what is there on Earth that can better deserve the name of Divine? – There should be some mark, some Cross or Heap of Stones to direct the Traveller to turn off on his Left, 15 or 20 yards thro' the Coppice, about a 100 yards or so before he comes to the road-view of the Lake of Keswick / 20 yards thro' this open Coppice brings him 40

suddenly to the Edge of a finely wooded Precipice, with Lodore beneath him at a small Distance on his Left, & on his Right the Promontory of Birches on the Lake / the House at the Foot of Lodore, the Bridge, the Road seen in 3 different distances, so very beautiful – the Lake of Keswick – & of Bassenthwaite / – the Height from the extreme steepness & direct 45 plumb-down Look on the Lake seems vast – the breezes rush in pencil brushes over it – / you *look down* on every thing, & every thing spreads in consequence, broad & long & vast! – – This is / I have no hesitation in saying it – / the best, every way the best & most impressive View in all the Lake Country – why not in all the Island? – Bowder Stone, the Stone 50 under Dumbarton Rock, & the Bull Stone in the foot of Glenfalloch, the 3 great Stones of the Island / of these Bowder is the least, by far. How could Wordsworth think otherwise? – – Go & build up a pile of Stones, by that Coppice – measure the Strides from the Bridge where the water rushes down a rock in no mean cataract if the Rains should have swoln 55 the River – & the Bridge itself hides a small cataract – from this Bridge measure the Strides to the Place, build the Stone heap – & write a Poem, thus beginning – From the Bridge &c [–] repeat such a Song, of Milton, or Homer, so many Lines as I must find out may be distinctly recited during a moderate healthy man's walk from the Bridge thither – or better 60 perhaps from the other Bridge – so to this Heap of Stones – there turn in – & then describe the Scene. – O surely I might make a noble Poem of all my Youth – nay *of all my Life* – – One section on plants & flowers, my passion for them, always deadened by their learned names. – Yet ever to note those that have & may hereafter affect me – 65

260 a most unpleasant Dispute with W. & Hazlitt Wednesday Afternoon, Oct[ober] 26. 1803. – I spoke, I fear too contemptuously – but they spoke so irreverently so malignantly of the Divine Wisdom, that it overset me. Hazlitt how easily roused to Rage & Hatred, self-projected / but who shall find the Force that can drag him up out of the Depth into one 5 expression of Kindness – into the shewing of one Gleam of the Light of Love on his Countenance. – Peace be with *him!* – But *thou*, dearest Wordsworth – and what if Ray, Durham, Paley, have carried the observation of the aptitudes of Things too far, too habitually – into Pedantry? – O how many worse Pedantries! how few so harmless with so much 10 efficient Good! – Dear William, pardon Pedantry in others & avoid it in yourself, instead of scoffing & reviling at Pedantry in good men in a good cause, & *becoming* a Pedant your self in a bad cause – even by that very act becoming one! – But surely always to look at the superficies of Objects

for the purpose of taking Delight in their Beauty & sympathy with their 15
real or imagined Life, is as deleterious to the Health & manhood of
Intellect, as always to be peering & unravelling Contrivances may be to
the simplicity of the affections, the grandeur & unity of the Imagination.
– O dearest William! Would Ray, or Durham, have spoken of God as you
spoke of Nature? 20

261 Frid[ay] Morning 5 o'clock – Dosing, dreamt of Hartley as at his
Christening – how as he was asked who redeemed him, & was to say,
God the Son / he went on, humming and hawing, in one hum & haw,
like a boy who knows a thing & will not make the effort to recollect it – so
as to irritate me greatly – Awakening gradually I was able compleatly to 5
detect that it was the Ticking of my Watch which lay in the Pen Place in
my Desk on the round Table close by my Ear, & which in the diseased
State of my Nerves had *fretted* on my Ears – I caught the fact while
Hartley's Face & moving Lips were yet before my Eyes, & his Hum
& Ha[w], & the Ticking of the Watch were each the other, as often 10
happens in the passing off of Sleep – that curious modification of Ideas by
each other, which is the Element of *Bulls*. — I arose instantly, & wrote it
down – it is now 10 minutes past 5.

262 To return to the Question of Evil – woe to the man, to whom it is an
uninteresting Question – tho' many a mind, overwearied by it, may shun
it with Dread / and here, N.B scourge with deserved & lofty Scorn those
Critics who laugh at the discussion of old Questions – God, Right &
Wrong, Necessity & Arbitrement – Evil, &c – No! forsooth! – the 5
Question must be new, *new spicy hot* Gingerbread, a French Constitu-
tion, a Balloon, change of ministry, or which had the best of it in the
Parliamentary Duel, Wyndham or Sheridan / or at the best, a chemical
Theory, whether the new celestial Bodies shall be called Planets or
Asteroids – &c – Something new, something *out* of themselves – for 10
whatever is *in* them, is deep within them, must be *old* as elementary
Nature. To find no contradiction in the union of old & novel, to contemplate the Ancient of Days with Feelings new as if they then sprang
forth at his own Fiat – this marks the mind that feels the Riddle of the
World, & may help to unravel it. But to return to the Question – the 15
whole rests on the Sophism of imagining Change is a case of positive
Substitution. – This, I fully believe, *settles* the Question / – The assertion
that there is in the essence of the divine nature a necessity of omniform
harmonious action, and that Order, & System / not number – in itself
base & disorderly & irrational – / define the creative Energy, determine 20

& employ it – & that number is subservient to Order, regulated, organized, made beautiful and rational, an object both of Imag[ination] & Intellect, by Order – this is no mere Assertion / it is strictly in harmony with the Fact, for the world appears so – & it is proved by whatever proves the Being of God – . Indeed, it is involved in the Idea of God. — 25

263 What is it, that I employ my Metaphysics on? To perplex our clearest notions, & living moral Instincts? To extinguish the Light of Love & of Conscience, to put out the Life of Arbitrement – to make myself & others *Worthless*, *Soul*-less, *God*less? – No! To expose the Folly & the Legerdemain of those, who have thus abused the blessed Organ of Language –, 5 to support all old & venerable Truths, to support, to kindle, to project, to make the Reason spread Light over our Feelings, to make our Feelings diffuse vital Warmth thro' our Reason – these are my Objects – & these my Subjects. Is this the metaphysics that bad Spirits in Hell delight in?

264 Sat. Morn. Oct[ober] 29. 1803. Three o'clock. The Moon hangs high over Greta, & the Bridge, on the first step of her Descent, & three hours at least from the Mountain, behind which she is to sink: nearly full – not a Cloud in Heaven, the Sky deep sable blue, the Stars many & white in the height of the Sky, but above around, & beneath the Moon, not a Star; she 5 is starless as the Sun. Yet there is no gleam, much less silver whiteness, on the Lake: simply it is easily seen; & even the Greta stretching strait in an oblique line underneath is not silver-bright, or any where brilliant; but rather the gleam of some baser Composition imitating Silver [–] it is a grey brightness like the colour of an ash grove in keenest December 10 Moonlight. The Mountains are dark, low, all compact together, quiet, silent, asleep – the white Houses are bright throughout the vale, & the evergreens in the Garden. The only Sound is the murmur of the Greta, perpetual Voice of the Vale.

265 Oct[ober] 31. 1803. The full moon glided behind a black cloud / & what then? & who cared? – It was past 7 o'clock in the morning – There is a small Cloud in the East, not larger than the moon & ten times brighter than she! So passes Night & all her favors vanish in our minds, ungrateful! —— 5

266 Wednesday Morning, 20 minutes past 2 o'clock. November 2nd. 1803. The Voice of the Greta, and the Cock-crowing: the Voice seems to grow, like a Flower on or about the water beyond the Bridge, while the Cock crowing is nowhere particular, it is at any place I imagine & do not distinctly [?see]. A most remarkable Sky! The Moon, now waned to a 5

perfect Ostrich's Egg, hangs over our House almost – only so much beyond it, garden-ward, that I can see it, holding my Head out of the smaller Study window. The Sky is covered with whitish, & with dingy *Cloudage*, thin dingiest Scud close under the moon & one side of it moving, all else moveless: but there are two great Breaks of Blue Sky – the one stretching over our House, & away toward Castlerigg, & this is speckled & blotched with white Cloud – the other hangs over the road, in the line of the Road in the shape of a I do not know what to call [it]: but this is the Figure – this is unspeckled, all blue – 3 Stars in it / more in the former Break – all unmoving. The water leaden white, even as the grey Gleam of Water is in latest Twilight. – Now while I have been writing this & gazing between whiles (it is 40 M[inutes] past Two) the Break over the road is swallowed up, & the Stars gone, the Break over the House is narrowed into a rude Circle, & on the edge of its circumference one very bright Star – see! already the white mass thinning at its edge *fights* with its Brilliance – see! it has bedimmed it – & now it is gone – & the Moon is gone. The Cock-crowing too has ceased. The Greta sounds on, for ever. But I hear only the Ticking of my Watch, in the Pen-place of my Writing Desk, & the far lower note of the noise of the Fire – perpetual, yet seeming uncertain / it is the low voice of quiet Change, of Destruction doing its work by little & little.

267 Derwent (Nov[ember] 6. Tea time) came in, & all the *Cake* was eat up, & he was by no means willing to accept dry Toast & butter as a Substitute[.] 'Don't eat all the Cake!' – Well, we will not tomorrow! – [']O but don't eat the Cake! You have eat the cake[.] O but don't eat up all the cake!' – His Passion had compleately confounded his Sense of Time & its Consequences – He saw that it *was* done; & yet he passionately entreated you not to do it – & not for the time to come / but for the Present & the Past. 'O but you have! O but don't now!' – This Mem. for the effect of the Passions on the reasoning power imprimis in producing *Bulls*

268 Anecdote of myself
Frere with false heart complimenting me at Cambridge as if I was almost sure of getting the prize. I told him, I was sure of the contrary – namely, that he or some one of King's would obtain it. 'But why?' – Why, Sir! the Boot fits you, Sir! I cannot get my Leg in.

269 Derwent's *Bull* from eager Desire & Disappointment – Nov[ember] 6 in g—w Mem: book. – at the same time I noticed the remarkable disposition of all Children of his Age, who are any way kindly treated, to *contra-*

dict – the pleasure they find in it / when there is any plausibility in their own counterassertion it often rises into passion & self-willedness; when none, it is *fun* – & *wit* – . It hangs in a String with their love of calling white black &c. – as Derwent when he had scarce a score of words in his whole Tonguedom comes holding up a pair of filthy Pawlets, & lisps – Here's *clean white* Hands! – & then laughed immoderately.—

270 Southey's (Nov[ember] 13th, 1803) notion of Godwin – My close Stool was right opposite to him, as he sate by my bedside – he compared him to a close stool pan, most often empty, & better empty than when full

271 a pretty optical fact occurred this morning. As I was returning from Fletcher's, up the back lane, & just in sight of the River, I saw floating high in the air, somewhere over Mr Banks's, a noble *Kite* – I continued gazing at [it] for some time; when turning suddenly round I saw at an equidistance on my right, i.e. over the middle of our field, a pair of Kites – floating about – I looked at them for some seconds when it occurred to me that I had never before seen two Kites together – instantly the vision disappeared – it was neither more or less than two pair of Leaves, each pair on a separate Stalk, on a young Fruit tree that grew on the other side of the wall, not two yards from my eye. The leaves being alternate did, when I looked at them as leaves, strikingly resemble wings – & they were the only leaves on the Tree. – The magnitude was given by the imagined Distance; that Distance by the former Adjustment of the Eye, which *remained* in consequence of the deep impression, length of time, I had been looking at the Kite, the pleasure, &c – & a new Object impressed itself on the eye / &c &c.

272 My nature requires another nature for its support, & reposes only in another from the necessary Indigence of its Being. – Intensely similar, yet not the same; or may I venture to say, the same indeed, but dissimilar, as the same Breath sent with the same force, the same pauses, & with the same melody pre-imaged in the mind, into the Flute and the Clarion shall be the same Soul diversely incarnate.

273 Tuesd[ay] Nov[ember] 22 – 1803 – The prodigious effect of the Love of Spices on the human Race / the cause of the E[ast] India Voyages, [?] of Columbus, &c &c &c —

274 Die Bäume und die Felsen sagen mir nichts, said Socrates[;] & the endless superiority of Christ over him in this respect / Tant pis pour vous —

275 When some wretched Poets have run down some beauty or licence in the mechanism of Verse, or Diction, & it has been noticed with disgust, then come your still more wretched Critics (the same perchance who at the first had hugely admired the thing), & if they find in any poem even a single Instance of this, it is instantly *detected* with all the airs of offended 5 Wisdom / here, Judiciously used – & so used by him, as that it would always have been felt as excellent, if none had ever used it otherwise – so for instance, in putting the emphasis on the adjective – Each fond word utters with a fond delight.

276 Thursday, Nov[ember] 24th, 1803. – Lo! on this day *we change Houses!* – all is in a bustle / and I do not greatly like *Bustle*; but it is not that that depresses me / it is the *Change!* – *Change!* – O Change doth trouble me with Pangs untold! – But change, and change! change about! – But they shall not get me out – from Thee, Dear Study! – – I must write a Poem on 5 this. – But this is not the only thing – it is Nov[ember] 24th, 1803. Nov[ember] 24th, 1799 – it was a Sunday, & I was at Sockburn! – /

277 True & easy Test of Poetry – If it relate to sight, might a well educated man born blind have written it – Examine Blacklock. [?And if to] ear or sound[,] the deaf / if to feelings, a man utterly heartless.

278 To analyse the pleasures received from Gates, in corners of Fields, at twilight / Vide Wordsworth Evening Walk
[']The sound of closing Gate across the water borne['] /

279 The common Fern fades into an Orange / the Stone Fern into a *rich* Brown

280 [On] the simplicity or manifoldness of the human Being? In what sense is it one? Sense, Appetite, Passion, Fancy, Imagination, Understanding, & lastly, the Reason & Will?

281 Dec[ember] 6. 1803. – Adam travelling in his old age – came to a set of the descendants of Cain, ignorant of the origin of the world; & treating him as a Madman killed him. A sort of Dream, which I had this Night.

282 We ought to suspect reasoning, founded wholly on the differences of man from man, not on their commonnesses – which are infinitely greater. So I doubt the wisdom of the Treatment of Sailors, & criminals; because it is wholly grounded on their vices, as if the vices formed the whole or major part of their Being. 5

283 Abstruse Reasoning : the inductions of common sense :: reaping : delving. But the Implements with which we reap, how are they gained? By Delving. – Besides[,] what is common sense [–] it was abstruse Reasoning with earlier Ages.

284 Tuesday ½ past 3. beautiful Sun set – the Sun setting behind Newlands across the foot of the Lake. The Sky cloudless, save that there is a cloud on Skiddaw, one on the highest Mountain in Borrodale, some on Helvellin, and the Sun sets in a glorious Cloud / these Clouds are of various shapes, various Colours – & belong to their Mountains, & have 5 nothing to do with the Sky. — N.B. Something metallic, silver playfully & imperfectly gilt, & highly polished; or rather something mother of pearlish, in the Sun gleams upon Ice, thin Ice.

285 I have repeatedly said, that I could have made a volume, if only I had noted *down*, as they occurred to my Recollection or Observation, the instances of the Proverb, Extremes Meet / – This Night, Sunday, Dec[ember] 11, 1803, ½ past 11, I have determined to devote the last 9 pages of my Pocket [Book] to the collection of the same. 5

EXTREMES MEET.

The parching Air
Burns frore, and Cold performs the Effect of Fire.
Par[adise] Lost, Book 2. 594.

Insects by their smallness, the Mammoth by its hugeness, terrible. 10

Sameness in a Waterfall, in the foam Islands of a fiercely boiling Pool at the bottom of the Waterfall, from infinite Change.

The excess of Humanity & Disinterestedness in polite Society, not to give Pain, e.g. not to talk of your own Diseases or misfortunes, & to introduce nothing but what will give pleasure, destroys all Humanity & 15 Disinterestedness by making it intolerable thro' Desuetude, to listen to the Complaints of our Equals or of any where the Listening does not gratify or excite some vicious Pride, & sense of Superiority.

A perfectly unheard of Subject, & a crambe bis cocta, chosen by a Man of Genius – difficult to say, which would excite in the higher degree the 20 sense of Novelty. E.g. the Orestes of Sotheby

Dark with excess of Light.

7. Self-absorption & Wor[l]dly-mindedness [–] N.B. The latter a most philosophical word

8. The dim Intellect *sees* an absolute Oneness, the perfectly clear Intellect *knowingly perceives it*. Distinction & Plurality lie in the Bewtixt. 25

9. The naked Savage, & the Gymnosophist.

10. Nothing & intensest absolutest Being.

11. Despotism & ochlocracy.

286 The paradise of Flowers' & Butterflies' Spirits.

287 The Soul within the Body, can I any way compare this to the Reflection of the Fire seen thro' my window on the solid Wall, seeming of course within the solid wall, as deep within as the distance of the Fire from the Wall? – I fear, I can make nothing out of it / but why do I always turn away from any interesting Thought to do something uninteresting – as 5 for instance, when this Thought struck me, I turned off my attention suddenly, & went to look for the Wolff which I had missed – / Is it a cowardice of all deep Feeling, even tho' pleasurable? or is it Laziness? or is it some thing less obvious than either? Is it connected with my epistolary Embarrassments? 10

288 A great Man's Book in this Country like a Candle in Lapland, extinguished the moment after it was lit by Insects, Gnats, & Buzzflies —

289 Good & ill-natured name of the same Thing / a Fish of a clumsy Shape is, when alive, phosphoric from Sides & belly / this the Germans call Klumpfisch, the French Lune de Mer, the English Sun-Fish

290 Passionately fond of the Hebrew Poetry I often have thought of the loss of the Library therein contained of Oracles & History, of which our present Bible is but a meagre & fortuitous extract, of but few Times &c with grief & so [on] of the Greek Hymns & Dythyrambics & Corybyntics, many perhaps equal to the Atys of Catullus, w[hi]ch I deem 5 a Translation from the Greek, & think it high Genius in a Roman to feel, and to represent an inspired Greek / but what if all these had been preserved? A Life would not have sufficed to the Reading thereof, and the admiration would have killed all original Power, all Hope / we have enough to excite Emulation, more would overlay it. Dec[ember] 18. 1803 10

291 Between each one of these Lines another might have been written with ease & perfect Legibility [–] I am extravagant. This Pocket book cost 9[s], 6[d] / more Shame to Mr G. Ward!

292 What a beautiful Thing urine is, in a Pot, brown yellow, transpicuous, the Image, diamond shaped of the Candle in it, especially, as it now appeared, I having emptied the Snuffers into it, & the Snuff floating about, & painting all-shaped Shadows on the Bottom.

293 I will at least make the attempt to explain to myself the Origin of moral Evil from the *streamy* Nature of Association, which Thinking = Reason, curbs & rudders / how this comes to be so difficult / Do not the bad Passions in Dreams throw light & shew of proof upon this Hypothesis? – Explain those bad Passions; & I shall gain Light, I am sure – A Clue! A Clue! – an Hecatomb a la Pythagoras, if it unlabyrinths me. – Dec[ember] 28, 1803 – Beautiful luminous Shadow of my pencil point following it from the Candle – rather going before it & illuminating the word, I am writing. 11 o'clock / – But take in the blessedness of Innocent Children, the blessedness of sweet Sleep, &c &c &c: are these or are they not contradictions to the evil from *streamy* association? – I hope not: – all is to be thought *over* and *into* – but what is the height, & ideal of mere Association? – Delirium. – But how far is this state produced by Pain & Denaturalization? And what are these? – In short, as far as I can see any thing in this Total Mist, Vice is imperfect yet existing Volition, giving diseased Currents of association, because it yields on all sides & *yet is* – So think of Madness: – O if I live! Grasmere, Dec[ember] 29. 1803

294 Egotistic Talk *with me* very often the effect of my Love of the Persons to whom I am talking / My Heart is talking of them / I cannot talk continuously of them to themselves – so I seem to be putting into their Heart the same continuousness as to me, that is in my own Heart as to them. ——

295

My Spirit with a fixed yet leisurely gaze
Following its even yet quietly
changing Clusters of Thoughts,
as the outward Eye of a happy
Traveller a flock of Starlings —

296 The two Apparition-Birch Trees, close together, abreast, with the *chocolate mist* of winter branches and tresses around and above its silver body – by the side of the steep steep Noisy Syke with two sheep-tracks inclosing an irregular oval area. – picture of a robe round a Spirit.

297 The waterfall at the head of the Vale, (the circular mountain walled vale) white, stedfast, silent from Distance / – the River belonging to it, smooth, full, silent – the Lake into which it empties itself silent / yet the noise of waters every where / Something distant, something near, [']Tis far off, & yet every where / – and the pillar of smoke / the smooth winter fields – the *indistinct* Shadows in the Lake [are all] eloquent of Silence

298 Remember to describe water (apparition / tadpoles) pulsating / really gliding down under ice / water – black[,] under Ice – silver.

299 Wednesday, Jan[uary] 4th / in the highest & outermost of Grasmere Wordsworth read to me the second Part of his divine Self-biography — 3 basons – 1 misty Tairn / sattiny dove colour painted Petticoat rocks / & a slope /

300 a boy sucking an Icicle with what affectionate Remembrance of a Lollipop

301 Thursday, Jan[uary] 5. 1804. – Snow on the ground – frosty particles full of – snatched up by the wind that seemed to rush from the valley up the Mountain, it galloped transversely from the middlemost of the mountains to their very Top, & along their summits, like a vast Ghost Cavalry scouring a Country — Item / I distinctly & repeatedly saw the wind raise up from the mountain a true genuine Cloud of Snow, that rose high (seemingly to the eye, but not really, as high as the highest Clouds) sailed along, a true genuine large white cloud with all the form & varied outline of a Cloud / – & this in several Instances dropped again, snow at second Hand, & often in the Sun resembled a Shower of diamond Spearlets.

302 The character of Australis a striking Illustration of the Basis of Morals. With truth, & with the warm coloring of one who feels the Truth, detail his Life, as a History, & the Tenor of his Life, as a system of Habits of [?Action –] his never once stumbling Temperance, his unstained Chastity from his Infancy to the present Hour, purus maritus puram, virgo virginem, the simplicity of his daily Life, the Industry & vigorous Perseverance in his Pursuits, the worthiness & dignity of these Pursuits, his Liberality & fatherly conduct to his Brothers & Relatives – & for their sakes how he submits to *review & Job*, yet by unexampled Industry can do this & yet do more than almost any other man, in the Subjects of his Choice & Ambition / his punctuality in all things – he inflicts none of those small Pains & Discomforts, which your irregular men scatter about them / & vice versâ, bestows all the pleasures which regular correspon-

dence, & a *reliability* in all things great & small can give / – he is kind to his servants, & he is more than kind – he is *good* to them / Bella for 15 instance / – all his works subserve Humanity, & the great cause of Peace, Equality, & pure Religion – and above all, of domestic Fidelity & Attachments of which as a Husband (& no doubt, he will as a Father) he is himself in his real Life a Pattern in the eyes of ordinary good men / – All this Australis *does*, & if all Goodness consists in definite, observable, 20 & rememberable *Actions*, Australis is only not perfect, his good Actions so many, [?his unadmirable] ones so few, & (with one or two exceptions) so venial. But now what *is* Australis? I can tell you, what he is *not*. He is not a man of warmth, or delicacy of Feeling, *he is not* self-oblivious or self-diffused, or acquainted with his own nature; & when warped by 25 Resentment or Hatred, not incapable of doing base actions, at all events most, *very*, or *damn'd*, indelicate actions, without hesitation at the moment, or any after[-]remorse (Recensio ασματιων λυρικων, Epistolæ permalæ Carolorum, calumniæ versus me, et animus quoad το Επος pro[rsus] ingratus, domus ex adverso mea, 'Novi Sara tuam, Novi istam 30 Meek Sister in the Family of Christ' / Furta et furtula poetica, et quicquid incongrui et parum decori follows from an unfathoming and (not only self-unfathomed, but even) self-unsounded, Spirit.) The smiles, the emanations, the perpetual Sea-like Sound & Motion of Virtuousness, which is Love, is wanting – / He is a clear handsome piece of Water in a 35 Park, moved from without – or at best, a smooth stream with one current, & tideless, & of which you can only avail yourself to one purpose.

303 Monday Morning, Jan[uary] 9. 1804 in the Dark with my eyes shut / a loud Thaw wind.

Derwent asleep in the other Bed, God love little dear Heart – & Dorothy, in the Parlour,

o dear Dorothy – 5

& O dear Sara Hutchinson —

304 Shadows in Snow weather on the Lake / I have observed indistinct just like Derwent's Face when the Wanton has veiled it in the thin white Window Curtain in a pretty strong Light, the white Calico strained tight to his Face.

305 Of the Hardheartedness of healthy People.

306 Tuesd[ay] Morn[ing] Jan[uary] 10 1804. – After I had got into bed last night, I said to myself, that I had been pompously enunciating, as a difficulty, a problem of easy & common solution / viz. that it was the effect of Association, we from Infancy up to Manhood under Parents, Schoolmasters, Tutors, Inspectors, &c having had our pleasures & 5 pleasant self-chosen Pursuits [self-chosen because pleasant, and not *originally* pleasant because self-chosen] interrupted, & we forced into dull unintelligible Rudiments or painful Labor / – *Now*, all Duty is felt as a *command*, commands *most often*, & therefore by Laws of Association felt as if *always*, from without / consequently calling up the Sensations &c, of 10 the pains endured from Parents', Schoolmasters', &c &c– commands from without. — But I awoke with gouty suffocation this morning, ½ past one / & as soon as Disease permitted me to think at all, the shallowness & falsity of this Solution flashed on me at once [/] I saw, that the phænomenon occurred far far too early – in early infancy, 2 & 3 15 months old, I have observed it / & have seen it in Hartley, turned up & lay'd bare to the unarmed Eye of merest common sense, that *Interruption* of itself is painful because & as far as it acts as Disruption / & then, without any reference to or distinct recollection of my former theory, I saw great Reason to attribute the effect wholly to the streamy nature of the 20 associating Faculty and especially as it is evident that *they most* labor under this defect who are most reverie-ish & streamy – Hartley, for instance, & myself – / This seems to me no common corroboration of my former Thought on the original of moral Evil in general.

307 The dignity of passiveness to worthy Activity[:] when men shall be as proud within themselves of having remained an hour in a state of deep tranquil Emotion, whether in reading or in hearing or in looking, as they now are in having figured away one hour / O how few can transmute activity of mind into emotion / yet there are [those] who[,] active as the 5 stirring Tempest & playful as a May blossom in a Breeze of May, can yet for hours together remain with hearts broad awake, *& the Understanding* asleep in all but its retentiveness and *receptivity* / yea, & the Latter evinces as great Genius as the Former /

THREE

LONDON, MALTA, ITALY
1804–1806

308 Left Grasmere, Saturday noon, Jan[uary] 14. 1804 – on foot / arrived at Kendal after a sweltring walk thro' heavy hot air & the latter half of the Journey / thro' Drizzle, at 5 o'clock in the evening – 19 miles in 5 hours, & I rested once to lunch.

309 Images of Calmness on Rydale Lake. Jan[uary] 14 / fresh Delves in the Slate Quarry I *mistook* for smoke in the reflection / –
an islet Stone, at the bottom of the Lake, the reflection so bright as to be heaved up out of the water / the Stone & its reflection looked so compleatly one, that Wordsworth remained for more than 5 minutes trying to 5
explain why that Stone had no Reflection / & at last found it out by me / the shore, & green field, a Hill bank below that Stone, & with Trees & Rock forming one brilliant picture without was such, that look at the Reflection & you annihilated the water / it is all one piece of bright Land / just half wink your Eyes & look at the Land, it is then *all* under water, or 10
with that glossy Unreality which a Prospect has, when seen thro' Smoke.

310 O May we All avoid Hazletts on Jury!

311 Friday Evening, Jan[uary] 20, 1804 Observed in the garden of Eaton House the flight of the Brown Linnets, a large flock of whom I had repeatedly disturbed by my foot-fall as I walked by the thicket. / 1. Twinkling of wings. 2 Heavy & swanlike rise & fall, yet so that while one was rising, another was falling – & so 4. Their sweet straight onward 5
motion / they swam on, not with *speed* or haste, much less *hurry*, but with easy natural Swiftness – & then [a] graceful wheel round one half of a circle or more, & then cut straight the diameter of it – 4. their change of position among themselves / right to left, hindw[ard] to the front,

vanguard to the rear – these four motions all at once in one beautiful Whole, like a Machine — 10

312 Bought this pocket-book in Pall Mall, Thursday Jan[uary] 26 / having arrived in London, Tuesday Night, 7 o'clock, Jan[uary] 24, 1804 – proceeded to T. Poole's, 16, Abingdon St, Westminster, & lodged at Mrs Segurs, next door to the House of Lords —

313 Dirty business — Now – said I, with a great effort to conquer my laziness, & a great wish to rest in the generality, what do you mean under the words, dirty Business. – I note this to remember the reluctance of the Mind in general to *analyse* —

314 Sunday Morning, Feb[ruary] 5. 1804 – called on Lamb fully expecting him to be from home, & intending all the way to write a note to him, of apology – found him at home, & while sitting & talking to him, took the pen & note paper, & began to write.

315 We are not inert in the Grave [–] St Paul's Corn in the ground proves this scripturally: Infants growing in their Sleep by natural analogy — What if our growth then be in proportion to the length & depth of the Sleep – with what mysterious grandeur does not this Thought invest the Grave? How poor compared with this an immediate Paradise —— 5

316 When Lady Beaumont was a child, she told me, that previously to her saying her Prayers she endeavored to think of a mountain, or great River, or something *great*, in order to raise up her Soul & kindle it – Sunday Morning, Feb[ruary] 13, 1804

317 Painting & Engravings send us back with new Eyes to Nature – as for instance the picture of the Cottagers by D^oe^ Sart Engraved by Woolelett / the reciprocating Influences of Poetry, Painting &c – and Nature.

318 Will you ask the maid to get me a Hackney Coach? Rickman's, Tuesday Night, Feb[ruary] 21. 1804, 11 o'clock / the day of the Receipt of that heart-wringing Letter from Sara, that put Despair into my Heart, and not merely as a Lodger, I fear, but as a Tenant for Life.

319 Poems in the Soother of Absence –
Ode on a Suicide for Love, whose punishment after his Death consisted in the continuance of the same appetiteless heart-gnawing Passion which he could not reveal: The wanderings of this Ghost – thro' the world may be finely worked up —— 5

320 N.B. in my great Critical Work give a direct close character of all the English Books of Criticism, of Note /

321 The generic how superior to the particular illustrated in Music, how infinitely more perfect in passion & its transitions than even Poetry – Poetry than Painting – & yet Genius how marvellous in all implements!! – March 10th / Lamb + John Lamb. Saturday Night – Knight[']s Bronzes with eyes – Statues — 5

322 The huge Organ Pipe at Exeter larger than that at Haerlem – but *dumb!* Green determined to make it speak / tried all ways & means in vain / till at last he made a second Pipe precisely alike, & placed it by it / – Then it spoke.

323 . . .
Here lies a true Soldier whom all must applaud,
Much hardship he suffer'd at home & abroad,
But the hardest Engagement he ever was in
Was the Battle of Self in the conquest of Sin. 5

Here lies I kill'd by a Sky-
Rocket in the Eye In the year forty

Here *I* lies all putrefaction
Waiting for the Resurrection = a fair statement of Priestley's
intermediate State / 10

324 Friday, April 6th, 1804 – got on board the Speedwell, expecting to sail instantly / but the wind wester[e]d again / Saturday April 7th / quite calm / beautiful sight / Isle of Wight, & the Ships below it / and on the other side 9 men of war in zigzag semicircle, & in the interspaces all sorts of smaller Ships, some with sails reefed, others all flying – the Sun on some, 5 some in shade / their different Shapes & sizes & distinctnesses, & the Portsea Land &c a fine background, into which the sight dies away & is satisfied. The different Signals, Drums, Guns, Bells, & sound of Voices weighing up & clearing Anchors. Wind all against us / Saturday, went on shore / but slept aboard. Dined on board on Sunday. 10

Monday, April 9th, really set sail. In weighing anchor the men grumbled aloud a sort of mutiny – not half our complement of men – Two pressed in the Downs / one ran away at Portsmouth, a rascal of a one-armed Cook better gone than stay[e]d / – Now we are Captain, Mate, 2 boys, 4 men, 3 passengers, one Sheep, 3 pigs, several Ducks & Chicken, 1 Dog, a Cat & 2 Kittens. — Was sickish & feverish for a few Hours on Monday; 15

but mended before dinner, eat a better dinner than my usual – and continued well. But by the Captain's persuasion lay on my bed – in consequence of which I dosed all night diseasedly, & all the morning – got upon deck, & formed different notions. No Health or Happiness without Work / In consequence partly of the Build of the Brig, & partly of its being so heavily laden at its bottom, the Cabbin rocks like a Cradle, when a cruel nurse rocks a screaming Baby. – / On Monday night we travelled like a Top Bough on a Larch Tree in a high wind / pitching & rocking at anchor in a Breeze that would have carried us 9 or 10 knots an hour / 20 25

This morning, Tuesday, April 10th, 1804, a fine sharp morning – the Sea rolls rough & high / but the Ships are before us & behind us. I count 35, and the blue Land, the Start, to our right, & the lonely Gulls fish in among the Ships / & what a beautiful object even a single wave is! I shall employ this morning if only I can lay down a Plan for the rest of my Voyage. 30

1. Being broad awake, & it being day-light, get up, drink a dish of ginger Tea / & do all I can to clean myself then read Italian till breakfast Time /

1. Up – wash – ginger Tea hot. 35
2. Italian till Breakfast Time.
3 Breakfast
4 Write or transcribe my Journal.
5th read the Theodicee & take notes for my Consolations.
6th Then write my Letters on literary Detraction / or a review of Wordsworth / in short, something, beginning with this. 40
7th / between dinner & tea what I can /. Read some Italian if possible.
after tea till bed time try to compose. God grant me fortitude & a perseverant Spirit of Industry!

325 an exquisite purple upon part of the Sea – such as I have often seen [in] the glass of waterglasses.

326 Wednesday, April 11, 1804 / Sea & Sky, & an irregular circle of Ships of which we seem the Center. Saw a nice black faced bright black-eyed white toothed Boy running up to the Main Top with a large Leg of Mutton swung, Albatross-fashion about his neck / – 'Rear'd[')] for a Ship lad, taught every thing by Curses – yet well-behav'd the while, & his Master shed a tear when he died – for the Boy would sing on the Top Mast, a Song neither of Love nor of Wine, & come down with Tears on his Cheeks / 5

327 April 12th / Thursday / the wind from N.E. has changed 5 points to S.E. / but we go on pretty well, & with far less Rocking. 'A neat handed Fellow who could shave himself in a storm, without drawing blood.' We are in the Bight of the Bay of Biscay, & tho' the Breeze blows fresh, yet I feel the Air more warm & genial and the Sky seems bluer. —

This day noon we are in 47 degrees 28 min[utes] of Latitude. —

Delightful weather, motion, relation of the convoy to each other, all exquisite / – and I particularly watched the beautiful Surface of the Sea in this gentle Breeze! – every form so transitory, so for the instant, & yet for that instant so substantial in all its sharp lines, steep surfaces, & hair-deep indentures, just as if it were cut glass, glass cut into ten thousand varieties / & then the network of the wavelets, & the rude circle hole network of the Foam /

And on the gliding Vessel Heaven & Ocean smil'd!

328 Why an't you here? This for ever / I have no rooted thorough thro' feeling – & never exist wholly present to any Sight, to any Sound, to any Emotion, to any series of Thoughts received or produced / always a feeling of yearning, that at times passes into Sickness of Heart.

329 The Sea with its interminable &[,] within the ken of the eye[,] innumerable *multitude* of Sunshine – / Have I not seen masses of plumbago like the Sea / or rather Fire sides, Hobbs, &c, that in certain slant reflections resemble it?

330 N.B. In my Consolations[:] on narrowness of Heart – Lamb can't like the Brothers / *Fox* does not like the Blank Verse Poems / Misery! how is this possible without pleading guilty to some defect of moral Being. If I do not like a poem, I can in my own conceit at least shew a reason why *no* one ought to like [it] / or that they would be better off if they did not. Satur[day] April 14

331 Saturday Morning, Apr[il] 14, 1804 / fine, but we go on slowly and we purchased the loveliness of last night by almost a calm. The Lark alive and brisk.

The elements of this picturesque Effect of a Ship / a man of war, for instance.

1. Its height upon a flat surface / if a Steeple be so uniformly pleasing on a diversified meadow, how much more the Masts of a man of war, referring as with a finger to the Sky, on this vast Level?

2. The proportion of the solid height to the Height above the Hull, about as 40 to 160, made graceful & right by the strongly felt Lightness & Airiness of the Sails / while yet 10
3. The elliptical figure of the Hull & its kindred motion prevent all abrupt or harsh contrast between the wood & the Canvass – to which the masts & in a [?fresh] gale the *stiff* Bellying of the Sails are aidant.
4. The height of the naked mast above the sails, connected however with them by the Pennant & Vane, associated, I think, with the human form on a watch-tower / a general feeling – ex.gr. the *Men* on the tops of conical mountains & of others in Cumberland & Westmor[land] / 15
5. The harmony of the Lines – the ellipses & semicircles of the bellying Sails & of the Hull, with the variety from the permanence of the one & the contingency of the other / 20
6. The terminating Lines of the Sails forming a similar curve with the sail, yet by its determinateness producing a threefold effect / 1. of a strongly felt variety in the Canvassage of the Vessel; / 2 / Secondly, I scarcely know how but its stiffness & determinateness always mingles a notion of natural Straightness which seems to form a link of union with the masts, & so thro' the masts with [the] Hull making one whole of the whole Vessel / while the mast above the Sails connects it with the beholder by obscure resemblance of the human form as seen at a distance or on a height / 3. This determinateness of the stiff rope-hemm'd Edge Lines of the Sails, not dying away into each other, weakening the *sensuous beauty* raises it to the picturesque, giving the whole a greater facility of connecting itself with other Ships as Forms, & of forming an interesting part of a common whole: which if it were a complete visual whole in itself, as a circle with its radii, &c it could not so easily do – 25 30 35
7thly / Every one of these Sails is *known* by the Intellect to have a strict & necessary action & reaction on all the rest, & that the whole is made up of parts, each part referring at once to each & to the whole / – and nothing more administers to the Picturesque than this phantom of complete visual wholeness in an object, which visually does not form a whole, by the influence ab intra of the sense of its perfect Intellectual Beauty or Wholeness. —— To all these must be added the Lights & Shades, sometimes *sunshiny*, sometimes *snowy*: sometimes shade-coloured, sometimes dingy – whatever effect distance, air tints, reflected Light, and the feelings connected with *the* Object (for all Passion unifies as it were by natural Fusion) have in bringing out, and in melting down, differences & contrast, accordingly as the mind finds it necessary to the completion of the idea of Beauty, to prevent sameness or discrepancy. — Of a Fleet of 40 45

Ships more may be said; & probably more will suggest itself, & of less obvious kind, on after quiet Looking, now that the Intellect has done its 50 main business & rests.

They begin to cheat with the metallic pencils. I am forced to take a new one from another Book, having compleatly worn out the one belonging to it / instead of being about 2 inches it was scarcely one; & the metal far softer & more wasteful. 55

No.2 proved by the ill look of a large Vessel with bare sails or the greater part of them reefed / unless it be made more than beautiful by becoming the Language of passion & peril / tho' it is most worthy of Observation, that in such circumstances there is such a wonderful correspondency of the surrounding objects, clouds & billows, & Ships, & their new relations 60 to each other, & to the Stars, the Hull of One to the Masts of the other, &c &c – such a correspondency, I say, either by likeness or counteraction, that the whole Field of Vision becomes sensuously picturesque, & *the parts* acquire as *parts* a charm which they have not as Things per se. — I mean to say, that divested of the passion that makes such a combination 65 of Forms Sublime, it would even sensuously *be grand* / if there be no other & better word. – Pursue this: – & add to the above the *outline* of the whole Ship, which especially in Merchant Ships, Brigs, &c is a beautiful Approach to the oval / – the height of the whole Vessel taken in with the length of the whole / – & forget not to observe what a vast number of 70 incidents the masts & sails of a Ship can represent, a sort of natural Telegraph, the distinctness of a Signal with the eloquence & absolute unarbitrary appropriateness of passion & reality.

332 Blue *pierced* white.

333 Thursday Morning, April 19th, 1804. – Yesternight with a bright moon, the Light of which rolled, like an Island of grey white Reeds on a tossing Lake – how hard to describe that sort of Queen's metal plating, which the Moonlight forms on the bottle-green Sea / the water bright, but the *Green* of the water not bright – & therein Moonlight bright as if [?even it] yet 5 seemed to partake of or rather to be modified by, the color in which it floated – made a different color from its natural blue whiteness without or very obscurely resembling that of the Sea water – *this* as a Mem. that the moon silvering the Sea is not *lively* to Nature – / However, under this moon we sailed at a large rate, and now about 10 o'clock I[,] sitting at 10 the Rudder Case, my Desk, on the Duck Coop, my Seat, have Spain, the Coast of Cadiz to wit, on my left-hand, & Africa, the Barbary Coast, on

my Right – perhaps 6 miles distant from the Spanish Coast, 13 from the Barbary[,] under mountain ridges both / but the Spanish Coast is of course more distinct / I am right abreast of a high Bank, black brown Heath with interspaces & large & small scarifications of light red Clay – beyond this Mountain islands, alongside, & in file resembling Canoes & Boats with their Keels upward. We have a Breeze that promises to let us laugh at Privateers & Corsairs that in a calm will run out, & pick up a Merchant Vessel under the very stern of the Commodore, as a Fox will a Fowl when the Wolf dog that guards the poultry yard, can only bark at him from his Chain / This is Spain! – That is Africa! Now, then, I have seen Africa! &c &c – / Power of Names to give Interest! – When I first sate down, with Europe on my left and Africa on my right, both distinctly visible, I felt a quickening of the movements in the Blood; but still it felt as a pleasure of *amusement* [rather] than of Thought, or Elevation / and at the same time, and gradually winning on the other, the nameless silent Forms of Nature were working on me, like a tender Thought on a man, who is hailed merrily by some acquaintance in his work, & answers it in the same Tone — . This is Africa! That is Europe! – There is *division*, sharp boundary, abrupt Change! – and what are they in Nature – two Mountain Banks, that make a noble River of the interfluent Sea, existing & acting with distinctness and manifoldness indeed, but at once & as one – no division, no Change, no Antithesis! – Of all men, I ever knew, Wordsworth himself not excepted, I have the faintest pleasure in things contingent & transitory. I never, except as a forced Courtesy of Conversation, ask in a Stage, Whose House is that – nor receive the least additional pleasure when I receive the answer. Nay, it goes to a disease in me – as I was gazing at a wall in Caernarvon Castle, I wished the Guide 50 miles off that was telling me, in this Chamber the Black Prince was born / or whoever it was – / I am not certain, whether I should have seen with any Emotion the Mulberry Tree of Shakespere / If it were a Tree of no notice in itself, I am sure, that I should feel by an effort with self-reproach at the dimness of the Feeling – if a striking Tree, I fear, that the Pleasure would be diminished rather than increased / that I should have no unity of Feeling & find in the constant Association of Shakespere's having planted it an intrusion that prevented me from wholly & as a whole man losing myself in the flexures of its Branches & interweaving of its Roots. No doubt, there are times & conceivable Circumstances, in which the contrary would be true, in which the Thought, under this Rock by this Sea shore I know that Giordano Bruno hid himself from the Pursuit of the enraged Priesthood, & overcome with the power & sublimity of the

Truths, for which they sought his Life, thought his Life therefore given him that he might bear witness to the Truth; & morti ultro occurrens, returned & surrendered himself – or here on this Bank Milton used to lie, 55 in late May, when a young man, & familiar with all its primroses made them yet dearer than their dear selves by that sweetest line in the Lycidas / [']And the rathe Primrose that forsaken dies['] / or from this Spot, the immortal Deer Stealer, on his Escape from Warwickshire, had the first View of London, & asked himself – And what am I to do there? — at 60 certain times, uncalled & sudden, subject to no bidding of my own or others, these Thoughts would come upon me, like a Storm, & fill the Place with something more than Nature. — But these are not contingent or transitory / they are Nature, even as the Elements are Nature / yea, more to the human mind / for the mind has the power of abstracting all 65 agency from the former, & considering [them] as mere effects & instruments [–] but a Shakespere, a Milton, a Bruno, exist in the mind as *pure Action*, defecated of all that is material & passive / – And the great moments, that formed them – it is hard & an impiety against a Voice within us, not to regard as predestined, & therefore things of Now & For 70 Ever and which were Always — But it degrades this sacred Feeling, & is to it what stupid Superstition is to enthusiastic Religion, when a man makes a Pilgrimage to see a great man's Shin Bone found unmouldered in his Coffin, &c. – Perhaps the matter stands thus: I could feel amused by these things, & should be[,] if there had not been connected with the 75 great Name, upon which the amusement wholly depends, a higher & deeper Pleasure, that will endure the Co-presence of so mean a Companion; while the mass of mankind, whether from Nature or as I fervently hope from Error of Rearing & the Wor[l]dliness of their after Pursuits, are rarely susceptible of any other Pleasures than those of *amusement*, 80 gratification of curiosity, Novelty, Surprize, Wonderment from the Glaring, the harshly Contrasted, the Odd, the Accidental; and find the reading of the Paradise Lost‡ a Task, somewhat alleviated by a few entertaining Incidents, such as the Pandæmonium and Self-endwarfment of the Devils, the Fools' Paradise, & the transformation of the infernal 85 Court into Serpents, and of their intended Applause into Hisses.

‡ N.B. To attack Johnson with all due severity on this phrase – Yes! and the Bible too! / & all good works / & the Fields, & Rivers, & Mountains / they – & Dr J. among the rest – die of Ennui in them —

This perhaps in the Consolations – on the virtues connected with the 90 Love of Nature, & vice versâ.

334 Soother of absence. / O that I had the language of Music / the power of infinitely varying the expression, & individualizing it even as it is / – My heart plays an incessant music, for which I need an outward Interpreter / – words still over & over again! – and each time I feel differently, tho' children of one family. 5

335 What change of place, Country, climate, company, situation, health of Shrubs, Flowers, Trees / – moving Seasons / & ever is that one Feeling at my Heart / felt like a faint Pain, a spot which it seems I could lay my finger on / – I talk loud or eager, or I read or meditate the abstrusest Researches, or I laugh, jest, tell tales of mirth / & ever as it were, within & 5 behind I think, & image *you* / and while I am talking of Government or War or Chemistry, there comes ever into my bodily eye some Tree, beneath which we have rested, [?some Rock] where we have walked [?together or] on the perilous road edging, *high above* the Crummock Lake / where we sate beneath the rock, & those dear Lips pressed my 10 forehead / – or that Scale Force in its pride, as we saw it – when they laughed at us for two lovers. /

336 Afternoon could not but go to Bed / incessant Rocking, & this from a Sea that crossed us, worse far worse than before —. I passed a wretched time / retained not a morsel of my Saturday Dinner, & took no food whatsoever till Sunday afternoon when I swallowed & with some difficulty retained a little Rice. The Bilge-fury broke loose again – all Saturday & 5 all Sunday, April 29th, 1804[.] Rocked into unwholesome & painful Dozings; passed a better night on Sunday – and on Monday Morning, April 30th, find the wind still against us as before, but the rocking less violent. All Sunday Night it rained & lightened incessantly. N.B. Is it excess of Sympathy in *me* beyond others? or is it from a cause common to 10 all men, namely, that we abstract the pleasant or the painful Sensations of others & so contemplate & sympathize with them as pure pain or pure pleasure? – However this be[,] 20 times since my Departure from Portsmouth, I have felt as if it were impossible that I could sustain the *presence* of Sara, or Mary & Dorothy, on board a vessel for Malta [–] 15 suffering only what I suffer – much less endure the imagination of their being there & coming to *me* – yet all along feel that I could undergo it many times for them & for less ends & that with such an end it would be greatly lightened. . . .

Mem. To write to the Recluse that he may insert something concerning 20 *Ego* / its metaphysical Sublimity & intimate Synthesis with the principle of Co-adunation – without *it* every where all things were a waste – nothing, &c –

337 In my Soother of Absence to note my utter want of sympathy with all the ordinary Love poems, complaining of the Cruelty of my Mistress, of her attachment to another, &c – in short, all that supposes that I could love with no knowle[d]ge of being loved in return – or even with the knowle[d]ge of the contrary. – In short, I shall have abundant matter for 5 contemplation on the Subject in my Perusal of the Italian Love-poems.

338 . . . Poetry a rationalized Dream dealing [?out] to manifold Forms our own Feelings, that never perhaps were attached by us consciously to our own personal Selves. – What is the Lear, the Othello, but a divine Dream / all Shakespere, & nothing Shakespere. — O there are Truths below the Surface in the subject of Sympathy, & how we *become* that which we 5 understandly behold & hear, having, how much God perhaps only knows, created part even of the Form. —— [?] good night ——

339 To Cockermouth / & why I never went thither – to remain a Dream.

340 Hawk with ruffled Feathers resting on the Bowsprit – now shot at, & yet did not move – how fatigued – a third time it made a gyre, a short circuit, & returned again / 5 times it was thus shot at / left the Vessel / flew to another / & I heard firing, now here, now there / & nobody shot it / but probably it perished from fatigue, & the attempt to rest upon the wave! – 5 Poor Hawk! O Strange Lust of Murder in Man! – It is not cruelty / it is mere non-feeling from non-thinking.

341 O dreary words! – the Captain comes off watch, & I am in bed. Says Mrs I. inquiring about the noise – They are setting the [?mainsail] – it is [?almost] calm again! – I will go to bed, tho' I have no sleep in my eyes – I have been trying to read W. Wordsworth's Poem on the Formation of his mind, but I have not been able to deliver myself up to it. – O bless you, all 5 you / Mary, William, the Babe, Dorothy, Sara / & my little ones! – and Good Southey! – and thee, the Mother of my Children, tho' we have lived in Bitterness!

342 Monday, May 14th /. Thank Heaven, 'the almost calm again' was but for a few minutes. The Breeze did its duty broad awake all night, even to this Noon – Indeed not quite so much as there was, at this present time, but still a nice little Breeze.

Mem. I have marked down, I believe, in some one of my pocket books, an Idea from Darwin, meant to prove the entire dependence of all Sublimity on Association. – The sound of Thunder? – Sublime – No! it is a mistake [–] it is a cart over a hollow road, or going under an arch way. – Where is the Sublimity[?] – This fairly took me in; but now I see the fallacy. There is here no dependence of Sublimity &c, but a true actual *Substitution* of the visual Image of a Cart and its low accompaniments[,] and of the word *Cart* & its associations[,] for the Sound first heard which was & always will be sublime if indeed it can be mistaken for Thunder. It is false that the Thunder clap depends for all its sublimity [?on our notion] of the danger [?of Lightning] & Thunder – [?with its] height &c – These *aid* but do not constitute / for how divinely grand in beauty is the great Aurora Borealis / yet no one will pretend that its crackling, tho' strange & impressive, is either sublime or grand or beautiful. But the fairest Proof a contra, & that which darted this Truth thro' my mind was the Commodore's Signal – which is truly sublime even as a Star is / so truly so, as long as I look at it or keep its Image before me, that even the word & visual Image [']Lanthorn['] & [']Candle['] only stands near it or under it, inert. – Let that noise be produced by the Chariot Wheels of Salmoneus – So too recollect the Hawk's flying all that cloudy day falling like a shooting Star thro' a Jacob's Ladder or slanting Column of Sunshine — I am much pleased with this Suggestion, as with every thing that overthrows or illustrates the overthrow of that all-annihilating system of explaining every thing wholly by association / either *conjuring* millions *out* of o, o, o, o, o, o, o o – or into noughts.

343 In the men of continuous and discontinuous minds explain & demonstrate the vast difference between the disjunction conjunctive of the sudden Images *seized* on from external Contingents by Passion & Imagination (which is Passion eagle-eyed) – [']The Breeze I see, is in the Tree – It comes to cool my Babe and me['] – which is the property & prerogative of continuous minds of the highest order, & the conjunction disjunctive of Wit – [']And like a lobster boil'd the Morn From black to red began to turn['], which is the excellence of men of discontinuous minds —

arrange & classify the men of continuous minds — the pseudo-continuous, or *juxta-ponent* mind / metaphysician not a poet – poet not a metaphysican? – poet + metaphysician / – *the faithful* in Love &c ——

344 The very persons who deem you a strange Anachronism of Bigotry for connecting any Horror with the Catholic Faith & its consequences, these so temperate, so smiling, so all-tolerating, '*there-are-good-&-bad-in-all-religions*' People, when Jacobinism came up, & some of its opinions appear to war against the rights of *Property* and for that all its other arti- 5 cles, with what horror! how dangerous! Gog & Magog! – tho' common sense told aloud, that it was [a] monster that would die of the convulsions it was born in /

345 Wednesd[ay] Morn[ing] July 4th, 1804. At Breakfast at Sir Alex. Ball's saw a Lady with Hair, Complexion, and a certain Cast of Countenance that on the first glance of her troubled me inconceivably – after a while I perceived the likeness to S.H. & was near fainting – O what an inconceivable faintness with fondness – / as I went away, I seemed to see clearly the 5 possibility of loving A. and B.[,] A being dead, & B. strikingly like, as truly one soul in two resembling Bodies – A 18 and A 35 years old.

346 Saw in early youth as in a Dream the Birth of the Planets; & my eyes beheld as *one* what the Understanding afterwards divided into 1. the origin of the masses, 2. the origin of their motions, and 3. the site or position of their Circles & Ellipses [–] all the deviations too were *seen* in one intuition of one, the self-same, necessity – & this necessity was a Law 5 of Spirit – & all was Spirit. — And in matter all beheld the past activity of others or their own – this Reflection, this Echo, is matter – its only essence, if essence it be [–] and of this too I saw the necessity and understood it – but I understood not, how infinite multitude and manifoldness could be one. Only I saw & understood, that it was yet more out of 10 my power to comprehend how it could be otherwise – & in this unity I worshipped in the depth of knowle[d]ge that passes all understanding the Being of all things – and in Being their Sole Goodness – And I saw that God is the one, *the* Good – possesses it not, but is it. —
For my own Life – written as an inspired Prophet, – *throughout*. 15

347 Thursday Night at the Opera. Sept[ember] 27, 1804. [I]n reflecting on the cause of the '*meeting* soul' in music, the seeming recognizance, &c &c, the whole explication of *memory* as in the nature of *accord* struck upon me / accord produces a phantom of memory, because memory is always an accord. 5

348 Syracuse, Saturday, Oct[ober] 5. 1804. A Serious Memorandum!
Mem. In company, indeed with all except a very chosen few, never dissent from any one as to the *merits* of another[,] especially in your own supposed department / but content yourself with praising in your turn the really good. Praises of the unworthy are felt by a good man & man of 5
genius as detractions from the worthy, as robberies, so the *flashy* moderns seem to *rob* the ancients of the honors due to them / & Bacon & Harrington are *not* read because Hume & Condilliac *are*. This is an evil; but oppose it, if at all, in books in which you can evolve the whole of your reasons & feelings [–] not in conversation, where it will be inevitably 10
attributed to Envy. Besides, they who praise the unworthy, must be the injudicious: and the eulogies of critics without taste or judgment are the natural pay of authors without feeling or genius – & why rob *them*. Sint unicuique sua præmia.

Coleridge! Coleridge! will you never never learn to appropriate your con- 15
versation to your company? Is it not desecration, indelicacy, a proof of great weakness & [?even vanity to talk to] &c &c, as if you [?talked with Wordswor]th & Sir G. Beau[?mont?]

349 Philosophy to a few, Religion with many, is the Friend of Poetry; as producing the 2 conditions of pleasure from poetry, namely, tranquillity & the attachment of the affections to *generalizations*. God, Soul, Heaven, the Gospel, miracles, &c are themselves a sort of *poetry*, compared with the Lombard St & 'Change alley Speculations. *Oct[ober] 5. 1804.* 5

350 Oct[ober]. 13. 1804. Saturday. Syracuse. – Each man having a spark (to use the old metaphor) of the Divinity, yet a whole fire-grate of Humanity / each therefore will legislate for the whole, spite of the De gustibus non est disputandum, even in trifles[,] till corrected by experience – and at least in this endless struggle of presumption, really occasioned by the ever 5
working Spark of the Universal, and the disappointments & baffled attempts of each, all are disposed to the Jus extrinsecum fortioris (Spinoza) & recognize that reason as the highest, which may not be understood as the best, but of which the Concrete Possession is felt to be the strongest — Then comes Society, Habit, Education, Sleepiness, 10
misery, intrigue, oppression – then *Revolution* / & the circle begins anew / ! – Each man will universalize his notions, & yet each is variously finite. To *reconcile* therefore is truly the work of the Inspired! This is the true *Atonement* – / i.e. to reconcile the struggles of the infinitely various Finite with the *Permanent*. 15

351 To defend the *Opera* = all the objections against *equally* applicable to Tragedy & Comedy without music, & all proceed on the false principle, that Theatrical representations are *Copies* of nature whereas they are imitations.

352 Oct[ober] 21st. 1804 – Monday night – Syracuse. — O my God! or if I dare not continue in that awful feeling! yet oh whatever is good in me, even tho' not in the *Depth*, tho' not in that which is the Universal & Perfect in us, yet oh! by all the ministering Imperfections of my Nature that were capable of subserving the Good – O why have I shunned & fled like a 5 cowed Dog from the Thought that yesterday was my Birth Day, & that I was 32 – So help me Heaven! as I looked back, & till I looked back[,] I had imagined I was only *31* – so completely has a whole year passed, with scarcely the fruits of a *month*! – O Sorrow & Shame! I am not worthy to live! – Two & thirty years – & this last year above all others! – I have done 10 nothing! No I have not even layed up any materials, any inward stores, of after action! – O no! still worse! still worse! body & mind, habit of bedrugging the feelings, & bodily movements, & habit of dreaming without distinct or rememberable . . .

353 Amid cruelly unlike Thoughts as I was passing up the green Lane with the garden on my left on my way to the Theatre, Nov[ember] – Monday, the aromatic Smell of the Poplars came upon me! What recollections, if I were worthy of indulging them.

354 Those crinkled ever varying circles, which the moonlight makes on the not calm, yet not wavy, sea. –
Quarantine, Malta. Nov[ember] 10. Saturday 1804.

355 Beasts & Babies remember: man only recollects. This distinction was made by Aristotle. ——

356 Friday, Nov[ember] 23, 1804
One of the heart-depraving Habits & Temptations of men in power, as Governors, &c &c[,] is to make *instruments* of their fellow-creatures – & the moment, they find a man of Honor & Talents, instead of loving & esteeming him, they wish to *use him* / hence that self-betraying side & 5 down look of cunning &c – and they justify & inveterate the habit by believing that every individual who approaches has selfish designs upon them.

357 Hard to express that sense of the analogy or likeness of a Thing which enables a Symbol to represent it, so that we think of the Thing itself – & yet knowing that the Thing is not present to us. – Surely, on this universal fact of words & images depends by more or less mediations the *imitation* instead of *copy* which is illustrated in very nature s*hakespearianized* / – that 5
Proteus Essence that could assume the very form, but yet known & felt not to be the Thing by that difference of the Substance which made every atom of the Form another thing / – that likeness not identity – an exact web, every line of direction miraculously the same, but the one worsted, the other silk — 10

358 Soother of Absence. Days & Weeks & months pass on / & now a year / and the sun, the Sea, the Breeze has its influences on me, and good and sensib[le] men – and I feel a pleasure upon me, & I am to the outward view of all cheerful & have myself no distinct consciousness of the contrary / for I use my faculties, not indeed as once, but yet freely – but oh 5
[?]! I am never happy, never deeply gladdened [–] I know not, I have forgotten, what the *Joy* is of which the Heart is full as of a deep & quiet fountain overflowing insensibly, or the gladness of Joy, when the fountain overflows ebullient — S.T.C.

359 How like Herrings, and onions[,] our vices are the morning after we have committed them / & even lawful pleasures like the smell of a dinner-room, when you have gone out & re-entered it, after dinner.

360 Nothing & yet the very thing, like the white or blank in a wooden cut, that serves for hair &c. ——

361 Final causes answer to *why?* not to *how?*. & who ever supposed, they did —

362 It is often said, that Books are companions [–] they are so, dear, very dear, Companions! But I often[,] when I read a book that delights me on the whole, feel a pang that the Author is not present – that I cannot *object* to him this & that – express my sympathy & gratitude for this part, & mention some fact that self-evidently oversets a second – start a doubt 5
about a third – or confirm & carry a fourth thought. At times, I become restless: for my nature is very social

363 Well! (says Λαδι βαλλ) the Catholic Religion is better than none / why, to be sure, it is called a Religion: but the ? is, is it, a Religion? Sugar of Lead / Well! better that than no Sugar. Put Oil of Vitriol into my Sallad – well, better that than no oil at all – or a fellow vends a poison under the name of James's Powders – well! we must get the best we can – better that than 5 none! So did not our noble Ancestors reason, or feel – or we should now be Slaves, and even as the Sicilians are at this day – or worse: for even they have been made less foolish in spite of themselves by others' wisdom.

364 To deduce instincts from obscure recollections of a pre-existing State – I have often thought of it – Ey! have I said, when I have seen certain tempers & actions in Hartley, that is *I* in my future State / so I think oftentimes that my children are my Soul. / that multitude & division are not (o mystery) necessarily subversive of Unity. I am sure, that two very 5 different meanings if not more lurk in the word, *one*. S.T.C.

365 Among my wild poem on strange things put into an artificial Brooding-machine or Sand in the Sun three eggs[:] an eagle[']s, a Duck[']s, & a Serpent's — .

366 O said I as I looked on the blue, yellow, green, & purple green Sea, with all its hollows & swells, & cut-glass surfaces – O what an Ocean of lovely forms! – and I was vexed, teazed, that the sentence sounded like a play of Words. But it was not / The mind within me was struggling to express the marvellous distinctness & unconfounded personality of each of the 5 million millions of forms, & yet the undivided Unity in which they subsisted.

367 A brisk Gale, and the spots of foam that peopled the *alive* Sea most interestingly combined with the numbers of white Sea Gulls so that repeatedly it seemed, as if the foam-spots had taken Life and Wing & flown up / – the white precisely same-color Birds rose up so close by the ever perishing white wave head, that the eye was unable to detect the 5 illusion which the mind delighted in indulging —

368 One travels along with the Lines of a mountain / I wanted, years ago, to make Wordsworth sensible of this – / how fine is Keswick Vale, would I repose? My Soul lies & is quiet, upon the broad level vale – would it act? it darts up into the mountain Tops like a Kite, & like a chamois goat runs along the Ridges – or like a Boy that makes a sport on the road of running 5 along a wall, or narrow fence ——

369 To trace the if not absolute birth yet the growth & endurancy of Language from the mother talking to the Child at her breast – o what a subject for some happy moment of deep feeling, and strong imagination. / – [Sara! Sara!] o those dear [children!]

370 The adventures, rivalry, warfare, and final union & partnership of Dr Hocus, & Dr Pocus.

371 Idly talk they who speak of Poets as mere Indulgers of Fancy, Imagination, Superstition, &c – They are the Bridlers by Delight, the Purifiers, they that combine them with *reason* & order, the true Protoplasts, Gods of Love who tame the Chaos.

372 Not to[o] hastily to abandon & kick away the means after the end is or seems to be accomplished / so have I in blowing out the Paper or match with which I have lit a Candle, blown out the Candle at the same instant.

373 Saturday, Dec[ember] 22nd, 1804. The duty of stating the power and in the very formation of the Letters, perceived during the formation, the meaning of the injured mind. The Best remains! Good God! wretched as I may be bodily, what is there good and excellent which I would not do – ? — But this is written in *involuntary* Intoxication. God bless all! 5

374 Sunday, Dec[ember] 23rd / I do not understand the first sentence of the above. I wrote them after that convulsed or suffocated by a collection of wind in my stomach & alternately tortured by its colic pangs in my bowels, I in despair drank three glasses running of whisky & water / the violent medicine answered – I have been feeble in body during the next 5 day, & active in mind – & how strange that with so shaken a nervous System I never have the Head ache! – I verily am a stout-headed, weaker-bowelled, and o! most pitiably weak-*hearted* animal! But I leave it as I wrote it, & likewise have refused to destroy the stupid drunken Letter to Southey which I wrote in the sprawling characters of Drunkenness[.] If I 10 should perish without having the power of destroying these & my other pocket books, the history of my own mind for my own improvement, O friend! Truth! Truth! but yet Charity! Charity! – I have never loved Evil for its own sake, no! nor ever sought pleasure for its own sake, but only as the means of escaping from pains that coiled round my mental powers, as 15 a serpent around the body & wings of an Eagle! My sole sensuality was *not* to be in pain! —

375 How opposed to nature & the fact to talk of the one *moment* of Hume; of our whole being [as] an aggregate of successive single sensations. Who ever *felt* a *single* sensation? Is not every one at the same moment conscious that there co[-]exist a thousand others in a darker shade, or less light; even as when I fix my attention on a white House on a gray bare Hill or rather long ridge that runs out of sight each way (How often I want the german [']unübersehbar[']?) the pretended single sensation is it any thing more than the *Light*-point in every picture either of nature or of a good painter; & again subordinately in every component part of the picture? And what is a moment? Succession with *interspace?* Absurdity! It is evidently only the Licht-pun[k]t, the *Sparkle* in the indivisible undivided Duration. Christmas Day, 1804. . . .

376 A Rainbow strangely preserving its form on broken clouds, with here a bit out, here a bit in, & yet still a rainbow even as you might place bits of colored ribbons at distances so as still to preserve the form of a Bow to the mind. Dec[ember] 25. 1804 —

377 There are two sorts of talkative fellows whom it would be injurious to confound / & I, S.T. Coleridge, am the latter. The first sort is of those who use five hundred words more [than] there needs to express an idea – that is not my case – few men, I will be bold to say, put more meaning into their words than I or choose them more deliberately & discriminatingly. The second sort is of those who use five hundred more ideas, images, reasons &c than there is any need of to arrive at their object / till the only object arrived at is that the mind's eye of the bye-stander is dazzled with colors succeeding so rapidly as to leave one vague impression that there has been a great Blaze of colours all about something. Now this is my case – & a grievous fault it is / my illustrations swallow up my thesis / I feel too intensely the omnipresence of all in each, platonically speaking – or psychologically my brain fibres, or the spiritual Light which abides in the brain marrow as visible Light appears to do in sundry rotten mackerel & other *smashy* matters, is of too general an affinity with all things – and tho' it perceives the *difference* of things, yet is eternally pursuing the likenesses, or rather that which is common / bring me two things that seem the very same, & then I am quick enough to shew the difference, even to hair-splitting – but to go on from circle to circle till I break against the shore of my Hearer's patience, or have my Concentricals dashed to nothing by a Snore – that is my ordinary mishap. At Malta however, no one can charge me with one or the other. I have earned the general character of being a quiet well meaning man, rather dull indeed – & who would have thought,

that he had been a *Poet!* 'O very wretched Poetaster, Ma'am! As to the reviews, it is well known, he half ruined himself in paying cleverer fellows than himself to write them' &c — 25 Dec[ember] 1804

378 How far one might imagine all the association System out of a system of growth / thinking of the Brain & Soul, what we know of an embryo – one tiny particle combines with another, its like[,] & so lengthens & thickens. – & this is at once Memory & Increasing vividness of impression / one might make a very amusing Allegory of an embryo Soul up to Birth! – Try! it is promising! – You have not above 300 volumes to write before you come to it – & as you write perhaps a volume once in ten years, you have ample Time, my dear Fellow! – Never be ashamed of scheming – you can't think of living less than 4000 years, & that would nearly suffice for your present schemes – / To Be sure, if they go on in the same Ratio to the Performance, there is a small difficulty arises / but never mind! look at the bright side always – & die in a Dream! *Oh!*

379 In the Preface of my Metaphys[ical] Work I should say – Once & all read Tetens, Kant, Fichte, &c – & there you will trace or if you are on the hunt, track me. Why then not acknowle[d]ge your obligations step by step? Because, I could not do in a multitude of glaring resemblances without a lie / for they had been mine, formed, & full formed in my own mind, before I had ever heard of these Writers, because to have fixed on the partic[ular] instances in which I have really been indebted to these writers would have [been] very hard, if possible, to me who read for truth & self-satisfaction, not to make a book, & who always rejoiced & was jubilant when I found my own ideas well expressed already by others, & [it] would have looked like a *trick*, to skulk there not quoted[;] & lastly, let me say, because (I am proud perhaps but) I seem to know, that much of the matter remains my own, and that the Soul is *mine*. I fear not him for a Critic who can confound a Fellow-thinker with a Compiler.

380 Good Heaven! that there should be any thing at all – and not nothing – ask the bluntest faculty that pretends to reason / & if indeed he have felt and reasoned, and he must feel that something is which is to be sought after out of the vulgar track of Change-alley Speculation. If my researches are shadowy, what in the name of Reason, are you – or do you resign all pretence to reason, & consider yourself – nay, even that is a contradiction – as a passive o among Nothings?

381 . . . not always, *at all*, & seldom *harshly* to chide, those conceits of words which are analogous to sudden fleeting affinities of mind / even as in a dance – touch & join & off again, & rejoin your partner that leads down with you the whole dance spite of these occasional off-starts, all still not merely conform to, but of and in, & forming, the delicious harmony – Shakespere is not a 1000th parts so faulty as the o o o believe him / [']Thus him that over-rul'd I oversway'd &c &c['] [–] I noticed this to that bubbling ice-spring of cold-hearted mad-headed Fanaticism, the late Dr Geddes — in the [']Heri vidi fragilem frangi; hodie mortalem mori[']

382 It is a most instructive part of my Life[,] the fact, that I have been always preyed on by some Dread, and perhaps all my faulty actions have been the consequence of some Dread or other on my mind / from fear of Pain, or Shame, not from prospect of Pleasure / – So in my Childhood & Boyhood the horror of being detected with a sorehead; afterwards imaginary fears of having the Itch in my Blood – / then a short-lived Fit of Fears from sex – then horror of *Duns*, & a state of struggling with madness from an incapability of hoping that I should be able to marry Mary Evans (and this strange passion of fervent tho' wholly imaginative and imaginary Love uncombinable by my utmost efforts with any regular Hope – / possibly from deficiency of bodily feeling, of tactual ideas connected with the image) had all the effects of direct Fear, & I have lain for hours together awake at night, groaning & praying — Then came that stormy time / and for a few months America really inspired Hope, & I became an exalted Being – – then came Rob. Southey's alienation / my marriage – constant dread in my mind respecting Mrs Coleridge's Temper, &c – And finally stimulants in the fear & prevention of violent Bowel-attacks from mental agitation / then almost epileptic night-horrors in my sleep / & since then every error I have committed, has been the immediate effect of the Dread of these bad most shocking Dreams – any thing to prevent them / – all this interwoven with its minor consequences, that fill up the interspaces – the cherry juice running in between the cherries in a cherry pie / procrastination in dread of this – & something else in consequence of that procrast[ination] &c / – and from the same cause the least languor expressed in a Letter from S.H. drives me wild / & it is most unfortunate that I so fearfully despondent should have concentered my soul thus on one almost as feeble in Hope as myself. 11 Jan[uary] 1805. —

Important metaphysical Hint [–] the influence of bodily vigor and strong Grasp of Touch in facilitating the passion of Hope: 5, 21, 14, 21, 3, 8, 19 – in all degrees even to the full 5, 14, 19, 8, 5, 1, 20, 8 ment and the 2, 15, 20, 8 at once.

383 Every one of tolerable education feels the *imitability* of Dr Johnson's & other such's, style / the inimitability of Shakespere &c – hence I believe arises the partiality of thousands to Johnson – they can imagine *themselves* doing the same / Vanity is at the bottom of it. The number of Imitators proves this in some measure. 5

384 Seeing a nice bed of glowing Embers with one Junk of firewood well placed, like the remains of an old Edifice, and another well nigh mouldered one, corresponding to it, I felt an impulse to put on three pieces of wood, that exactly completed this perishable architecture, tho' it was 11 o'clock, tho' I was that instant going to bed, & there could be in 5 common ideas no possible use in it. Hence I seem (for I write, not having yet gone to bed) to suspect, that this desire of totalizing, of perfecting, may be the bottom-impulse of many, many actions, in which it never is brought forward as an avowed, or even agnized as a conscious, motive / – thence I proceed to think of restlessness in general, its *fragmentary* nature, 10 and its connection if not identification, with the *pains correlative* to the pleasures derived from *Wholeness* – i.e. plurality in unity – & the yearning left behind by those pleasures often experienced.
Mem. To collect facts for a Comparison between a *wood* and a *coal*, fire as to sights, sounds, & bodily Feeling. 15

385 That one language may have advantages, which another has not, that the English language may excel all others in the immense number of its practical words, the trivial names of the operations & component Parts of Ships, of manufactories, &c / that the French may bear the palm in the scientific words of Trades, of military and diplomatic operations &c / that 5 the German exclusive of its world of mining, metallurgic, & mineralogical technical & scientific words has an incomparable army of metaphysical & psychological Phrases, & both by its structure & greek-rivalling facility of composition is of all others the best adapted to logic & intellectual analysis, that the Italian is the sweetest, the Spanish the most 10 majestic in its sounds, (capable indeed of as much sweetness as is desirable, adding falernian strength, & thus calling forth all worthy powers of articulation [,] it may be considered as the perfection of Sound – at all events, very very far more above the Latin, than it is below the Greek[)] – that the English by its monosyllabic, naturalizing, and marvellously 15 metaphorical Spirit (for the excellence wholly out of the Question [–]

What language can exhibit a style that resembles that of Shakespere, Jeremy Taylor, or Burke?) can express more meaning, image, and passion *tri-unely* in a given number of articulate sounds than any other in the world, not excepting even the ancient Greek / that on the other hand the 20
French is at once the most perspicuous & the most pointed language, & therefore the very own language of conversation, & colloquial writing, of light passion, and the social Vanity, which finds its main pleasure in pleasing so as to be admired for pleasing, & attains its end by turns of phrase (that like the painted dust-plumes on the Butterflies wing, or the 25
colours of a Bubble must not be examined by the grasp) by turns of phrase, that, like flowery Tufts covering & wholly concealing a Hollow, seem to have, but have not, a Substratum[,] & preeminently too by a perpetual Tampering with the morals without offending the ‡ Decencies / all this I can fully comprehend, & do most readily admit / consequently, I 30
can admit that in the narrative Epic and all the simpler modifications of Thought, and Passion, and general Imagery the Italian may yield only to the Spanish, & the Spanish only to the Greek, and that the It[alian] and Span[ish] really beyond the other living Languages be adapted to the sorts of Poetry implied in this description, & that the English not by 35
accidental Production of Genius, but by its natural constitution stands unequalled for all kinds of Poetry, in which the more complex and profounder Passions are united with deep Thought, for the Drama, whether Comedy or Tragedy, so that it is *Poetry* ° [( ]for in modern Comedies that professedly *copy* elegant conversation I am disposed to believe that 40
the French are our Superiors) for dramatic poetry, for impassioned and *particularized* Description, (see Burns' description of a Brook, and Wordsworth's Poetry in a hundred places) for rapid associations of sensuous Images – and that species of Delight from unexpected combinations of them which when it excites a disposition to laughter or even to a smile, 45
is usually called wit / and fancy in other cases [this tho' the common distinction, I perceive to be deficient / a better & perhaps the true & only tenable distinction would be, that where the manifest intention of the passage is to direct the attention chiefly to the combination for its own sake, for the sake of the pleasure derived from the surprize[,] it is properly 50
called *wit* – but where the combination is introduced either for the sake of some Reasoning or Fact to be illustrated by it [even tho' the illustration should bedazzle the res illustrate into obscurity by error of Judgment in the writer] or if introduced for its own sake, yet for the pleasure produced by the picture as gratifying the mental eye either by its colours, or its 55
picturesque combination or both, and not chiefly for the electric sensa-

tion derived from the surprize, then it is properly called Fancy / the difference is indeed only in the Tone of mind of the writer or speaker, & in the intention of the sentence or sentences / but these two dispositions are according to the *predominance* of the one or the other characteristic of 60 two very, very different sorts of intellectual power / the first belongs to men of Cleverness and Talent, the latter tho' by no means essentially constitutive of Genius, has yet a close affinity to it, and is most often an effect and attendent of it /] end. Now how to get back, having thus belabyrinthed myself in these most parenthetical parentheses? Cut thro' 65 at once, & now say in half a dozen Lines what a half a dozen Lines would have enabled me to say at the very beginning / but my Thoughts, my Pocket-book Thoughts at least, move like a pregnant Polypus in sprouting Time, clung all over with young Polypi each of which is to be a thing of itself – and every motion out springs a new Twig of Jelly-Life / – The 70 Spanish including the Portugese, & Italian Languages from their sweetness and pomp of sound, & from many political causes having less connection with the low and ludicrous in the words and consequent power of expressing common things with dignity without deviating from nature and simplicity (I am speaking, of the language not of the Thoughts) is 75 better suited than the other Eur[opean] Tongues to certain sorts of poetry, the English better to the *drama poetry*, to distinct painting, rapid association & combination both of images with images, & of images, & combinations of images[,] with the moral and intellectual world, and vice versa[,] words of passion and thought with natural images. 80

Full many a glorious morning have I seen
Flatter the mountain Tops with sov'ran eye /

and of the former take this as an illustration

Was it the proud full Sail of his Great Verse &c

all this seems to me Just and true / 85

° but I cannot admit that any language can be unfit for poetry, or that there is any language in which a divinely inspired Architect may not sustain the lofty edifice of Verse on its two Pillars of Sublimity and Pathos. Yet I have heard Frenchmen, nay even Englishmen, assert this of the German / which contains perhaps an hundred passages equal to the 90

Ein Gott ist, ein heiliger Wille lebt
Wie auch der menschliche wanke:
Hoch über der Zeit und dem Raume webt
Lebendig der höchste Gedanke!

Und ob alles in ewigem Weschel kreist, 95
Es beharret im Weschel ein ruhiger Geist.

and I have heard both Germans and Englishmen (and these too men of true feeling & Genius, & so many of them that such a company of my betters makes me not ashamed to the having myself being guilty of this Injustice) assert that the French Language is unsusceptible of Poetry, in 100 its higher and purer sense, of Poetry, which excites emotion not merely creates amusement, which demands continuous admiration, not regular recurrences of conscious Surprize, and the effect of which is Love and Joy. Unfortunately, the Manners, religion, and government of France, and the circumstances of its emergence from the polyarchy of feudal Barony, have 105 given a bad taste to the Parisians – so bad a one as doubtless to have mildewed many an opening Blossom. I cannot say, that I know & can name any one French writer, that can be placed among the great Poets – but when I read the Inscription over the Chartreux

C'est ici que la Mort et que la Verité 110
Elevent leur[s] flambe[a]ux terribles,
C'est de cette demeure au monde inaccessible
Que l'on passe à l'Eternité.

I seem to feel, that if France had been for ages a free and a protestant nation, and a Milton had been born in it, the French Language would not 115 have precluded the Production of a Paradise Lost / tho' it might perhaps that of an Hamlet or Lear.

386 It is not without a certain sense of self-reproof as well as self-distrust, that I ask, or rather that my understanding suggests to me the Quere, whether this divine poem (in so original a strain of thought and feeling honorable to human nature) would not have been more perfect, if the 3rd, 4th, and 5th Stanzas had been omitted, and the 10th and 11th transposed so as to stand 5 as the 3rd & 4th. It is not – perhaps not at all, but certainly not principally – that I feel any meanness in the '*needles*'; but not to mention that the words 'once a shining store' [are] a speck in the diamond, (in a less dear poem I might perhaps have called it more harshly a *rhyme-botch*) and that the word 'restless' is rather too strong an impersonation for the serious tone, 10 the *real*ness, of the Poem, & seems to tread too closely on the mock-heroic; but that it seems not true to poetic feeling to introduce the affecting circumstance of dimness of Sight from decay of nature on an occasion so remote from the *το καθολου* / and that the 5th Stanza, graceful and even affecting as the *spirit* of the playfulness is, or would be at least in 15 a poem having less depth of feeling, breaks in painfully here / the age and

afflicting infirmities both of the Writer & his Subject seem abhorrent from such trifling of – scarcely Fancy, for I fear if it were analysed that the whole effect would be found to depend on phrases hackneyed, and taken from the Almshouse of the Muses. The test would be this – read the 20 poem to a well-educated but natural Woman, an unaffected gentle Being endued with sense and sensibility, substituting the 10th & 11th Stanzas for these three / & some days after shew her the Poem as it now stands / I seem to be sure, that she would be shocked / an Alien would have intruded himself, & be found sitting in a circle of dear Friends whom she 25 expected to have found *all to themselves* . . . . S.T.C.

387 of my Mahometan Superstition – dread as to the destruction of Paper. I am almost ashamed to confess to myself, what pulling back of Heart I feel whenever I wish to light a candle or kindle a fire with a Hospital or Harbour Report / and what a cumulus lie upon my Table, I not able to conjecture what use they can ever be, and yet trembling lest what I thus 5 destroyed might be of some use, in the way of knowle[d]ge. This seems the excess of a good feeling; but it is ridiculous. Monday Feb[ruary] 11, 1805.

388 Tuesday, an hour and ½ after Noon (½ after 1.) Feb[ruary] 12, 1805 – Thinking during my perusal of Horsley's Letters in Rep[ly] to Dr P[riestley's] objections to the Trinity on the part of Jews, Mahometans, and Infidels, it burst upon me at once as an awful Truth what 7 or 8 years ago I thought of proving with a *hollow Faith* and for an *ambiguous purpose*, 5 my mind then wavering in its necessary passage from Unitarianism [which as I have often said is the Religion of a man, whose Reason would make him an Atheist but whose Heart and Common sense will not permit him to be so] thro' Spinosism into Plato and St John / No Christ, No God! – This I now feel with all its needful evidence, of the Under- 10 standing: would to God, my spirit were made conform thereto – that No Trinity, no God. – That Unitarianism in all its Forms is idolatry, and that the remark of Horsley is most accurate, that Dr Priestley's mode of converting the Jews & Turks is in the great essential of religious Faith to give the name of Christianity to their present Idolatry – truly the trick of 15 Mahomet, who finding that the Mountain would not come to him went to the Mountain. O that this Conviction may work upon me and in me / : and that my mind may be made up as to the character of Jesus, and of historical Christianity, as clearly as it is of the Logos and intellectual or spiritual Christianity – that I may be made to know either their especial 20 and peculiar Union, or their absolute disunion in any peculiar Sense.

389 Friday + Saturday 12–1 o'clock / What a sky, the not yet orbed moon, the spotted oval, blue at one edge from the deep utter Blue of the Sky, a *mass* of *pearl*-white Cloud below, distant, and travelling to the Horizon, but all the upper part of the Ascent, and all the Height, such *profound* Blue, *deep* as a deep river, and deep in color, & those two depths so entirely *one*, as to 5 give the meaning and explanation of the two different significations of the epithet (here so far from divided they were scarcely *distinct*) scattered over with thin pearl-white Cloudlets, hands, & fingers, the largest not larger than a floating Veil / Unconsciously I stretched forth my arms as to embrace the Sky, and in a trance I had worshipped God in the Moon / the 10 Spirit not the Form / I felt in how innocent a feeling Sabeism might have begun / O not only the Moon, but the depth of Sky! – the Moon was the *Idea*; but deep Sky is of all visual impressions the nearest akin to a Feeling / it is more a Feeling than a Sight / or rather it is the melting away and entire union of Feeling & Sight / and did I not groan at my unworthiness, 15 & be miserable at my state of Health, its effects, and effect-trebling Causes? O yes! – Me miserable! O yes! – Have Mercy on me, O something *out* of me! For there is no *power* (and if that *can* be, less *strength*) in aught *within* me! Mercy! Mercy!

Sat[urday] Morn[ing] 2 o'clock. S.T.C. 20

390 Those Whispers just as you have fallen or are falling asleep – what are they and whence?

391 In Illustration of what I have written in my Cottle-book on Envy suspected where only resentment is felt, & an uneasiness at a non-harmony, the wish not to see any thing admirable where you find, especially in the moral character, any thing low or contemptible, and the consequent wish to avoid the struggle within, this anti monadic feeling, this (what shall I 5 say?) *knowing*, *feeling*, a man to be *one*, yet not understanding how to think of him but as two —— in illustration of this I confess that it has cost & still costs my philosophy some exertion not to be vexed that I must admire – aye, greatly, very greatly, admire *Richardson* / his mind is so very vile a mind – so oozy, hypocritical, praise-mad, canting, envious, concu- 10 piscent / – But to understand & draw *him* would be to produce almost equal to any of his own, but in order to do this, '*down proud Heart down!*' as we teach little Children to say to themselves – *bless them!* – (N.B. my fat Boy, Derwent!) – all hatred down! – Charity, Calmness, an heart fixed on the good parts, tho' the *Understanding* is surveying all. – Richardson felt 15 truly the defect of Fielding – or rather what was not his excellence, & made that his *Defect*, a trick of Uncharitableness often played, chiefly, tho'

not exclusively by Contemporaries. Fielding's Talent was *Observation* not *Meditation* – But Richardson was not Philosopher enough to know the difference — say rather, to understand and develope it / Strange! to bring two such names together, as Cottle's and Richardson's – Yet amid & in spite of the vast difference there are points of resemblance / & I must not be afraid to look steadily at them. —

N.B. That deep intuition of our *oneness* – is it not at the bottom of many of our faults as well as Virtues / the dislike that a bad man should have any virtues, a good man any faults / & yet something noble and incentive is in this /

392 8 March 1805
But yesternight I pray'd aloud
In Anguish and in Agony —
Help, Lord! or I perish.

393 9th / 1 o'clock Sunday Morning —. 1805.
O keep me from utter Despair! ah
what Hope?
S.T.C.

394 March 16. 1805. Cause of the offence or disgust received by the *mean* in good poems when we are young, and its diminution and occasional evanescence when we are older in true taste / that at first we are from various causes delighted with *generalities* of Nature which can all be expressed in dignified words / but afterwards becoming more intimately acquainted with Nature in her detail we are delighted with *distinct* vivid ideas, and with vivid ideas most when made distinct / & can most often forgive and sometimes be delighted with even a low image from art or low life when it gives you the very thing by an illustration / as Cowper's stream '*inlaying*' the level vale as with silver / & even Shakespeare's shrill-tongued Tapster, answering shallow wits applied to echoes in an echo-full place /

395 Wednesday Night, 20th March, 1805, has past into Thursday Morning, ½ past 2. I arose & as I past by the last window of the Room made *a vow* aloud / O me! that I ever should have had need to make such a Vow! – and *Mss σετκο9* / Can I wonder that good men have joined in the cry of the Vileness of Human Nature! Their mistake was either logical or of nomenclature / they either said – H.N. was *evil* because there was *evil* in H.N. = false logic, since they might equally say, H.N. is good for there is good in H.N. – & so either involve contradiction in terms, or destroy the

unity of H.N. – or else they *do* destroy the Unity of H.N. & make the Association without *will* or *reason*, fantasms and fantastic feelings, the concupiscent, vindictive, and *narcissine*‡ part of our nature one separate, dividuous being, and the pure Will and ever benevolent *Reason* they make another Thing, & call it Grace, or the Holy Spirit, or God / Now this appears imprudent, as furnishing excuses for Despair and spiritual Sloth, and instead of that best prayer of putting our shoulders to the wheel with upturned eyes, & heart, so that the co-operating muscles themselves *pray*, we stand idle & gossip to Hercules with our Tongues / The Cart will never be out of the Slough or Rut. Merciful God! grant that this Rising out of my Bed may be a Resurrection to my better Spirit! . . .

‡ I mean, the not me becoming great and good by spreading thro' and combining with all things, but all [things] becoming mean to me by the phantom-feeling of their being concentered *in me* / & only valuable as associated in the symbolical sense (the eye in the seeing; the ear in the blind / the taste in infants, the feeling in the adult deaf, and blind, (& consequently dumb) – Stallmaster at Hanover) with our own Symbol / = to men in general, our visual Form. /

396 [']Tis one source of mistakes concerning the merits of Poems that to those read in youth men attribute all that praise which is due to Poetry in general, merely considered as select language in metre (Little children should not be taught verses, in my opinion / better not seen till ten or eleven years old –)[. T]wo kinds of pleasure are procured, in the two master-movements & impulses of man, the gratification of the Love of Variety with the grat[ification] of the Love of Uniformity – and that by a recurrence, delightful as a painless and yet exciting act of memory, tiny breezelets of surprize, each one destroying the ripplets which the former had made, yet all together keeping the surface of the mind in a bright dimple-smile. Hatred of Vacancy reconciled with the Love of Rest — These and other causes often make Poetry an overpowering Delight to a Lad of Feeling, as I have heard Poole relate of himself respecting Edwin and Angelina / – But so it would be with a man bred up in a Wilderness by unseen Beings, who should yet converse and rationalize – how beautiful would not the first other Man appear, whom he saw, & knew to be a man by the resemblance to his own image seen in the clear Stream / he would in like manner attribute to the man all the divine attributes of humanity, tho' haply it should be a very ordinary or even almost ugly man, compared with a hundred others. Many of us have felt this with respect to women, who have been bred up where few are to be seen / and I

acknowle[d]ge that both in persons and in poems it is well *on the whole* that we should retain our first Loves; tho' alike in both cases evils have happened as the consequence — 1 April, 1805.

397 *31 March, 1805.* Sunday Night, 11 o'clock. – This day noon, a little after one o'clock Sir A. Ball sent for me – he not being in his study, I went into the Drawing Room, which was full of Visitors – Lady Ball addressed me, asking me if I knew Capt[ai]n Wordsworth / I said, a little – Is he not a Brother of the Mr Wordsworth, you so often talk of? – No, I replied, still 5 imagining she meant the Cousin / But you have heard his melancholy fate? What? said I / & the Ship? – Here I turned pale & repeated the Question / Going from England, it sunk / & 300 men are lost – & only but one hundred saved / . But the Captain / he is lost, said Lady Ball, her voice faltering, for she saw my Emotion / I could just say – Yes! it is the 10 Brother / & retired from the Room / Sir Alexander followed me, upon Business – and Dr Sewel to invite me to dine with him / I was nearly strangled – and at last just got out – I have just heard of the Death of a dear Friend, Sir! excuse me / – & got home, led by the Sergeant & followed to the Door by Sir A.B. O what an Afternoon! – O William, O 15 Dorothy, Dorothy! – Mary – & you loved him so! – And o blessed Sara, you whom I in my imagination at one time I so often connected with him, by an effort of agonizing Virtue, willing it with cold sweat-drops on my Brow! – How shall I ever visit Langdale / O it will look like a hollow Vault – like a Cenotaph / his Tomb & a more heart-rending sight 20 because O Christ! – Dear dear John! these Tears tho' from eyes that throb and smart are pleasure compared to what I have felt, to what I shall feel. – Methinks, it is impossible to live / I shall hear next of Sara's Death / no, not of William's – no! no! – surely not – no surely, if there be intention in any thing, or goodness in Providence / God forgive me! – I for myself 25 despair of ever seeing my home. They are expecting me – did they not even so expect him! – O God have pity on us! O may Almighty God bless you, my Friends! and comfort you – dearest Dorothy, Mary, dear dear Mary – & Sara, deepest yet hopeless Hope! Ah venerated William / how will you and Dorothy look at times . . . 30

398 2 April, 1805 The first yellow green leaves of the figures scattered all over‡ the Tree, & yet thinly, & yet disclosing every branch & every grey twig[,] resembled to a wonder a flight of large green Butterflies alighted on the leafless Tree / all shot through with Sunshine

‡ no! only at the extremities of each twig. 5

399 The beautiful Milk Thistle with the milk-blue-white veins or fibres up & athwart its dark green Leaves.

400 Midnight 5 April 1805. I will write as truly as I can from *Experience* [–] actual individual *Experience* – not from Book-knowle[d]ge. But yet it is wonderful how exactly the Knowle[d]ge from good books coincides with the experience of men of the World, as I have often noticed when much younger / in men of the World who beginning to withdraw a little into 5 themselves, commonly by reading – I have noticed in them their deep delight in so many passages which had escaped me – so much in so many others which I had never heard of *but from Books* / Experience necessary no doubt, if only to give a *light* and *shade* in the mind, to give to some ideas a greater vividness than others, & thereby to make it a thing of Time 10 and outward reality – practical – for all being equally vivid = the whole becomes a dream. But notwithstanding this & other reasons, I yet believe that the saws against Book-knowle[d]ge are handed down to us from Times when Books conveyed only abstract Science or abstract Morality & Religion / whereas in the present day what is there of real Life, in all 15 its goings on, Trades, Manufacturies, high Life, low life, animate & inanimate that is not *in books*. Books are conversation at present. Evil as well as Good in this, I well know / but Good too as well as Evil —

401 O dear John! and so ended thy dreams of Tairns & mountain Becks, & obscure vales in the breasts and necks of Mountains! So thy dream of living with or among thy Brother & *his* – O Heavens! Dying in all its Shapes; shrieks; and confusion; and mad Hope; and Drowning more deliberate than Suicide; – these, these were the Dorothy, the Mary, the 5 Sara Hutchinson, to kiss the cold Drops from thy Brow, & to close thy Eyes! – Never yet has any Loss gone so far into the Life of Hope, with me. I now only fear. – 6 Ap[ril] 1805

402 8 Apr[il] 1805. Monday. – The favorite Object of all oriental Tales, & that which inspiring their Authors in the East inspires still their Readers every where is the impossibility of baffling Destiny, & that what we considered as the means of one thing becomes in a strange manner the direct means of the Reverse. O dear John Wordsworth! what Joy at 5 Grasmere that you were made Capt[ai]n of the Abergavenny & so young too! / now it was next to certain that you would in a few years settle in your native Hills, and be verily one of *the Concern*. – Then came your Share in the brilliant action with Linois – I was at Grasmere in spirit only! but in Spirit I was one of the Rejoicers – as Joyful as any, & perhaps more 10

Joyous! – This doubtless not only enabled you to lay in a larger & more advantageous Cargo, but procured you a voyage to India instead of China / & in this a next to certainty of Independence / – and all these were Decoys of Death! – Well! – but a nobler feeling than these vain regrets would become the Friend of the man whose last words were – 'I have 15 done my Duty! let her go![’] – – Let us do our *Duty*: all else is a Dream, Life and Death alike a Dream / this short sentence would comprize, I believe, the sum of all profound Philosophy, of ethics and metaphysics conjointly, from Plato to Fichte – S.T.C. —

403 I humbly thank God, that I have for some time past been more attentive to the regulation of my Thoughts – & the attention has been blessed with a great measure of Success. There are few Day-dreams that I dare allow myself at any time; and few & cautiously built as they are, it is very seldom that I can think myself entitled to make lazy Holiday with any one of 5 them. I must have worked hard, long, and well, to have earned that privilege / . So akin to Reason is Reality, that what I could *do* with exulting Innocence, I can not always *imagine* with perfect innocence / for Reason and Reality can stop and stand still, new Influxes from without counteracting the Impulses from within / and *poising* the Thought. But 10 Fancy and Sleep *stream on*; and (instead of outward Forms and Sounds, the Sanctifiers, the Strengtheners!) they connect with them motions of the Blood and nerves, and images forced into the mind by the feelings that arise out of the position & state of the Body and its different members. I have done innocently what afterwards in absence I have like- 15 wise day-dreamed innocently, during the being awake; but the Reality was followed in Sleep by no suspicious fancies / the Day-dream *has* been. Thank Heaven! however / Sleep has never yet desecrated the images, or supposed ‡ Presences, of those whom I love and revere. ‡ There is often a dim sense of the Presence of a Person in our dreams, whose form does not 20 appear.

All the above-going throw lights on my mind with regard to the origin of Evil. $\upsilon\lambda\eta$ = confusio = passio = finiri // Reason, Action, Forma efformans. [= means 'the same as': // 'opposed to'.]

404 A Treasure of Trash!

405 Saturday Night, April 14, 1805 – In looking at Objects of Nature while I am thinking, as at yonder moon dim-glimmering thro' the dewy window-pane, I seem rather to be seeking, as it were *asking*, a symbolical language for something within me that already and forever exists, than

observing any thing new. Even when that latter is the case, yet still I have always an Obscure feeling as if that new phænomenon were the dim Awaking of a forgotten or hidden Truth of my inner Nature / It is still interesting as a Word, a Symbol! It is Λογος, the Creator! and the Evolver!

What is the right, the virtuous Feeling, and consequent action, when a man having long meditated & perceived a certain Truth finds another, [?] foreign Writer, who has handled the same with an approximation to the Truth, as he had previously conceived it? – Joy! – Let Truth make her Voice *audible.*

While I was preparing the pen to write this remark, I lost the train of Thought which had led me to it. I meant to have asked something else, now forgotten: for the above answers itself – it needed no new answer, I trust, in my Heart. 14 April, 1805 –

406 . . .

that all the realities about me lose their natural *healing* powers / at least, diminish the same, & become not worthy of a Thought. Who that thus lives with a continually divided Being can remain healthy! I work hard, I do the duties of common Life from morn to night / but verily I raise my limbs, [']like lifeless *Tools*' — The organs of motion & outward action perform their functions at the stimulus of a galvanic fluid applied by the *Will*, not by the Spirit of Life that makes Soul and Body one / Thought and Reality two distinct corresponding Sounds, of which no man can say positively which is the Voice and which the Echo. O the beautiful Fountain or natural Well at Upper Stowey – . . .

The images of the weeds which hung down from its sides, appeared as plants growing up, straight and upright, among the water weeds that really grew from the Bottom / & so vivid was the Image, that for some moments & not till after I had disturbed the water, did I perceive that their roots were not neighbours, & they side-by-side Companions. So – even then I said – so are the happy man's *Thoughts* and *Things* – (in the language of the modern Philosophers, Ideas and Impressions.) — . . .

407 Schiller disgusted with Kotzebueisms deserts from Shakespere. What? cannot we condemn a counterfeit, & yet remain admirers of the Original? This is a sufficient Proof, that the first Admiration was not sound, or founded on sound distinct perceptions / it was a sound feeling, but cloathed & manifested to the consciousness by false Ideas. And now the French Stage, is to be re-introduced / O Germany! Germany! – why this

endless Rage of Novelty! Why, this endless Looking-out of thyself? – – But stop! let me not fall into the Pit, I was about to warn others of – let me not confound the discriminating character & genius of a nation with the conflux of its Individuals, in *Cities* & *Reviews* / Let England be 10 Sir P. Sidney, Shakespere, Spenser, Milton, Bacon, Harrington, Swift, Wordsworth, and never let the names of Darwin, Johnson, Hume, *furr* it over! – If these too must be England, let them be another England / — or rather let the first be old England, the spiritual platonic old England / & the second[,] with Locke at the head of the Philosophers & Pope of 15 the Poets, with the long list of Priestleys, Paleys, Hayleys, Darwins, Mr Pitts, Dundasses, &c &c – be representative of commercial G[reat] Britain / these have their merits, but are as alien to me, as the Mandarin Philosophers & Poets of China / even so Leibnitz, Lessing, Voss, Kant, shall be *Germany* to me, let whatever Coxcombs rise up, & *shrill* it away in 20 the Gras[s]hopper-vale of Reviews / and so shall Dante, Ariosto, Giordano Bruno be my Italy / Cervantes my Spain / and o! that I could find a France for my Love! / but ah! spite of Paschal, Madame Guyon, and Moliere[,] France is my Babylon, the Mother of Whoredoms in Morality, Philosophy, Taste – / the French themselves feel a 25 foreign[n]ess in these Writers / How indeed is it possible at once to *love* Paschal & Voltaire?

408 The ψευδο-poets, Campbell, Rogers, Cottle etc, both by their writings & moral characters tend to bring poetry into disgrace / and but that men in general are the Slaves of the same wretched infirmities, they would do it and it would be well / The true Poet could not smother the sacred fire / 'his Heart burnt within him, and he spake' — & Wisdom would be 5 justified by her Children / but the false Poet (i.e the No-poet) would be prevented from scribbling, finding poetry in contempt among the Many, of whose Praise, whatever he may affirm, he is alone ambitious.

409 Gravitation, all in all / nothing in any one part, as fluid, ether, or such like / – analogy of this to *Soul*, to Consciousness / that nothing-something, something-nothing /

410 The more I reflect, the more exact & close appears to me the Similie of a *Watch* and Watches : the Sun & motion of the heavenly Bodies in general, to the conscience and consciences : : to the reason & goodness of the Supreme / Never goes quite right, any one; no two go exactly the same, they derive their dignity and use as being Substitutes and 5 Exponents of heavenly motions / but still in a thousand instances they are

& must be our instructors, by which we must act, in practice presuming a co-incidence, while theoretically we are aware of incalculable *Variations*.

411 20th October, 1805 – My Birth Day! – O Thought [of] Agony! O Thought of Despair! drive me not to utter Madness –

412 The understanding of Metaphor for Reality (Loaves and Fishes = Apostles, Fishermen, Christ's Doctrine / &c &c) one of the Fountains of the many-headed River of Credulity which overflowing covers the world with miscreations & reptile monsters, & then gives its huge supply thro' its many mouths into the Sea of Blood. 5

413 To W.—— in the progression of Spirit / once Simonides, or Empedocles or both in one? – O that my Spirit purged by Death of its Weaknesses, which are alas! my *identity* might flow into *thine*, & live and act in thee, & be Thou.

414 God knows, that at times I derive a comfort even from my infirmities, my sins of omission & commission, in the joy of the deep feeling of the opposite Virtues in the two or three whom I love in my Heart of Hearts / Sharp therefore is the pain when I find faults in these Friends, opposite to my Virtues. I find no comfort in the notion of *average* for I wish to love even 5 more than to be beloved & am so haunted by the conscience of my many Failings that I find an unmixed pleasure in esteeming & admiring, but in Esteem & Admiration I feel as a man whose good dispositions are still alive feels in the enjoyment of a *darling* Property on a doubtful Title. My instincts are so far dog-like / I love beings superior to me better than my 10 Equals – but inferior is so painful to me, that I never in common Life, feel a man my Inferior except by after-reflection. What seems vanity in me is in great part attributable to this Feeling but of this hereafter I will cross examine myself—

415 Modern Poetry charaterized by the Poets' <u>*anxiety*</u> to be always *striking* – The same march in the Greek & Latin Poets / Claudian, who had powers to have been any thing – observe in him the anxious craving Vanity! every Line, nay, every word *stops*, looks full in your face, & asks & *begs* for Praise. A Chinese Painting [–] no distances no perspective / all in the 5 fore-ground – and this is all *Vanity*. I am pleased that when a mere Stripling I had formed the opinion, that true Taste was Virtue / & that bad writing was bad feeling.

416 Σωμα ψυχοπλαστον Ψυχη σωμαπλατт[ου]σα
Reo = reor[,] probably an obsolete Latin word, and res the second person singular of the Present Indicative – / If so, it is the Iliad of Spinozo-Kantian, Kanto-Fichtian, Fichto-Schellingian Revival of Plato-Plotino-Proclian Idealism in a Nutshell *from* a Lilliput Hazel. Res = thou art 5 thinking. – Even so our 'Thing': id est, thinking or think'd. Think, Thank, Tank = Reservoir of what has been *Thinged* — Denken, Danken – I forget the German for Tank / The, Them, This, These, Thence, Thick, Thing, Thong, Thou, may be all hocus-pocused by metaphysical Etymology into Brothers and Sisters – with many a Cousin-German / all 10 little Miss Thetas, the Θ being a Circle, with the Kentron, or central Point, creating the circumference & both together the infinite Radii / – the central point is primary Consciousness = living Action; the circumference = secondary Consciousness or Consc[iousness] in the common sense of the Word[;] and the passing to and fro from the one to the other 15 Thought, Things, necessary Possibilities, contingent Realities / = Father, Son, Holy Ghost / the *Το Ον, Ο Λυγος, η Σοφια* / — The · is I which is the articulated Breath drawn inward, the O is the same sent outward, the ⊙ or Theta expresses the synthesis and coinstantaneous reciprocation of the two Acts, the Dualism of *Thought* by *Distinctions*, the Unity of *Thing* 20 by Indivisibility / and then the Radii, *Ακτῖνες* = Res in Theta (or perhaps Delta) = *Αγω* (acta) *εν θητα* (or Tau) — [O Lord! What thousands of Threads in how large a Web may not a metaphysical Spider spin out of the Dirt of his own Guts / but alas! it is a net for his own super-ingenious Spidership alone! It is so thin, that the most microscopical Minitude of 25 Midge or Sand-flea – so far from being detained in it – passes thro' without seeing it. —] These Words within the Crotchets – are Truth for the Worldlings, all without are Crotchets with a Vengeance to them / but to me those Words are the Crotchets, the Capapee Masquerade Domino of my own Convictions in the Opinions of the men of supposed gesunder 30 Menschenverstand / the former are the naked Flesh & Blood, Bone and Muscle of my own individual Faith /

Rome – Jan[uary] 1. 1806. Monday

417 1 Jan[uary] 1806. Heard from Mr Jackson of the arrival of the French at Rome, to be expected on the 5th / To stay or not to stay —

418 'He works too much with the Pipe in his mouth – looks too much at the particular Thing, instead of overlooking – übersehen.' – *Alston* / Thursday Feb[ruary] 15. 1806.

419 What Tone [is] to colors, chiaro-Oscuro [is] to Light & Shade; viz. such a management of them that they form a beautiful whole, independent of the particular Images colored, lit up, or shaded.

420 The quiet circle, in which Change and Permanence *co-exist*, not by combination or juxtaposition, but by an absolute annihilation of difference / column of smoke, the fountains before St Peter's, waterfalls / God! – Change without loss – change by a perpetual growth, that [at] once constitutes & annihilates change. [T]he past, & the future included in the 5 Present // oh! it is aweful.

421 June 7th, 1806.
O my children – ! — whether, and which of, you are dead, whether any, & which among you, are alive, I know not / and were a Letter to arrive this moment from Keswick (Saturday Night, June 7th, 1806, Leghorn – Gasparini's, or Arms of England Hotel) I fear, that I should be unable to open it, so deep and black is my Despair – O my Children, my Children! 5 I gave you life once, unconscious of the Life, I was giving / and you as unconsciously have given Life to me – Yes! it has been lost — many many months past I should have essayed whether Death is what I groan for, absorption & transfiguration of Consciousness – for of annihilation I cannot by the nature of my Imagination have any idea / yet it may be true 10 — O mercy, mercy! — Even this moment I could commit Suicide but for you, my Darlings (of Wordsworths / – of Sara Hutchinson / that is *passed* – or if remembered[,] thoughts to make a Hell of / [)] O me! now racked with pain, now fallen abroad & su[?ffocated wi]th a sense of intolerable Despair / & no other Refuge than Poisons that degrade the Being, while 15 they suspend the torment, and which suspend only to make the Blow fall heavier /

FOUR

THE LAKES, LONDON 1806–1810

422 Let me try – that I may have at least one good thought to alleviate the pang of dying away – to pursue steadily the plan of opening the eyes of the public to the real situation of Needle-workers, and [of] women in general. Mary Lamb has promised me Facts in abundance.

423 St[od]d[a]rt / passes over a poem as one of those tiniest of tiny night-flies runs over a leaf, casting its shadow, 3 times as long as itself, yet only just shading one or at most two letters at a time. Minute Criticism.

424 A maid servant of Mrs Clarkson's Parents had a great desire to hear Dr Price, & accord[ing]ly attended his Congreg[ation]. On her return being asked, well, what do you think &c – [']'[']A *īī* / ['] replied she / [']There was neither the Poor nor the Gospel'. Excellent Hit on the fine *respectable* attendants of Unitarian Chapels, and the moonshine heartless Head- 5
work of the Sermons.

425 Arrived at Keswick on Thursday Evening, *Oct[ober] 30th 1806.*

426 Memory, a wan misery-Eyed Female, still gazing with snatches of the eye at present forms to annihilate the one thought into which her Being had been absorbed – & every form recalled & refixed – In the effort it seemed to be fluttering off – the moment the present form had been seen, it returned — She fed on bitter fruits from the Tree of Life – & often she 5
attempted to tear off from her forehead a seal, which Eternity had placed there; and instantly she found in her Hand a hideous phantom of her own visage, with that seal on its forehead; and as she stood horror-struck beholding the phantom-head so wan & supernatural, which she seemed to hold before her eyes with right hand too *numb* to feel or be felt / itself 10
belonging to the eye alone, & like a distant rock in a rain-mist, distin-

guishable by one shade only of substance / (i.e. the vision enriched by sub-consciousness of palpability by influent recollections of Touch [)]

427 To be sure, some good may be imagined in any evil – as he whose house is on fire in a dark night, his Loss gives him Light to run away —

428 – like a Lake beneath the Sun seemed to possess in its own right & prodigally give the fiery Light, which by not receiving it flashed forth /

429 Æolian Harp motive for opening the Sash; & at once lets in Music & sweet air; purifies & delights, = moral Eloquence — Poetry —

430 O Elpizomene! When shall I have to write a letter to you, with no *other* Sorrow to communicate, than that absence from you, which writing itself implies?

Friday Nov[ember] 28.
1806 – 5

I know, you love me! – My reason knows it, my heart feels it / yet still let your eyes, your hands tell me / still say, o often & often say, My beloved! I love you / indeed I love you / for why should not my ears, and all my outward Being share in the Joy – the fuller my inner Being is of the sense, the more my outward Organs yearn & crave for it / O bring my 10 whole nature into balance and harmony.

431 Moonlight gleams, and massy glooms —

432 In the forest the spots of moonlight of the wildest outlines, not unfrequently approaching so near to the shape of man, & the domestic animals most attached to him, as to be easily conjured into them by fancy, and mistaken by terror, moved & started as the winds stirred the Branches; that it almost seemed, like a flight of lucent spirits, of light, Sylphs and 5 Sylphids dancing & capering in a world of Shadows / once where our path was completely overcanopied by the meeting Boughs for a stone-throw, as I halloo[']d to those behind me, a sudden flash of Light darted down as it were, upon the path close before me, with such rapid & indescribable effect, that my life seemed snatched away from me – not by 10 terror, but by the whole attention being suddenly, & unexpectedly, seized hold of – if one could conceive a violent Blow given by an unseen hand, yet without pain, or local sense of injury – of the weight falling here, or there – it might assist in conceiving the feeling – This I found was occasioned by some very large Bird, who, scared by my noise, had suddenly 15 flown upward, and by the spring of his feet or body had driven down the branch on which he was a-perch.

433 I fall asleep night after night watching that perpetual feeling, to which Imagination [–] or the real affection of that organ or its appendages by that feeling, beyond the other parts of the body (tho' no atom but seems to share in it) [–] has given a place and seat of manifestation, a Shechinah in the heart. – Shall I try to image it to myself, as an animant self-con- 5 scious pendulum, continuing for ever its arc of motion by the for ever anticipation of it? – or like some fairer Blossom-life in the centre of the Flower-polypus, a Life within Life, & constituting a part of the Life, th[at] includes it? a consciousness within a Consciousness, yet mutually penetrated, each possessing both itself & the other – distinct tho' indivis- 10 ible! – S.T.C. –

434 All the Linen at the Bridgewater Arms mark'd 'Stoln from the Bridgwater Arms['].

435 Blue Sky through the glimmering interspaces of the dark Elms at Twilight rendered a lovely deep yellow green / all the rest delicate Blue.

436 It is not the W's knowle[d]ge of my frailties that prevents my *entire* Love of them / no! it is their Ignorance of the Deep Place of my Being – and o! the cruel cruel misconception of that which is purest in me, which alone is indeed pure – My Love of *ασρα* could not be, did I not know that she knew it as if she was it – herself & the Conscience of that self, beyond the 5 bounds of that form which her eyes behold when she looks up on herself / O there is a form which seems irrelative to imprisonment of Space!

437 Every thing, that has been known or deemed fit to win woman's Love, I have an impulse to make myself – even tho' I should otherwise look down upon it – I cannot endure not to be strong in arms, a daring Soldier – yet I know, I have no fear of Life or dread of Pain, & that I am not that because I cannot respect it — again, I must be the high Intellect, that despises it – 5 & both at once. I must be a graceful & bold Horseman / I must sing & play on the Harp / I must be beautiful instead of what I am [–] and yet she must love me for what I now am, even for myself & my exceeding Love / & what then mean these vain wishes? O I well know! even to make her already loving me love me to that unutterableness, that impatience at the 10 not enoughness of dependence, with which I love her! Oh and likewise because, if indeed she do love me, I feel myself unworthy, not able to repay the debt – I want, I yearn to make her Love of me delightful to her own mind / I want to be every thing good & that good wearing every attraction, w[hi]ch even Evil has more often around it; & why? because 15 she is all my Vanity & all my Virtue – Loving *her* I intensely desire all that

could make the greatest & (be it viceless) the weak, if they be amiable, love *me* – I am so feeble that I cannot yearn to be perfect, unrewarded by some distinct soul – yet still somewhat too noble to be satisfied or even pleased by the assent of the many – myself will not suffice – & a stranger is 20
nothing / It must be one who is & who is not myself – not myself, & yet (The very Breath owes its power [to] moral feeling) so much more my Sense of Being, than myself that myself is therefore only not a feeling for reckless Despair, because she is its object / Self in me derives its sense of Being from having this one absolute Object, including all others that but 25
for it would be thoughts, notions, irrelevant fancies – yea, my own Self would be – utterly deprived of all connection with her – only more than a thought, because it would be a Burthen – a haunting of the dæmon, Suicide. O! What mad nonsense all this would sound to all but myself – and perhaps even She would despise me for it – no! not despise – but be 30
alarmed – and learn from *W*— to pity & withdraw herself from my affections. Whither? – O agony! O the vision of that Saturday Morning – of the Bed / – O cruel! is he not beloved, adored by two – & two such – Beings! and must I not be beloved *near* him except as a Satellite? – But O mercy mercy! is he not better, greater, more *manly*, & altogether more 35
attractive to any the purest Woman? And yet, and yet, methinks, love so intense might demand love – otherwise, who could be secure? who could know, that his Beloved might not meet his Superior? – W. is greater, better, manlier, more dear, by nature, to Woman, than I – I – miserable I! – but does he – O No! no! no! no! he does not – he does not 40
pretend, he does not wish, to love you as I love you, Sara! – he does not love, he *would* not love, it is not the voice, not the duty of *his* nature, to love *any* being as I love you. NO! he is to be beloved – but yet, tho' you may feel that if he loved you, tho' only even *partly* as *I* love you, you should inevitably love him, love him to a degree in which you *cannot* love 45
me – yet still he does not *so* love you – no! not in kind, much less degree – I alone love you so devotedly, & therefore, therefore, love me, Sara! Sara! love me!

awakened from a dream of Tears, & anguish of involuntary Jealousy, ½ past 2 / Sept[ember] 13. 1807 50

N. Stowey.

438 To lie in ease yet dull anxiety for hours, afraid to think a thought, lest some thought of Anguish should shoot a pain athwart my body, afraid even to turn my body, lest the very bodily motion should introduce a train of painful Thoughts —

439 Our mortal existence a stoppage in the blood of Life – a brief eddy in the everflowing Ocean of pure Activity, from wind or concourse of currents – who beholds Pyramids, yea, Alps and Andes, giant Pyramids the work of Fire, raising monuments like a generous Victor, o'er its own conquest, tombstones of a world destroyed – yet, these too float adown the Sea of 5 Time, & melt away, Mountains of floating Ice /

440 Accords and Dissonances in their texture exquisite, a seeming Intertangle, yea, to the grosser eye a matted mass, & witch-lock of confusion.

441 The Blast Rises & falls & trembles at its height – – –

442 The moulting Peacock with only two of his long tail feathers remaining, & those sadly in tatters, yet proudly as ever spreading out his ruined fan in the Sun & Breeze —

443 Water wagtails, 7 or 8, following the feeding Horse in the pasture / fluttering about & hopping close by his hoofs, under his belly and even so as often to tickle his nostrils with their pert Tail / The H[orse] shortens the grass – & they get the insects.

444 W – W – &c

It is not in nature to love those, who after my whole manhood's service of faithful self-sacrificing Friendship have wantonly stripped me of all my comfort and all my hopes – and to hate them is not in *my* nature. What remains? – to do them all the good, I can; but with a blank heart! 5

445 Quere – Whether we may not, nay, ought not, to use a neutral pronoun relative, or representative, to the word 'Person', when it hath been used in the sense of homo, *ανθρωπος*, mensch, or noun of the common gender, in order to avoid particularizing man or woman, or in order to express either Sex indifferently? If this be incorrect in syntax, the whole use of the word 5 Person is lost in a number of instances, or only retained by some stiff and strange position of words – as 'not letting the *person* be aware, *wherein offence has been given*['] – instead of – [']wherein he or she has offended.' – In my [opinion] both the specific intention and general *etymon* of 'Person', in such sentences, fully authorize the use of *It*, & *which*, instead 10 of He, She, him, her, who, whom.

446 Rival Editors have recourse to Necromancy to know from Shakspeare himself who of them is the fittest to edit and illustrate him. The meeting described – the ceremonies of Conjuration – the appearance of the Spirit – Effect on the Rival Invokers – Resume courage – ask the Question –

that is, the Arbiter appointed by them / they listen / Malone leaps up, while the rest hang their heads at the same instant that the Arbiter re-echoes the words of the Spirit, Let Malone! – – the Spirit shudders – then exclaims in the dread And angry utterance of the Dead – No! No! Let me alone, I said, Inexorable Boobies! 5

O that eternal Bricker-up of Shakspeare – Registers, Memorandum Books, and Bill, Jack, and Harry, Tom, Walter, & Gregory, Charles, Dick, and Jim &c &c lived at that time, but that nothing more is known of them – but oh the importance when half a dozen Players' Wills can be made to stretch thro' half a hundred or more of pages – tho' not one word in them that by any force can be made to illustrate either the times or life or writings of Shakspere / or indeed of any times / – and yet no Edition but this Gentleman's name *burs* upon it – *Bur*glossa with a vengeance / like the Genitive Plural of a Greek Adjective, it is Malone, Malone, Malone. 10 15

Μαλῶν, Μαλῶν, Μαλῶν. 20

447 Shakespere, Milton, Boyle,
all the great living-dead men of our Isle.

448 4 Sorts of Readers. 1. Spunges that suck up every thing and, when pressed give it out in the same state, only perhaps somewhat dirtier – . 2. Sand Glasses – or rather the upper Half of the Sand Glass, which in a brief hour assuredly lets out what it has received – & whose reading is only a profitless measurement & dozing away of Time – . 3. Straining Bags, who get rid of whatever is good & pure, and retain the Dregs. – and this Straining-bag Class is again subdivided into the Species of the Sensual, who retain evil for the gratification of their own base Imaginations, & the calumnious, who judge only by defects, & to whose envy a beauty is an eye-sore, a fervent praise respecting an other an ear-grievance; and the more virulent in its action because the miserable man does not dare confess the Truth to his own Heart – . 4 and lastly, the Great-Moguls['] Diamond Sieves – which is perhaps going farther for a Simile than its superior Dignity can repay, inasmuch as a common Cullender would have been equally symbolic / but imperial or culinary, these are the only good, & I fear the least numerous, who assuredly retain the good, while the superfluous or impure passes away & leaves no trace / 5 10 15

449 1. Sense of Beauty – this thro' the whole poem, even to almost effeminacy of sweetness – good sign / painter who begins with old men's and old women's faces, a bad sign – coarse & strong is easily done so as to *strike* – –
2. With things remote from his own feelings – and in which the romanticity gives a vividness to the naturalness of the sentiments & feelings —
3. Love of natural Objects – quote the Hare, p.23 – there is indeed a far more admirable description precedent, but less fitted for public recitation /
4. Fancy, or the aggregrative Power – 13th.p. – [']Full gently now['] &c – the bringing together images dissimilar in the main by some one point or more of Likeness – – distinguished – read from Pocket book – / both common in the writers of Shakspere's time /
5. – That power of & energy of what a living poet had grandly & appropriately. [']To flash upon that inward Eye Which is the Bliss of Solitude['] – & to make every thing present by a Series of Images — This an absolute Essential of Poetry, & of itself would form a poet, tho' not of the highest Class – It is however a most hopeful Symptom, & the V[enus] & A[donis] is one continued Specimen /
6. Imagination / power of modifying one image or feeling by the precedent or following ones – . – So often afterwards to be illustrated that at present I shall speak only of – one of its effects – namely, that of combining many circumstances into one moment of thought to produce that ultimate end of human Thought, and human Feeling, Unity[,] and thereby the reduction of the Spirit to its Principle & Fountain, who alone is truly *one*. (Quote the passage p.28. *before this* observation.) – & p.29 – for
7. The describing natural Objects by cloathing them appropriately with human passions:
[']Lo, here the gentle Lark[']
8. Energy, depth, and activity of Thought without which a man may be a pleasing and affecting Poet; but never a great one. Here introduce Dennis's – enthus[iasm] & vulgar pass[ion] – & from the excess of this in Shakespere be grateful that circumstances probably originating in choice led him to the Drama, the subject of my next lecture – & end with Chapman's —

Previous to 1. – notice the unpleasing nature of the Subject – which would not be introduced but that this very reason makes it so illustrative of Shakespere's character – – – There are men who can write most eloquently, and passages of deepest pathos & even Sublimity, on circumstances personal & deeply exciting their own passions; but not therefore poets –

Mothers – Deborah's Song – Nature is the Poet here — but to become by 40
power of Imagination another Thing – Proteus – a river, a Lion, yet still
the God felt to be there – – Then his thinking faculty & thereby perfect
abstraction from himself – he writes exactly as if of an other planet, or as
describing the movement of two Butterflies —

450 For a future Lecture on the moderns
Milton in three incidental words has implied all which for the purposes of
more direct apprehension, which at first must be slow-paced in order to
be distinct, I have endeavored to develope in a precise & strictly adequate
definition / Speaking of Poetry, he says, (as in a parenthesis) which is – 5
'simple, sensuous, passionate.' – How awful is the power of Words! –
fearful often in their consequences when merely felt not understood! but
most aweful when both felt and understood! Had these three words only
been properly understood, and present in the minds of general Readers,
not only almost a Library of false Poetry would have been either pre- 10
cluded or still-born, but what is of more consequence, works truly excellent, and capable of enlarging the understanding, warming & purifying
the heart, and placing in the centre of the whole Being the Germs of
noble & manlike Actions, would have been the common Diet of the
Intellect, instead. – For the first condition – namely, simplicity, while it 15
distinguishes Poetry from the arduous processes of Science laboring
towards an end not yet arrived at, & supposes a smooth and finished Road
on which the Reader is to walk onward easily, with streams murmuring
by his side, & Trees & Flowers, & human dwellings to make his journey
as delightful as the Object of it is desirable, instead of having to toil with 20
the Pioneers, & painfully make the road, on which others are to travel,
precludes every affectation – & so on ———

451 In the preceding Lecture we have examined with what armour cloathed
& with what titles authorized Shakespere came forward, as a poet, to
demand the throne of Fame, as the dramatic poet of England; we have
now to observe and retrace the excellencies which compelled even his
Contemporaries to seat him on that Throne, altho' there were Giants in 5
those days, contending for the same honor – hereafter we shall endeavor
to make out the title of the English Drama, as created by & existing in
Shakespere, & its right to the Supremacy of Dramatic Excellence, in
general. — I have endeavored to prove that he had shewn himself a *poet*,
previously to his appearance, [as] a dramatic poet – & that had no Lear, 10
no Othello, no Henry the Fourth, no Twelfth Night, appeared, we must
have admitted that Shakespere possessed the chief if not all the requisites

of a Poet – namely, deep Feeling & exquisite sense of Beauty, both as exhibited to the eye in combinations of form, & to the ear in sweet and appropriate melody [with the except[ion] of Spenser, he is &c] –. That these feelings were under the command of *his own Will* – that in his very first productions he projected his mind out of his own particular being, & felt and made others feel, on subjects no way connected with himself, except by force of Contemplation – & that sublime faculty, by which a great mind becomes that which it meditates on. — To this we are to add the affectionate Love of Nature & natural Objects, without which no man could have observed so steadily, or painted so truly & passionately the very minutest beauties of the external world —

Next, we have shewn that he possessed Fancy, considered as the faculty of bringing together & / &c. – 'Full gently now she' &c – Still mounting, we find undoubted proof in his mind of Imagination or the power by which one image or feeling is made to modify many others, & by a sort of *fusion to force many into one* — that which after shewed itself in such might & energy in Lear, where the deep anguish of a Father spreads the feeling of Ingratitude & Cruelty over the very Elements of Heaven —. Various are the working of this greatest faculty of the human mind – both passionate & tranquil – in its tranquil & purely pleasurable operations it acts chiefly by producing out of many things, as it would have appeared in the description of an ordinary mind, described slowly & in unimpassioned succession, a oneness / even as Nature, the greatest of Poets, acts upon us when we open our eyes upon an extended prospect – Thus the flight of Adonis from the enamoured Goddess in the dusk of the Evening –

> Look! how a bright star shooteth from
> the Sky, So glides he in the night
> from Venus' Eye –.

How many Images & feelings are here brought together without Effort & without discord – the beauty of Adonis – the rapidity of his flight – the yearning yet hopelessness of the enamoured gazer – and a shadowy ideal character thrown over the Whole – / Or it acts by impressing the stamp of humanity, of human feeling, upon inanimate Objects – The Pines shorn by the Sea-wind & seen in twilight /

Then /

> Lo! here the gentle Lark —

and lastly, which belongs only to a great poet, the power of so carrying on the Eye of the Reader as to make him almost lose the consciousness of words – to make him *see* every thing – & this without exciting any painful or laborious attention, without any *anatomy* of description, (a fault not uncommon in descriptive poetry) but with the sweetness & easy movement of nature —

Lastly, he – previously to his Drama – gave proof of a most profound, 55 energetic & philosophical mind, without which he might have been a very delightful Poet, but not the great dramatic Poet / but this he possessed in so eminent a degree that it is to be feared &c &c – if — –
But Chance & his powerful Instinct combined to lead him to his proper province – in the conquest of which we are to consider both the 60 difficulties that opposed him / & the advantages —

452 Sudden connection of the Understanding in a very quick mind[,] before the Imagination & general Habit of Thought & Sensation are reconciled thereto[,] makes a man feel as if he stood on his Head. His State is the direct Antipode of a *Bull* – the latter is the feeling without the sense of connection, the former the perception without the Feeling. 5

453 Speaking of the original unific Consciousness, the primary Perception, & its extreme difficulty, to take occasion to draw a lively picture of the energies, self-denials, sacrifices, toils, trembling knees, & sweat-drops on the Brow, of a philosopher who has really been sounding the depths of our being – & to compare it with the greatest & most perseverant Labors 5 of Travellers, Soldiers, and whomever else Men honor & admire – how trifling the latter! And yet how cold our gratitude to the former – Say not, that they were vainly employed – compare the mind & notions of a vulgar Sensualist, or wild Savage[,] with the mind of a Plato or an Epictetus – & then say if you dare that there is any more comparision between *the effects* 10 of the toils of the Philosopher & the Worldling, than there is between the intensity of the toils themselves.

454 24th March, 1808. In how kind and quiet a manner the *Conscience* talks to us, in general, & at first – how *long-suffering* it is, how delicate, & full of pity – and with what pains when the Dictates of Reason made impulsive by its own Whispers have been obstinately pushed aside, does it utter the sad, judicial, tremendous Sentence after which nothing is left to the 5 Soul but supernatural aid. O what an aweful Being is Conscience! And how infra-bestial the Locks, Priestleys, Humes, Condilliacs and the dehumanizing race of fashionable Metaphysici[ans.] *Metapothecaries*, said one *sportively* – but I *seriously*, should say *Cata*physicians (i.e. *Contra*-naturalists) when I spoke of them as *agents*; but when I regard them 10

merely in *themselves*, & *passive*, I should call them *Hypo*physicians, i.e. *below Nature. Zoophytes?* Nay, there is no contradiction in any thing but degraded man.

455 There lives within the very flame
of Love,
A kind of wick or Snuff,
that will abate it.
Hamlet. —

Merciful Wonder-making Heaven! What a man was this Shakespear! I know no better epithet than that given by a Greek Monk of the lower Empire to some other Monk – *μοριον*[*ου*]*ς*, myriad-minded. –

456 O that sweet Bird! where is it? – it is encaged somewhere out of Sight – but from my bedroom at the Courier office, from the windows of which I look out on the walls of the Lyceum, I hear it, early Dawn – often alas! then lulling me to late Sleep – again when I awake – & all day long. – It is in Prison – all its Instincts ungratified – yet it feels the Influence of Spring – & calls with unceasing Melody to the Loves, that dwell in Fields & Greenwood bowers – ; unconscious perhaps that it calls in vain. – O are they the Songs of a happy enduring Day-dream? has the Bird Hope? Or does it abandon itself to the Joy of its Frame – a living Harp of Eolus? – O that I could do so! –

— 16 May, 1808. —

457 Assuredly, a Thrush or Blackbird encaged in London is a far less shocking Spectacle, its Encagement a more venial Defect of just Feeling than (which yet one so often sees) a Bird in a gay Cage in the heart of the Country – yea, as if at once to mock both the poor Prisoner, and its kind Mother, Nature, in a cage hung up in a Tree – where the free Birds after a while, when the gaudy Dungeon is no longer a scare-crow to them, perch on the wires, drink the water, & peck at the seeds. —

But of all Birds I most detest to see the nightingale encaged – & the Swallow & the Cuckoo, – motiveless! monstrous! – but the *Robin* – o woe! woe! woe! he, sweet cock my head & eye, pert-bashful darling, that makes our kitchens its chosen Cage —

458 *1808*

Need we wonder at Plato's opinions concerning the Body, at least, need that man wonder whom a *pernicious Drug* shall make capable of conceiving & bringing forth Thoughts, hidden in him before, which shall call

forth the deepest feelings of his best, greatest, & sanest Contemporaries? 5
And this proved to him by actual experience? – But can subtle strings set in greater tension do this? – Or is it not, that the dire poison for a delusive time has made the body, i.e. the *organization*, not the articulation (or instruments of motion)[,] the unknown somewhat, a fitter Instrument for the all-powerful Soul. – As the Instrument, so will be the Manifestation, 10
the Epiphany, of the Soul. – How greatly does this both exalt soul & body – what a grand exposition of St Paul's 15th Chapter of the Corinthians – . We are finite – an instrument we must have – but it may be a glorified Instrument – the Soul varies only as its Instrument varies – & yet that by the action of the Soul, or Arbitrement! – Infinite incomprehensible 15
Mystery, yet absolute Truth! It seems, as if the Soul or Arbitrement were a Spring, as a steel Spring, struggling up against an indefinite weight, and increasing or diminishing its powers apparently, as the weight increases or diminishes – this is comprehensible! But in what way this indestructible uncrushable Spring (Stahl-feder, as the Germans more happily have 20
it, avoiding the equivoque of this with *Fountain*) in what way it of itself acts toward the increase or diminution of the superincumbent weight – this is the mystery! – this that which has caused the grand controversies of Protestants & Catholics, & afterwards, of Calvinists & Arminians – finally, this is that which forms the Boundary between the material & 25
spiritual World – & by its very incomprehensibility gives the condition of Hope & Faith.

459 *Important.*
The great injury done to mankind by a man of *no genius*, *no real wisdom*, attaining to the very height of that reputation / as Dr Johnson, the most fertile instance / in (among many, many other bad effects) the destroying the influence of truly great minds on those of their inferiors in the 5
establishment of aweful Truths, – or the removal of pernicious Errors – Take for instances, Johnson's silly opinion, concerning the *Origin of Evil* in opposition to Leibnitz whom he could not understand – his authority in favor of Ghosts and all other selfish & base Anti-religions – These men easily obtain reputation, which they call *fame*, by sympathizing with 10
Ignorance, & with vulgarity of Head & Heart in pompous archi-parnassian Language. And having obtained this mock-Fame they harden that Ignorance & Vulgarity into Pride & proud Bigotry by their authority —.

S.T.C.

460 Wednesday Night, 18th May, 1808. – Important remark of Stuart, with whom I never converse but to receive some distinct and rememberable Improvement – (and if it be not remembered, it is the defect of my memory, which, alas! grows weaker daily, or a fault from my Indolence in not noting it down, as I do this) that there is a period in a man's Life, 5 varying in various men, from 35 to 45 – & operating most strongly in Batchelors, Widowers, or those worst & *miserablest of Widowers, unhappy Husbands*, in which a man finds himself at the *Top of the Hill* – & having attained perhaps what he wishes begins to ask himself – what is all this for? – begins to feel the *vanity* of his pursuits – becomes half-melancholy, 10 gives into wild dissipation, or self-regardless Drinking – and some not content with these – not *slow* – poisons, destroy themselves – & leave their ingenious female or female-minded friends, to fish out some *motive* for an act which proceeded from a motive-making Impulse, which would have acted even without a motive – even as the Terror in Night-mairs[,] a 15 bodily sensation, tho' it most often calls up ‡ consonant Images, yet – as I know by experience, can affect equally without any – or if not so, yet like gunpowder in a Smithy, tho' it will not go off without a spark, is *sure* to receive one – if not this hour, yet the next. — I had *felt* this Truth; but never saw it before so clearly; it came upon me at Malta, under the 20 melancholy dreadful feeling of finding myself to be *Man*, by a distinct division from Boyhood, Youth, and '*Young man*' – Dreadful was the feeling – before that Life had flown on so that I had always been *a Boy*, as it were – and this sensation had blended in all my conduct, my willing acknowlegement of superiority, & *in truth*, my meeting every person, as a 25 superior, at the first moment —— O Hope! O Hopelessness!

Yet if men survive this period, they commonly become chearful again – that is a comfort – for mankind – *not for me!*

S.T.C.

‡ O Heaven! 'twas frightful! now run down, and star'd at 30
By shapes more ugly, than can be remember'd –
Now seeing nothing and imagining nothing
But only being afraid – stifled with *fear*
And every goodly, each familiar Form
Had a strange somewhat that breath'd Terror on me – 35
From my Mss. Tragedy —

461 N.B. to read Chalmers' History of Scotland with a Mem: Book by me —

462 My inner mind does not justify the Thought that I possess a Genius – my *Strength* is so very small in proportion to my Power – I believe, that I first from internal feeling made, or gave light and impulse to this important distinction, between Strength and Power – the Oak, and the tropic Annual, or Biennial, which grows nearly as high and spreads as large, as 5 the Oak – but the *wood*, the *heart* of Oak, is wanting – *the vital* works vehemently, but the *Immortal* is not with it —

And yet I think, I must have some *analogon* of Genius; because, among other things, when I am in company with Mr Sharp, Sir J. Mackintosh, R. and Sydney Smith, Mr Scarlet, &c &c, I feel like a Child – nay, rather 10 like an Inhabitant of another Planet – their very faces all act upon me, sometimes as if they were Ghosts, but more often as if I were a Ghost, among them – at all times, as if we were not *consubstantial.*

463 Ah! dear Book! Sole Confidant of a breaking Heart, whose social nature compels *some* Outlet. I write more unconscious that I am writing, than in my most earnest modes I *talk* – I am not then so unconscious of talking, as when I write in these dear, and only once profaned, Books, I am of the act of writing – So much so, that even in this last minute or two that I have 5 been writing on my writing, I detected that the former Habit was predominant – I was only *thinking.* All minds must think by some *symbols* – the strongest minds possess the most vivid Symbols in the Imagination – yet this ingenerates a *want*, *ποθον*, *desiderium*, for vividness of Symbol: which something that is *without*, that has the property of *Outness* (a word 10 which Berkley preferred to 'Externality') can alone fully gratify / even that indeed not fully – for the utmost is only an approximation to that absolute *Union*, which the soul sensible of its imperfection in itself, of its *Halfness*, yearns after, whenever it exists free from meaner passions, as Lust, Avarice, love of worldly power, passion for distinction in all its forms of 15 Vanity[,] unmodified by those Instincts which often render it ‡ venial, sometimes ‡‡ almost amiable, namely, ostentation of Wealth & Rank, as in Routs (1100 persons present, all of more or less distinction in one House! – The Prince of Wales, Townshend the Thief-catcher, & the Intelligencer from the Morning Post, all present! – what glory! – and the 20 whole Street unpassable for those poor Creatures, who happen to have to drive thro' it, when their Wife is in labor, or their Mother dying, or some such Trifle) or in the more deceiving form of being the active man in a Patriotic Fund, or a Society for the Prevention of Vice, or for the Amelioration of the Poor, or any other of those danity devices for turning 25 the labouring *Nobles* of England into Neapolitan Lazzaroni – (I say

Nobles: for if to be a *Roman* Citizen was itself a Patent of Nobility, in the good Times of Rome, why should not the 'to be an Englishman' have the same claim, while he has hands to maintain himself, if Justice were done him, & both hand & heart to defend his Country?) – or, lastly, in 30 the pursuit of literary Reputation, which a few disguise to himselves as an honorable Love of *Fame*, & betray the truth to all sharp-sighted minds by their undue Irritation & vehemence of Language concerning every Review which attacks them, and every acquaintance, whose Opinion of them does not soar so high as their own of themselves – (ex.gr. 35 [Wordsworth] in relation to [Sharp] at [Sir George Beaumont's] –) — I say, every generous mind not already filled by some one of these passions feels its *Halfness* – it cannot *think* without a symbol – neither can it *live* without something that is to be at once its Symbol, & its *Other half* – (That phrase now so vulgar by the profane Use of it was most beautiful in 40 its origin –) — Hence I deduce the habit, I have most unconsciously formed, of *writing* my inmost thoughts. I have not a soul on earth to whom I can reveal them – and yet

'I am not a God, that I should stand alone'

and therefore to you, my passive, yet sole true & kind, friends I reveal 45 them. *Burn you I certainly shall, when I feel myself dying*; but in the Faith, that as the Contents of my mortal frame will rise again, so that your contents will rise with me, as a Phœnix from its pyre of Spice & Perfume. /

464 May 20th – Went in a cocked hat, one of the *on* head and *under* arm, deformities of fashion to ———; on my return, purposely put it on, and went into a Cook's Shop, and bought half-a-pound of cold beef – and into another for half a pound of Beef Sausages, in order to help to make the Cock'd-hat Gentry ridiculous among the lower Classes. — 5 Detestable Coxcombry!

465 Of a too witty Book. I like Salt to my Meat so well that I can scarce say Grace over Meat without Salt – But Salt to one's Salt – ! / A sparkling dazzling lit-up Saloon or subterraneous Minster in a vast Mine of Rock-Salt – what of it? – full of white Pillars, and Aisles, & Altars of eye-dazzling Salt – well what of it? [It] is uncomfortable Lodging and 5 Boarding – in short *all my Eye*. Now I am content with a work if it be but my Eye & Betty Martin; because having never heard any charge against the Author of this Adage, candour obliges me to conclude that

Eliza Martin
Is *sense* for sartain. — 10

In short, never was a metaphor more lucky, apt, ramescent, and fructiferous, a hundred branches and each hung with a different graft-fruit, than Salt as typical of Wit: – the uses of both being the same, not to nourish, but to season & to preserve nourishment. – Yea, even where there is plenty of good substantial Meat to incorporate with, stout Aitch-bone & 15
Buttock, still there may be too much – & they who confine themselves to such meals, will contract a scorbutic Habit of Intellect (i.e. a *scurvy* Taste) and with loose Teeth & tender gums become incapable of chewing & digesting hard matters of mere plain Thinking. —

466 He was grave & solid from his Infancy, like that most *useful* of domesticated Animals, that even as a Piggie never runs but with some prudent motive, to the Mast or the Wash-tub, and at no time a slave to the Present Moment[,] never even grunts over the acorns before him without a scheming Squint,‡ toward those on one side, which his Neighbour is, or 5
may be about, to enjoy. —

‡ and a Segment at least of its wise little eye, cast toward &c—

467 Lord of Light and Fire – what is the universal of Man in all, but especially in savage states – fantastic ornaments, and in general, the most frightful Deformities – slits, &c &c (here enumerate them from books of Travels) – What is the solution? – Man will not be a mere thing of Nature – he will be & will shew himself a power of himself – hence these violent dis- 5
ruptions of himself from all other creatures. What they are made, that *they* remain / they are Nature's & wholly Nature's.

468 If one thought leads to another, so often does it blot out an other – This I find, when having lain musing on my Sopha, a number of interesting Thoughts having suggested themselves, I conquer my bodily indolence & rise to record them in these books / alas! my only Confidants. – The first Thought leads me on indeed to new ones; but nothing but the faint 5
memory of having had them remains of the others, which had been even more interesting to me. — I do not know, whether this be an idiosyncracy, a peculiar disease, of *my* particular memory – but so it is with *me.* – My Thoughts crowd each other to death.

469 O misery! when the occasion of premature Death is that which makes Death terrible! Savage Stab! that transpierces at once Health and Conscience! Body and Spirit. — *ωΠΜ.*

470 Alas! my Heart seems of very truth palsy-stricken / It is dead-alive, yet trembles ceaselessly. O mercy! O for the *power* to cry out for Mercy from the inmost [–] That would be Redemption! Now I understand, now I feel the anguish of not feeling savingly the prayer – I believe! Lord help my unbelief! 5

471 Plucked up my Soul from its Roots.

472 Re-arrived at Grasmere and entered the new House for the first time Thursday Night, ½ past Eleven, 1 Septemb[e]r, 1808.

473 Essay – Influence of Property on the Affections of Families – W.W.

474 you never sate with or near me ten minutes in your life without shewing a restlessness, & a thought of *going*, &c, for at least 5 minutes out of the 10

475 *Extremes meet*. One Essay in the Upholder – perhaps, in these first explain my system of balanced opposites – & thence the Like in the Unlike / —

476 O! Heaven! the thousandfold combinations of Images that pass hourly in this divine Vale, while I am dozing & muddling away my Thoughts & Eyes — o let me rouse myself – If I even begin mechanically, & only by aid of memory look round and call each thing by a name – describe it, as a trial of skill in words – it may bring back fragments of former Feeling – 5 For we can live only by feeding abroad ——

477 The vicious taste of our modern Ratcliffe, Monk Lewis, German Romances – Take as a specimen the last, I have read, the Bravo of Venice / in the combination of the highest sensation, wonder of effects produced by supernatural power, without the means – thus gratifying our instinct of free will that would fain be emancipated from the thraldom of ordinary 5 nature – & would indeed annihilate both space & time — with the lowest of all human scarce-human faculties – viz – Cunning – low thieves' Cunning – Trap door – pick-locks – low confederacies &c / Can these things be admired without a bad effect on the mind —

478 Poetry is

The species of composition, which represents external nature, or the human mind, – both in relation to human affections – so as to produce immediate pleasure – / and the greatest quantity of immediate pleasure in each part, that is compatible with the largest possible sum of Pleasure in 5 the whole. ——

Poetry is – simple, sensuous, passionate. —

479 O my Heart was transparent to you as a Dew-drop, which you saw thro' & thro', and wherever you fixed your eye, beheld the image of yourself—

480 It is not that the Philosophy of the Fathers or moderate *Realists* is more abstruse or difficult to be believed than that of the Nominalists & *Materialists* (who are indeed *the true Realists*) [–] so far from it that the philosophy of Plato & his systematic followers is only a display of the *possibility* of that which Mankind in general believe to be *real* – such as, 5
that there is some ground in *Nature* or a common essence, why Peter & John are two *men* / whereas the Philosophy of the Nominalists is abhorrent from all the common feelings of all mankind – but this it is, that gives the latter its fashion & favor – that according to the former there is a wide connected System, including a wide scheme of natural & revealed 10
Religion, requiring hard thinking & close self-energy (αυτοενεργεια) to master – whereas the latter consists in unbelieving as far as possible[,] till we come to *words* that convey all their separate meanings at once, no matter how incomprehensible or absurd the *collective* meaning may be – for the collective meaning cannot be inquired after but by an effort of 15
Thought – and to avoid this is the aim of those who embrace this philosophy.

481 We understand Nature just as if at a distance we looked at the Image of a Person in a Looking-glass, plainly and fervently discoursing – yet what he uttered, we could decypher only by the motion of the Lips, and the mien, and the expression of the muscles of the Countenance—

482 Water forms on the Lake, first Mountains, then the triangles blend at their bases & intermingling made the most exquisite Alpine Scenery of Mountain Tops – then a net /

Novemb[e]r 28. 1809.
Grasmere Lake. 5

483 What should we think of Music, if all airs were composed to the tune of God save the King – & Rule Britannia? – Yet this is not a very unfair statement of the truth respecting our Style since the writings of Johnson, Junius, and the Scotch Translators of their Thoughts into English

484 One lifts up one's eyes to Heaven as if to seek there what one had lost on Earth /   Eyes –

Whose Half-beholdings thro' unsteady tears
Gave shape, hue, distance, to the inward Dream /

485 Of a swan shot on the water / a delightful image as description or as simile

486 Pope like an old Lark who[,] tho' he leaves off soaring & singing in the heights, yet has his *Spurs* grow longer & sharper, the older he grows.

487 Soother of Absence – distant 2000 miles – what seas, what wildernesses, &c &c between us! – And yet how incalculably farther might a single Thought separate us – a suspicion or jealousy, a wound brooded over! —

488 Sometimes when I earnestly look at a beautiful Object or Landscape, it seems as if I were on the *brink* of a Fruition still denied – as if Vision were an *appetite*: even as a man would feel, who having put forth all his muscular strength in an act of prosilience, is at that very moment *held back* – – he leaps & yet moves not from his place. — 5

489 Sunday Night – 4 Feb[ruary] 1810 – I eat a red Herring for supper, & had a dreadful night in consequence. Before I fell asleep, I had a spectrum of the fish's back bone which immediately & perceptibly formed itself by lengthening & curving the cross bone threads into a sort of Scorpion – with a sense of fright – which doubtless was the sensation which produced it – 5

J. Bœhmen's mind may be well illustrated from Dreams – there is meaning, important meaning, in both; both the exponents are almost accidental – such [an] infinity of synonimes exist in the language of vision, considered as the language or representatives of Sensations & Notions. 10

490 For great Estates enlarge not little Hearts.

491 Christabel – my first cries mingle[d] with my Mother's Death-groan / – and she beheld the Vision of Glory ere I the earthly Sun – when I first looked up to Heaven, consciously, it was to look up after or for my Mother – &c &c —

492 Why is true Love like a Tree? – A Poem.

493 Facts – stubborn facts! – none of your Theory. — A most entertaining & instructive Essay – the sooner the better — Hunt it from the most absurd credulity – in Fracastorius de Sympathiâ, I. Cap – & the Alchemy Book – even to those of your modern Agriculturists, relating their *own facts* – & swearing against each other, like Ships' Crews – 5

O! it is your *relation* of the *Facts*, not the fact / Friend –

494 I dare avow – & hope, I shall give no offence to serious Believers – that it appears to me scarcely possible, that a young man of ingenuous dispositions, warm sensibility, and an enquiring mind should avoid Socinianism – educated as we all are – 1[.] The grounds are – the application of common Logic, i.e. the law of incongruity (regula contradictionis) to premises abstracted from Matter, & falsely applied to Spirit – . Thus in the word *one* – Logic[,] in short[,] applied without any previous analysis of the faculties of the mind, and the seat or source of different notions – thus, time & space / – cause and effect – are all applied to Deity & to human Soul in the same sense & with the same confidence as to the phænomena of the Senses / — 2. The custom so inveterate of disputing a Religion by Texts – Text marshalled against Text – the consequence of which must necessarily be, that one class of Texts appearing to contradict the other, the preference will – & indeed ought to [–] be given to that sense which is the most congruous with Reason — 3. Young men ignorant of the corruption & weakness of their own hearts, & therefore always prone to substitute the glorious *Ideal* of human nature for the existing reality — This may be most affectingly shewn by the fervent friendships & bitter quarrels of young men, each expecting the other to be an Angel, & taking their generous wishes in their most generous moods for Virtue — / Hence no need is felt of Redemption – . – 4. a subtler & abstruser ground – why young men are inclined to necessitarianism, in addition to the pleasure from clear & distinct notions, which those must needs be which are but in truth material Images by a sophism of metathesis passed off for operations of mind – in addition to this, strange as it may appear, yet it is true, that we least value & think of that which we enjoy in the highest degree – this free-agency, the unsettled state of Habit not yet Tyranny – we begin to think of, & intellectually to know, our freedom when we have been made to feel its imperfections, & its loss – From these causes I explain & justify the fact of the Trinity not being taught to young Christians, to the catechumens – . And this is a glorious proof that to *acquiesce* in a doctrine was, by no means, all that the Christian Church required – till Christianity had already done part of its work, in turning the mind in upon itself, & leading it gradually to a deep faith in its free-agency in *posse*, the Trinity could not be understood or believed, in the Christian sense of the word *belief* – therefore, it was not taught – This is a most important fact – and places or shews the true corner stone, or foundation of Christian Faith / which is not κατανοεῖν το προσωπον εν εσοπτρῳ, but παρακυψαι εις νομον τελειον τον της Ελευθεριας – . This is the great fundamental Article of Christian Faith. – – The last ground, I

have now to mention, in addition to all said in another Memorandum Book is – the Chillingsworthian Touch, that the whole Religion of Protestants not only is in the Bible, but is capable of being demonstrated from it, without assistance of Tradition, or the writings of the Fathers – – – Prove that this is not the orthodox Faith of the Church of England – & its dangerous Consequences – — 45

495 Tho' the dependence of all theologic speculation on the practical Reason & its moral postulates will always preserve the religious faith of a true philosopher within the modesty of the Gospel; yet it would not be amiss if our belle esprits had made part of their intellectual voyages in the groves & enchanted Islands of Plato, Plotin[us] & even Proclus – – rendering 5 the mind lofty and generous & *abile* by splendid Imaginations that receive the beauty of form by the proportions of Science / Fancy moulded in Science, & thence no unbecoming Symbols – Counters at least – of moral Truth / holding to truth the same ascetic & preparatory relations as the Game of Chess to War. 10

496 Sarah Coleridge says, on telling me of the universal Sneeze produced in the Lasses while shaking my Carpet, that she wishes, my Snuff would *grow*: as I sow it so plentifully.

497 I wish, I dared use the Brunonian phrase[,] & define Poetry – the Art of representing Objects in relation to the *excitability* of the human mind, &c — or what if we say – the communication of Thoughts and feelings so as to produce excitement by sympathy, for the purpose of immediate pleasure, the most pleasure from each part that is compatible with the 5 largest possible sum of pleasure from the whole – ?

The art of communicating whatever we wish to communicate so as to express and to produce excitement – or, in the way best fitted to express &c &c — or as applied to all the fine arts[:]

a communication of mental excitement for the purposes of immediate 10 pleasure, in which each part is fitted to afford as much pleasure as is compatible with the largest possible Sum from the whole –

Many might be the equally good definitions of Poetry, as metrical Language – I have given the former the preference as comprizing the essential of all the fine Arts, and applying to Raphael & Handel equally as 15 to Milton / But of Poetry commonly so called we might justly call it – A mode of composition that calls into action & gratifies the largest number of the human Faculties in Harmony with each other, & in just proportion

– at least, it would furnish a scale of merit if not a definition of *genus* — Frame a numeration table of the primary faculties of Man, as Reason, *unified per Ideas*, Mater Legum, Judgement, the discriminative, Fancy, the aggregative, Imagination, the modifying & *fusive*, the Senses & Sensations – and from these the different Derivatives of the Agreeable from the Senses, the Beautiful, the Sublime / the Like and the Different – the spontaneous and the receptive – the Free and the Necessary – And whatever calls into consciousness the greatest number of these in due proportion & perfect harmony with each other, is the noblest Poem. —

Not the mere quantity of pleasure received can be any criterion, for that is endlessly dependent on accidents of the Subject receiving it, his age, sensibility, moral habits, &c – but the worth, the permanence, and comparative Independence of the Sources, from which the Pleasure has been derived.

498 Mem . – If I should die without having destroyed this & my other Memorandum Books, I trust, that these Hints & first Thoughts, often too cogitabilia rather than actual cogitata a *me*, may not be understood as my fixed opinions – but merely as the Suggestions of the disquisition; & acts of obedience to the apostolic command of Try all things: hold fast that which is good.

499 The German Unitarians (Paulus & his Disciples) have thrown aside even the poor hollow Caterpillar Skin of transmigrated Christianity which the English Unitarians still hold in worship in their musæum of cut & dried Faith / – The English Unitarians = the Hermit Crab, naked Philosophers (whose instinctive motion is retrograde) finding out the empty shell of some other Crab, which is however 9 times out of 10 still large for the Tenant-alien, & never rightly fits it.

500 One excellence of the Doctrines of Plato, or of the Plotino-platonic Philosophy, is that it never suffers, much less causes or even occasions, its Disciples to forget themselves, lost and scattered in sensible Objects disjoined or *as* disjoined from themselves. It is impossible to understand the Elements of this Philosophy without an appeal, at every step & round of the Ladder, to the fact within, to the mind's Consciousness – and in addition to this, instead of lulling the Soul into an indolence of mere attention (for a comparative *Indolence* it is, even as, relatively to mere passive amusement (a musâ) or positively passive affections of Sense & Sensation, it is likewise a comparative *Effort*) but rouses it to acts and energies of creative Thought, & Recognition – of conscious re-

production of states of Being. I was not originally led to the study of this Philosophy by Taylor's Translations; but in consequence of early, half-accidental, prepossession in favour of it sent in early manhood for Taylor's Translations & Commentaries – & this I will say, that no man 15 worthy the name of man can read the many extracts from Proclus, Porphyry, Plotinus, &c, those[,] I mean, those chiefly, that relate to the moral claims of our Nature, without an ahndung, an inward omening, of a system congruous with his nature, & thence attracting it – / The boast therefore of the modern Philosophy is to me a decisive proof of its being 20 an Anti-philosophy, or at best a *psilo*sophy, that it calls the mere understanding into exertion without exciting or awakening any interest, any tremulous feeling of the heart / as if it heard or began to *glimpse*, something which had once belonged to it, its Lord or its Beloved – even as a man recovering gradually from an alienation of the Senses or the 25 Judgment, on beginning to recollect the countenances of his Wife, Mother, Children, or Betrothed — But yet it must not be denied or even withheld, that Taylor could not have understood the System, he teaches – for had he done so, he must have understood the difficulties that oppose its reception, the objections which immediately occur to men formed 30 under notions so alien from it – Whereas he no where prepares the mind, no where shews himself in a state of Sympathy with the hesitating Examiner /

501 In talking to Southey, 7 July, a weighty thought suggested itself to me – viz – the conditio sine quâ non of expanse of Time (offence against the probabilities of Time –) aye, and of place too, [–] to the endurance, much more to the empassioned delight in, the *humour*, the wild schein-comœdia *το κομωδιοιδες*, of Shakespere in his Lear & other Tragedies – 5 and likewise, of his delicious poetry *stationes* fluvii torrentis, the pools & smooth expanses between his rapids & his Cataracts, on the very edge of the Cataract – & then the impossibility of his having actualized his deep knowle[d]ge of human Nature (how? by the perpetual balance yet union of individuali[t]y with the *το καθαλου* – almost unattempted by any *prior* 10 writer, unattained by any [ )] — And yet these criticastors abuse him for that in their vile Johnsonian Antithesis of Black & White / One would suppose from Johnson's Preface that Sh[akespeare] was a pie-bald Poet – & that he, the Critic, was standing by, in the worthy employment of counting & pointing out, black spots against white – [?hence]: a black 15 spot[']s on his right ear, just half an inch in diameter – but just on his forehead there is a white spot, of the same size – & so on thro' the whole skin

of the poor becritick'd Animal — Further, illustrate this damnable rage of judging by the faults, imprimis, instead as of yore by his excellences – (the School of Rafael – what did that mean? – The Flemish School – the 20 Venetian School – the School of Milan &c – but now! The Southeian *School*, the Wordsworthian / &c !! – O the spirit of envy & baseness & more than all, indolence of heart & mind amounting to & manifesting itself in an impotence of *intelligent* admiration) – & 2[ndo]. in pointing out as faults the conditio sine quâ non of the acknowle[d]ged beauties! – The 25 expecting of contradictions! – The Poet & his Subject, are they not as the *Δημιουργος* & *ὑλὴ* of Plato – if the *υλη* were not of itself reluctant & naked & ungratifying, what need of the Demiurge – and tho' he may [?hinder] this, and alter it & form, & educe perpetual good even out of the worst evil, can he annihilate the *υλη* without evanishment of the 30 *ιδεα* ? . . .

502 Wordsworth's enemies – especially that Mistress Bare and Bald – the reason – that his works make them restless by forcing them in on their own worthless Selves – and they recoil from their Heart, or rather from the place, where the Heart ought to be, with a true *Horror Vacui*.

503 Monday Noon, Sept[embe]r. 1810 – The Lady of the Lake.

Canto the I. – p.3. (1st of the Poem). – unmeaning use of common-place poetic metaphors, which are mere slang –

> O minstrel Harp! still must thy accents *sleep*?
> Mid rustling Leaves and Fountains murmuring 5
> Still must thy sweeter sounds their silence *keep*,
> Nor *bid* a warrior smile, nor *teach* a maid to weep?

In the preceding Lines the Harp of the North is addressed, first as *mouldring* on a witch-elm over St Fillan's Spring, and yet notwithstanding this had flung its numbers down the fitful Breeze, till envious Ivy 10 clung round it, and muffled it – now whatever may be the Substrate of this allegory, which I profess I do not clearly understand, yet surely the Harp of the North must have been a *Harp* and not an Eolian Lute – yet how a common Welch Harp or any Harp while mould'ring on a tree can fling its *numbers* (which assuredly if it signify any thing, must signify *tunes*[ )] 15 down the Breeze is to me inconceivable – and at least equally so, how the silence enforced by having been muffled can be called *Sleep?* – and as to the vile phrases *bid* and *teach*, it is sufficient, I think, to ask what they mean 1. in themselves, & 2. in their antithesis – – Surely, to *bid* a man smile, is rather ridiculous – what if a Jokist after one of his Jokes were to 20 say to his Servant, Laugh, Sir! or Strip! (N.B. My Father's Comedy) and surely to weep is not an attainment so very foreign to a young Lady's Nature as to require being *taught?*

p.4. Thine ardent symphony *sublime* & *high* – wherein differ these words applied to a Harp? – Besides, in this Stanza it becomes a *real* Harp, distinguished from the Lay – My God! with what a grand contempt of all *thought* do our modern Poets write? (a man of education early determined to be a poet, tho' without poetic rapture, how easy in the present day to make the [?intense] wish supply a *sort* of power? – But tho' he may filtrate & distill, & redistill the salt water, till to those accustomed to it it may seem excellent, yet it is but to taste the water from the spring that bursts from the rock — &c —)

Ditto. Strange position of words – [']Fair Dames and crested Chiefs *attention bow'd* ['] – for bow'd in mark of attention.

In the third Stanza this Proteus Harp becomes once more an allegory for a particular kind of Poetry —
Well but now the Poem is to begin –

P. 5. & 6. – very well & spirited, till the Tempter appears in the 4 last lines (& 4 first of Stanza 3)

> Yell'd on the view the opening pack,
> Rock, glen, & cavern – *paid them back* *vulgarism*
> To many a mingled sound at once
> The awaken'd Mountain *gave* response – – The rock,

glen & cavern *pay'd*, the mountain *gave* – Generous Mountain! – –

The first, 2, 3 &c Stanzas comprize the description of a *Chace* – / and this is a Poem, i.e. a composition with a Beginning, Middle, & End, the parts of which are to be proportionate to their common purpose, and to each other. – This chase therefore – how large is its verbal proportion, & what its real? – This to be kept in mind, but now for minutiæ.

Stanza IV. p.8. [']Stayed perforce['] – a not uncommon, yet great fault, is the placing [of] the participle passive where it requires the skill of the printer, & utmost skill of the reader, to prevent it from being understood as the Perfectum of the Verb active –

> And many a gallant stayed perforce. –

No! – it is –

> And many a gallant, stayed perforce,
> Was fain to breathe his faultering Horse –

D[itt]o. last line –

Had the bold Burst *their mettle tried*

I will not say, that *tried their mettle* is too mean, too I do not [know] what a phrase (but to *my* feeling it borders on *grossness*) but what I object principally to these and some 50 other phrases of the kind is the dislocation of the words for the purpose of rhyme & metre — It appears to me little less than a general rule, that wherever a phrase confessedly trivial & colloquial is introduced in poetry, it ought not to be disguised by position – but placed as it would be *in prose* – otherwise it makes poetry absolutely ludicrous – and the reason is this: that the original ground of the metathesis of words is *passion* suggesting one idea before others [–] in Greek & Latin where there are cases, mere logic is sufficient [–] but with us where there are no cases (i.e. in all instances but pronouns) there must be a *passion* / and in such phrases passion must be supposed to have place for this purpose – because if there be any passion, it is that very passion which brought to the mind the trivial instead of a thought-created sentence — thus Othello – [']Not a Jot! Not a Jot![’] – Where if he had said – [']No! not a jot even![’] — this for a hint to myself – the remark is true; but I have not happily exprest it – 60 65 70 75

And I must not forget in speaking of the certain Hubbub, I am to undergo for hypercriticism, to point out how little instructive any criticism can be which does not enter into minutiæ – & to contrast it with the common reviews – take for instance any half dozen from the Edingburgh – 80

504 Not *Loved* but one whose Love is what has given pleasure / O this is a sad mistake! How perceptibly has ———’s love for poor C lessened since he has procured other enthusiastic admirers! – As long as C. almost all dissenting, was the *sole* Admirer & Lover, *so long* he was loved. – But poor C. *loved*, truly loved! — 5

Of this accursed analysis or rather anatomy of a friend’s Character, as if a human Soul were made like a Watch, or loved for this & that tangible & verbally expressible quality! —

W. authorized M. to tell me, he had no Hope of me! – O God! what good reason for saying this? The very belief takes away all excuse, because all kind purpose for the declaration 10

W. once — was unhappy: dissatisfied, full of craving [–] then what Love & Friendship, now all calm & attached – and what contempt for the moral comforts of others —

505 O merciful God! and was Hume right in making the agreeable & disagreeable the sole principle of Love or Dislike, Esteem or Disapprobation?

506 Sunday Night. No Hope of me! absol[ute] Nuisance!

507 Horrid Thought! it seems as if I alone of all men had *Love!* as if it were a sense, a faculty to which there was no corresponding Object! – Oct[ober] 29. 1810 –

508 Whirled about without a center – as in a nightmair – no gravity – a vortex without a center.

FIVE

LONDON, WILTSHIRE 1810–1816

509 Man of genius places things *in a new light* – this trivial phrase better expresses the appropriate effects of Genius than Pope's celebrated Distich

What oft was thought but ne'er so well exprest /

It has been *thought distinctly*, but only possessed, as it were, unpacked & unsorted – the poet not only *displays* what tho' often seen in its unfolded 5 mass had never been opened out, but he likewise adds something, namely, Lights & Relations. Who has not seen a Rose, or a sprig of Jasmine, of Myrtle, &c &c – But behold these same flowers in a posy or flowerpot, painted by a man of genius – or assorted by the hand of a woman of fine Taste & instinctive sense of Beauty? 10

510 Mere knowle[d]ge of the right, we find by experience, does not suffice to ensure the performance of the Right – for mankind in general. How indeed should it, if mankind need instruction? that is, if they are sick & weak in their moral Being; when it is the very prime & the essential character of a Soul made perfect that the Knowle[d]ge of the Right is to 5 Him the adequate, & the sole adequate, motive to the performance – i.e. to do our Duty exclusively because it is our duty. — Much less shall we be led to our Duty by calculations of pleasant or harmful consequences – to our *Duty* indeed, this is impossible, & a contradiction in terms; but even to the outward acts & conventional Symbols of Duty, i.e. Legality, 10 Experience demonstrates what the acquaintance with the Human Soul would indeed render almost certain a priori, such selfish Promises & Threats have little effect — for the more the selfish principle is set into fermentation, the more imperious & despotic does the Present Moment become – till at length to love our future Self is almost as hard as to love 15 our Neighbour – it is indeed only a difference of Space & Time – my

Neighbour is my *other* Self, *othered* by Space – my old age is to my youth an other Self, *othered* by Time. — How then shall he act upon imperfect & enslaved man? By all together – but chiefly, by setting them in *action* – Now what is the medium between mere conviction & resolve, & suitable 20 *action?* For such a medium is absolutely necessary, since there is no saltus in nature – This medium is found in Prayer, & religious Intercommunion between Man & his Maker – . Hence the necessity of Prayer ———

511 Man the only animal who can *sing*; music is his Invention, if not God's gift by Inspiration / for unlike painting, it is not an imitative Art — To man alone it is given to make not only the air articulated, and the articulated Breath a symbol of the articulations & actualities of his Heart & Spirit, but to render his gestures, his postures, & all his outward 5 Habiliments symbolical – Are these gifts of God? And dare we despise them, or neglect them? Nothing less than a positive divine precept could justify us – – But if to be cultivated, are they to be excluded from God's service, that which most requires the exaltation of the Sum total of our Being, Body & Soul, to him who made, who redeemed, who sanctified, 10 who will raise again both Body & Soul – Are our affections to be roused by Music for an earthly Love, in which we so easily exceed unexcited, & shall it be with held from aiding his Love on which we cannot feel enough – for sorrow for the absence or displeasure of a friend – of triumph for a bloody Victory, &c – & not for & &c. 15

512 Sir Philip Sidney – he dwells in our thoughts as in an element of his own effluviation, a divine Empyræum of Love and Wonder, ever like some rare Balsam insulated by an atmosphere of its own delightful Odors.

513 The Love of Nature is ever returned double to us – not only the Delighter in our Delight, but by linking our sweetest but of themselves perishable feelings to distinct & vivid Images, which we ourselves at times & which a thousand casual associations will often recall to our memory. She is the preserver, the Treasuress of our Joys – even in Sickness & nervous 5 Diseases she has peopled our Imaginations with lovely Forms which have sometimes overpowered the inward pain & brought with them their old sensations – and even when all men have seemed to desert us, & the Friend of our heart has passed on with one glance from his 'cold disliking eye', yet even then the blue Heaven spreads it out & bends over us, & the 10 little Tree still shelters us under its plumage, as a second Cope, a domestic Firmament, and the low creeping Gale will sigh in the Heath-plant & sooth us as by a sound of Sympathy, till the lulled Grief loses itself in fixed

gaze on the purple Heath-blossom, till the present beauty becomes a Vision of Memory — 15

514 Jan[uary] 25. 1811. –
Elucidation of my all-zermalming argument on the subject of ghosts & apparitions by what occurred last night in my sleep – I drew up my legs suddenly: for a great pig was leaping out direct against them. No! a great pig appeared to leap out against me because by a fear-engendering 5 disease of the stomach, affecting the circulation of the Blood or nervous powers[,] my Legs were suddenly twitched up.

Night-mair is, I think, always – even when it occurs in the midst of Sleep, and not as it more commonly does after a waking Interval [–] a state not of Sleep but of Stupor of the outward organs of Sense, not in 10 words indeed but yet in fact distinguishable from the suspended power of the senses in true Sleep; while the volitions of *Reason*[,] i.e. comparing &c, are awake, tho' disturb'd / This stupor seems occasioned by some painful sensation, of unknown locality, most often, I believe, in the lower gut, tho' not unseldom in the Stomach, which withdrawing the attention 15 to itself from its sense of other realities present makes us asleep to them indeed but otherwise awake – and when ever this derangement occasions an interruption in the circulation, aided perhaps by pressure, awkward position, &c, the part deadened – as the hand, or his arm, or the foot & leg, on this side [–] transmits double Touch as single Touch: to which the 20 Imagination therefore, the true inward Creatrix, instantly out of the chaos of the elements or shattered fragments of Memory puts together some form to fit it – which derives an over-powering sense of Reality from the circumstance, that the power of Reason being in good measure awake most generally presents to us all the accompanying images very 25 nearly as they existed the moment before, when we fell out of anxious wakefulness into this *Reverie* — ex.gr. the bed, the curtains, the Room, & its furniture, the knowle[d]ge of who lies in the next room &c— . . .

515 I have never seen the evening Star set behind the mountains but it was as if I had lost a Hope out of my Soul – as if a Love were gone, & a sad Memory only remained – / O it was my earliest affection, the Evening Star / – One of my first utterances in verse was an address to it, as I was returning from the New River, and it looked newly-bathed as well as I – I 5 remember that the substance of the Sonnet was that the woman whom I could ever love, would surely have been emblemed in the pensive serene brightness of that Planet – that we were both constellated to it, & would after death return thither / – –

516 All intense passions have faith in their own eternity, & thence in the eternity of their objects –

517 What a swarm of Thoughts & Feelings, endlessly minute fragments & as it were representations of all preceding & embryos of all future Thought lie compact in any one moment – So in a single drop of water the microscope discovers, what motions, what tumult, what wars, what pursuits, what stratagems, what a circle-dance of Death & Life, Death hunting Life & Life renewed & invigorated by Death – – the whole world seems here, in a many-meaning cypher – – What if our existence was but that moment! – What an unintelligible affrightful Riddle, what a chaos of limbs & trunks, tailless, headless, nothing begun & nothing ended, would it not be! And yet scarcely more than that other moment of 50 or 60 years, were that our all! each part throughout infinite diminution adapted to some other, and yet the whole means to nothing – ends every where, and yet an end no where. ——

518 One fruitful remark on or against Hartley's *one* Law of Time for Association is that in different moods we naturally associate by different laws – as in Passion, by Contrast – in pleasurable states, by Likeness – &c. To be able to shew the possibility of explaining these things verbally with Time – as Cause & effect always coming together, therefore remembered by *Time* – does not prove the *fact* that they are so – on the contrary, we clearly feel the difference in our own minds & know well when we remember a thing by accident & passively, & when actively – This important distinction of active & passive Remembrance is among the many Omissions of Hartley's System –

519 2 April, 1811. – An argument that suggested itself to me against the immortality or rather the usual argument for it (as in Addison's Cato Soliloquy) turned in its favour – All passions have a tendency to make us think them lasting, & for ever – Love, for instance – but what is the *feeling* of Life, but a feeling which when thought of, involves all others – in giving man therefore *prospective* Thoughts, *any* future at all, Nature compels him to think himself immortal – especially, when to this we add the unimaginability of passing from Something to Nothing, between which there is no medium / sed nusquam in naturâ Saltus – / or of believing in a negative – & this too, a negative of that Positive which is the perpetual presence of our Being, and the menstruum of all our Thoughts, Feelings, Acts, & Experiences — . Now this is therefore no arbitrary fancy conjured up by our desires – but a necessity inwoven in our Being – just as much reason therefore for affirming the future State as for denying that

Nature ever *tells a Lie generically* – never makes animals have milk, when they are never to have sucklings / &c. 15

520 The image-forming or rather re-forming power, the imagination in its passive sense, which I would rather call Fancy = Phantasy, a Φαιν[ειν], this, the Fetisch & Talisman of all modern Philosophers (the Germans excepted) may not inaptly be compared to the Gorgon Head, which *looked* death into every thing – and this not by accident, but from the 5 nature of the faculty itself, the province of which is to give consciousness to the Subject by presenting to it its conceptions *objectively*[;] but the Soul differences itself from any other Soul for the purposes of symbolical knowle[d]ge by *form* or body only – but all form as body, i.e. as shape, & not as forma efformans, is dead – Life may be *inferred*, even as intelligence 10 is from black marks on white paper – but the black marks themselves *are truly 'the dead* letter'. Here then is the error – not in the faculty itself, without which there would be no *fixation*, consequently, no distinct perception or conception, but in the gross idolatry of those who abuse it, & make that the goal & end which should be only a means of arriving at it. 15 Is it any excuse to him who treats a living being as inanimate Body, that we cannot arrive at the knowle[d]ge of the living Being but thro' the Body which is its Symbol & outward & visible Sign? —

From the above deduce the worth & dignity of poetic Imagination, of the fusing power, that fixing unfixes & while it melts & bedims the Image, 20 still leaves in the Soul its living meaning –

521 O me – April 1811 – what strange anguish I felt in writing the names at the top of the Page – ! It was as if I had kissed *Falsehood as Truth*, having been used to adore it as such, & yet knowing it to be Falsehood! – O if she were lying dead by me, I should kiss her – & not be able to imagine her to be dead – & tho' *false & cruel*, yet how can I cease to think her true & 5 loving! – *O agony!* –

O my poor Book! no other friend on earth have I but thee, unto whom I can discharge what yet my heart almost bursts with! – But I shall soon die.

– S.T.C. –

522 The sick and sleepless Man after the Dawn of the fresh Day watching the Smoke now from this, & then from the other chimney of the Town from his Bedchamber, as if willing to borrow from others that sense of a new Day, of a discontinuity between the Yesterday & the ToDay, which his own Sensations had not afforded – / – Barrier between Day & Day 5

523 To understand fully the mechanism in order fully to feel the incomparable Excellence of Milton's Metre, we must make four Tables, or a fourfold Compartment: the first for the Feet, single & composite, for which the whole 26 feet of the Ancients will be found necessary; the second, to note the construction of the Feet, whether from different or from single 5 words: for who does not perceive the difference to the Ear between

'Inextricable Disobedience' and
'To love or not: in this we stand or fall:'

yet both lines are composed of five Iambics. – The Third, of the strength and position, the concentration or diffusion of the *Emphasis*. Fourth, the 10 Length and Position of the Pauses. — Then compare his Narrative with the Harangues. – I have not noticed the Ellipses, because they either do not affect the Rhythm, or are not Ellipses but comprehended in the Feet. —

524 Why do you make a book? Because my Hands can extend but a few score Inches from my body; because my poverty keeps those Hands empty when my Heart aches to empty them; because my Life is short, & my Infirmities; & because a Book, if it extends but to one Edition, will probably benefit three or four on whom I could not otherwise have acted; & 5 should it live & deserve to live, will make ample Compensation for all the afore-stated Infirmities. O but think only of the thoughts, feelings[,] radical Impulses that have been implanted in how many thousands of thousands by the little Ballad of the Children in the Wood! The Sphere of Alexander the great's Agency is trifling compared with it. – – 10

525 Wine — some men = musical Glasses – to produce their finest music you must keep them *wet* —

526 O that perilous moment (for such there is) of a half-reconciliation, when the Coldness & the Resentment have been sustained too long – each is drawing toward the other – but like Glass in the midstate between fusion & compaction a single sand will splitter it –

527 How got the Atheist his Idea of that God which he denies? – I have always held Des Cartes' Proof the best & tenable. The Materialist is the Idealist of the intelligible World – as the Idealist constrains the realities ab extra into illusions ab intra, so the Mat[erialist does] the realities *in* us into reflexes and echoes of things without us. – To the one the Universe is 5 but an echo-chamber of the Soul; to the other the Soul is but an empty echo-chamber or whispering Labyrinth of the World — . Both alike

deduce the 'Is' from the 'Appears', the Substance from the Shadow, the Sound from the Echo – both mistake Analysis for preformation – both confound the Genealogist with the Proto-Patriarch. —

528 Nature! sweet Nurse! O take me in thy Lap – And tell me of my Father yet unseen Sweet Tales & True, that lull me into Sleep, & leave me dreaming. —

529 On a better-most sort of Remark of Dr Johnson's recorded by Boswell –

a notable Flea-skip for so grave a Bug.

530 His Imagination, if it must be so called, is at all events of the pettiest kind – it is an Imagunculation. – How excellently the German Einbildungs-kraft expresses this prime & loftiest Faculty, the power of co-adunation, the faculty that forms the many into one, *in eins Bildung*. Eisenoplasy, or esenoplastic Power [in opposition to, or as contradistinguished from] Fantasy, or the Mirrorment, either catoptric or metoptric – repeating simply, or by transposition – & again, involuntary (as in dreams) or by an act of the will. –

531 The ear-deceiving Imitation of a steady soaking Rain, while the Sky is in full uncurtainment of sprinkled Stars and milky Stream and dark blue Interspaces – the Rain had held up for two Hours or more – but so deep was the silence of the Night, that the *Drip* from the Leaves of the Garden Trees *copied* a steady Shower –

20 Sept[embe]r, 1814. – Ashley, Box, Bath. —

532 Symbol = 'the whole, yet of the whole a part' – P. Fletcher's Purple Island. —

533 Thicker than rain-drops on November Thorn. —

534 A philosopher's ordinary Language and Admissions in general conversation or writings ad populum is as his Watch compared with his astronomical Time-piece – He sets the former by the Town Clock, not because he believes it right, but because his Neighbors, & his Cook, *go* by it. –

535 The immense difference between that admiration felt in consequence of a pre-existent *Ideal* excited into developement, as a young Poet-urus for a contemporary Poet – & the admiration of curiosity; & – I shall like to see, how the odd fish looks! – Shark? – Or Camelo pardalus? —

536 If a man could pass thro' Paradise in a Dream, & have a flower presented to him as a pledge that his Soul had really been there, & found that flower in his hand when he awoke – Aye? And what then?

537 Floods & general Inundations render for the time even the purest springs turbid.

538 For compassion a human Heart suffices, but for full adequate sympathy with Joy[,] an Angel's —

539 The evening primrose – its sudden[n]ess – and irrevocability – the strange *Feder* = Spring.

540 Virtue makes us not worthy of Happiness, only worthier – Existence itself gives a claim to Joy – Virtue & Happiness incommensurate quantities – how much Virtue must I have before I have paid off the old debt of my happiness in Infancy and childhood – O we all outrun the Constable with Heaven's *Justice* – We have to earn the Earth before we can think of earning Heaven. – against the doctrine of books. 5

541 We all look up to the blue Sky for comfort, but nothing appears there – nothing comforts nothing answers us – & so we die —

542 Lie with the ear upon a dear friend's grave —

543 Feb[ruary] 23rd 1816. Calne – I thought, I exprest my Thoughts well when I said – There is no Superstition but what has a Religion as its Base (or Radical) and Religion is only Reason, seen perspectively by a finite Intellect.

S.T. Coleridge 5

CODA

HIGHGATE
1816–1820

544 Sunday, April 30 – 1816. Reflections on my four gaudy Flower-pots, compared with the former Flower-poems – – After a certain period, crowded with Poetry-counterfeiters, and illustrious with true Poets, there is formed for common use a vast *garden* of Language – all the shewy, and all the odorous Words and Clusters of Words, are brought together – and to 5 be plucked by mere mechanic and passive Memory — In such a state, any man of common practical reading, having a strong desire (to *be?* oh no! but –) to be thought a Poet will present a Flower-Pot / – gay and gaudy – but the *composition!* – That is wanting — : we carry our judgements of Times & Circumstances, into our Pleasures – A Flower-Pot which would 10 have inchanted us before Flower-gardens were common, for the very beauty of the component Flowers, will be rightly condemned as *common-place out of place* – (for such is a common-place *Poet* – it involves a contradiction both in Terms & Thought – –)[.] So Homer's Juno, Minerva, Battles, are still read with delight; but Blackmore? / This is the reason 15 why the Judgement of those who are Newlings in poetic reading, is not to be relied on – – the Positive, which belongs to all, is taken as the Comparative, which is the individual's Praise – A good ear, who had never heard Music, with what raptures would it praise one of Shield's or Arne's Pasticcios & Centos! But it is the human Mind it praises, not the 20 Individual — Hence it may happen, & (I believe) has happened, that Fashionableness may produce Popularity / 'The Beggar's Petition' is a fair instance – and what if I dared add Gray's 'Elegy in a Country Churchyard' /

545 *ΣΑΡΑ* Written as of yore Christmas, 1816 Coleridge
ΣΑΡΑ Does the Past live with me alone? Coleridge

546 31 March 1817. Highgate. – Monday Morning, six o'clock. *Hen Pen* resenting the being washed, in the nursery, opposite the drawing Room in which I sit.

I will not say, that in our present religious controversies we are disputing about *trifles*: for nothing can be a trifle which tends to keep up even the 5 memory, that there is or may be, or has been supposed to be, such a power as Religion. But I say, that we dispute about the neutral or interjacent ground, not about the territory itself – and that in this sense 9990 in every 10,000 are *Αθεοι* – if there be a personal God, with will, foresight, and all other attributes of personal Intelligence that distinguish the living God 10 (the idea of) from the Spinozistic Ground of the Universe, or infinite Modificable. – If so, every pang, we feel, every error, we commit, much more every sin, proves an alienation from that God – We must be away from him / for an omnipotent Father would never suffer an *innocent* Son to be tormented in his presence, by mere force of *general Laws* – he must 15 needs give then his own happiness. — Our misery may be a merciful mode of recalling us from our Self-chosen Exile, but only in exile can the Prodigal Son be groaning over the refuse of the Hog-trough – not in his Father's house. The local notions of Heaven (ex. gr. we shall *go* to a better place &c) have been very injurious. Is God then confined to a Place? Or is 20 not rather Place the phantom, which our limited faculties create, as the *picture*, the *word*, of our own *State* of Being. Is it not the dream of one who in full sun shine has bricked himself up, or excluded the Light by voluntary Blindness? – What can shew more clearly the hollowness of Unitarianism, than that boastfully distinguishing itself as a belief *in one* 25 *God*, so far from drawing the necessary conclusions from *a* one living God it, more than any other theory in religion, has lost the idea in the vague notion of a – Solution of the material World / an arbitrary Attribution of intelligence to Gravity, Attraction, Repulsion, &c. —

547 . . .

As soon as the human mind is intelligibly addressed by any outward medium, exclusive of articulate Speech, so soon does *Art* commence. But please to observe, that I have layed stress on the words, *human mind* – excluding thereby all results common to man and all sentient creatures – 5 and consequently, confining it to the effect produced by the congruity of the animal impression with the reflective Powers of the mind – so that not the Thing presented, but that which is *re*-presented, by the Thing, is the source of the Pleasure – . In this sense Nature itself is to a religious Observer the Art of God – and for the same cause Art itself might be 10 defined, as of a middle nature between a Thought and a Thing, or, as before, the union and reconciliation of that which is Nature with that which is exclusively Human. – Exemplify this by a good Portrait, which becomes more and more like in proportion to its excellence as a Work of *Art* – while a real *Copy*, a Fac Simile, ends in shocking us. — 15

Taking therefore *mute* as opposed not to sound but to articulate Speech, the oldest definition of Painting is in fact the true and the best definition of the Fine Arts in general – *muta Poesis* – mute Poesy – and of course, *Poesy* – / – (and as all Languages perfect themselves by a gradual process of desynonymizing words originally equivalent, as Propriety, Property – 20 I, Me – Mister, Master — &c – I have cherished the wish, to use the word, Poesy, as the generic or common term, distinguishing that species of Poesy, which is not *muta* Poesis, by its usual name, *Poetry* /) – while of all the other species, which collectively form the *Fine Arts*, there would remain this as the common definition – that they all, like Poetry, are to 25 express intellectual purposes, Thoughts, Conceptions, Sentiments that have their origin in the human Mind, but not, as Poetry, by means of articulate Speech, but as Nature, or the divine Art, does, by form, color, magnitude, Sound, and proportion, silently or musically. —

Well – it may be said – but who has ever thought otherwise. We all know, 30 that Art is the imitatress of Nature. – And doubless, the Truths, I hope to convey, would be barren Truisms, if all men meant the same by the words, *imitate* and *nature*. But it would be flattering mankind at large, to presume that this is the Fact. – First, imitate – The impression on the wax is not an imitation but *a Copy* of the Seal – the Seal itself is an Imitation. / 35 But farther – in order to form a philosophic conception, we must seek for the *kind* – as the *heat* in Ice – invisible Light – &c – but for practical purposes, we must have reference to the degree. It is sufficient that philosophically we understand that in all Imitation two elements must exist, and not only exist but must be perceived as existing – Likeness and 40 unlikeness, or Sameness and Difference. All Imitation in the Fine Arts is the union of Disparate Things. – Wax Images – Statues – Bronze – Pictures — the Artist may take his point where he likes – provided that the effect desired is produced – namely, that there should be a Likeness in Difference & a union of the two – *Tragic Dance*. 45

So Nature. *346*. – i.e. natura naturata – & hence the natural Question / What *all* and every thing? – No, but the Beautiful. – And what is the Beautiful? – The definition is at once undermined. – – / If the Artist painfully *copies* nature, what an idle rivalry! If he proceeds from a Form, that answers to the notion of Beauty, namely, the many seen as one – what an emptiness, an unreality – as in Cypriani – The *essence* must be mastered – the natura naturans, & this presupposes *a bond* between *Nature* in this higher sense and the Soul of Man – . — . . .

The wisdom in Nature is distinguished from Man by the coinstantaneity of the Plan & the Execution, the Thought and the Production – In Nature there is no reflex act – but the same powers without reflection, and consequently without morality. (Hence *Man* the *Head* of the visible Creation – *Genesis.*) Every step antecedent to full Consciousness found in Nature, – so to place them as for some one effect, totalized & fitted to the limits of a human Mind, as to elicit and as it were superinduce *into* the forms the reflection, to which they approximate – this is the mystery of Genius in the Fine Arts – Dare I say that the Genius must act on the feeling, that *Body* is but a striving to become Mind – that it is *mind*, in its essence? ——

As in every work of *Art* the Conscious is so impressed on the Unconscious, as to appear *in* it / ex.gr. Letters on a Tomb compared with Figures constituting a Tomb / – so is the Man of Genius the Link that combines the two – but for that reason, he must partake of both – Hence, there is in Genius itself an unconscious activity – nay, that is *the* Genius in the man of Genius. — . . .

Difference of Form as proceeding and Shape as superinduced – the latter either the Death or the imprisonment of the Thing; the former, its self-witnessing, and self-effected sphere of agency —

Art would or should be the Abridgment of Nature. Now the Fullness of Nature is without character as Water is purest when without taste, smell or color – but this is the Highest, the Apex, not the whole – & Art is to give *the whole* ad hominem / hence each step of Nature has its Ideal, & hence too the possibility of a climax up to the perfect Form, of harmonized Chaos —

To the idea of Life Victory or Strife is necessary – As Virtue not in the absence of vicious Impulses, but in the overcoming of them, so Beauty not in the absence of the Passions, but on the contrary – it is heightened by the sight of what is conquered . . .

548 S.T.C = who with long and large arm still collected precious Armfuls in whatever direction he pressed forward, yet still took up so much more than he could keep together that those who followed him gleaned more from his continual droppings than he himself brought home – nay, made stately Corn-ricks therewith, while the Reaper himself was still seen only with a [?strutting] Armful of newly cut Sheaves. – But I should misinform you grossly, if I left you to infer that his Collections were a heap of incoherent Miscellanea – No! – the very Contrary – Their variety conjoined with the too great Coherency, the too great both desire & power of referring [to] them in systematic, nay, genetic subordination was that which rendered his schemes gigantic & impracticable, as an Author – & his Conversation less instructive, as a man / – Inopes sua *Copia* fecit, too much was given, all so weighty & brilliant as to preclude choice, & too many to be all received – so that it passed over the Hearer[']s mind like a roar of waters —

549 Trees in winter neither dead nor inactive – nor, tho' the sap may not flow, are they sapless – but they are forming new radicles underground, for an additional Supply for Spring & Summer – not merely to supply the same as last year[,] but more – to be progressive

550 2 Sept[ember] 1819. Ramsgate. I *begin* to understand the above poem: after an interval from 1805, during which no year passed in which I did not reperuse, I might say construe, *parse* and spell it, 12 times at least, such a fascination had it, spite of its obscurity! A good instance, by the bye, of that soul of *universal* significance in a true poet's Compositions in addition to the specific meaning.

S.T.C.

P.S. After the 4 first lines the Hand writing is that of my old, dear, and honored Friend, Mr Wade of Bristol.

551 Ad Lectorem.

The Author's one Request.

Do not hold yourself authorized to scoff at this work, till you have read it. What? throughout? Yes. – But will that be possible? For him who puts this question without having read any part of it, probably not. But there is another thing not only possible but easy, – and honest to boot. Say nothing about it.

This work is the Labor of five and twenty the best and ripest years of my Life. I brought to it the advantages and preparatory aids of a learned

Education – and I have woven into it the flower of constant study, Travel, 10
Conversations and Correspondence with a very large proportion of the greatest Geniuses in Arts, Science, and Literature, at home and abroad, among our Contemporaries, and much and multiform experience in more and more various relations & circumstances of life than have fallen to the Lot of literary men in general, and above all, habitual commune 15
with the moods and movements of my own moral and intellectual Being. I seek not money or reputation; and it would indeed betray a pitiable simplicity, and specially an ignorance of the existing State of Society and the present Fashion of Literature, in this Country, if I expected either. Yet I have one request to make, Christian Reader! and only one. 20
—— &c.

But I have it to review! – O! – You are a Reviewer? I beg your pardon. Farewell.

552 Amid the profoundest and most condensed constructions of hardest Thinking, the playfulness of the Boy starts up, like a wild Fig-tree from monumental Marble.

Commentary

Note: Cross-references are made to the number of the entry (not of the page).

1 **Gutch 2 § 2.** *CN* i. 10. *RX* 13. 1794/5.
The Gutch Notebook, so called because it was once owned by John M. Gutch (1776–1861), a friend of STC's since schooldays at Christ's Hospital; he played an important (and not entirely happy) role in the publication of *BL* (see *BL* i, pp. xlix; lvii–lxii). The Gutch Notebook is charismatically described in *RX* 5–31.

RX points to a note appended to Erasmus Darwin's *The Botanic Garden* (1791), which speculates about the moon's future habitation. Lowes calls STC's interest 'inscrutable' (*RX* 35); but a poem about life beginning afresh in an unspoiled new world might hold an explicable charm for putative émigrés: see 22 n. CL was to suggest in February 1797 (among other proposals) that STC write 'the description (from a vision or dream, suppose) of an Utopia in one of the planets, (the Moon for instance) –': *LambL* i. 97 (cited *RX* 472 n. 12).

2 **Gutch 2v § 2.** *CN* i. 15. *AP* 7; *DCP* 453. 1794/5.
An augmentation of the more conventionally sentimental theme of 'The faded Flower', sent in a letter (22 July 1794: *CL* i. 95) while STC was touring Wales: 'had *I* seen | Thy modest Beauties dew'd with evening's Ge[m,] | I had not rudely cropt thy parent stem.' A similar feeling appears a hallmark of natural piety in WW's Coleridgean lines of *c.*1798, 'I would not strike a flower | As many a man would strike his horse' (*Prel.* 493); and cf. STC's 1805 notebook entry: ' I would not willingly kill even a flower, but were I at the head of an army, or a revolutionary Kingdom, I would do *my Duty*' (*CN* ii. 2551).

1. Quid si vivat: 'What if it should live?'

3 **Gutch 3 § 4.** *CN* i. 22. 1795/6.
Cf. the blest, with 'celestial courage, inly armed' marching beneath 'Banners of Omnipotence' in 'Religious Musings' (ll. 65; 69: *CPW* i. 111), published in 1796, and allegedly written on Christmas Eve 1794; also *W* 242 (19 April 1796). STC's professed belief at this time, under the influence of the leading Unitarian Joseph Priestley (1733–1804), was Necessitarian (that is, disbelieving in the freedom of the will) and

Optimist (that is, holding that whatever occurs is divinely intended and tending to the good): see *CL* i. 145; 205. The *Essay on Man* (1733) by Alexander Pope (1688–1744), subsequently one of STC's principal dislikes, voices the Optimist position most famously in English verse: 'All Discord, Harmony, not understood; | All partial Evil, universal Good: | And spite of Pride, in erring Reason's spite, | One truth is clear, "Whatever IS, is RIGHT"' (1, ll. 291–4)—lines STC alludes to in his 1795 lectures as part of his case for 'the evident and vast predominance of Good in the natural World' (*LPR* 151).

The attraction of this philosophy was the intimate involvement of all worldly phenomena with the good agency of God: that, as Priestley says, God's 'power is the very *life and soul* of everything that exists; and, strictly speaking, *without him we* ARE, as well as, *can* DO *nothing*' (*Disquisitions Relating to Matter and Spirit* (2nd edn.; 2 vols.; Birmingham, 1782), i. 42). (See H. W. Piper, *The Active Universe* (1962), 29–59; and Jonathan Wordsworth, *The Music of Humanity* (1969), 188–200.) The major difficulty of Optimism, as expounded by Priestley in *The Doctrine of Philosophical Necessity Illustrated* (1777; 1782), was that 'evil' ceased to exist, except as a means to further good (see *LPR* 103–6, and nn.): much of STC's thinking over the next few years worried at the point. The most lucid account of Priestley remains Basil Willey's in *The Eighteenth Century Background* (1940), 168–204; and see the sympathetic portrait in Roy Porter, *Enlightenment: Britain and the Creation of the Modern World* (2000), 406–15.

1. Optimism: Optimist *CN*. The last letter is crunched and could well be a 't'; but the abstract noun perhaps fits the definition-form better: cf. the entry defining 'Anti-optimism' (143).

4 **Gutch 3 § 5.** *CN* i. 23. 1795/6.
1. Cf. ''Tis the sublime of man, | Our noontide Majesty, to know ourselves | Parts and proportions of one wondrous whole' ('Religious Musings', ll. 135–7: *CPW* i. 113–14). STC's religious thinking at this time, besides being Priestleian, was heavily indebted to 'the great and excellent' David Hartley (1705–57) (*CL* i. 200), also Necessitarian and Optimist, whose *Observations on Man* (1749) STC adduced in 'Religious Musings' as proof that the soul gradually ascended by innate disposition from selfhood to selfless participation in the Deity (*CPW* i. 110): see 27. The mechanism which effected this was the association of ideas: 'Since God is the source of all good, and consequently must at last appear to be so, *i.e.* be associated with all our pleasures, it seems to follow, even from this

proposition, that the idea of God, and of the ways by which his goodness and happiness are made manifest, must, at last, take place of, and absorb all other ideas, and HE himself become, according to the language of the scriptures, *all in all*' (*Observations on Man* I. i, § iii, prop. xxii). Much of STC's intellectual career would revolve around his rejection of the purely associative picture of mental life that Hartley drew. (See Willey, *Eighteenth Century Background*, 136–54; and Porter, *Enlightenment*, 180–3.)

5 **Gutch 3 § 6.** *CN* i. 24. 1795/6.
1. Presumably, as *CN* says, the *Reflections on the Revolution in France* (1790) by Edmund Burke (1730–97), the founder of modern conservativism and the French Revolution's most eloquent opponent. Cf. *Conciones ad Populum* (a lecture delivered February 1795): 'while I shudder at the excesses, I must admire the strength, of this Hercules Furens of Oratory' (*LPR* 63). Le Grice, a Cambridge contemporary, remembered STC devouring Burke's prose as it emerged from the press and quoting 'whole pages verbatim'; according to WH, STC was maintaining in early 1798 that Burke was 'almost a poet' (*IR* 11; 58).

6 **Gutch 3v § 4.** *CN* i. 28. *AP* 2. 1795/6.
'Miseries' are said to arise from 'artificial Wants' in STC's 'Lecture on the Slave-Trade' (16 June 1795); but there is 'Imagination' a gift from God, 'that stimulates to the attainment of *real* excellence by the contemplation of splendid Possibilities' (*LPR* 235).
1. cure us of : cure of us of *MS*.

7 **Gutch 3v § 7.** *CN* i. 31. *AP* 3. 1795/6?
One of many attempts to ameliorate the doctrine of Necessity. Cf. 38 n.

8 **Gutch 4 § 2.** *CN* i. 35. *AP* 4. 23 March–6 April 1795.
CN points to a similar sentiment in Edward Young's 'A Discourse on Lyric Poetry', from a passage describing the inspired, unruly virtues of the ode: *Complete Works* (2 vols.; 1854), i. 419. STC borrowed Young's works from the Bristol Library, 23 March–6 April 1795 (*WB* 119.)
1. correction : corrections *NB*. (correction *AP*.)

9 **Gutch 4 § 3.** *CN* i. 36. 23 March–6 April 1795.
CN again identifies a source in Young (*Complete Works*, i. 418; 419): the last sentence, however, is largely STC's own. For the deeply Coleridgean notion of poetry as a 'union' of diverse elements, see 205, 497; and cf. *BL*: 'GOOD SENSE is the BODY of poetic genius, FANCY its DRAPERY, MOTION its

LIFE, and IMAGINATION the SOUL that is every where, and in each; and forms all into one graceful and intelligent whole' (ii. 18). The changing role of imagination between 1795 and 1815 (when *BL* was dictated) is especially telling.

10 **Gutch 4 § 4.** *CN* i. 37. *RX* 14. 1795?
The Upas was a legendary Javan tree so toxic that no life could persist within miles of it (*OED*). Erasmus Darwin (see 33 n.) talks about it in *The Botanic Garden*, II (*The Loves of the Plants*) (1789; London, 1799), III, ll. 219–38. The best account is Geoffrey Grigson's, in *The Harp of Aeolus and Other Essays on Art Literature and Nature* (1947 [i.e. 1948]), 56–65; and see too Grigson's *The Romantics: An Anthology* (1942), 114; 340–1.

1. article. Mem. : autob. Mon. *CN*. (article. Mem. *RX*) The *CN* reading is inspired (short for 'autobiographical Monody'), and both are certainly possible; but 'Mem.' tallies with other entries in the Gutch Notebook noting ideas for compositions, and 'article' seems a more likely alternative to a 'poem'.

11 **Gutch 4ᵛ § 3.** *CN* i. 40. *RX* 15. 1795.
'The first former, fashioner, or creator' (*OED*). Cf., from STC's contribution to RS's epic *Joan of Arc* (1796): 'NIGHT | An heavy unimaginable moan | Sent forth, when she the PROTOPLAST beheld | Stand beauteous on Confusion's charmed wave' (II. 233–6), later to reappear in 'The Destiny of Nations' (ll. 288–92: *CPW* i. 140). STC's contribution seems to have been written by November 1795 (*CL* i. 172). (STC's later note by the passage reads: 'These are very fine Lines, tho' I say it, that should not: but, hang me, if I know or ever did know the meaning of them, tho' my own composition': *CPW* i. 140). God's taming of chaos into Creation serves repeatedly as a Coleridgean analogy for imaginative activity: see 371, 449, 501.

12 **Gutch 5 § 1.** *CN* i. 42. Early 1795?
The image appears in 'On the Present War' (February 1795), in *Conciones ad Populum* (*LPR* 69).

13 **Gutch 5ᵛ § 1.** *CN* i. 45. *RX* 15. 1795/6?
The Wandering Jew is Ahasuerus, who taunted Christ on the way to his Crucifixion, and was thereafter doomed to wander the earth. Within STC's circle, the myth also drew WW ('Song of the Wandering Jew' in the second edition of *Lyrical Ballads*) and Thomas De Quincey (in *Suspiria de Profundis*). STC's romance did not emerge, but he did write part of a prose piece, 'The Wanderings of Cain', a planned collaboration

with WW (*CPW* i. 285–92); and he later described his own Ancient Mariner as 'the everlasting Wandering Jew' (*TT* i. 273–4). *RX* relates the 'romance' to 'The Ancient Mariner', 244–52, 257–60; and see *CV* 145–6, 165–6.

14 **Gutch 5v § 2.** *CN* i. 46. 1795/6.

15 **Gutch 6 § 4.** *CN* i. 52. Before 4 July 1796.
The phrase appears in a poem included in a letter of 4 July 1796, later published as 'On a Late Connubial Rupture in High Life' in the *Monthly Magazine* (September): 'thy poor heart | 'Mid all the "pomp and circumstance" of state | Shivers in nakedness' (ll. 2–4: *CPW* i. 152; cf. *CL* i. 223)—hence *CN*'s suggested date. The Prince of Wales had acrimoniously separated from Princess Caroline: STC's lines address her sympathetically. *CN* cites a self-reference of a few months later: 'my Soul seems so mantled & wrapped round by your Love & Esteem, that even a dream of losing but the smallest fragment of it makes me shiver – as tho' some tender part of my Nature were left uncovered & in nakedness' (*CL* i. 235).

16 **Gutch 6v § 2.** *CN* i. 54. 1795/6.
The Leviathan leaves billowing ocean behind him in STC's contribution to RS's *Joan of Arc* (II. 387–90); later 'The Destiny of Nations', ll. 412–15 (*CPW* i. 145). STC's attraction to the 'quiet Life' he must nevertheless resign is the subject of 'Reflections on Having Left a Place of Retirement' (*CPW* i. 106–8), published October 1796.

17 **Gutch 6v § 4.** *CN* i. 56. 1795/6.
Robespierre, for instance, 'possessed a glowing ardor that still remembered the *end*, and a cool ferocity that never either overlooked, or scrupled, the *means*' (*LPR* 35). The point is a nice one for an Optimist Necessitarian, obliged to 'deny the existence of any Evil, inasmuch as the end determines the nature of the means and I have been able to discover nothing of which the end is not good' (*LPR* 105).

18 **Gutch 7 § 1.** *CN* i. 57. *RX* 15. 1795/6?

19 **Gutch 7 § 4.** *CN* i. 60. 1795/6?

20 **Gutch 7v § 1.** *CN* i. 62. *DCP* 454. 1795/6.
DCP points us to the 'Preface' to *Poems on Various Subjects* (1796): 'Compositions resembling those of the present volume are not unfrequently condemned for their querulous egotism. But egotism is to be condemned then only when it offends against time and place, as in an

History or an Epic Poem. To censure it in a Monody or Sonnet is almost as absurd as to dislike a circle for being round' (*CPW* ii. 1135–6). In *BL*, on the other hand, he recalls writing sonnets under the name of Nehemiah Higginbottom (*CPW* i. 209–11) partly to satirize 'the spirit of *doleful egotism*' in modern verse (*BL* i. 27). For egotism, see 21, 141, 294.

21 **Gutch 8ᵛ § 1.** *CN* i. 74. 1796.
6–7. egotizes in tuism: 'talks of himself in the guise of talking of another'.
9. fellow : felow *CN*
11. recentment: an obsolete form of 'resentment'. Phlogiston was the substance supposed present in inflammable bodies which was discharged during burning: a dephlogisticated heart would be one whose fires have burnt out. Phlogiston lost prestige toward the end of the eighteenth century: Lavoisier denied its existence; but Priestley, who discovered oxygen (and hence the germ of a better account of combustion), held to it, thinking of oxygen as 'dephlogisticated air'.

22 **Gutch 9ᵛ § 1.** *CN* i. 75. 1796.
Since the summer of 1794, STC's hopes had been largely invested in 'Pantisocracy', a 'System of no Property', upon which he, with RS and others, planned to establish a utopian community in unspoiled countryside. Initially, they had in mind the banks of the Susquehannah river in America; by March 1795, plans had dwindled to somewhere in 'Wales – near some Town, where there is a speedy Communication with London' (*CL* i. 90; 97; 155). (For the theory of Pantisocracy, see J. R. MacGillivray, 'The Pantisocracy Scheme and its Immediate Background'; in Malcolm W. Wallace (ed.), *Studies in English* . . . (Toronto, 1931), 131–69; and Nicholas Roe, *Wordsworth and Coleridge: The Radical Years* (Oxford, 1988; 1990), 113–15.) *CN* suggests STC has in mind *Reasons for Contentment, Addressed to the Labouring Poor of the British Public* (1793) by William Paley (see 39 n.): the discussion was presumably destined for STC's work on Pantisocracy (see 39 n.). The lessons of such '*Christianity* – I mean – that mongrel whelp that goes under it's name' were, no doubt, what STC had feared his mother-in-law would spread among the settlers were she among the Pantisocrats (*CL* i. 123).

23 **Gutch 9ᵛ § 4.** *CN* i. 78. 1796?
1. poor and the rich : poor & and the rich *MS.*

24 **Gutch 9ᵛ § 6.** *CN* i. 80. 1796/7?
STC was converted to Unitarianism while at Cambridge, under the influence of the Jesus College don William Frend (as related in *GLC*

53–5). Unitarianism asserts the unity of the Godhead, and so denies the doctrine of the Trinity, and hence the divinity of Jesus, who is supremely good but nevertheless merely human.

1. why? : why, *CN*. *CN* identifies a possible source for the question in William Wilberforce's *A Practical View of the Prevailing Religious Systems of Professed Christians in the Higher and Middle Classes of this Country* (1797). The Unitarian STC would have disagreed with the analysis, of course.

25 **Gutch 9ᵛ § 7.** *CN* i. 81. 1796/7?
'The real source of inconstancy, depravity, & prostitution, is *Property*, which mixes with & poisons every thing good – & is beyond doubt the Origin of all Evil', a recurrent theme in STC's radicalism: he intended to write about 'The origin of Property & the *mode of removing it's* evils' (*CL* i. 214; 253). In the *Lectures on Revealed Religion* he cites Acts 2: 44–5 ('And all that believed were together, and had all things common; And sold their possessions and goods, and parted them to all *men*, as every man had need'), glossing it provocatively as 'almost the whole' of Christian doctrine (*LPR* 229).

26 **Gutch 10ᵛ § 2.** *CN* i. 87. *AP* 5. 1795/6?
An effect of *bad* poetry, presumably. Later, in 1805, commenting on an Italian sonnet, the instinct was still obviously strong: 'I cannot but think, that this mode of belying the lovely countenance of Things & *red-ochring* the rose, must be injurious to the moral tact both of the authors & their admirers' (*CN* ii. 2625). The sentiment is close to WW's in the 1800 'Preface' to *Lyrical Ballads*, resisting the artificiality of 'poetic' diction in favour of 'the very language of men' (*WPrW* i. 130); and cf. the 'false and bastard sensibility' of the 'fine lady' who 'sips a beverage sweetened with human blood, even while she is weeping over the refined sorrows of Werter or of Clementina' (*W* 139).

27 **Gutch 11ᵛ § 4.** *CN* i. 98. *LR* i. 279; *DCP* 454; *CPW* ii. 989. 1795/6.
Cf. the self-annihilating spiritual climax in 'Religious Musings': 'Self, spreading still! Oblivious of its own, | Yet all of all possessing! This is Faith! | This the Messiah's destined victory!' (ll. 156–8: *CPW* i. 115).

28 **Gutch 12 § 3.** *CN* i. 102. 1795/6?

29 **Gutch 15ᵛ § 1.** *CN* i. 123. 1795/6?
The Pleasures of the Imagination (1757), I, ll. 285–7. STC read it in *Poems* (1772), borrowed from the Bristol Library over Christmas 1795 (*WB* 122).

Mark Akenside (1721–70) was an early favourite (*CL* i. 215): STC quotes from him several times in the 1795 lectures.

30 **Gutch 16 § 1.** *CN* i. 127. 1795/6?
Gloucester has his eyes gouged out in *King Lear* (III. vii), a scene Dr Johnson thought 'too horrid to be endured in dramatick exhibition' (*Johnson on Shakespeare*, ed. Walter Ralegh (Oxford 1908; 1968), 160). STC later grew more doubtful about the scene, though he still sought to justify it (*LL* ii. 333).

2. Humanité: the French word (odd but almost certainly the right reading) is presumably meant to imply a false refinement.

31 **Gutch 16 § 2.** *CN* i. 128. 1796?
STC began his journal *The Watchman* with a discussion of the importance of printing and Protestantism in the diffusion of knowledge (*W* 9–10). Later, gathering himself for an attack on contemporary journals, STC conceded 'the services which the EDINBURGH REVIEW, and others formed afterwards on the same plan, have rendered to society in the diffusion of knowledge' (*BL* ii. 108). (The *Edinburgh* was founded in 1802.)

32 **Gutch 16ᵛ § 2.** *CN* i. 131. 1796?
In *W*, STC writes satirically about the 'establishment of political schoolmasters' spreading government propaganda in the absence of a free diffusion of print (*W* 11–12).

33 **Gutch 16ᵛ § 3.** *CN* i. 132. 1796.
1. Dr Darwin: Erasmus Darwin (1731–1802), polymathic scientist, as well as author of the poems *The Botanic Garden* and *Zoönomia*. STC read widely in Darwin, but his reservations were strongly felt: 'I absolutely nauseate Darwin's Poem', he wrote in May 1796 (*CL* i. 216); but he was indebted nevertheless. (See Desmond King-Hele, *Erasmus Darwin and the Romantic Poets* (Basingstoke, 1986), 88–147.) Cf. 'During my first Cambridge vacation, I assisted a friend in a contribution for a literary society in Devonshire: and in this I remember to have compared Darwin's work to the Russian palace of ice, glittering, cold and transitory' (*BL*, i. 19–20). Beer points out (*CV* 228–9) that the ice palace comes from Cowper's *Task*, V, ll. 127–76.

4–5. The distinction between poetry and painting would remain important: Milton's verse, for instance, gives you '*creation* rather than painting' (*BL* ii. 128). But cf. his description of himself as a young poet, roaming the Quantocks: 'With my pencil and memorandum book in my hand, I was *making studies*, as the artists call them, and often moulding my thoughts into verse, with the objects and imagery immediately before my senses' (*BL* i. 196).

34 **Gutch 17 § 1.** *CN* i. 133. 1795/6?
The sense of the imminent Millennium—the period of a thousand years during which Christ is to reign on earth—was an important element in much Nonconformist radicalism in the 1790s: for instance, Priestley's 'The Present State of Europe compared with Antient Prophecies' (in *A Farewell Sermon* (1794)) had confidently interpreted contemporary events in the light of the Book of Revelation; and both Hartley and Godwin had a millennial inflection. (For a sense of STC's place in the millennialism of a wider radical culture, see Jonathan Wordsworth, *William Wordsworth: The Borders of Vision* (Oxford, 1982), 341–62; and, for an exhaustive discussion, Morton D. Paley, *Apocalypse and Millennium in English Romantic Poetry* (Oxford 1999), 91–153.) *CN* reminds us that Priestley was also the author of *Experiments and Observations on Different Kinds of Air*, so he may have been especially in mind: STC regarded 'every experiment that Priestly [*sic*] made in Chemistry, as giving *wings* to his more sublime theological works' (*CL* i. 372).

35 **Gutch 18 § 1.** *CN* i. 142. *AP* 6; *RX* 18. Before 4 July 1796.
RX (463 n. 74) compares 'To an unfortunate Princess', ll. 19–20: 'Then bid your Souls inseparably blend, | Like two bright Dew-drops bosom'd in a flower!' (*CL* i. 224).

36 **Gutch 18 § 2.** *CN* i. 143. *RX* 18. Early 1796.
RX points us to an encounter on the tour gathering subscriptions for *The Watchman*: 'The moment I entered the Coach I stumbled on a huge projection, which might be called a Belly with the same propriety that you might name Mount Atlas a Molehill'; *CN* prefers 'Mr Meanly – that tobacco-toothed Parson with a majestic periphery of guts' (*CL* i. 175; 182). Such observations mildly raise one's hopes for the novel STC once contemplated writing (*CL* i. 585).

37 **Gutch 19 § 5.** *CN* i. 153. 1796?

38 **Gutch 20 § 1.** *CN* i. 156. 1796?
That the doctrine might *need* rendering harmless is telling (cf. 7): the point seems to be that our imagination's absorption in the proximate causes of things means we are not preoccupied with the ultimate necessity that, actually, wholly governs them. STC had personally experienced the

dilemmas of attempting to live out a belief in 'the Automatism of Man': when RS talked about entering the Church, STC struggled to believe that 'That Being, who is "in will, in deed, Impulse of all in all" whichever be your determination, will make it ultimately the best', and was outraged when RS took that as approval—'you *knew* that sentence to imply no more than the pious confidence of Optimism' (*CL* i. 147; 159; 168).

CN points to a passage in Priestley's *Disquisitions on Matter and Spirit* (1782), describing the way we imagine immaterial powers (like magnetism) to explain physical events the direct cause of which we cannot discern.

3. [? monotonous] : monotonous *CN*. The passage is in smudgy pencil and has faded.

39 **Gutch 21 § 1.** *CN* i. 161. *RX* 20. Early 1796.
One of several lists of projected works; most did not materialize.

2. This book was advertised in the *Cambridge Intelligencer* in the summer of 1794, and he was still looking to finish the work in October 1795 (*CL* i. 77; 161); but it never appeared.

4. Oct[avo] : 1 ~~vol.~~ Oct *CN*. Holbach's *Système de la nature* had appeared in an English translation in 1795: the 'Answer' would doubtless address its atheism, reclaiming nature for God.

5. CL remembered STC talking about this (*LambL* i. 97). That the 'origin' should be addressed is easily comprehensible, since in an Optimistic scheme 'evil' does not properly exist at all: see 3 n.

6. An enthusiasm for the sonnets of William Lisle Bowles (1762–1850), poems of sensitive recollection within landscapes, that STC recalled in *BL* (i. 17). STC wrote an admiring sonnet to him (*Morning Post*, 26 December 1794: *CPW* i. 84).

7. The 'answer to Godwin' was announced several times, and was still under way in April 1797, but did not appear either: it was to be an unfavourable comparison with the 'System' of Jesus (*CL* i. 267; 320; 293). William Godwin (1756–1836), later a member of STC's circle, was the subject of a warm sonnet in the *Morning Post* (*CPW* i. 86); but STC's full attitude was ambivalent. Godwin's *Enquiry Concerning Political Justice* (1793) was the philosophical manifesto of the rationalist left: STC disliked its atheism and opposition to marriage, and attacked it as 'vicious' and 'a Pandar to Sensuality' (*W* 196). (See Nicola Trott, 'The Coleridge Circle and the "Answer to Godwin"', *Review of English Studies*, 41 (1990), 212–29.) STC admired the *Horae Paulinae* (1790), a work of biblical scholarship by William Paley (1743–1805), but was scornful of his defence

of the political status quo in *Principles of Moral and Political Philosophy* (1794) (*LPR* 310–11).

8. STC's ambitions for 'The book of Pantisocracy' crossed with those of his essay on Godwin (*CL* i. 115): neither appeared. TP wrote down what STC said about the practicalities of Pantisocracy, so we have some idea (*IR* 32–4).

10. *Carthon* (1765) is a tragical Ossian poem by James Macpherson (1736–96). STC borrowed *Ossian* from the Bristol Library in January 1796 (*WB* 122).

11. STC's *Poems on Various Subjects* appeared in April 1796 (*CL* i. 204).

12. STC told a correspondent that the 'Ode on the Poetical Character' by William Collins (1721–59) had 'inspired & whirled *me* along with greater agitations of enthusiasm than any the most *impassioned* Scene in Schiller or Shakspere' (*CL* i. 279). For STC's less enthused view of Gray, see 544.

14. Which became *Osorio* (1797), written (as STC thought) on commission from Richard Brinsley Sheridan, for the Drury Lane theatre: having submitted it, he heard nothing, and the scheme eventually fell through (*CL* i. 304; 384–5; 604). The play, revised, was eventually performed, with some success, in 1813.

15. *CN* prints this as part of the entry for 'Litany'. In MS it appears alongside that entry, halfway across the page, a little above the bottom: a line is drawn down the centre of this part of the page, creating a new column. (The *RX* transcription is useful: 20.) I take it to be a separate item, placed opposite 'A Litany' because STC ran out of space. ('On the different sects' seems odd contents for a *litany*, but an essay topic perfectly in line with 'on the abolition of Indiv[id]ual Property'.)

40 **Gutch 21ᵛ § 1.** *CN* i. 162. *RX* 22–3. 1795–6?

11. a Gallon Barrel : a Gallon of Barrel *MS*. The government suspended Habeas Corpus on 23 May 1794, allowing detention without charge: STC attacked the move in his Bristol lectures (*LPR* 61–2).

41 **Gutch 22 § 1.** *CN* i. 163. *RX* 23. 1796?

An odd thing to require a memorandum, but true anyhow: 'I am remarkably fond of Beans & Bacon', he told TP, attributing the attachment to his father's encouragement when a boy (*CL* i. 347). See *RX* 23.

42 **Gutch 22ᵛ § 2.** *CN* i. 165. *RX* 24. 1796?

1. the Swedenborgian: that is, a follower of the Swedish mystic Emmanuel Swedenborg (1688–1772), whose works include *The True*

Christian Religion and *Heaven and Its Wonders and Hell from Things Heard and Seen*. STC's surviving marginalia to Swedenborg (*CM* v. 403–74) are extensive, but of a later date.

43 **Gutch 22ᵛ § 3.** *CN* i. 166. *RX* 24. 1796?

44 **Gutch 23ᵛ § 1.** *CN* i. 170. *RX* 25. 1796?
STC refers admiringly to Dante throughout his life. (He later befriended Henry Cary, whose translation of *The Divine Comedy* he championed in his literary lectures (*LL* ii. 395, 401).) There is a good discussion of influence in Ralph Pite, *The Circle of Our Vision: Dante's Presence in English Romantic Poetry* (Oxford, 1994), 68–118.

1. Book : Books *MS.* STC originally wrote 'three Books', but then made a modest revision, evidently forgetting to change the number of the noun. Dante : Dantè *CN.* (Dante *RX.*)

45 **Gutch 24ᵛ § 1.** *CN* i. 174. *RX* 26–8; 467. 1795/6?
Another list of intended works.

1. Tobit is an apocryphal book of the Bible, full of fantastic incidents.

3. STC's defence of marriage was one of the main points of difference from progressives like Godwin or John Thelwall, radical and poet, with whom STC had been in correspondence since April 1796, and with whom he had disagreed on the point. (*CL* 204; i. 213–14).

4. Jacob Behmen, or Boehme or Böhme (1757–1624), German theosophist and mystic, author of *Aurora* (1612), a book that STC later said he had '*conjured over* at School' (*CL* iv. 751); *BL* speaks admiringly of him (i. 147–51) as a counter-influence to the empiricism of the age. See *CPT* 325–32; and Tim Fulford, 'Coleridge, Böhme, and the Language of Nature', *Modern Language Quarterly*, 52 (1991), 37–52.

5. John Henderson (1757–88), a renowned scholar of humble origins, was posthumously subjected to a monody by JC ('Mem'ry turns from *little men* to THEE, | And views, with smiles that light her trembling tear, | Thy Genius destin'd for a nobler sphere'), published in his *Poems* (1795; 1796).

6. For his continuing attraction to the subject, see *CN* iv. 5192.

7. Thomas Burnet (1635?-1715) was author of *Telluris Theoria Sacra* (1681), translated as *The Sacred Theory of the Earth* (1684–9), one of the works STC singles out in *BL* as poetry although not written in verse (ii. 14). *RX* (462 n. 64) speculates which passages about mountains STC may have had in mind.

9–10. Some good Coleridgean candles are gathered by Lowes (*RX* 474 n. 10).

12. For a reproduction see *RX* 26. It is a bewildering piece of joke Greek for which *RX* (604–604a) offers the gloss 'The Lover's Hat': it refers to 'Mary, the Maid of the Inn', a poem by RS.

13. St Withold appears in one of poor Tom's mad songs from *King Lear* (III. iv., ll. 120–4): STC wrote to RS in December 1796, 'Would not this be a fine subject for a *wild* Ode . . . I shall set about one, when I am in a Humour to *abandon* myself to all the Diableries, that ever met the Eye of a Fuseli!' (*CL* i. 135). The paintings of Henry Fuseli (1741–1825) included *The Nightmare* and wild illustrations of Shakespeare.

14. Presumably, 'crotchet' as 'fanciful device' (*OED*): the title of a volume of poems? See 416.

18–21. The case against Godwin again, whose Necessitarianism was not coupled (as STC's was) with a theist Optimism, but relied precariously on the supposedly irresistible claim of human Reason. The choice is made clear in a letter of January 1796 about Darwin: 'whether we be the outcasts of a blind idiot called Nature, or the children of an all-wise and infinitely good God' (*CL* i. 177).

21. ideot : STC's archaic spelling of 'idiot'. 'Ideotisme' is 'the condition of being void of intellect or reason' (*OED*).

24. Presumably, to be an attack on the Church's complicity with the war: the Revd Dr Randolph had recently consecrated the colours of the Essex cavalry before the Duke of York (*CN*).

26. 'From the prison of the warring clouds'—a second thought connected by the cross symbol with the entry 'Slave of an ideot Nature!'

27. Egomist : *CN* tracks 'Egomism' (not in *OED*) to Andrew Baxter's *Enquiry into the Nature of the Soul* (1745). The reference is to the philosophical position that rejects the material reality of the external world, while insisting on the reality of the self and its mental experience: a view STC evidently inclined to rhapsodize.

28. George, Bishop Berkeley [*sic*] (1685–1753), was a favourite author of the young STC: he was declaring himself 'a *Berkleian*' in 1797 (*CL* i. 335), enthused by the combination of theistic immediacy and Platonic transcendence he found in Berkeley's idealism. STC borrowed the second volume of Berkeley's works from the Bristol Library in March 1796 (*WB* 122); and he drew upon Berkeley's *Maxims Concerning Patriotism* in his analysis of 'Modern Patriotism' in *W* for 17 March 1796 (98–100). The gist of page 345 is 'a believer [rather] than an infidel [has] a better chance of being [a] patriot' (*W* 100 n. 1).

30–1. The 'system', as set out in Berkeley's *Principles of Human Knowledge* (1710), although philosophically quite distinct, overlapped in certain respects with the Priestleian Unitarianism which had already drawn STC: Berkeley says that 'everything we see, hear, feel, or anywise perceive by Sense, [is] a *sign* or *effect* of the power of God . . . It is therefore plain that nothing can be more evident to any one that is capable of the least reflection than the existence of God, or a Spirit who is intimately present to our minds – producing in them all that variety of ideas or sensations which continually affect us, on whom we have an absolute and entire dependence, in short "in whom we live, and move, and have our being"' (§§ 148, 149).

33. A satire on private property, presumably.

34. Fletcher Christian (1764–?), ringleader of the mutiny on HMS *Bounty* (1789)—and, incidentally, a distant relative of WW.

35. In a fit of emotional and financial desperation, STC had enrolled in the Dragoons in December 1793. He was discharged the following April, after a remarkably unsuccessful career as a horseman. (See *IR* 18–25.) Was this period to be the source of his anecdotes?

36. A recruiting slogan: in *Conciones ad Populum*, associated with the enlisting poor (*LPR* 70).

37. For STC's interest in the imagery of the ancient Orphic hymns, see *CV* 238.

38. The 'Two Bills', severe measures to suppress dissent and demonstration against the government, were passed in December 1795: one of the objectives of *The Watchman* was to campaign against them (*W* 5).

40. Edingburgh : Edinburgh *CN*. STC's customary spelling in the Notebook. STC habitually associated the city with the excesses of 'Enlightenment': the medical training it offered would presumably base itself on inadequate, materialist theories of life (cf. *CL* i. 294–5).

46 **Gutch** 79 § 1. *CN* i. 276. Before 27 February 1796?
An abridged quotation from Jonathan Richardson's *Explanatory Notes and Remarks on Milton's Paradise Lost* (1734), identified by James Thorpe, *Modern Language Notes*, 63 (1948), 130–1. STC used the passage in the preface to the second edition of his *Poems* (1797), which is dated 27 February 1797. That the greatest poetry justifies all its verbal choices is a favourite Coleridgean axiom: 'it would be scarcely more difficult to push a stone out from the pyramids with the bare hand, than to alter a word, or the position of a word, in Milton or Shakespeare, (in their most important works at least)' (*BL* i. 23).

47 **Gutch** 76[v] § 3. *CN* i. 265. *DCP* 457. 22 September–12 October 1796 (*CN*).
Cf. 'Ode to the Departing Year', ll. 72–3: 'The Spirit of the Earth made

reverence meet, | And stood up, beautiful, before the cloudy seat' (*CPW* i. 164). STC reportedly demurred at the line's merits in later life (*IR* 90).

48 **Gutch 26ᵛ § 6.** *NB* i. 181. *DCP* 455; *CPW* ii. 991. 22 September–18 October 1796 (*CN*).
2. Chalcography is the art of engraving on copper.

49 **Gutch 26ᵛ § 7.** *CN* i. 182. September–October 1796 (*CN*).
An idea repeated in a letter of December 1796 (*CL* i. 267).

50 **Gutch 27ᵛ § 2.** *CN* i. 188. 1796?
Dreams would become one of the recurring subjects of the Notebook. *CN* compares Christabel's experience of 'such perplexity of mind | As dreams too lively leave behind' (ll. 385–6: *CPW* i. 228); and cites a note from *Osorio*: 'Prophetical dreams are things of nature, and explicable by that law of the mind in which where [*sic*] dim ideas are connected with vivid feelings' (*CPW* ii. 566). Many of STC's dream writings are usefully gathered in Jennifer Ford, *Coleridge on Dreaming* (Cambridge, 1998).

51 **Gutch 27ᵛ § 3.** *CN* i. 189. *AP* 2. 1796?
A recurring idea about the self: cf. 'That which intuitively it at once beholds and adores, praying always, and rejoicing always – *that* doth it tend to become' (*LS* 90). For a poetic mind (Shakespeare's) becoming that which it contemplates, see 451.

52 **Gutch 27ᵛ § 3.** *CN* i. 190. 1796?
STC defended himself against the charge of being 'an *Enthusiast*' in *W* (197). More generally, his view of enthusiasm was highly ambiguous: 'Enthusiasm . . . implies an undue (or when used in a good sense, an unusual) vividness of ideas' (*CM* i. 270).

53 **Gutch 28 § 2.** *CN* i. 193. 1796?
2. *inward*: the underlining is not beyond dispute.

54 **Gutch 28 § 6.** *CN* i. 197. *LR* i. 278; *CDP* 455; *CPW* ii. 991. 1795/6?
Cf. 'The Destiny of Nations', ll. 257–8: 'Such strange vivacity, as fires the eye | Of Misery fancy-crazed!' (*CPW* i. 139). The fiery eye of genius invokes a Platonic type of the poet that often features in STC, most magnificently at the end of 'Kubla Khan', but cf., from February 1797: 'You would smile to see my eye rolling up to the ceiling in a Lyric fury, and on my knee a *Diaper* pinned, to warm' (*CL* i. 308). DW's first impressions of STC's 'eye' are to the point: 'it has more of "the poet's eye in a fine frenzy rolling" than I ever witnessed' (*IR* 45).

55 **Gutch 28ᵛ § 1.** *CN* i. 199. *LR* i. 278; *DCP* 455; *CPW* ii. 991. Before 26 December 1796.
DCP compares 'Ode to the Departing Year', ll. 33–7 (published in the *Cambridge Intelligencer*, 31 December 1796): 'Seiz'd in sore travail and portentous birth | (Her eyeballs flashing a pernicious glare) | Sick Nature struggles! Hark! her pangs increase! | Her groans are horrible! but O! most fair | The promis'd Twins she bears – Equality and Peace!' (*CPW* i. 161 n.).

56 **Gutch 29 § 1.** *CN* i. 203. 9 November–13 December 1796.
Another unwritten essay on an abiding preoccupation: 'the cold System of Newtonian Theology' (*CL* ii. 866). Cf. STC's note in *Joan of Arc*: 'It has been asserted that Sir Isaac Newton's philosophy leads in its consequences to Atheism: perhaps not without reason. For if matter, by any powers or properties *given* to it, can produce the order of the visible world and even generate thought; why may it not have possessed such properties by inherent *right*? and where is the necessity of a God?' (*CPW* ii. 1112). The position is attributed to atheistical scoffers in lines that become ll. 26–35 of 'The Destiny of Nations': 'Their subtle fluids, impacts, essences, | Self-working tools, uncaused effects, and all | Those blind Omniscients, those Almighty Slaves, | Untenanting creation of its God' (ll. 32–5: *CPW* i. 132). STC takes the reference to Aristotle's *Metaphysics* from Ralph Cudworth's *True Intellectual System of the Universe* (1678), a favourite work of English Platonism which STC borrowed from Bristol Library in May–June 1795 and again in November–December 1796 (*WB* 120; 124).

57 **Gutch 29 § 3.** *CN* i. 205. 9 November–13 December 1796.

58 **Gutch 29 § 4.** *CN* i. 206. *TT* ii. 142; *AP* 7. Late 1796?

59 **Gutch 45ᵛ § 1.** *CN* i. 240. *DCP* 457. Early 1796–early 1797? (*CN*).
Notes for one of the Hymns listed in 45? A passage from Thomas Maurice's *History of Hindostan* (1795): its Coleridgean afterlife (in 'Kubla Khan' especially) is discussed by *RX* 379–83 and *CV* 246–7, 263–4.
4. An English ell is about 45 inches (*OED*).

60 **Gutch 30 § 1.** *CN* i. 212. *RX* 28–9. 1796/7?
The life of idiots would shortly feature in WW's 'The Idiot Boy'.
4. famished : famish'd *CN*.

61 **Gutch 30v § 1.** *CN* i. 213. *LR* i. 278 (no. 3); *DCP* 455–6 (nos. 1, 3, 4, 5, 6); *CPW* ii. 992. 1796/7?
Fragments, as *CPW* speculates, for 'The Brook': 'I sought for a subject, that should give equal room and freedom for description, incident, and impassioned reflections on men, nature, and society, yet supply in itself a natural connection to the parts, and unity to the whole. Such a subject I conceived myself to have found in a stream . . . Many circumstances, evil and good, intervened to prevent the completion of the poem, which was to have been entitled "The Brook"' (*BL* i. 195–6). Among the 'good' circumstances, we should count the presence in STC's life of WW, whose poetic task they had collaboratively decided by spring 1798: a philosophical epic poem to be called '*The Recluse or views of Nature, Man, and Society*' (*WEY* 214).
10. [-top] : -top *LR*, *DCP*, *CPW*, *CN*. The ink is now very faint.
15. 'furr'd' is not easy; but *DCP*, *CPW*, *CN* all have it.

62 **Gutch 31 § 2.** *CN* i. 215. 1796/7?
1–2. Shakespeare, Sonnet 107, ll. 1–2.
4–5. Shakespeare, Sonnet 110, ll. 5–6. look'd : looked *CN*.

63 **Gutch 31 § 3.** *CN* i. 216. *LR* i. 277; *DCP* 456; *CPW* ii. 992. 1796/7?
1–3. Cf. 'Christabel', ll. 16–17: '"The thin gray cloud is spread on high, | It covers but not hides the sky' (*CPW* i. 216)—which, in turn, is associated with an entry in DW's journal (31 January 1798): 'When we left home the moon immensely large, the sky scattered over with clouds. These soon closed in, contracting the dimensions of the moon without concealing her' (*DWJ* i. 5)—one of several 'Christabel'-like phrases in the journal during this period.

64 **Gutch 31 § 4.** *CN* i. 217. *LR* i. 278; *DCP* 456; *CPW* ii. 993. 1796/7?
1. *DCP* compares 'The Picture', ll. 149–50: 'The smoke from cottage-chimneys, tinged with light, | Rises in columns' (*CPW* i. 373).

65 **Gutch 32 § 1.** *CN* i. 219. *DCP* 456. Autumn–winter 1797/spring 1798?
HC was born 19 September 1797, named after STC's first philosopher. The incident finds a poetic home in 'The Nightingale' (written 1798):

> once, when he awoke
> In most distressful mood (some inward pain
> Had made up that strange thing, an infant's dream –)
> I hurried with him to our orchard-plot,
> And he beheld the moon, and, hushed at once,

Suspends his sobs, and laughs most silently,
While his fair eyes, that swam with undropped tears,
Did glitter in the yellow moon-beam! (ll. 98–105: *CPW* i. 267)

66 **Gutch 32 § 2.** *CN* i. 220. Autumn–winter 1797/spring 1798?
RX (364–70) traces the 'wilderness-plot' to William Bartram, *Travels through North and South Carolina, Georgia, East and West Florida, the Cherokee Country [etc.]* (Philadelphia, 1791). *RX* connects it with 'Kubla Khan' (probably written November 1797), and also with the Xanadu-like landscape in a letter of April 1798: 'Laudanum gave me repose, not sleep: but YOU, I believe, know how divine that repose is – what a spot of inchantment, a green spot of fountains, & flowers & trees, in the very heart of a waste of Sands!' (*CL* i. 394). For the unhappier place of opium in his later life, see 374n.

67 **Gutch 35 § 1.** *CN* i. 223. *TT* ii. 38; *RX* 10. 1797/8?
An early example of a perpetual fascination: extremes meeting. The musky dead dog reappears in *Omniana* (*SWF* i. 321), *AR* (122), and *TT* (ii. 38) to warn against the delusive attractions of far-off things.

68 **Gutch 35 § 2** *CN* i. 224. 1797/8?
1. *suspicious* : suspicions *CN.*

69 **Gutch 35[v] § 2.** *CN* i. 226. 1797/8?

70 **Gutch 36 § 1.** *CN* i. 227. 1797/8?

71 **Gutch 36 § 3.** *CN* i. 229. *DCP* 456; *CPW* ii. 993. 1797/8?
2. A shining : Ashining *CN.* (A-shining *DCP*, *CPW*). A nice decision; but I can see no hyphen.

72 **21. 3[v] § 2.** *CN* i. 314. December 1797/January 1798.
CN identifies a source for the joke in Richard Bentley's *Remarks upon a Late Discourse of Free-Thinking* (1713). It appears in *Omniana* (*SWF* i. 300) to typify 'modern criticisms on the works of our elder writers'.

73 **21. 3[v] §§ 3, 4, 5, 6.** *CN* i. 315–18. *CPW* ii. 1000. December 1797/1798.
Printed as separate entries in *CN*, but as a single collection of fragments in *CPW*.

12. heaven, : heavens *CN.* (heaven *CPW.*) The *CN* reading makes slightly better sense; but the 's' really is elusive.

74 **21. 3[v] § 7.** *CN* i. 319. December 1797/1798.
CN tracks this (and the next entry) to Robert South's *Sermons* (1737).

75 21.4 § 5. *CN* i. 326. December 1797/1798.

76 21.4^{v} § 1. *CN* i. 328. *AP* 6. December 1797/1798.
A phrase recycled in *Omniana* (*SWF* i. 319). *CN* suggests another source in South, describing Thomas's refusal to credit the Resurrection until he had felt the wound in Christ's side; but 'Snails' (which is what matters) is STC's own word. Cf. his letter to Poole, 16 October 1797: 'from my early reading of Faery Tales, & Genii &c &c – my mind had been habituated to the vast . . . I know no other way of giving the mind a love of "the Great", & "the Whole". – Those who have been led to the same truths step by step thro' the constant testimony of their senses, seem to me to want a sense which I possess' (*CL* i. 354).

77 21.4^{v} § 2. *CN* i. 329. Winter 1797/8.
Lines that, reworked, make their way into 'Frost at Midnight' (February 1798): 'while the nigh thatch | Smokes in the sun-thaw' (ll. 69–70: *CPW* i. 242).

78 21.5 § 1. *CN* i. 330. *AP* 3–4. 1798? with later additions.
The children in question in the earliest entries in the list must be Hartley and Berkeley (b. 14 May 1798). STC planned a series of 'poems on Infancy' (*CN* i. 605).

8. The relationship between means and ends is a perennial topic for STC: the child's self-sufficiency of means-without-ends anticipates a later formulation of one kind of genius, for which 'the love of the *means* is their end' (*CN* iii. 3249).

10. The last phrase is a later addition. He means the workhouse: WW shared his hostility toward the 'House, misnamed of INDUSTRY' in 'The Old Cumberland Beggar', written January–March 1798 (l. 179: *WPW* iv. 239).

13. A Lapland baby appears on his mother's back in 'The Destiny of Nations', while his father 'Wins gentle solace as with upward eye | He marks the streamy banners of the North' (ll. 76–7: *CPW* i. 134).

17–18. 'Princess unkissed & foully husbanded' is an addition, tucked in *after* the '&' which originally introduced 'the infants': I have restored the '&' to its original company, which seems what is meant. (For the kindred wretchedness of rich and poor children, see 23.) Like items 15 and 16, added to this list of projects and observations, the phrase has been transcribed from Notebook 4, an entry originally made in November–December 1799 (*CN* i. 605).

19. *AP* reads 'William' (thinking of WW?): indeed, the 's' is not

emphatic. *CN* suggests a reference to Edward Williams, the Welsh bard (1746–1826), mentioned by STC in a letter (*CL* i. 214): the reference is apparently confirmed elsewhere (*CN* i. 605). This entry to the list is an addition, squeezed in the edge of the page: 'vision' (*CN*) is not easy to make out (*AP* has 'union').

22. Swedenborg discusses infants in heaven in his *Heaven and Hell* (§§ 329–45): among his insights is that to earthly, almost as much as to heavenly children, 'Each and every object seemed to them to be alive; and thus in every least idea of their thought there is life' (§ 338). Cf. STC's contribution to WW's 'We Are Seven' (ll. 1–4: *WPW* i. 236; and see 361–2).

24–5. Another interpolation, in a small hand.

26. *Στοργη*: i.e. affection, especially of a parental or filial kind.

29–33. The fat baby is DC (born 14 September 1800); the whirling child is HC. An addition from *c.*28 September 1802: cf. 'Hartley & little Derwent running in the Green, where the Gusts blow most madly – both with their Hair floating & tossing, a miniature of the agitated Trees below which they were playing / inebriate both with the pleasure – Hartley whirling round for joy – Derwent eddying half willingly, half by the force of the Gust – driven backward, struggling forward, & shouting his little hymn of Joy' (*CL* ii. 872).

79 3.1 § 1. *CN* i. 335 (excerpt). 18 September 1798.

STC, the Wordsworths, and John Chester (a friend of STC's) left Yarmouth for Germany on 16 September, with the intention of 'learning the language, and for the common advantages to be acquired by seeing different people and different manners', as DW put it (*WEY* 220). Originally, SC and the children were to go as well, but financial prudence dissuaded them from the plan (*CL* i. 414). The first page has been damaged, obliterating several characters.

1. The month is missing through damage to the page.

4. transversely /: the line attempts to represent the transverse road of moonlight.

6. 35 : 37 *CN*. STC has changed the number.

20. [']Tis the mouth : From this the mouth *CN*. An obscure passage: 'from' (if it *is* 'from') appears crossed through; I cannot make out 'this'.

80 3.4 § 1. *CN* i. 336. 19 September 1798.

The entry should be compared with the letter to TP (*CL* i. 431–4).

5. Wordsworth went to seek : Wordsworth went ~~with the agreeable French~~ Em. to seek *CN*. 'Em' (the beginning of 'Emigrant') is crossed out too.

6. Von Axen was an agent of the Wedgwoods (see *CL* i. 457).

8. William Remnant, a bookseller, on whom STC had an order for £25, given to him by his generous publisher Joseph Johnson (see *WPrW* i. 92; *CL* i. 417).

9. Chatterley was an English businessman (*CN* i. 337).

13. The 'Emigrant' was a Frenchman who had travelled with them (*CL* i. 424). 'Der Wilder Man' is 'Der Wilde Mann': 'i.e. The Savage – an hotel not of the genteelest Class', he told TP (*CL* i. 433).

81 3. 4ᵛ § 1. *CN* i. 337 (excerpt). 20 September 1798.

2. He goes on to work out his accounts. (Cf. *CL* i. 434.)

82 3. 8 § 1. *CN* i. 339 (excerpt). 21 September 1798.

1. 21st : 21th *MS*. STC wrote '20th' and then changed the number.

2. Klopstock : Klopstock's *MS*. Klopstock was Chatterley's business partner, and the brother of the poet Friedrich Gottlieb Klopstock (1724–1803). There is an account of the meeting in *BL* (ii. 194–205), and WW also left one (*WPrW* i. 91–5). STC contrasted *Der Messias* (1748–73) unfavourably with *Paradise Lost* in his lectures (*LL* ii. 425).

4. STC had seen an impressive bust in the house of the poet's brother the day before (*CN* i. 337).

7. WW spoke to Klopstock in French (*WPrW* i. 91).

8. Richard Glover (1712–85), whose forgotten works in blank verse included *Leonidas* and *The Athenaid*.

12. now : new *CN*.

20. Toupee Periwig : Toupee, Perriwig *CN*. Gotthold Ephraim Lessing (1729–81), playwright and aesthetician, whose life STC planned to write (*CN* i. 377). He had seen the picture of Lessing at Klopstock's brother's (*CN* i. 337).

83 21. 134ᵛ § 1. *CN* i. 357. 10 October 1798.

WW and DW separated from STC at the beginning of October, and headed for Goslar where lodgings were cheap; STC and Chester headed for the scenic town of Ratzeburg, where STC settled down to learn German – a relief after 'the filth, the noise and the tallow-faced Roguery of Hamburg' (*CL* i. 445; 440; 420).

1. After the date STC has added, sometime after, '1798.!!': the entry comes as a surprise, way out of chronological sequence, toward the back of the book. He describes Ratzeburg to his wife in a letter (*CL* i. 460–1), including an account of the pleasures of ice-skating: the letter was later reworked to form an article, 'Christmas out of Doors', in *F* (28 December

1809: ii. 257–8), introducing an excerpt from WW's unpublished *Prelude* (cf. *1805*, I, ll. 427–89) also describing the pleasures of skating.

84 **21. 6 § 2.** *CN* i. 381. Winter 1798/9.
1. The German winter was bitter: 'for two days it was twenty degrees under the Freezing Point' (*CL* i. 458). Cf. WW, 'Written in Germany on One of the Coldest Days of the Century' (*WPW* iv. 64–5).

85 **21. 6 § 5.** *CN* i. 383. *AP* 5. Winter/spring 1799.
8. Bard : *Bard CN*. The Bard : *The Bard CN*.

86 **3. 20 § 1.** *CN* i. 401. 25 March–April 1799.
After the long winter, STC and Chester left Ratzeburg for Göttingen, arriving on 12 February 1799. There, STC matriculated in the university, met the expatriate community, and threw himself into university life (*CL* i. 475–6). Does the entry describe a piece of student wit observed there? He wrote to SC: 'Such an Evening I never passed before – roaring, kissing, embracing, fighting, smashing bottles & glasses against the wall, singing – in short, such a scene of uproar I never witnessed before, no, not even at Cambridge. – I drank nothing.' Back home, his little boy Berkeley had died, though he was not to learn the news until April (*CL* i. 476; 478–9).

87 **5. 61ᵛ § 1.** *CN* i. 454. 11 September 1799.
STC and RS went on a short tour of Devon, 10–16 September (see *CN* i. 1580).

88 **5. 61ᵛ § 2.** *CN* i. 455. 12 September 1799.
A sighting at Dartmouth (see *CN* i. 1581, where the date is given).
3–4. [?in the cloud] : in the cloud *CN*. The last three words are obscured by a stain. *J* is not much help.

89 **5. 2ᵛ § 1.** *CN* i. 470. *AP* 59. Autumn 1799.

90 **5. 2ᵛ § 3.** *CN* i. 472. Autumn 1799.

91 **5. 60 § 2.** *CN* i. 488. 25 October 1799.

92 **5. 60 § 4.** *CN* i. 490. 25 October 1799.
1. Aspens : Aspen *CN*.

93 **5. 4 § 2.** *CN* i. 498. October 1799.
A regular target (e.g. *HCR* i. 28), sometimes jocularly; cf. *CN* iii. 4134: 'Bitch, Botch, Stitch, Blotch, Ditch, Grutch . . . crutch, clutch, Witch, Scritch . . . a catalogue of Characteristics, equally consonant with the

Thing, as with the *Word*, "Scotch", in short, a monosyllabic yet compleat Compendium of *its* qualities, habits, customs, doings, sufferings, and circumstances' (*CN* iii. 4134). The writers he has most in view are presumably, from the past, Hume (see 375 n.), and, from the present, Sir James Mackintosh (see 104 n.) and Francis Jeffrey (1773–1850), editor of the *Edinburgh Review*.

94 5. 58^{v} § 2. *CN* i. 493. *AP* 8. 26 October 1799.
This was STC's first meeting with SH: he and JC arrived at the Hutchinsons' farm at Sockburn in County Durham, where WW and DW were staying. (See *WEY* 269; 271 n.) STC, WW, and JC set off the next day for a tour of the Lake District. JC parted company from them on 30 October, returning to Bristol; WW and STC went on: it was STC's first experience of the Lakes.

95 5. 41 § 1. *CN* i. 537 (excerpt). 11 November 1799.
This day, they walked from Ouse Bridge to Buttermere, southwards down Lorton Vale. The mountain which STC calls Grasmere is properly Grasmoor; the peak of Melbreak is on the western side of Crummock Water. The most useful guide is Dave and Kerry Walker, *Wordsworth and Coleridge Tour of the Lake District 1799* (Blackpool, 1997).

4. Scale Hill is at the northern tip of Crummock Water; Loweswater lies a mile or so to the west.

7. Estatesmen, or Statesmen, were the small land-holders of the Lake Country, like WW's Michael.

9. round : around *CN*.

25. Island : Islands *CN*.

27–8. Buttermere is circled about by mountains: Buttermere Fell to the south and Robinson to the north.

96 5. 27 § 1. *CN* i. 549 (excerpt). 16 November 1799.
From Threlkeld to Patterdale. The waterfall (line 20) is Aira Force: viewing arrangements have improved.

6. House too! : House too *CN*. An uncertain reading.

10. black mountain! : black mountain *CN*.

20. [visited] : the word is likely but difficult, written over another, perhaps (as *CN* says) 'now'.

24. running // athwart : STC is using the lines as a quick sketch. 'is original' is a difficult reading though a little clearer in *J*.

28. After 'half-wheel', STC here draws a half-circle.

33. and now I have : and I now I have *MS*.

34. Pooley Bridge is at the northernmost tip of Ullswater.
37–8. Cliff / : Cliff! *CN*.

97 5. 23 § 1. *CN* i. 551. 17 November 1799.
Leaving Patterdale, looking across Ullswater.
7. [?] : Mist *CN*. The initial letter looks more of a 'W'; but I have no suggested alternative to *CN*.
12. forks : forke *CN*. A doubtful reading.

98 5. 12ᵛ § 1. *CN* i. 556. November 1799.
The mystery of Spinozism is a version of the imponderable STC had encountered in Priestley's theology: if God is *identical* with the multifarious world, how does he retain the unity of his Godhead? (Cf. *AR* 402–3 and n.) The One and the many is an ancient philosophical question, and perhaps the central concern of STC's metaphysics. What is the relationship between the unity of God and the immense plurality of the sensory world? Or, putting it another way: how can a *uni*verse be diverse? (For a cogent account of the problem, and a sympathetic treatment of STC's later, Trinitarian attempt to resolve it, see Colin E. Gunton, *The One, the Three and the Many: God, Creation and the Culture of Modernity*... (Cambridge, 1993), esp. 17–21.) STC would revive his idea for the poem a few years later, altering the scheme subtly (see 248). For Spinoza, see 110 n.

99 5. 13 § 1. *CN* i. 557. November 1799.

100 5. 14ᵛ § 3. *CN* i. 563. 20 November 1799.
Extremes meet again. Ending their tour, WW and STC visited the Clarksons. Thomas Clarkson (1760–1846), the famous slave campaigner, lived at Eusemere at the top of Ullswater; he was married to Catherine (1772–1856), an old friend of DW. STC left on 18 November, and, at Scotch Corner, headed east again, now alone, to revisit the Hutchinsons.

101 5. 15 § 2. *CN* i. 565. 20–7 November 1799.
A continuing interest in the politics of no property? He suggested in December that RS write 'a History of the Levellers and the Levelling Principle under some goodly Title, neither praising or abusing them' (*CL* i. 554).

102 5. 18ᵛ § 1. *CN* i. 578. 25–7 November 1799.
Written at Sockburn: the beginning of his long-lived, hopeless love for SH. Cf. 'The Keepsake' (published in the *Morning Post* in 1802), l. 36: 'the entrancement of that maiden kiss'. A little earlier in that poem (ll. 26–31)

we have, perhaps, another recollection of this visit: 'There, in that bower where first she owned her love, | And let me kiss my own warm tear of joy | From off her glowing cheek, she sate and stretched | The silk upon the frame, and worked her name | Between the Moss-Rose and Forget-me-not – | Her own dear name, with her own auburn hair!' (*CPW* i. 346). His love for Sara becomes one of the dominating themes of the Notebook over the next ten years or more, not just as a cause of personal wish and despair, but also involving itself with STC's speculations about dreams, consciousness, imagination, and poetry. Sara often appears as 'Asra', or '*Ασρα*'; also in some other guises. The relationship is treated with much sympathy by Richard Holmes (*Coleridge: Early Visions* and *Coleridge: Darker Reflections* (1989; 1998)). The fullest account remains George Whalley, *Coleridge and Sara Hutchinson and the Asra Poems* (1955).

103 4. 2v § 2. *CN* i. 591. 29 November 1799.
The first entry made in this pocket-book (dated 27 November) is a description of a flock of starlings seen from the coach, which STC later transcribed into Notebook 21 (see 251); page 2v is headed: 'Remarks made in London at which place I arrived Wednesday midnight, Nov[ember] 27 1799' (*CN* i. 590). This entry was also written up later (252). The Notebook is mostly in pencil, and many entries were already badly faded when Coburn saw them (*CN* i (n.), pp. xxvii–xxviii); many entries are clearer in *J*.

104 4. 7 § 2. *CN* i. 609. 14–16 December 1799.
Sir James Mackintosh (1765–1832), lawyer, essayist, and STC's rival as conversationalist of the age. STC attended his lectures on 'The Law of Nature and Nations' given at Lincoln's Inn in 1800: 'Lord have pity on those Metaphysics, of which he is a competent Judge . . . such a wretched patch work of plagiarisms from Condilliac – of contradictions, and blunders in matters of fact, I never heard from any man's mouth before,' STC told TP in February 1801 (*CL* i. 675). (Condillac [*sic*] (1715–80) was a French proponent of Locke, not a combination set to appeal to STC.) See John Beer, 'Coleridge, Mackintosh and the Wedgwoods', *Romanticism*, 7 (2001), 16–40.

1. [N]othing : Nothing *CN*. There is a tail which just might suggest 'Nothings'.

3–4. [si]ck : sick *CN*. aff[?liction. The] : affection. The *CN*. The reading 'sick' seems sure; might the second word be 'affliction'? This is the bottom of the page, and has suffered not only normal rubbing but perhaps water damage too: it was a Notebook he used outdoors.

4. For STC's long fascination with the serpent as an emblem of genius, see *CV* 70–1. Shakespeare's serpentine genius, 'writhing in every direction, but still progressive', appears in *LL* ii. 278; and cf. *BL* ii. 14.

7. [are] : are *CN*. The word is lost in *J* too.

8–19. Milton's description of the serpent from *Paradise Lost*, IX, ll. 498–503, run on to ll. 516–17 (to 'wanton wreath'), when STC's own words take over ('yet still . . .'). STC re-lineates to fit his page.

105 4. 9ᵛ § 3. *CN* i. 617. 21 December 1799.
STC later told a story of HC, 'scarcely five years old': 'On some one asking him, if Anny Sealy (a little girl, he went to school with) was an Acquaintance of his, he replied very fervently, pressing his right hand on his heart – No! She is an *In*quaintance' (*CL* v. 466). HC's remarks were frequently recorded admiringly: 'he said one night, coming thro' the Streets – "Stars are dead Lamps – they *be'nt* naughty – they are put up in the Sky." –Two or three weeks ago he was talking to himself while I was writing, & I took down his soliloquy – It would make a most original Poem' (*CL* i. 563).

106 10. 50 § 1. *CN* i. 658. February 1800?

107 10. 47 § 2. *CN* ii. 672. February–April 1800.
In the 1818 *Friend*, STC invokes 'an ignorant man . . . describing or relating' as an example of immethodical thought in which 'memory alone is called into operation', rather than the well-educated man's 'unpremeditated and evidently habitual *arrangement* of his words'. His Shakespearian examples include the nurse from *Romeo and Juliet* and Mistress Quickly (*F* i. 449; 450–1).

108 10. 46ᵛ § 1. *CN* i. 673. February–April 1800.
Though metaphysical poetry (in STC's terms) was an enthusiasm: 'why so violent against *metaphysics* in poetry,' he asked John Thelwall, 'Is not Akenside's a *metaphysical* poem?' (*CL* i. 215).

109 10. 44ᵛ § 1. *CN* i. 681. February–April 1800.
'Clarkson' presumably means the entry was written at Clarkson's house: see 100 n.

110 21. 7ᵛ § 7. *CN* i. 705. March 1800.
Apparently, Spinoza is the source of the remark, but it is not his own opinion (*CN*). This is an early mention in the Notebook of Baruch Spinoza (1632–77), with whose philosophy STC would long wrestle. In his *Ethics* (1777) Spinoza asserts: '*Except God, no substance can be or be conceived*' (I, prop. 14): God, that is, is identical with the totality of the

universe—hence 'pantheism' ('All-God-ism'). STC talked about Spinoza while walking in Germany in 1799 (*IR* 81), in which his 'Spinosism (if Spinosism it be and i'faith 'tis very like it)' (*CL* i. 551) sounds practically Unitarian. He would later dismiss Priestley's claims to philosophical stature (e.g. *BL* i. 136), but his attitude toward Spinoza became almost parodically ambivalent, intensely reverent while repelled by his Pantheism (see *IR* 156). (The best account remains *CPT*, especially 53–106.)

111 21. 8 § 3. *CN* i. 713. *AP* 9. March–August 1800.

112 21. 8 § 4. *CN* i. 714. *AP* 10. March–August 1800.
2. As *CN* remarks, 'from affright' is difficult, crushed into the bottom of the page: *AP* reads 'paleness, wan affright'.

113 10. 37ᵛ § 2. *CN* i. 737. 2 June 1800.
STC and his family spent most of June 1800 returning from a stay with TP, through Bristol and Liverpool, and arriving back at Grasmere on 29 June 1800 (*CN* i. 749). They stayed at Dove Cottage for almost a month.

114 5½. 6ᵛ § 2. *CN* i. 760. 20–3 July 1800.
William Gilpin's *Observations, On Several Parts of England, Particularly the Mountains and Lakes of Cumberland and Westmoreland, Relative Chiefly to Picturesque Beauty* (1786) was an indispensable guide for the picturesque tourist. Cf. 'Of the fashionable travellers, who pass through Grasmere in the summer months, I have observed no small number *asleep*. A much greater number are *reading* descriptions of the place, or lost in admiration of the landscape in aqua-tinta' (*EOT* i. 406).

115 5½. 6ᵛ § 3. *CN* i. 761. 20–3 July 1800.
The incident behind the fourth of WW's 'Poems on the Naming of Places', about 'Point Rash-Judgment' (*WPW* ii. 115–17).

116 5½. 14 § 1. *CN* i. 785. August 1800.
The Coleridges moved into their new house, Greta Hall, Keswick, on 24 July 1800 (*CL* i. 608). The house, about thirteen miles from Dove Cottage, commanded marvellous views, as STC wrote to RS: 'In front we have a giant's camp – an encamped army of tent-like mountains, which by an inverted arch gives a view of another vale. On our right the lovely vale and the wedge-shaped lake of Bassenthwaite; and on our left Derwentwater and Lodore full in view, and the fantastic mountains of Borrodale. Behind us the massy Skiddaw, smooth, green, high, with two chasms and a tent-like ridge in the larger. A fairer scene you have not seen in all your wanderings' (*CL* ii. 717).

117 5½. 14 § 2. *CN* i. 786. August 1800.

118 5½. 41ᵛ § 1. *CN* i. 799. *AP* 10. 1 September 1800.
AP notes that this too made its way into the fourth of WW's 'Poems on the Naming of Places': 'And, in our vacant mood, / Not seldom did we stop to watch some tuft / Of dandelion seed or thistle's beard' (ll. 16–18).

119 5½. 55ᵛ § 1. *CN* i. 806. 14 September 1800.
The child was eventually named Derwent. Bracy is the name of the bard in part II of 'Christabel', written during this year.

120 5½. 56ᵛ § 1. *CN* i. 812. 19–27 September 1800.
The illness of the new baby (see 121) evidently called to mind Berkeley, who had died on 10 February 1799, while STC was in Germany. 'I cannot truly say that I grieve – I am perplexed – I am sad – and a little thing, a very trifle would make me weep; but for the death of the Baby I have *not* wept!' (*CL* i. 479).

121 5½. 56ᵛ § 2. *CN* i. 813. 27 September 1800.

122 5½. 57ᵛ § 1. *CN* i. 817. 29 September 1800.

123 5½. 58ᵛ § 1. *CN* i. 819. 29 September–10 October 1800.
A nice example of STC's natural observation suggesting a simile.

124 5½. 58ᵛ § 2. *CN* i. 820. 29 September–10 October 1800.
Brandelhow is on the west side of Derwentwater: the 'Castle' is Castle Crag, which looms up within the jaws of Borrowdale to the south of the lake.

125 4. 49 § 4. *CN* i. 662. 1800–1803?
Cf. 'A man of maxims like Cyclops with one eye, but that eye placed in the back of his head' (*TT* i. 83), in connection with Polonius from *Hamlet*. Experience without the informing presence of antecedent ideas is elsewhere described as 'a cyclops walking backwards': Pitt is once cited as an instance (*LS* 42–3, 43 n.).

126 4. 35 § 1. *CN* i. 834. 30 October 1800.
As *CN* remarks, a particularly bad time for STC. Is he writing about the doomed attempts to get on with 'Christabel', dropped from the second edition of *Lyrical Ballads* at the beginning of the month (*DWJ* i. 64)?

127 4. 35 § 2. *CN* i. 835. 30 October–18 November 1800.

128 4. 36 § 1. *CN* i. 838. 18 November 1800.
3. [?talk] : talk *CN*. The bottom of the page has faded badly.

129 4. 34 § 2. *CN* i. 848. 28 November 1800.
3. catching hold of : catching holding of *MS*.
5. [my] : my *CN*. [&] : & *CN*. Words now lost.
7. Ebn Ebn : Ebon Ebon *CN*. If there be an 'o' in each of the words, it is swallowed up; but 'Ebn Ebn' is not unlikely. A druggist called 'Ebn Thaher' appears in the translation of the Arabian Nights that STC would have known (as *CN* notes), introduced in Night CLXXXV and featuring in several subsequent stories: *Arabian Nights Entertainments*, from the French of M. Galland (12 vols.; 11th edn.; 1763), v. 69.

130 4. 33ᵛ § 1. *CN* i. 849. 29 November 1800.
3. Was STC thinking of WW's Lakeland scene from *An Evening Walk*—'Bright'ning the cliffs between where sombrous pine | And yew-trees o'er the silver rocks recline' (139–40: *WPW* i. 16)?

131 4. 33ᵛ § 2. *CN* i. 858. November 1800–1801?

132 4. 18ᵛ § 3. *CN* i. 899. 1800? (*CN*).

133 4. 19 § 2. *CN* i. 901. 1800? (*CN*).
1. knew from : knew – from *MS*.
2. burned : burnt *CN*. The word is not neat, but a 't' is not obvious.

134 21. 18 § 1. *CN* i. 864. *AP* 11. November/December 1800.
1. For STC's admiration for Luther, see *F* i. 136–43, where his background is contrasted with that of 'the political and moral philosophy of English Free-thinkers re-modelled by *Parisian Fort Esprits*' (142–3)—presumably Condillac, Holbach, and other representatives of the French Enlightenment.

135 21. 18 § 4. *CN* i. 867. *AP* 11. November/December 1800.
1. For children's disposition to analogy, see 142.

136 21. 18 § 5. *CN* i. 868. *AP* 11. November/December 1800.
2. M. & H.: Probably, as *CN* says, Sir James Mackintosh, 'the great Dung-fly' (*CL* i. 588) (see 104 n.); and Thomas Holcroft (1745–1809), radical, atheist (see *IR* 161–2 for a run-in), playwright, and novelist.
4. *I said* : I *said CN*. (*I said AP*.)

137 21. 20ᵛ § 1. *CN* i. 875. *AP* 12. 19 December 1800.

138 **21. 20ᵛ § 2.** *CN* i. 876. *AP* 12. December 1800/January 1801.
1. seeth : seeeth *MS*. The phrase is from 'Via Pacis: A Short Method of Peace and Holiness', in Jeremy Taylor's *The Golden Grove* (1655). Taylor (1613–67) was one of STC's favourite writers (see *CL* i. 245; *SWF* i. 300). The sentence summarizes one of STC's most abiding intellectual passions: he reuses it prominently in *BL* i. 294.

139 **21. 21ᵛ § 3.** *CN* i. 886. *AP* 12. December 1800/January 1801.
By the end of 1800 STC was thinking of himself as 'a kind of Metaphysician'. He was sick much of the winter, but emerged in early February to announce that he had been '*thinking* vigorously during my Illness' about 'the Relations of Thoughts to Things, in the language of Hume, of Ideas to Impressions'; and, by March, he was telling TP about plans for a great philosophical work (*CL* i. 658; ii. 662; 671–2; 707).

1. 'to walk' is from [']to feel the ground under you['] : 'to walk' is 'from' to feel the ground under you *MS*. The entry seems originally to have stopped with 'under you', before a further thought occurred.

3. *nisus*: i.e. 'Effort, endeavour, impulse' (*OED*). The defining attribute of thinking.

140 **21. 21ᵛ § 4.** *CN* i. 887. *AP* 12. December 1800/January 1801.
Immanuel Kant (1724–1804), whose works, STC would recall, 'took possession of me as with a giant's hand' (*BL* i. 153). Dating his serious reading in Kant is not easy, but it perhaps began in 1801–2 (see *CN* i. 1517 n.). Space, says Kant, 'is not an empirical concept which has been derived from outer experiences' but 'a necessary *a priori* representation, which underlies all outer intuitions': *Critique of Pure Reason*, trans. Norman Kemp Smith (1929; repr. 1990), 68. For Kant's influence on STC, a complex and immense subject, see Basil Willey, *Samuel Taylor Coleridge* (1972), 86–96; D. M. MacKinnon, 'Coleridge and Kant', in John Beer (ed.), *Coleridge's Variety: Bicentenary Studies* (1974), 183–202; and Rosemary Ashton, *The German Idea: Four English Writers and the Reception of German Thought 1800–1860* (Cambridge, 1980), 36–48. For an accessible account of the essential creativity of mind in STC's thought (creative even in ordinary acts of 'passive' perception), see Kathleen M. Wheeler, *The Creative Mind in Coleridge's Poetry* (1981).

141 **21. 22ᵛ § 2.** *CN* i. 904. *AP* 14–15. February 1801.
The ancient Empirics were physicians who based their practice upon experience rather than theory (*OED*). STC is presumably linking them with the proponents of modern empiricism, pre-eminently John Locke

(1632–1704), whose *Essay on Human Understanding* (1690), the central text of British empiricism, sets out from the presumption that the answer to the question 'Whence has [the mind] all the materials of Reason and Knowledge?' is, 'in one word, From *Experience*' (II. i, § 1)—and not, that is to say, from any innate, pre-experiential ideas or principles. Locke would become, along with Hobbes and Hume, symbolical of the philosophical opposition STC faced: 'The pith of my system is to make the Senses out of the Mind – not the Mind from the Senses, as Locke etc.' (*TT* i. 312).

4. Paracelsus (1493–1541), alchemist and celebrated physician.

5. *The Watchman* had noted how the private intrigues of the revolutionary Jacobins gave rise to harsh laws (*W* 288). STC was currently reading Christian von Wolff (1679–1754), philosopher and scientist, and advocate of the counter-Lockean philosophy of Leibniz (see 407 n.). (See *CN* 902 n., 905 n.)

6. John Brown (1735–88), deviser of the Brunonian system, which held life to be dependent upon 'excitability', an excess or deficiency of which would equally induce disease. (For a vivid account of STC's interest in the subject, see Neil Vickers, 'Coleridge, Thomas Beddoes, and Brunonian Medicine', *European Romantic Review*, 8 (1997), 47–94.) Milton's 'intense egotism' would later become refigured as evidence of his especial genius (*TT* i. 420).

10–11. A defence of egotism with personal reference? (See 294.)

17. Lætitia mixta cum odio: i.e. 'pleasure mixed with ill-will'.

19. 'tho not formidable' is an afterthought. There is a final phrase to the entry, omitted by *AP*: ' – *Die Bette Thut*'. *CN* finds it 'meaningless'; and I certainly do not know what to make of it.

142 **21. 24[v] § 1.** *CN* i. 918. *AP* 13. February/March 1801.

4–5. An added thought.

143 **21. 24[v] § 2.** *CN* i. 919. *AP* 13. February/March 1801.

144 **21. 24[v] § 3.** *CN* i. 920. *AP* 14. February/March 1801.

145 **21. 24[v] § 4.** *CN* i. 921. *AP* 15. February/March 1801.

1–2. WW, 'Lines Composed a Few Miles above Tintern Abbey', ll. 48–9 (*WPW* ii. 260). In WW's poem, the '*Life* of Things' seems to be a near-relation of the 'one Life' of STC's Unitarianism: an in-dwelling force or energy interfused throughout natural Creation. The Notebook's revisionary reading appears to place the '*Life* of Things' instead within the self (the 'I'), a relocation of vitality which is also recorded in 'Dejection:

An Ode' (1802): 'in our life alone does Nature live' (l. 48: *CPW* i. 365). A wall perceived is uncomplicatedly an object set before a perceiving subject. In an act of introspective self-reflection, the *self* becomes the object of perception (in something like the way the wall was) *as well* as being the contemplating subject, thus 'identifying the Percipient & the Perceived'—in the later words of *BL*, 'object and subject, being and knowing, are identical, each involving and supposing the other' (i. 273). See Stephen Bygrave, *Coleridge and the Self: Romantic Egotism* (Basingstoke, 1986), 78–9.

5. here I necessarily : here. I necessarily *CN*. I can make out no period; which is not conclusive, but the sense without seems good: an argumentative 'here' (meaning 'in this case') set against 'Now' in line 5.

146 **21. 24ᵛ § 5.** *CN* i. 922. *AP* 14. February/March 1801.
1. Pantheism : ~~a~~ Pantheism *CN*. STC seems first to have written 'Atheism' and then crossed out the 'A', writing in above it 'Pan'. (The *CN* note makes this clearer.) An Anthropomorphite is one who ascribes a human form to God: STC's Unitarianism disapproved of such habits. Cf. a letter of 1802: 'Even the worship of one God becomes Idolatry, in my convictions, when instead of the Eternal & Omnipresent, in whom we live, & move, & *have* our being, we set up a distinct Jehovah tricked out in the *anthropomorphic* Attributes of Time & *Successive* Thoughts – & think of him, as a PERSON, *from* whom we *had* our Being' (*CL* ii. 893). The alternative positions given in this entry pointedly exclude Unitarianism; embracing Trinitarianism would prove a long struggle, its trials often recorded in the privacy of the Notebook.

147 **21. 25 § 1.** *CN* i. 923. *AP* 15–16. 17 March 1801.
Mirrors were much on HC's mind that winter: on 9 February, STC had written to DW, 'I had a very long conversation with Hartley about Life, Reality, Pictures, & Thinking, this evening . . . he pointed out without difficulty that there might be five Hartleys, Real Hartley, Shadow Hartley, Picture Hartley, Looking Glass Hartley, and Echo Hartley / and as to the difference between his Shadow & the Reflection in the Looking Glass, he said, the Shadow was black, and he could not see his *eyes* in it' (*CL* ii. 673).

7. Abstract: i.e. 'epitome'.

148 **4. 24 § 1.** *CN* i. 957. June 1801–June 1803.
An essential element, but one held in balance with others, according to *BL*, where the Imagination, 'while it blends and harmonizes the natural

and the artificial, still subordinates art to nature; the manner to the matter; and our admiration of the poet to our sympathy with the poetry' (ii. 17).

149 4. 30ᵛ § 4. *CN* i. 968. June 1801–June 1803.
Cf. STC's parenthetical remark, 'it is with similies, as it is with jests at a wine table, one is sure to suggest another' (*BL* i. 39).
1. [As] : The *MS.* '& easily opened' is an addition. STC evidently forgot his original grammar.

150 6. 12ᵛ § 2. *CN* i. 932. 1801?
Habitual imagery: cf. 'alas! you will find me the wretched wreck of what you knew me, rolling, rudderless' (*CL* iii. 22).

151 6. 13 § 1. *CN* i. 935. 1801–2.

152 6. 14 § 2. *CN* i. 944. 1801–2.

153 6. 4ᵛ § 2. *CN* i. 978. August 1801?

154 21. 32 § 3. *CN* i. 982. *AP* 18. 14 September 1801.

155 21. 32ᵛ § 2. *CN* i. 984. September 1801.
1. 'infinitely beloved Darling' has been erased, though it is still discernible, especially in *J*.

156 21. 34 § 1. *CN* i. 989. *AP* 18. September 1801.
Cf. 'It is not enough, that we have once swallowed it – The *Heart* should have *fed* upon the *truth*, as Insects on a Leaf – till it be tinged with the colour, and shew it's food in every the minutest fibre' (*CL* i. 115; and cf. *LPR* 49; 297). In *BL*, Shakespeare is said similarly to have combined 'knowledge become habitual and intuitive' with 'his habitual feelings' (ii. 27).

157 21. 34ᵛ § 1. *CN* i. 996. *AP* 19. 19 October 1801.
The river Greta runs behind Keswick, bending sharply below Greta Hall (where is is bridged), and joining the Derwent just north of Derwentwater.

158 21. 34ᵛ § 2. *CN* i. 997. *AP* 19. 20 October 1801.
'A life-long mistake. He was born October 21, 1772' (*AP*).

159 21. 34 § 4. *CN* i. 999. *AP* 19–20. 22 October 1801.
4, 5. Some letters are now lost thanks to damage to the page, but they are clearly recorded in *J*. Mary was SH's sister (see 203 n.).

160 **21. 34^{v} § 6.** *CN* 1001. *CHH* 138. 1 November 1801.
'Hartley was breeched last Sunday – & looks far better than in his petticoats. He ran to & fro in a sort of dance to the Jingle of the Load of Money, that had been put in his breeches pockets; but he did [not] roll & tumble over and over in his old joyous way – No! it was an *eager* & solemn gladness, as if he felt it to be an awful aera in his Life. – O bless him! bless him! bless him! If my wife loved me, and I my wife, half as well as we both love our children, I should be the happiest man alive – but this is not – will not be!' (*CL* ii. 774–5).

161 **21. 35^{v} § 5.** *CN* i. 1013. *AP* 18. November 1801.
1. Religions : religion *CN*. (religions *AP*.) There is a firm downstroke of some kind after the 'n' of 'religion' which is interpretable as an 's'—a multiplicity which 'all' might confirm. The analogy appears in *Omniana* (*SWF* i. 304) as one for 'The state, with respect to the different sects of Religion under its protection', which also suggests that the plurality of religious positions is the point at stake.

162 **21. 35^{v} § 6.** *CN* i. 1014. November 1801.

163 **6. 16^{v} § 2.** *CN* i. 1032. 25 November 1801–25 January 1802.

164 **21. 37 § 2.** *CN* i. 1056. *AP* 20. December 1801/early 1802.
For Taylor, see 138 n.; and for STC's admiration for his prose (and that of some of his contemporaries) see *LL* ii. 233–4.
3. junctions &c : junction &c *CN*. Scribbly.

165 **21. 39 § 2.** *CN* i. 1072. *AP* 27. December 1801/early 1802.

166 **21. 39 § 3.** *CN* i. 1073. *AP* 27. December 1801/early 1802.
That the universe at large should exemplify the republican virtues of equality and fraternity was an axiom of STC's early Unitarianism: ''Tis the sublime of man, | Our noontide majesty, to know ourselves | Parts and proportions of one wondrous whole! | This fraternises man, this constitutes | Our charities and bearings' ('Religious Musings', ll. 126–30: *CPW* i. 113–14)—a fraternity that extended, in the exuberance of principle, to asses ('I hail thee *Brother*': 'To a Young Ass', l. 26: *CPW* i. 75) and cats (*CL* i. 121).
1. [the] : the *CN*.

167 **21. 40^{v} § 1.** *CN* i. 1081. *AP* 28. December 1801/Spring 1802.
STC was in London in December 1801, writing for the *Morning Post*; he was back in Nether Stowey on Boxing Day, and returned to the capital on

21 January (*CL* ii. 776; 778; 779). By late February, he was homesick, and, hearing SH was ill, headed north at once for Gallow Hill, the Hutchinsons' farm; he arrived back at Greta Hall on 15 March.

3. plictri-plactri: as *CN* says, possibly imitating the noise of a plucked instrument.

168 **21.** 40^{v} § 2. *CN* i. 1082. *AP* 24; *CHH* 42 (both in part). December 1801/Spring 1802.

A list of reasons to believe in God's active presence in the universe.

1–3. The German might be translated: 'If there is a God, then there is a purpose—and our ends are subordinate to his—and so there is a connectedness [*ein Zusammenhang*], a totality [*ein Ganzes*], within which we act; we effect something which is not lost with our death.' The position has an obvious kinship with STC's own early belief in God's 'one all-conscious Spirit, which informs | With absolute ubiquity of thought | (His one eternal self-affirming act!) | All his involvéd Monads' ('The Destiny of Nations', ll. 44–7: *CPW* i. 133).

5. I follow *CN* reading 'thereby', but it is not well formed: indeed the whole entry is quite difficult. The Marquis de Condorcet (1743–94), philosopher and mathematician, as well as Girondist President of the Legislative Assembly after the Revolution in France, until deposed by the Jacobins. *CN* suggests STC has in mind his *Esquisse d'un tableau historique des progrès de l'esprit humain* (1795), which argued (like Godwin) for the 'perfectibility' of man. (STC quoted from it, *W* 272.)

7. Creation. [A]m I : Creation. am I *MS*.

7–9. Cf. the account in 'Religious Musings' of a world with no sense of God: 'whose presence lost, | The moral world's cohesion, | We become an Anarchy of Spirits!' (ll. 144–6: *CPW* i. 114). For the idiocy of a Godless nature, see 45.

10. STC misnumbers his list.

11. The comfort (allegedly) to be had from a knowledge of God's purpose, 'the Divine Providence that regulates into one vast harmony all the events of time, however calamitous some of them may appear to mortals' ('Argument' to 'Ode to the Departing Year': *CPW* i. 160). For problems of determinism, see 38 n.

12–13. Sold[iers] derive from : Sold[ier] derives from *CN*. B from God : B being God *CN*. B is Bonaparte (as *CN* suggests). I suppose the sense is: 'the soldiers gain courage from Napoleon, their general, and Napoleon from God, [whom he takes to be] *his* general.'

14. content[ion] : content. *CN*. The word is hastily finished off, perhaps abbreviated: 'contention' ('strife' or 'dispute') makes sense and ties in with other anxieties about the problem of evil: see 262.

16. An analogy : 'evils in the universe are like spots in the light of the sun'. William Herschel (1738–1822) had recently speculated a connection between sun-spots and climate fluctuation. Cf. 'Spots in the Sun' (*CPW* ii. 969), a scurrilous little poem about 'My father confessor' and Annette the 'lovely courtesan' (published in the *Morning Post* on 11 October 1802, a week after 'Dejection: An Ode' had appeared on WW's wedding day): it must allude to WW's affair with Annette Vallon, a rare lapse (STC may have puckishly thought) in a life of spotless virtue, and certainly a secret well kept within the WW circle.

18. A further point connected (by the symbol) to item 5.

169 8. 31ᵛ § 2. *CN* i. 1134. *AP* 22. Early 1802?

170 6. 43 § 2. *CN* i. 1087. January 1802?
2. *nothings* : nothings *CN*.

171 6. 19 § 2. *CN* i. 1101. 28 January–14 February 1802.

172 6. 20ᵛ § 1. *CN* i. 1108. 14 Febuary 1802.
STC recalled the incident in 1817. Mr 'Bellews', an Irish barrister, had thrown a jovial party, and STC had drunk 'two large Tumblers of very strong punch': from the hallucination he deduced 'an imitative sympathy in the nerves' (*CL* iv. 731).

173 6. 23 § 2. *CN* i. 1122. February–March 1802.
Worrying over the central point of Christian doctrine, the difficulty of which had been one of the spurs to his Unitarianism. The orthodox doctrine of Redemption (in which the Crucifixion serves as a sacrifice on behalf of man, somehow to God's satisfaction) was deplored in the 1795 lectures as 'the most irrational and gloomy Superstition that ever degraded the human mind' (*LPR* 204). Priestley's alternative was to offer Christ's voluntary death as an exemplary model of perfect sincerity, intended to arouse human emulation (not divine approval). At the end of his life, STC recalled of his youth: 'I had a strong sense of the repugnancy of the doctrine of vicarious atonement to the moral being, and I thought nothing could counterbalance that' (*TT* i. 489): one thing that works to 'counterbalance' it, of course, is the doctrine of the Trinity, which allows God to sacrifice his Son, yet mysteriously at the price of sacrificing himself. For a brilliantly tendentious account of such matters, see William

Empson, S. T. Coleridge, *Selected Poems*, ed. William Empson and David Pirie (1972; Manchester, 1989), 97–100.

2. Cross – i.e. : Cross or i.e. *CN*. A squiggle of a dash?

174 **6. 23 § 3.** *CN* i. 1123. February–March 1802.
A growing conviction: 'Believe me, Southey! a metaphysical Solution, that does not instantly *tell* for something in the Heart, is grievously to be suspected as apocry[p]hal' (*CL* ii. 961)—a position which anticipates the advice given years later in *Aids to Reflection*: 'Christianity is not a Theory, or a Speculation; but a *Life*. Not a *Philosophy* of Life, but a Life and a living Process . . . Try it' (*A* 202).

1. [Chri]stianity : Xstianity *MS*.

175 **6. 41ᵛ § 3.** *CN* i. 1124. February–March 1802.
CN compares 'The Picture, or The Lover's Resolution', ll. 51–4: 'here will I couch my limbs, | Close by this river, in this silent shade, | As safe and sacred from the step of man | As an invisible world – unheard, unseen' (*CPW* i. 370).

176 **6. 23ᵛ § 2.** *CN* i. 1142. 8–12 March 1802.
Cf. STC's 'Letter' to SH, written (according to its subtitle) 4 April 1802: '(The Larch, which pushes out in tassels green | It's bundled Leafits)' (*CL* ii. 790).

177 **6. 23ᵛ § 3.** *CN* i. 1143. 8–12 March 1802.

178 **6. 37ᵛ § 1.** *CN* i. 1152. March–April 1802.
A poem about SH, presumably. The 'Letter' to Sara Hutchinson (*CL* ii. 790–8) was supposedly written on 4 April.

179 **6. 37ᵛ § 2.** *CN* i. 1153. March–April 1802.
Daydreams prompted several poems during this period: 'Save when shy king-fishers build their nest | On thy steep banks, no loves hast thou, wild stream! || This be my chosen haunt – emancipate | From Passion's dreams, a freeman, and alone, | I rise and trace its devious course' ('The Picture', ll. 117–20: *CPW* i. 372). 'A Day-Dream' recounts a moment of intimacy with 'Asra' and Mary Hutchinson, also recollected in the 'Letter' (*CL* ii. 792–3); 'The Day-Dream' (published in the *Morning Post*, 19 October 1802), addressed to 'Sara', purports to be a verse letter from an emigrant to his wife (*CPW* i. 385–6; 386–7). The attempt to tame his day-dreams (often, one suspects, daydreams about SH) recurs: see 403.

1. day-dreams—note : day-dreams & note *CN*.

180 **6. 37 § 1.** *CN* i. 1154. March–April 1802.
A piece of fantastic Platonism: see 501 for the Demiurge myth.

181 **6. 37 § 2.** *CN* i. 1155. March–April 1802.
STC remained drawn by the metrical life of the choruses from Milton's *Samson Agonistes* (*CN* ii. 3180). The appearance of Samuel Johnson (1709–84)—poet, critic, lexicographer, and the greatest man of letters in late eighteenth-century England—usually occasions STC's displeasure or ridicule, a hostility which was quietly audacious: a display of characteristic irreverence earned him hisses during a lecture in 1812 (*LL* i. 411). (For a good account, see James Engell, 'Coleridge, Johnson, and Shakespeare: A Critical Drama in Five Acts', *Romanticism*, 4 (1998), 22–39.) STC thought Johnson's treatment of Milton in his *Lives of the English Poets* wholly inadequate (see 333), which is presumably the point at issue here.

182 **6. 37 § 3.** *CN* i. 1156. March–April 1802.
Whether a real excursion or an imaginary is not clear.
1. this night : 'this' is badly formed, and might almost as well be 'the'.

183 **6. 26 § 1.** *CN* i. 1163. 20 April 1802.
The Rock of Names was on the east side of Thirlmere midway between Grasmere and Keswick. The Wordsworth circle carved their initials on it. Its fragments led a difficult and peripatetic life after Thirlmere was turned into a reservoir for Manchester and engineers blew it to pieces. A photograph is reproduced (plate 6) in Stephen Gill, *William Wordsworth: A Life* (Oxford, 1989): you can see 'DW' some way above 'SH' (for Sara Hutchinson), with 'STC' and 'JW' (for John Wordsworth, the brother of DW and WW) in between. See John Worthen, *The Gang: Coleridge, the Hutchinsons, and the Wordsworths in 1802* (New Haven, 2001), 181–3.

184 **6. 27 § 1.** *CN* i. 1168. April–May 1802.
Versified into a poetic fragment: *CPW* ii. 1002.
1. [on] : on *CN*. [a] : a *CN*. The words have been lost through wear.

185 **6. 35 § 2.** *CN* i. 1176. April-May 1802.
His nightmares often returned to school-days at Christ's Hospital. CL recalled him as a garrulous prodigy (*IR* 2–3); but his own memories were of a time when he, 'pent 'mid cloisters dim | . . . saw nought lovely but the sky and stars' ('Frost at Midnight', ll. 52–3: *CPW* i. 242).

186 **6. 34[v] § 2.** *CN* i. 1178. April–May 1802.
3. as if : as of *CN*.

187 6. 31[v] § 2. *CN* i. 1186. April–May 1802.
In legend, the sacred geese gave the alarm when Rome was infiltrated by the Gauls.

188 6. 31[v] § 4. *CN* i. 1192. April–May 1802.
1. [calls] : calls *CN*. STC omits the word.

189 21. 40 § 3. *CN* i. 1189. *AP* 28. May 1802?
Rocks and stones are invested with life in WW's poetry: there is a sea-beast-like stone in 'Resolution and Independence' (as *CN* points out), written May–July 1802 (*WPW* ii. 235–40); and the Pedlar, an idealized self-portrait WW had described in blank verse written in the Coleridgean spring of 1798, enjoys the same sort of enlivening vision: 'To every natural form, rock, fruit, and flower, | Even the loose stones that cover the highway, | He gave a moral life' ('The Pedlar', ll. 332–4: Jonathan Wordsworth, *The Music of Humanity* (1969), 182).

4. The route from Ambleside to Patterdale passes over the Kirkstone Pass, a route to Ullswater, locally known as 'The Struggle'. (See David McCracken, *Wordsworth and the Lake District: A Guide to the Poems and their Places* (Oxford, 1984), 127–8.) STC describes rapt experiences ('God is every where') journeying over a stormy Kirkstone in two letters of January 1803 (*CL* ii. 914; 915–16).

190 6. 30 § 2. *CN* i. 1200. 8 June 1802.

191 6. 29[v] § 3. *CN* i. 1203. 8 June 1802.
The compelling question of sameness and difference, but now meditated under the influence: the word 'interfused'—from 'Religious Musings' (l. 405: *CPW* i. 124), where it describes the inhabiting presence of divine energies within the world—links the entry to more obviously profound concerns.

1. inter[?fused] : interfused *CN*. The second half of the word appears to contain a long 's' as part of a double 's'; but the hand seems more than half-tipsy.

2. destr[?oyed] : [?destroyed] *CN*.

192 2. 15[v] § 2. *CN* i. 1218. 5 August 1802.
This is one of several entries describing STC's great solitary tour of the Lakes in the summer of 1802. There is a vivid account in Molly Lefebure, *Cumberland Heritage* (1970), 140–7; and see too Alan Hankinson, *Coleridge Walks the Fells: A Lakeland Journey Retraced* (Maryport, 1991). The descent he describes here follows what Lefebure calls 'the first

known ascent of Scafell by one other than a local dalesman' (142). Having decided to go on to climb what he calls Bowfell (but what is really Scafell Pike), STC attempted to scramble down to the 'low Ridge' which joins Scafell and Scafell Pike: it is called Broad Stand. The descent requires some pluck ('dropping from Precipices'): walkers are warned off it now. Having made it, and abandoning thoughts of climbing 'Bowfell', he came down into Upper Eskdale by Cam Spout (the waterfall of line 21). The entry should be compared with his description of it to SH: *CL* ii. 841–4. (The entry continues on 17 as STC turns over two pages by mistake.)

3. lownded: a local word, as in 'I was sheltered (in the phrase of this country, *lownded*)' (*CL* ii. 858).

7. hazy : *hazy CN*.

13. STC more colourfully describes the several drops the descent required in his letter to SH: 'My Limbs were all in a tremble . . . O God, I exclaimed aloud – how calm, how blessed am I now / I know not how to proceed, how to return / but I am calm & fearless & confident' (*CL* ii. 842).

31. STC draws a triangle in the space after 'with': the mountain looking down over the scene. The Bowder Stone is a celebrated petrific feature of Borrowdale: see 260 n.

31. weeds : weed *CN*.

193 21. 48 § 2. *CN* i. 1231. September 1802.

The page 21. 48 is headed 'Transcripts from my Velvet-writing-paper Pocket Books'. STC is transcribing entries from Notebook 5, one of the smaller notebooks he took with him on various expeditions (see *CN* i (n.), pp. xxix–xxx): these notes originally date from autumn 1799, when STC was in the Lakes for the first time, and their transcription (*CN* proposes) from the same time as the retrospective additions made to the note on infants (78). The first *aperçu*, about parodies (from *CN* i. 463), reappears in *Omniana* (*SWF* i. 304).

194 21. 48 § 4. *CN* i. 1233. *AP* 26. September 1802.

Adapted from *CN* i. 467. Socinianism, named after the Italian theologians Laelius Socinus and his nephew Faustus (1525–62, 1539–1604), is the doctrine that denies the divinity of Jesus: it becomes the pejorative term which STC uses for the Unitarianism he is seeking to refute. If Unitarianism was (as STC thought) too rationalist to excite the heart, then Methodism aroused his wariness about 'enthusiasm' (see 52): see Basil Willey, *Samuel Taylor Coleridge* (1972), 86–7.

195 **21.48 § 6.** *CN* i. 1235. September 1802.
Adapted from *CN* i. 469. In the rhyme (*The Oxford Nursery Rhyme Book*, ed. Iona and Peter Opie (Oxford, 1955, corr. repr., 1957), 169), the dog barks and the disorientated woman worries she is not herself after all. The rhyme appears again in *Omniana* (*SWF* i. 322). The question of personal identity proved a difficult problem for the empiricist tradition: for Hume, 'there was no question in philosophy more abstruse', for the mind seemed 'nothing but a heap or collection of different perceptions . . . suppos'd, tho' falsely, to be endow'd with a perfect simplicity and identity' (*Treatise of Human Nature* I. iv, § ii). The point at issue in STC's adducing of the rhyme, I take it, is his belief that metaphysics should *begin* from the fact of a unitary consciousness, a self: that it thereby obey the ancient advice, 'Know Thyself' (*BL* ii. 240 n.; and many other places), and take as its starting point the internal reality of 'I am', rather than the external reality of 'It is' (see *HCR* i. 112). Kant (by contrast with the empiricists) begins by seeking to describe how the mind must be for experience to be possible in the first place.

1. ab extra : *ab extra CN*. 'From the outside'.

196 **21.48 § 7.** *CN* i. 1236. *AP* 59. September 1802.
Adapted from *CN* i. 470. Cf. 275.

197 **21.48v § 1.** *CN* i. 1241. *AP* 60. September 1802.
Adapted from *CN* i. 523.

198 **21.48v § 4.** *CN* i. 332. *AP* 59. 1802?
To judge by its appearance, this entry was not made at the same time as those preceding: *CN* places it much earlier in the sequence, but gives the date only as '1797–1802' (that is, from the beginning of the use of the Notebook to the date of the other entries on the page). If this entry (and the three neighbouring entries that *CN* groups with it, including the next here) are additions to a list of ideas for 'Poems' (197), then a date circa that of the upper part of the page does not seem unreasonable.

199 **21.48v § 6.** *CN* i. 334. *AP* 59. 1802?
Cf. his letter to TP, *c.*16 March 1801, which begins: 'The interval since my last Letter has been filled up by me in the most intense Study. If I do not greatly delude myself, I have not only completely extricated the notions of Time, and Space; but have overthrown the doctrine of Association, as taught by Hartley' (*CL* ii. 706). It sounds as though Hartley was being pushed aside by a new enthusiasm for Kantian idealism.

200 **21. 49 § 1.** *CN* i. 1244. September/early October 1802.
The Arab was a Coleridgean touchstone for a super-alertness of sense. Cf. STC to the poet and translator William Sotheby (1757–1833): 'a great Poet must be, implicitè if not explicitè, a profound Metaphysician. He may not have it in logical coherence, in his Brain & Tongue; but he must have it by *Tact* / for all sounds, & forms of human nature he must have the *ear* of a wild Arab listening in the silent Desart', etc. (*CL* ii. 810).

201 **21. 49ᵛ § 1.** *CN* i. 1246. *AP* 61. September/early October 1802.
Extremes meet: see 67 n.

202 **21. 50 § 1.** *CN* i. 1248. September/early October 1802.
A analogy he repeats (almost verbatim) in a letter to TP of October 1803, where his sensitivity to passing thoughts being used against him is clear: he asks TP to destroy a letter attacking Newton (*CL* ii. 708–10) lest 'it should ever see the *Light*' (*CL* ii. 1011; 1014). The careless ostrich crops up again: e.g. *BL* i. 45–6.

203 **21. 41ᵛ § 2.** *CN* i. 1250. *CHH* 152. 3 October 1802.
2. Cloysters : Cloyster *CN*.
8. 'Mary' is Mary Hutchinson (1770–1859), who was to marry WW on 4 October (STC's wedding anniversary).
9. STC has lost track of his sentence and does not include a noun (presumably, 'person' or 'woman').
17. [?smokelike] : smokelike *CHH*, *CN*. The word is not obvious; it is doubtfully complete, as STC writes into the Notebook's bound margin. *CN* also suggests 'snakelike', which would have a resonance with the 'shrunken serpent eyes' of Geraldine in part II of 'Christabel' (l. 602: *CPW* i. 233).

204 **21. 42ᵛ § 1.** *CN* i. 1253. *AP* 24. October 1802.

205 **21. 42ᵛ § 3.** *CN* i. 1255. *AP* 24. October 1802.
That the diverse 'talents', far from proving incompatible, actually work in concert together (in great literary works) becomes a central point: 'The poet, described in *ideal* perfection, brings the whole soul of man into activity, with the subordination of its faculties to each other, according to their relative worth and dignity' (*BL* ii. 15–16); and see 497. Locke and Hume appear as prominent representatives of the native empiricist school of thought towards which STC was increasingly hostile.
4. Locke thought highly of Sir Richard Blackmore's *King Arthur*: see Samuel Johnson, *Lives of the English Poets*, ed. George Birkbeck Hill

(3 vols.; Oxford, 1905), ii. 238. For STC's surprisingly indulgent view of Blackmore (whose verses were 'in general . . . quite bad enough for a physician') see *TT* ii. 452.

5. Hume had described Shakespeare as a prodigy born in a 'rude age', whose works are irregular and absurd, in his *History of England* (1754–62; 6 vols.; Indianapolis, 1983), v. 151—a view STC resisted vehemently (e.g. *LL* i. 79). Hume criticizes Milton's 'stiff and pedantic' prose in 'On Civil Liberty': *Essays Moral, Political, and Literary*, ed. Eugene F. Miller (Indianapolis, 1987), 92.

206 **21. 42ᵛ § 4.** *CN* i. 1256. *AP* 25. October 1802.
Recalling his return from London earlier that year? Cf. *Prel.: 1805*, I, ll. 1–54.

2. Alders : alder *CN.* (alders *AP.*)

207 **8. 44 § 2.** *CN* i. 1295. 6–19 December 1802.
Not just mothers: the 'Conclusion to Part II' of 'Christabel' (*CPW* i. 235–6) was (said STC) a 'very metaphysical account of Fathers calling their children rogues, rascals, & little varlets – &c – ' (*CL* ii. 728–9).

208 **8. 44 § 3.** *CN* i. 1296. 6–19 December 1802.
A cosmic harmony so inclusive that even 'discordant' noises blended into it tunefully was a favourite metaphor for the diverse life of nature in a God-filled universe, as in 'To a Young Ass' (ll. 34–5) and, more impressively, 'This Lime-Tree Bower my Prison', which imparts the wisdom that 'No sound is dissonant which tells of Life' (l. 76) (*CPW* i. 76; 181). STC came greatly to admire the Pythagorean system, which adopted harmony as its central symbol (*PL* i. 117).

209 **8. 45ᵛ § 2.** *CN* i. 1302. *AP* 26. 19 December 1802.
STC would have walked by the Teme as he journeyed north with his patron and friend Tom Wedgwood (1771–1805): they left Crescelly on 16 December, and arrived in Keswick on Christmas Eve (*CL* ii. 898; 902). The point, I suppose, is the Protestant association of Catholicism with misplaced sensuousness. STC's religious life-history largely comprises a determined struggle to overcome the rapt wonder with which he responded to the experience of diverse natural beauty, and to relocate religious feeling squarely in the less worldly regions of spirit or mind—until old STC could confidently table-talk, 'The result of my system will be, to show, that, so far from the world being a goddess in petticoats, it is rather the Devil in a strait waistcoat' (*TT* ii. 76). See Norman Fruman, 'Coleridge's Rejection of Nature and the Natural Man', in Richard

Gravil, Lucy Newlyn and Nicholas Roe (eds.), *Coleridge's Imagination* (Cambridge, 1985), 69–78.

210 8. 46 § 1. *CN* i. 1304. 19–20 December 1802.
The meaning of 'mawwollop' is elusive: *CN* suggests 'inexplicable interpenetration'.

211 8. 46 § 3. *CN* i. 1306. 20–3 December 1802.

212 8. 46 § 4. *CN* i. 1307. *AP* 23. 20–3 December 1802.
'Outness' is a preferred term for externality that STC takes over from Berkeley: see 45 n. Cf. his account of near-disaster while descending Scafell (192): 'if this Reality were a Dream, if I were asleep, what agonies had I suffered! what screams!' (*CL* ii. 842); and for his needy reliance upon a world without the self, see 359, 476. For driving over a pavement, see 342.

213 8. 46[v] § 3. *CN* i. 1310. 24 December 1802.
STC wrote bravely to RS on Christmas Day: 'Sara was safely brought to bed the morning before – i.e. Thursday ½ past six, of a healthy – GIRL! I had never thought of a Girl as a possible event – the word[s] child & man child were perfect Synonimes in my feelings – however I bore the sex with great Fortitude – & she shall be called Sar*a*. Both Mrs Coleridge & the Coleridgiella are as well as can be – ' (*CL* ii. 902).

214 21. 45 § 5. *CN* i. 1374. *AP* 25. 1802/1803.
CN persuasively deduces the date from a reference on 44[v]; but the next *certain* date we have (31 March 1803) is appended to CL's transcription of Cowper's 'On the Loss of the Royal George' (*CN* i. 1381), a couple of pages later: so this and the following entry might conceivably be the work of 1802.

215 21. 45 § 7. *CN* i. 1376. *AP* 25. 1802/1803.

216 8. 54 § 3. *CN* i. 1387. April–June 1803.
For 'outness' see 212. Symbols become increasingly important in his thinking: see 357, 532.

217 8. 54 § 4. *CN* i. 1388. April–June 1803.

218 8. 55 § 1. *CN* i. 1392. *AP* 23. April–June 1803.
The entanglement of kindly and unkindly emotions is the subject of the 'Conclusion to Part II' of 'Christabel' (*CPW* i. 235–6), first sighted in a letter to RS of 1801 (*CL* ii. 728–9).

219 4. 30 § 3. *CN* i. 1400. 6 July 1803.

220 4. 29v § 1. *CN* i. 1401. 10 July 1803.
The story is retold in a letter to SH (*CL* ii. 1024).

221 4.27v § 1. *CN* i. 1416. *AP* 29. 19 July 1803.
After a confrontation with his brother Frank, STC (aged 7) fled into the countryside outside Ottery St Mary. He told TP about it in one of his 1797 autobiographical letters: 'I distinctly remember my feelings when I saw a Mr Vaughan pass over the Bridge, at about a furlong's distance – and how I watched the Calves in the field beyond the river' (*CL* i. 353). He was finally rescued from freezing the next morning by the local squire. '1803' has been written in the entry at a later date, and, *CN* suggests, by another hand.

4. [?that] : that *AP*, *CN*. The entry is in a small faded hand.

5. [?lowing] : lowing *AP*, *CN*. Neither for this word, nor for 'that' above, is *J* much help. The names of the rivers are also dim.

222 16. 2 § 1. *CN* i. 1426. 15 August 1803.
The pencil throughout Notebook 16 has faded, especially badly at the finger-tipped edges. In general, *J* is much easier to make out. This opening page is practically invisible (though *CN* made out more than I am able to), but these first lines have been inked in. For STC's itinerary during the Scottish tour, see Carol Kyros Walker, 'Breaking Away: Coleridge in Scotland', *Wordsworth Circle*, 31 (2000), 102–8; and my 'Coleridge's Scotland', *Coleridge Bulletin*, NS 17 (2001), 58–75.

2. 'We have bought a stout Horse – aged but stout & spirited – & an open vehicle called a Jaunting Car – there is room in it for 3 on each side, on hanging seats – a Dicky Box for the Driver / & a space or hollow in the middle, for luggage – or two or three Bairns' (*CL* ii. 975).

4. The description becomes legible again as STC turns the page (onto 2v): he is midway though the description of the waterfalls at Caldbeck (which he had seen while exploring the Lakes in the autumn of 1800: *CN* i. 828)—'a delicious spot in which to breathe out a summer's day', thought DW (*DWJ* i. 195).

7. [?whirl] : whirl *CN*. The word is unclear.

14. [?] : right *CN*. The missing word falls off the page's edge.

20. *CN* suggests for the indecipherable word 'flashing' or 'glinting'.

21–2. 'Slept at Mr Younghusband's publick-house, Hesket Newmarket' (*DWJ* i. 195). Did STC stay here in 1800?

25–9. Cf. the illusion of the two kites a few months later (below, 271).

30. Saw Dust : Sand Dust *CN*. The 'w' is ebullient, but I see no reason to suspect the obvious reading.

223 16.5 § 1. *CN* i. 1428. 16 August 1803.
3–4. i.e. 'as the Goose is to the Swan, so Wyndham is to Burke'. William Windham [*sic*] (1750–1810) was a follower of Burke, and Secretary of War under Pitt. 'This Wyndham is a professed imitator of Mr Burke, whom he resembles as nearly as a stream of melted lead resembles the lava from Mount Vesuvius' (*W* 122). For STC's ambivalent attitude toward Burke, see 5 n.

224 16.5ᵛ § 1. *CN* i. 1432. 17 August 1803.
At Carlisle, WW and STC saw John Hatfield (c.1758–1803) who, posing as an MP, had misled Mary Robinson, a serving girl, 'The Beauty of Buttermere', a sensation of the time: STC later told the story with much relish in the *Morning Post* (*EOT* i. 403–15). Hatfield was tried for forging franks, a capital offence: he was sentenced to death the day after STC interviewed him.

10. Cf. 'to *think* ourselves in to the Thoughts and Feelings of Beings in circumstances wholly & strangely different from our own / hoc labor, hoc opus / and who has atchieved [*sic*] it? Perhaps only Shakespere' (*CL* ii. 810).

225 7.10ᵛ § 1. *CN* i. 1454. 22 August 1803.
From Hamilton to Glasgow.

2. DW describes 'Bothwell Castle, which is in Lord Douglas's grounds' and its well-planted grounds (*DWJ* i. 232–3). (Freestone is a kind of limestone or sandstone.)

5. 'Ballantyre' is Blantyre.

6–7. DW: 'We were annoyed by carts and dirt, and the road was full of people, who all noticed our car in one way or another.' She also noticed the lack of 'coaches or gentlemen's carriages'; and remarked the arrangements for washing at the 'bleaching-ground'—that is, Glasgow Green (*DWJ* i. 235; 236).

226 7.11ᵛ § 1. *CN* i. 1455. 22–3 August 1803.
See 40. The suspension had to be re-enacted by Parliament annually.

227 7.26ᵛ § 1. *CN* i. 1471. 30 August 1803.
The party has reached Loch Katrine, the eastern end of which reaches into the Trossachs.

9. [?saw] : saw *CN*. The passage is mostly inked in, but this word (obscure to the inker-in no doubt) is left in pencil.

21. Galilæe, vicisti! : Galilæe vicisti *CN*. 'You have conquered, Galilean', supposedly the last words of Julian the Apostate to Christ. The connection is obscure: some kind of comical concession of the Scottish lake-scene's magnificence. The comparison with Borrowdale is made again, but to Cumberland's advantage: see 259.

28. Wil[?son] : [?Wilson] *CN*. A doubtful reading. STC wrote to SC: 'the Hovel . . . was varnished *so rich* with peat smoke, an apartment of highly polished [oak] would have been poor to it: it would have wanted the *metallic* Lustre of the smoke-varnished Rafters. – This was [the pleasantest] Evening, I had spent, since my Tour: for [Wordsworth's] Hypochondriacal Feelings keep him silent, & [self-]centered –' (*CL* ii. 978).

31. After 'My Friend' STC has added, at a later date (1812: see note to line 52): '*O me!* what a word to give permanance to the *mistake* of a Life!'

34–6. Retracing their steps, back to the east shore of Loch Lomond, which they had taken the ferry across to see Loch Katrine (*DWJ* i. 259–61). It was pouring with rain and they were soaked through (*DWJ* i. 279).

41–2. DW has a nice description of the locals returning from their Sabbath-day meeting (*DWJ* i. 282–3).

42. Tarbet, on the west side of Loch Lomond, is where they had stayed before the Loch Katrine excursion.

48–9. ribbon Finery : ribbon *Finery CN*. STC has returned to add the phrases 'those not subject to yearly Burning' and 'in the *apotheosis* of Finery' in a smaller hand.

50. Arrochar is at the head of Loch Long, a little to the west of Tarbet; the Cobbler is a nearby peak.

52. After 'D[orothy]', STC has returned to add: '*utinam nunq[uam] vidissem!*' (i.e. 'Oh that I had never seen them!'); and after 'now', 'alas! *now* it is June 5, 1812'. (In fact, STC seems to have written two years separated by a slash, perhaps '1812/1802': the figures are hard to decipher, but a little clearer in *J*.)

54. After 'Edingburgh', STC has returned to add: 'O Esteesee! that thou hadst from thy 22nd year indeed made *thy own* way & *alone*!' ('Esteesee' = 'STC', his preferred appellation: *CL* ii. 867.) DW says in her 'Tour': 'poor C. being very unwell, determined to send his clothes to Edinburgh and make the best of his way thither, being afraid to face much wet weather in an open carriage' (*DWJ* i. 287); but writing to SC, STC sounds keener to break away on his own ('somehow or other I had

not been quite comfortable': *CL* ii. 978). His twenty-second year included his first meeting with WW.

228 7. 30[v] § 1. *CN* i. 1472. 30 August 1803.

229 7. 30[v] § 2. *CN* i. 1473. 30 August 1803.
A simile for WW's perception of him, drawn from the recent boat across the loch?

230 7. 38[v] § 1. *CN* i. 1476. 30–1 August 1803.
3. flower Gardens : flower of Gardens *CN*. There is some attempt at a word before 'Gardens', but I think crossed through.

231 7. 56. *CN* i. 1489 (excerpt). 4 September 1803.
In fact, STC did not head for Edinburgh: instead, with a burst of new energy he set out on an enormous solitary tour that took him north, through Fort William, on to Fort Augustus (where he was briefly apprehended as a spy: *CL* ii. 984–5), and the length of Loch Ness. He wrote to SC, on 2 September: 'having found myself so happy alone – such blessing is there in perfect Liberty! – that I walked off – and have walked 45 miles since then' (*CL* ii. 979). This entry records his sighting of the landscape about Glen Nevis.

2. Cf. 'Dim similitudes | Weaving in moral strains': 'On Observing a Blossom on the First of February 1796', ll. 19–20 (*CPW* i. 149).

30. ind[eed] : indeed *CN*. The word has been lost at the page's edge.

31. After 'distant', he has tried to draw the scene, but scribbled it through, writing 'miserable'. (Not, I think, 'miserably', a first choice of epithet replaced by 'segmented', as *CN* sees; but 'miserable', a separate reference to his drawing.)

232 7. 72[v] § 1. *CN* i. 1503. September 1803.

233 7. 72[v] § 2. *CN* i. 1504. September 1803.
'Ode' appears crossed out. STC the ghost: cf. 197 and 462.

234 7. 72[v] § 3. *CN* i. 1505. September 1803.
2. [?moral] : moral *CN*. *MS* has faded, and *J*, which is helpful for most of the entry, does not illuminate this word much.

235 7. 72 § 4. *CN* i. 1509. September 1803.

236 7. 71[v] § 1. *CN* i. 1510. September 1803.
1. Tree : Trees *CN*.

237 **4. 25 § 1.** *CN* i. 1515. September–October 1803 (*CN*).
A very early hint of the idiosyncratic genre of *BL* (as *CN* notes), which was subtitled *Biographical Sketches of my Literary Life and Opinions*.

238 **4. 25 § 1.** *CN* i. 1517. September–October 1803 (*CN*).
1. [?whence] : [?whence/where] *CN*. Obscure.
9. [or] : or *CN*. The word has faded.

239 **16. 16 § 1.** *CN* i. 1528. 30 September–12 October 1803.
A favourite story (*TT* i. 76). Edward FitzGerald recalled: 'Coleridge used to relate how he formed a great notion of the understanding of a solid-looking man, who sat during dinner silent, and seemingly attentive to his discourse. Till suddenly, some baked potatoes being brought to table, Coleridge's disciple burst out, "Them's the jockeys for me!"' (*IR* 221).

240 **16. 16ᵛ § 3.** *CN* i. 1533. 12–28 October 1803.

241 **16. 17 § 1.** *CN* i. 1535. 12–28 October 1803.
Recollecting West Country days—the 1798 walk, perhaps, taken with WH along the Somerset coast to Linton, where, WH recalled, 'I pointed out to Coleridge's notice the bare masts of a vessel on the very edge of the horizon and within the red-orbed disk of the setting sun, like his own spectre-ship in the *Ancient Mariner*' (*IR* 65).

242 **16. 17ᵛ § 4.** *CN* i. 1541. 12–28 October 1803.
Opposite qualities meet in the creative act.
3. *substance* & *distinctness* : substance & distinctness *CN*. 'The Soother of Absence' was a projected topographical poem which STC 'had long mummel'd about in my mind', before finally resolving to write during his Lake excursion in August 1802 (*CN* i. 1225). See Max F. Schulz, 'The Soother of Absence: An Unwritten Work by S. T. Coleridge', *Southern Review*, 2 (1967), 289–97.

243 **21. 50 § 2.** *CN* i. 1546. *AP* 30. September–October 1803.
WW had (so STC hoped) left off writing the shorter poems that had occupied him in 1802 (*CL* ii. 830), and finally set his attentions upon *The Recluse*, the philosophical epic about 'Nature, Man, and Society' devised in the Alfoxden spring of 1798 (*WEY* 212), and for which STC had been impatiently waiting since: 'of nothing but "The Recluse" can I hear patiently' (*CL* i. 538) was already a complaint in October 1799. (WW, who largely shared STC's sense of poetic priorities, forlornly acknowledged in early 1804, 'I have great things in meditation but as yet I have only been doing little ones': *WEY* 436.) In a letter to TP (14 October 1803) STC

similarly regrets WW's 'multitude of small Poems' and repeats the simile of pushing on through the open ocean of native genius, adding: 'I have seen enough, positively to give me feelings of hostility towards the plan of several of the Poems in the L. Ballads: & I really consider it as a misfortune, that Wordsworth ever deserted his former mountain Track to wander in Lanes & allies; tho' in the event it may prove to have been a great Benefit to him . . . I must request of you, & do *rely* on it, that you will be so good as to destroy this Letter' (*CL* ii. 1013).

4. those little : these little *CN*. A nice decision.

244 **21. 50^{v} § 3.** *CN* i. 1551. *AP* 30. October 1803.
This, and the next four entries, return to (and mostly revise) entries made in Notebook 5 in November 1799.

The point about good judgement derives from *CN* i. 519; *CN* notes something similar in Jeremy Taylor.

245 **21. 50^{v} § 5.** *CN* i. 1553. *AP* 28–9. October 1803.
Expanding *CN* i. 521. Part of STC's growing disenchantment with the 'plan' of some of the *Lyrical Ballads*, perhaps. The 'Preface' had celebrated 'Low and rustic life' as an ennobling influence resisting 'arbitrary and capricious habits' (*WPrW* i. 124): cf. the account in *BL* of the dangers of growing 'selfish, sensual, gross, and hard-hearted' in the country (ii. 44–5). STC's own earlier position had been similar to WW's, of course: 'In the country, all around us smile Good and Beauty – and the Images of this divine *καλοκἀγαθόν* [the beautiful and good] are miniatured on the mind of the beholder, as a Landscape on a Convex Mirror' (*CL* i. 154).

246 **21. 50^{v} § 6.** *CN* i. 1554. *AP* 31. October 1803.
A revision of *CN* i. 524. The 'under-consciousness' appears in *The Statesman's Manual*: 'when the nervous system is approaching to the waking state, a sort of under-consciousness blends with our dreams, that in all, we imagine as seen or heard, our own self is the ventriloquist, and move the slides in the magic-lanthorn' (*LS* 80).

4. *solitary* : solitary *CN*.

247 **21. 51 § 3.** *CN* i. 1558. *AP* 31. October 1803.
The same as *CN* i. 528. STC's enthusiasm for Plato and the Platonist tradition is a constant in his intellectual life, sometimes (as here) couched in affectionate deprecation (cf. *CL* i. 295; see 458, 495): Plato's popular association with esoteric mysticism made him an ambiguous authority, and in *BL* STC complains about his reputation suffering through its association with 'the visionary flights of Plato' (ii. 240). The illuminated

mist recalls the strongly Platonic imagery of 'The Destiny of Nations': 'him First, him last to view | Through meaner powers and secondary things | Effulgent, as through clouds that veil his blaze' (ll. 15–17: *CPW* i. 132). See David Newsome, *Two Classes of Men: Platonism and English Romantic Thought* (1974); Keith Cunliffe, 'Recollection and Recovery: Coleridge's Platonism', in Anna Baldwin and Sarah Hutton (eds.), *Platonism and the English Imagination* (Cambridge, 1994), 207–16; and Mary Anne Perkins, 'Coleridge and the "Other Plato"', *European Romantic Review*, 8 (1997), 25–40.

248 **21. 51 § 6.** *CN* i. 1561. *AP* 61. October 1803.
A revision of 98 (*CN* i. 556).
4. copresence : co presence *CN*. (co-presence *AP*.)

249 **21. 53v § 1.** *CN* i. 1577. *CHH* 24–5. 19 October 1803.
6. The Men & the Times: STC had published 'Pitt' in the *Morning Post* (19 March 1800), the first of 'A Pair of Portraits', and gained some celebrity (*IR* 86); the second, on Bonaparte, never appeared—STC later claimed this was because he did not want to gratify Bonaparte, who was known to be eager to read what STC had to say about him (*EOT* i. 219–26).

9. Dark Ladié : Dark Ladie *CN*. 'The Maid of Orleans' is STC's contribution to RS's *Joan of Arc* (1796), later excerpted and re-presented as 'The Destiny of Nations: A Vision' in 1817 (*CPW* i. 131–48); 'The Ballad of the Dark Ladié' (1798) was finally published, a fragment, in 1834 (*CPW* i. 293–5); 'Christabel', of course, was never finished, though STC often discussed its unwritten conclusions (see *CV* 187–8).

11. Presumably, accounts of the tours he had undertaken with her brother Tom Wedgwood, STC's patron and fellow-metaphysician. They had travelled in Wales towards the end of 1802 (recorded in letters home, *CL* ii. 882–902).

12. The government frequently announced national fast days to solicit God's assistance in the war against France. It was an anxious time: uprising in Ireland and Bonaparte apparently preparing to invade.

22. 'O *Σαρα Σαρα* why am I' has been inked over, but is still just discernible, especially in *J*.

28. '*Ασρα*' has also been deleted, but can just be made out, especially with the help of *J*.

31. The Latin means: 'O ye gods! Strength and virtue to me, but you . . . alas! Hopeless love!' The missing words in between have been scratched out.

33. A second thought attached by the ‡ to line 30.

35. Edith and Mary, SC's sisters, were staying in Greta Hall, 'a large, a very large Bolus!', as STC bravely told TP, ' – but it is astonishing, how one's Swallow is enlarged by the sense of doing one's Duty – at least where the Pill is to pass off some time or other – & the Medicine to be discontinued' (*CL* ii. 1015).

36. dead : there is a faint chance of 'lead' (as in 'leaden') : the 'd' is unusually formed for STC.

250 **21. 54ᵛ § 1.** *CN* i. 1578. 19–21 October 1803.
This time a slight contraction of an earlier entry (*CN* i. 579), which read 'a society more approaching in their Laws & Habits to Nature —'. The observation first struck him during the fateful visit to the Hutchinsons' in 1799: did he return to that Notebook after the outburst of the previous entry?

251 **21. 56 § 1.** *CN* i. 1589. *CHH* 47; 52; 54–5 (in part). 19–21 October 1803.
Two pages of 'Images': a rewriting and tidying of several earlier entries in pocket notebooks (*CN* i. 494, 495, 496, 510, 515, 581, and 582). As *CN* says, 'my Scotch Tour' (line 10) helps date the writing-up to 1803.

4–5. Genesis 3: 24—or, perhaps, Milton's superb amplification at the end of *Paradise Lost* (XII, ll. 626–40). The likeness first occurred to him in 1802 (*CN* i. 1199).

6. Barnard Castle is on the Tees: STC and WW (and JC) travelled through it on the way from the Hutchinsons at Sockburn on their way to the Lakes, 28 October 1799.

11. Like the next few sightings, the persistent foam was seen on this same tour: 'The white Eddy-rose that blossom'd up against the stream in the scollop, by fits & starts, obstinate in resurrection – It *is the life* that we live' (*CN* i. 495).

19. That is, an inhabitant of Brobdingnag, the land of giants in Swift's *Gulliver's Travels* (1726). The scene is various yet harmonized into a kind of visual unity (hence beautiful: see 331): like the flock of starlings in a few lines' time, the sight is of many things yet one thing; but is the unity innate in the scene or is it an attribution of the comprehending eye? For STC's further speculations on the point, see 440.

25. sharp : steep *CN*. An uncertain reading, as the word is poorly formed; but the middle does not look like a Coleridgean 'e' to me, and some attempt has been made to insert a letter first omitted in haste: an 'r'?

29. Seen on STC's coach journey south to London in November 1799.

252 **21. 56[v] § 2.** *CN* i. 1592. *AP* 8–9. 19–21 October 1803.
An expansion of his first thoughts upon arrival in London in 1799: see 103.

253 **21. 67 § 1.** *CN* i. 1597. *AP* 31–2. 19–21 October 1803.
2. To 'dance the hay' is to dance in a ring.

254 **21. 67 § 2.** *CN* i. 1598. *AP* 32. 19–21 October 1803.
1. St Herbert's Island is in Derwentwater.

2. on : in *CN*. (on *AP*.) There is no visible dot for an 'i', which is not at all conclusive, but 'on' might make marginally better sense in connection with the metaphor of the pavement.

255 **21. 67 § 3.** *CN* i. 1599. *AP* 32. 19–21 October 1803.

256 **21. 68 § 1.** *CN* i. 1603 *AP* 34. 21 October 1803.
2. STC's square brackets, possibly added later.

7. Castle Crag, south of the Falls of Lodore: is STC recalling a view from within the valley, looking north-east?

18. consubstantiate: i.e. 'unite in one common substance' (*OED*), primarily a theological term.

20. Last sentence added later (after a change in the weather, no doubt).

257 **21. 69 § 1.** *CN* i. 1606. 21–3 October 1803.
A = STC; B = WW (*CN*'s suggestion.) Cf. STC's letter to TP, 14 October 1803: 'I owe it to Truth & Justice as well as to myself to say, that the concern, which I have felt in this instance, and one or two other more *crying* instances, of Self-involution in Wordsworth, has been almost wholly a Feeling of friendly Regret, & disinterested Apprehension – I saw him more & more benetted in hypochondriacal Fancies, living wholly among *Devotees* – having every the minutest Thing, almost his very Eating & Drinking, done for him by his Sister, or Wife – & I trembled, lest a Film should rise, and thicken on his moral Eye' (*CL* ii. 1013).

1. *Envy* : Envy *CN*.

9. this! : this? *CN*.

36. STC originally drew a line under the entry after 'Character', before returning to continue the note.

38. The Act of Union with Ireland was passed into law on 1 January 1801. William Pitt (1759–1806) was the Prime Minister 1783–1801, and returned to power in 1804. STC normally took a dismal view of his malformed intellect: see *EOT* i. 219–26.

42. a : as *CN*. STC's indefinite articles often trail a downward tail that emulates an 's': 'a' seems better sense in this case.

52. STC begins to list the stages of the process by the letters L, M, N, O, and P.

55–6. A telling piece of self-analysis: STC would later (1815) address WW as one 'to whom for the more substantial Third of a Life we have been habituated to look up: especially, where our Love, tho' increased by many and different influences, yet begun and throve and knits it's Joints in the perception of his Superiority' (*CL* iv. 571). The contribution STC's habitual self-abasement made to the relationship is well described by Thomas McFarland, *Romanticism and the Forms of Ruin: Wordsworth, Coleridge, and Modalities of Fragmentation* (1981), 56–103.

258 **21. 70ᵛ § 1.** *CN* i. 1607 and 1608. 23 October 1803.

2. The route between Keswick and Grasmere took STC past Thirlmere. The large single lake is now a reservoir, and the valley is rather drab; but in STC's day there were two smaller lakes, and the scene was evidently more impressive.

10. 'ending' has been partially crossed through and 'received into' written in.

11. '& connects' is an addition.

15. reflection, : reflections *CN*. If an 's' it is very indistinct; but it is not certainly a comma either.

16–18. *CN* prints the text after 'setting Sun. —' as a separate entry, though it runs on in *MS* without a break: STC's celebratory description leads without transition into thoughts of SH. (Tom Hutchinson was SH's brother.) As *CN* notes, the thought of SH living nearer to Greta Hall did not seem to stop STC's plans to find a better climate to improve his health.

259 **21. 71. § 1.** *CN* i. 1610. *CHH* 42; 43 (in part). 24 October 1803.

1. WH had been in the Lakes since the summer, and had painted WW and STC, 'masterly . . . very much in the manner of Titian's portraits'. By September, STC's assessment of his young friend was sharpening a little: 'a thinking, observant, original man', but also 'brow-hanging, shoe-contemplative, *strange* . . . jealous, gloomy, & of an irritable Pride – & addicted to women, as objects of sexual Indulgence' (*CL* ii. 960; 990). WH was shortly to become involved in a scrape of some kind: WW was later to maintain he fled an irate populace, outraged by his 'gross attacks on women' (*HCR* i. 169).

9. A comparison with the landscape seen on the Scottish tour earlier that year (see 227).

14. woods : Wood, *CN*.

27. The hamlet of Watendlath and the tarn (properly, not a lake) sit in the hills separating Borrowdale and the Thirlmere valley, above Rosthwaite. Watendlath Beck runs out of the tarn, down to the Lodore falls, just to the south of Derwentwater ('the lake of Keswick').

27–8. moss, too? : moss, too *CN*.

45. & of Bassenthwaite : & Bassenthwaite *CN*.

46. Look on : Look in *CN*. The word is hastily formed: either is possible.

50. The Bowder Stone, a large free-standing stone, and an object of tourist wonder, is a little over a mile south of the bottom tip of Derwentwater. STC and WW had disagreed about its size during their Scottish tour (*DWJ* i. 242).

53. pile of stones : pile of three *CN*.

59. Lines as I must : Lines I ~~will~~ must *CN*.

62–3. Is (as *CN* speculates) STC thinking of WW's poem on his youth (to become *The Prelude*)?

63. *all my Life!* : *all my Life CN*. Several pages earlier in the Notebook (13^{v}–18: *CN* i. 863) are filled with an alphabetical list of common names, written out (as *CN* identifies) by Sara Hutchinson.

260 21. 73^{v}. *CN* i. 1616 (excerpt). *AP* 35–6; *CHH* 43. 27 October 1803.
The first part of the entry as printed in *CN* is a night scene; STC then recalls an argument of the day before.

8. The naturalist-theologians John Ray (1627–1705), author of *The Wisdom of God Manifested in the Works of the Creation* (1691), and William Derham [*sic*] (1657–1735), author of *Physico-Theology: Or, A Demonstration of the Being and Attributes of God, from his Works of Creation* (1713), both of whom celebrated the ingenuity of God's contrivance in making the world. (See Basil Willey, *The Eighteenth Century Background* (1940), 34–42.) The *Evidences of Christianity* (1794) and *Natural Theology* (1802) of William Paley (see 39 n.) sought to prove God's existence by examining the nicety of his design manifest in the natural world. STC's early Optimism had some sympathy with such arguments in his 1795 lectures: 'the more nicely we examine the relations of Things the more clearly we perceive their astonishing aptitude' (*LPR* 93; cf. *TT* i. 462–3 for his later view).

WW seems to have spoken abrasively about the way such an approach to nature interferes with the spontaneous contemplation of her objects; STC's counter-charge, that having 'sympathy with their real or imagined Life' can be just as distorting, and his being disturbed that WW should speak about nature with an eloquence properly belonging to theology, anticipates later reservations about WW's 'vague misty, rather than mystic, Confusion of God with the World & the accompanying Nature-worship' (*CL* v. 95).

261 21. 76v § 1. *CN* i. 1620. *AP* 40–1. 28 October 1803.
The children were not actually baptized for another few days (*WEY* 418).

12. A bull 'consists in a mental juxta-position of incongruous ideas with the sensation, but without the sense, of connection' (*SWF* i. 308); or, 'the bringing together two incompatible thoughts, with the *sensation*, but without the *sense*, of their connection' (*BL* i. 72 n.); and cf. *LS* 153. A bull is a small-scale example of heterogeneous ideas being joined together by an act of the mind, and so close to STC's definitions of imagination (and fancy: see *TT* i. 489–90). There is a good account of bulls in Christopher Ricks, *Beckett's Dying Words* (Oxford, 1993), 152–203.

262 21. 77 § 1. *CN* i. 1622. *AP* 41–2. 28 October 1803.
5. Arbitrement means 'freedom of the will, free choice' (*OED*). It is a Miltonic word: *OED* cites *Paradise Lost*, VIII, ll. 640–1, 'to stand or fall | Free in thine own arbitrament it lies', besides *F* i. 109–10/ii. 73–4 (14 September 1809), where STC reworks this Notebook entry.

8. STC was no admirer of Windham (see 223). Richard Brinsley Sheridan (1751–1816), dramatist and man of the theatre (he had rejected STC's tragedy), MP, and Treasurer to the Navy, 1806–7.

11. *old* as : *old as CN*. 'To find no contradiction in the union of old and new', etc., will later appear as a characteristic of poetic genius: 'To carry on the feelings of childhood into the powers of manhood, to combine the child's sense of wonder and novelty with the appearances which every day for perhaps forty years had rendered familiar' (*F* i. 109–10; and quoted again, applied to WW, in *BL* i. 80–1).

16. is : in *CN*. Evil is a problem if you wrongly suppose the mutability of things to mean genuine alteration: in truth, all such change is superficial only, subsumed within the permanence of God.

17. If the world is subsumed within the inclusive goodness of God, how can we explain the presence within that divine unity of manifoldness, of multiplicity and alteration? Cf. 'if God *be* every Thing, every Thing is God – : which is all, the atheists assert – . An eating, drinking, lustful *God* – with no *unity* of *Consciousness*' (*CL* i. 192–3; and cf. *AR* 402–3). The

'Question' of Evil is settled if the apparently changeable multiplicity of the world is recognized as part of an abiding 'necessity of omniform harmonious action', a divine 'Order'. That 'number' (sheer numerousness) is intrinsically opposed to the Good, and that evil is 'antipathy to the One' (*CN* iv. 5076), is a Platonic instinct found throughout STC, complicating his seemingly innate delight in the multiform details of the material universe.

17–23. As the multiplicity of the world is recognized to be 'subservient to order, regulated, organized, made beautiful and rational' by God's 'creative Energy', so the apprehension of its order renders it a fit object for the 'Imag[ination] & Intellect' to contemplate: the Godlikeness of Imagination is a theme of increasing importance to STC. See 371.

263 21. 77v § 1. *CN* i. 1623. *AP* 42–3. 28 October 1803.
This self-defensive passage is reworked in *F* i. 108/ii. 73.

5. Legerdemain: i.e. *léger de main*, a trick pulled off by sleight-of-hand (*OED*)—that STC's phrase for such low behaviour is French is no accident, I suppose. That the 'machine' of language itself, suitably scrutinized, should lead our thoughts toward deep truths is a Coleridgean instinct: a good indication of the wrongness of a philosophical system is taken to be its discrepancy with the usage of 'all known languages' (*L* 129).

9. The fallen angels talked 'Of providence, foreknowledge, will and fate, | Fixed fate, free will, foreknowledge absolute, | And found no end, in wandring mazes lost' (*Paradise Lost*, II, ll. 559–61), lines STC later applies to his own precocious immersion in metaphysical questions (*BL* i. 16).

264 21. 77v § 2. *CN* i. 1624. 29 October 1803.
14. Voice : STC originally had 'Dweller'.

265 21. 57 § 4. *CN* i. 1625. 31 October 1803.

266 21. 78v § 1. *CN* i. 1635. *AP* 43–4. 2 November 1803.
4. [?see] : see *CN*. I find no trace of the word.

6. Egg : Eggs *CN*. (egg *AP*.)

11. Castlerigg, where a stone circle stands, is a mile or so to the east of Keswick.

13. After 'shape of a' STC attempts to draw the shape he cannot name: *AP* prints 'an ellipse or shuttle' in place of the drawing, which describes it well enough.

267 **16. 21 § 4.** *CN* i. 1643. 6 November 1803.
4. cake : cakes *CN*.
6. *was* : was *CN*.
9. imprimis: i.e. 'in the first place'. For STC on bulls, see 261 n.

268 **16. 22v § 1.** *CN* i. 1656. 6–13 November 1803.
John Hookham Frere (1769–1846), diplomat, translator, and contributor to the *Anti-Jacobin*, where STC was one among many targets. Another version of the story appeared in the *Monthly Magazine* in 1804 (*IR* 10). While an undergraduate, STC won the Brown Medal for a Greek ode, but failed to gain a university scholarship by competition (*IR* 9–10; 16).

269 **21. 83 § 1.** *CN* i. 1645. 7–9 November 1803.
2. 'g – w Mem: book' is short for 'George Ward's Memorandum Book' (Notebook 16: see 291 and *CN* i. 1628). The entry in question is 267.

270 **16. 23 § 1.** *CN* i. 1658. 13 November 1803.
An appealing vignette of life at Greta Hall.
1. The date is not unambiguous: it might be '14th'. STC's dates at this point in Notebook are a little muddled anyway (*CN* i. 1665, 1667). A close stool was a forerunner of the water-closet.

271 **21. 86 § 3.** *CN* i. 1668. *AP* 47–8. 16–20 November 1803.
An incident he remembered in 1811 and told to Crabb Robinson while busy discriminating between imagination and fancy, as exemplifying 'a sort of disease of imagination' (*IR* 132).
3. Mr : ~~Mr~~ the *CN*.

272 **21. 87 § 2.** *CN* i. 1679. *AP* 49. 21–4 November 1803.
CN connects the passage with the *Enneads* of Plotinus, which STC was reading at this time.
2. from the: i.e. 'because of the'.

273 **16. 26 § 1.** *CN* i. 1677. 22 November 1803.
2. [?] : viz *CN*. A malformed word whatever it is.

274 **16. 26v § 2.** *CN* i. 1686. 22–9 November 1803.
1. Die Bäume und die Felsen sagen mir nichts : 'Trees and rocks say nothing to me': cf. 'I'm a lover of learning, and trees and open country won't teach me anything' (*Phaedrus* 230d).
2. Tant pis pour vous : 'So much the worse for you.' An answer to Socrates, presumably: see *CPT* 205.

275 **16. 27 § 2.** *CN* i. 1688. 22–9 November 1803.
6. 'here': presumably, 'in this case, the licence is judiciously used'—STC apparently has a particular work in mind to defend. *CN* suggests WW's *Lyrical Ballads*.

276 **21. 89 § 1.** *CN* i. 1682. 24 November 1803.
The Southeys moved to Greta Hall after their daughter fell seriously ill, so that Edith could be near SC. 'What a nice Thing for us, if you & Edith were to take the other half of this House', wrote STC in August; returning from his Scottish tour, he found a letter awaiting him in Perth, telling him that the girl was dead, and wrote RS an anguished response: 'Change! change! change! – O God of Eternity! when shall we all be at rest in thee?' (*CL* ii. 975; 984). Obviously, some rearrangement of accommodation became necessary.

3. *Change! – Change!* : *Change! –* Change! *CN*.

7. 24 November 1799 was one of STC's fateful dates: the day he arrived at Sockburn, there to fall in love with SH (*CN* i. 576–80). See 102 n.

277 **16. 28 § 2.** *CN* i. 1692. 29 November 1803.
2. The blind Scottish poet Thomas Blacklock (1721–91), author of *A Collection of Original Poems* (1760). [?And if to] : And if to *CN*. The words have faded badly.

278 **16. 31ᵛ § 1.** *CN* i. 1707. 29 November–11 December 1803.
3. 'Sound of clos'd gate, across the water born': *An Evening Walk*, l. 441 (*WPW* i. 38).

279 **16. 31ᵛ § 3.** *CN* i. 1709. 29 November–11 December 1803.

280 **16. 32ᵛ § 1.** *CN* i. 1712. 29 November–11 December 1803.
The One and the many played out within the self: one way the diverse faculties may be harmonized into unity is in the making of poetry: see 497 n.

1. [On] : On *CN*. The word is lost, dimly visible in *J*.

281 **21. 89ᵛ § 2.** *CN* i. 1698. *AP* 51. 6 December 1803.
Thoughts still turning about the Cain story he had been drawn to in 1797: see 13 n.

282 **21. 89ᵛ § 3.** *CN* i. 1699. *AP* 51. 6 December 1803.

283 **21. 90 § 1.** *CN* i. 1700. *AP* 51. 6 December 1803.
1. That is to say: 'Abstruse Reasoning *is to* the inductions of common sense *as* reaping *is to* delving.' Cf. 'What was born and christened in the

schools passes by degrees into the world at large, and becomes the property of the market and the tea-table' (*BL* i. 86–7 n.; and cf. *CN* iii. 3549).

284 **21. 90 § 2.** *CN* i. 1701. 6 December 1803.
1. Newlands is the valley to the west of Derwentwater.

285 **16. 120 § 1.** *CN* i. 1725. *AP* 52–3. 11 December 1803.
STC's favourite proverb: all instances of 'the balance or reconciliation of opposite or discordant qualities' which he will later identify as the activity of the imagination (*BL* ii. 16).

2. *down* : down *CN*. Observation : observations *CN*.

6–7. *Paradise Lost*, II, ll. 594–5.

11–12. For the sameness-in-difference of waterfalls, see 222. Cf. WW's coincidence of opposites in 'The stationary blasts of waterfalls' (*Prel.: 1805*, VI, l. 558).

19. crambe bis cocta : 'twice-boiled cabbage', i.e. a worn-out topic.

21. William Sotheby's *Orestes: A Tragedy in Five Acts* (Bristol, 1802). STC mentions the play in the context of his proverb in a letter to Sotheby in August 1802 (*CL* ii. 857).

22. Cf. the hymn to God in *Paradise Lost*: 'Dark with excessive bright' (III, l. 380). STC must have somewhere in mind 'Lucus a non lucendo': that is, the etymological claim that 'dark grove' (lucus) comes from 'absence of *light*' (lux), and hence a phrase to describe any apparently paradoxical deduction.

23. *MS* clearly reads 'Wordly'; but the sense demands a missing 'l' (it is silently supplied by *AP*). Worldly-mindedness is a *philosophical* word, presumably, because it nicely catches the essence of a philosophy—materialism, in which the mind is the passive recipient of the world's impressions, 'a lazy Looker-on on an external World' (*CL* ii. 709). It is an irony of which STC was fond that the outcome of such a position, in which 'all is merged in the objective', is practically indistinguishable from its polar opposite, idealism, in which 'all is subject' (*PL* ii. 559; 558): each, by denying the distinction between self and world, 'removes all reality and immediateness of perception, and places us in a dream-world of phantoms and spectres, the inexplicable swarm and equivocal generation of motions in our own brains' (*BL* i. 137). Cf. 527.

22–3. An attempt to resolve the many and the One by casting its rival perceptions as stages in a biographical progress.

24. The Gymnosophists were a sect of Hindu ascetics who wore few or no clothes, and devoted themselves to mystical contemplation.

26. ochlocracy: i.e. government by the mob or lowest of the people (*OED*).

286 **16.39 § 3.** *CN* i. 1736. 13–18 December 1803.

287 **16.39 § 4.** *CN* i. 1737. *AP* 54. 13–18 December 1803.
The optical illusion by which STC saw 'the image or reflection of the fire, that seemed burning in the bushes or between the trees in different parts of the garden or the fields beyond it . . . and which still arranged itself among the real objects of vision' (*F* i. 145); cited in *AP*.

288 **16.40 § 5.** *CN* i. 1743. 13–18 December 1803.
STC's hostility to the culture of contemporary periodical criticism was often outspoken (e.g. *BL* ii. 107–18).

289 **16.40 § 6.** *CN* i. 1744. 13–18 December 1803.
STC has been reading the natural historian J. F. Blumenbach (see *CN* i. 1738), whose lectures and conversation he had enjoyed while at the University of Göttingen, and whose 'manual' he thought of translating (*CL* i. 494; 590).

1. Thing / : Thing // *CN*. The entry has been retraced in a sharper pencil, creating some double-lines, including this one. clumsy : clumbsy *CN*. The word is carelessly formed; a 'b' (an odd spelling) is not obvious.

290 **16.41 § 1.** *CN* i. 1749. 18 December 1803.
The point seems initially to have been his preference for Hebrew over Greek poetry (as in *CL* ii. 865–6); but the thought is temporarily sidelined by the phrase 'wh[ic]h I deem . . . an inspired Greek'.

5. In the poem of Catullus (*c.*84–*c.*54 BC), Atys is metamorphosed into a fir by the goddess Cybele.

291 **16.46v § 1.** *CN* i. 1764. 26 December 1803.
Referring to the previous entry in the Notebook. George Ward was a London bookseller, who at one stage was ready to publish STC's (unwritten) *Consolations and Comforts* (*CL* ii. 1046). Presumably, he sold the notebook to STC—unless the 'shame' is upon the extravagance of his gift.

292 **16.47 § 1.** *CN* i. 1766. *CHH* 48. 26–8 December 1803.
2. of the : of the of the *MS*. STC repeated the words as he turned the page of the Notebook.

293 **16.48 § 2.** *CN* i. 1770. *AP* 56–7; *CHH* 44; 45. 28–9 December 1803.
The case against association again: the thought that associations were

actually directed by something, and not simply self-governed by their own irresistible process, had cropped up (in slightly different terms) in a letter to RS in August: 'I almost think, that Ideas *never* recall Ideas as far as they are Ideas – any more than Leaves in a forest create each other's motion – The Breeze it is that runs thro' them / it is the Soul, the state of Feeling' (*CL* ii. 961).

6. A hecatomb was a great public sacrifice of oxen: Pythagoras, thanking the gods for his trigonometric discovery, offered up millet and honeycomb.

13. The proliferating association of ideas, unless controlled by a will, would be a state of delirium: cf. *BL* i. 111–12.

14. A 'denaturalized' mind is presumably one cut off from the influences of external nature, the complaint of 'Dejection'. Cf. his letter to Godwin (April 1801): 'I have been compelled . . . to seek resources in austerest reasonings – & have thereby so denaturalized my mind, that I can scarcely convey to you the disgust with which I look over any of my own compositions' (*CL* ii. 725).

16. *yet is* : *yet* is *CN*. (yet *is AP*.)

294 **16. 49 § 1.** *CN* i. 1772. 31 December 1803.

295 **16. 50^v § 3.** *CN* i. 1779. 31 December 1803.

2. even yet : ever yet *CN*. The word is not well formed.

296 **16. 52 § 1.** *CN* i. 1783. 31 December 1803.

3. A syke is a stream.

297 **16. 52 § 2.** *CN* i. 1784. 31 December 1803.

3. itself : also *CN*. Not a certain reading, but there seems some attempt at a letter extending below the line, like a Coleridgean 'f'.

6. [are all] : are all *CN*. The words have worn away.

298 **16. 53^v § 3.** *CN* i. 1800. 1–4 January 1804.

This, and the previous two entries, seem to describe scenes from a New Year's Eve walk with WW up Greenhead Gill—the setting of 'Michael', which WW read (*CN* i. 1776; 1782). STC spent Christmas and the first fortnight of the New Year at Grasmere, with DC (*CL* ii. 1026).

299 **16. 54 § 1.** *CN* i. 1801. 4 January 1804.

Presumably, the second part of the 1799 *Prelude*, written in October–December 1799 (*Prel.*, p. xv), which ends with a farewell to STC, first written when he was leaving to write journalism in London. Now, he was planning to leave WW's company again, this time for his health (*CL* ii. 1025). They walked up Easedale together (*CN* i. 1803).

1. STC has omitted a word after 'outermost': 'part' or 'reach' perhaps.

3. sattiny : satting *CN*. The word is badly formed, but could be 'sattiny' (an available spelling for 'satiny', i.e. 'satin-like').

300 **16. 54v § 1.** *CN* i. 1805. 4–5 January 1805.
Another sight from the excursion up Easedale with WW?

301 **16. 55 § 1.** *CN* i. 1809. 5 January 1805.
1–2. frosty particles full of – snatched up by the wind that seemed to rush : snatched up by the wind that full of frosty particles seemed to rush *CN*. STC has drawn a line from the first phrase that ends approximately at 'seemed to', so the intended order of the words is not obvious.

302 **16. 58 § 1.** *CN* i. 1815. 5–8 January 1805.
Australis is RS ('australis' meaning 'southern'), whose remorseless virtues often vexed STC.

4. [?Action –] : the word (omitted by *CN*) is obscure, although it does not appear to be crossed out.

5–6. purus maritus puram, virgo virginem: i.e. 'a chaste husband to a chaste wife, virginal for his virgin'.

7. Pursuits, the : pursuit, the *CN*.

9. sakes : sake *CN*.

19. Pattern: i.e. 'archetype'.

22. [?his unadmirable] : his unad[mirable] *CN*. Words lost at the foot of the page.

28–33. The poly-lingual parentheses are complicated: the attempt of *CN* to make sense of it should be read alongside James Diggle, 'Greek and Latin in Coleridge's Notebooks', *Notes and Queries*, NS 45 (1998) 193–9, 194–5, on which I am drawing here. It is a list of complaints, something like: 'Review of Lyrical Songs [i.e. the *Lyrical Ballads*, which RS reviewed unsympathetically]; mischievous letters by the Charleses [i.e. CL and Charles Lloyd, whose poems appeared with STC's and CL's in a collaborative volume in 1797]; malicious remarks about me; a completely ungrateful attitude so far as concerns the Epic [presumably *Joan of Arc*: RS's insufficient gratitude for STC's efforts had been a source of resentment since 1795 (*CL* i. 172)]; my house in opposition [presumably some reference to domestic disharmony, in which RS took SC's part]; "I know your Sara, I know that Meek Sister in the Family of Christ" [this last phrase a (mis)quotation from 'The Eolian Harp' (l. 53)—are we to imagine RS throwing STC's words back in his face, in defence of SC?]; poetic thefts and pilferings, and whatever is incongruous and insufficiently becoming'.

29. permalæ : per malæ *CN*. pro[rsus] : prout *CN*.

31. furtula : fustula *CN*.

32–3. STC's brackets within brackets. *CN* puts them in different places, and never closes the bracket opened in line 22.

37. avail yourself to one : avail yourself of to one *MS*.

303 **16. 130v § 1.** *CN* i. 1820. 9 January 1804.
Written on the last free page in the book.

304 **16. 60v § 4.** *CN* i. 1821. 9 January 1804.

305 **16. 62 § 2.** *CN* i. 1825. 9 January 1804.
His own health was by now very poor, undermined by the draughts and damp of life in Greta Hall as well as by his increasing dependency on opium: does the entry imply his hurt feelings at the impatience of his circle?

306 **16. 64v § 2.** *CN* i. 1833. 10 January 1804.
One theory: one feels duty as though a command from without because of the strong association formed in childhood between obligation and figures of authority. But children too young to have formed any such associations seem still to suffer when under external compulsion: the phenomenon might instead be attributed to a pain intrinsic to any interruption of the interior stream of the mind—and, thus, the mind's associative life finds itself at odds with the ethical obligations of duty.

6–7. STC's square brackets.

15. sense, that *Interruption* : sense. That interruption *CN*.

23–4. See 293.

307 **16. 65 § 1.** *CN* i. 1834. 10–11 January 1804.

7. *& the Understanding* : & the Understanding *CN*.

8. *receptivity* : receptivity *CN*.

308 **16. 70 § 1.** *CN* ii. 1843. 14 January 1804.

309 **16. 70 § 2.** *CN* ii. 1844. 14 January 1804.
Heading south, having left Grasmere, passing Rydal Water. WW accompanied him 'almost to Troutbeck' (*WEY* 429).

310 **16. 72 § 2.** *CN* ii. 1850. 19–20 January 1804.
The spelling is odd, but (as *CN* says) unmistakable.

311 16. 72 § 3. *CN* ii. 1851. 20 January 1804.
STC left Grasmere to visit Liverpool, where he stayed with Dr Crompton, an old friend who lived at Eton House, 'a noble seat four miles & a half from the town' (*CL* i. 607).
5. STC misnumbers his list of observations.
7. then [a] graceful : their graceful *CN*.
9. among : amongst *CN*. hindw[ard] : hindward *CN*. Letters lost at the page edge.

312 9. 2ᵛ § 1. *CN* ii. 1854. 26 January 1804.
STC was mostly resident in London for the first few months of 1804, working for the *Courier*, and seeking a place on a ship to take him to Malta where he hoped to regain his health.

313 9. 7 § 1. *CN* ii. 1861. *AP* 53. 26–7 January 1804.

314 9. 8ᵛ § 3. *CN* ii. 1875. *AP* 66. 5 February 1804.
1804 : 1803 *MS*. A mistake (*CN*).

315 16. 73 § 3. *CN* ii. 1896. *AP* 163–4. February 1804?
1. 1 Corinthians 15: 35–8: 'But some *man* will say, How are the dead raised up? and with what body do they come? *Thou* fool, that which thou sowest is not quickened, except it die: And that which thou sowest, thou sowest not that body that shall be, but bare grain, it may chance of wheat, or of some other *grain*: But God giveth it a body as it hath pleased him, and to every seed his own body.'
4. the Grave? : the Grave! *CN*.

316 9. 10ᵛ § 1. *CN* ii. 1906. 12 February 1804.
A recollection likely to appeal to STC. Margaret, Lady Beaumont (1755–1829), was married to Sir George (1753–1827), connoisseur and patron: he had met STC by chance in 1803, at Greta Hall, and been much impressed by his genius (*IR* 93–4). STC would later stay with the Wordsworths in a house on the Beaumont estate in Leicestershire. (The correction to the date of the entry is deduced by *CN*.)

317 9. 10ᵛ § 2. *CN* ii. 1907. 12–21 February 1804.
2. Dᵒᵉ Sart : Du Sart *CN*. Woolelett : Woollett *CN*. The painter in question is properly the Dutchman Cornelius Dusart (1660–1704); William Woollett [*sic*] (1735–85) was a celebrated engraver, especially famous (says *DNB*) for his engraving of the *Death of Wolfe*, but known too for versions of Dusart's *The Cottagers* and *The Jocund Peasants*. *CN* corrects 'Woolelett', blaming trouble with the 'pen', but the spelling seems clear. (The entry is in pencil.)

318 **9. 11v § 2.** *CN* ii. 1912. 21 February 1804.
The letter is lost; but its contents can be guessed. John Rickman (1771–1840) was secretary to the Speaker of the House of Commons and one of STC's favourite London friends: 'a wonderful man!' (*CL* ii. 1058).

319 **9. 11v § 3.** *CN* ii. 1913. 21 February–10 March 1804.
For 'The Soother of Absence', see 242 n.

320 **9. 13 § 1.** *CN* ii. 1922. 21 February–10 March 1804.
Writing about WW (to RS) in July 1802, and increasingly aware of 'a radical Difference in our theoretical Opinions respecting Poetry', STC had expressed his intention 'to lay down some plain, & perspicuous, tho' not superficial, Canons of Criticism respecting Poetry' (*CL* ii. 830); and an 'Essay on Criticism' had been floated in the privacy of the Notebook more than a year before that (*CN* i. 892).

321 **9. 22 § 1.** *CN* ii. 1963. 10 March 1804.
Home after an evening with CL and his brother. *CN* tracks down the reference to Richard Payne Knight (1751–1824), aesthetician and collector, upon whom STC had called earlier in the month.

322 **9. 24v § 2.** *CN* ii. 1972. *AP* 67. 10–24 March 1804.
Samuel Green was a celebrated organ-builder, responsible for the instrument at Lichfield Cathedral (among others). The episode has a symbolism reminiscent of 'The Blossoming of the Solitary Date-Tree' (*CPW* i. 395–7), inspired by the story of a date tree which, despite flowering profusely every year, produced fruit only when a branch from another such plant had been brought close to it.

323 **9. 28 § 1.** *CN* ii. 1992 (excerpt). 27 March–6 April 1804.
STC travelled from London to Portsmouth on 27 March, to board the *Speedwell* for Malta. This entry is, I suppose, a record of his attempt to spend the time (wandering about a churchyard, perhaps?). The likely resonance of the true soldier's 'Battle of Self' is not hard to imagine. The second epitaph turns out to be a not uncommon joke (see *CN*); and the third satirizes Priestley's curious mixture of stubborn materialism *and* belief in the bodily resurrection: what happens to the body between dying and rising again is the tricky point.

324 **9. 28v § 1.** *CN* ii. 1993. 10 April 1804.
Finally on board and, after a false start, heading for Malta.
2. wester[e]d: i.e. 'shifted to the west'.
4. Before the word 'zigzag', STC draws a rapid zigzag.

8. & sound : & the sound *CN.*

12. pressed: i.e. caught by the press-gang.

35. STC abandons his list of activities and begins again as he turns the page.

39. The 'Consolations and Comforts' was a work STC planned for some time, though it was never written. He gave its full title to TP as 'Consolations and Comforts from the exercise and right application of the Reason, the Imagination, and the moral Feelings, addressed especially to those in Sickness, Adversity, or Distress of Mind, *from speculative Gloom*, &c.' (*CL* ii. 1036). See Max F. Schulz, '*Comforts and Consolations*: An Unwritten Work by S. T. Coleridge', *Coranto: Journal of the Friends of the Libraries, University of Southern California* 4:2 (1967), 3–11.

41. something, beginning with this : *something, beginning with this CN.* Not an underlining, I think, but originally a ruling-off of the entry (as STC often does), before he was moved to continue it.

325 9.31[v] § 1. *CN* ii. 1994. 10 April 1804.

326 9.32 § 1. *CN* ii. 1997. 11 April 1804.
One of a number of events on the journey that brought his poem to mind: see 340.

327 9.33[v] § 1. *CN* ii. 1999. 12 April 1804.
4. Bight: i.e. the curve of the bay.

14. WW, 'The Female Vagrant' (from the 1798 *Lyrical Ballads*), l. 162: 'And on the gliding vessel Heaven and Ocean smiled' (*WPW* i. 114, *app. crit.*). WW's speaker is wretched and bereft.

328 9.34 § 1. *CN* ii. 2000. 12–13 April 1804.

329 9.36 § 1. *CN* ii. 2006. 18 April 1804.
1. interminable : intermination *CN.* Mine is the less interesting reading, but 'intermination' ('action of threatening or menacing': *OED*) does not obviously fit here; and 'interminable' ('boundless, endless') might carry for STC a Miltonic grandeur ('As if they would confine the interminable': *Samson Agonistes*, l. 307).

2. Plumbago is graphite, mined for pencils as well as the manufacture of armaments. STC would have seen it in the Lakes: the area around Keswick was the finest source of pure plumbago in the world.

330 9.37[v] § 2. *CN* ii. 2011. 14 April 1804.
Another memo for 'Comforts and Consolations': STC is worrying about unfavourable responses to WW. CL ventured some cautious reservations

about the second edition of *Lyrical Ballads* (1800), and wrote very amusingly to his friend Manning about the disgruntlement of both WW and STC at his remarks. WW had adduced the moment of homecoming in 'The Brothers' as an example of his own imaginative strength—a passage CL glossed, with comical irreverence: 'A Youth after years of absence revisits his native place, and thinks (as most people do) that there has been strange alteration in his absence' (*LambL* i. 273). Charles James Fox (1749–1806) was the most prominent parliamentary opponent of Pitt: STC and WW sent him a copy of the 1800 *Lyrical Ballads*, 'solely' (said WW in a covering letter) 'on account of two poems in the second volume', the blank verse poems 'The Brothers' and 'Michael'. Fox replied, contrarily, that it was the poems in rhyme which he had preferred (*WEY* 313; 337).

331 9.38 § 1. *CN* ii. 2012. 14 April 1804.
An extraordinary analysis of the picturesque effect of ships in convoy under sail, reworking the Coleridgean themes of sameness and difference, permanence and variety; and (in the seventh item in the list) describing the mind's contribution to the apprehension of a unified whole in a way which anticipates later remarks about the imagination's activity. In eighteenth-century terms, the 'picturesque' was found in landscapes and scenes distinguished by contrast or variety: a mild kind of sublime, its visual irregularity was meant to stir the viewer's imagination in a way that a more ordered or even sight would not; here, STC reworks the concept in a finely idiosyncratic way. The passage, with its neighbours, is well discussed in Raimonda Modiano, *Coleridge and the Concept of Nature* (Basingstoke, 1985), 23–6.

14. [?fresh] : [?brisk/fresh] *CN*. The word is undecidable; but the first letter has a very low loop for a 'b'.

16. by the Pennant : by Pennant *CN*.

17. There is a 'Man' on High Seat, and a 'Shivery Man' near Watendlath; the summit of Skiddaw has a 'Skiddaw Man'. The name probably comes from the Celtic 'maen': see Joan Lee, *The Place Names of Cumbria* (Carlisle, 1998), 62; and see too the indispensable H. H. Symonds, *Walking in the Lake District* (1933; pocket edn., 1935; repr. 1947), 130–1.

30. Edge Lines : Edge Line *CN*.

31–5. The lines of the ship allude to geometrical shapes, but do not fulfil them: it is this quality of suggestive incompleteness that makes them picturesque.

35. it could not so easily do : the words are squeezed in the remains of a torn-off page.

45. feelings : feeling *CN*.

56. No. 2: that is, the second item on the list (in line 8).

58. of Observation : of of Observation *MS*.

59. circumstances : circumstance *CN*.

60. billows : billow *CN*.

63. sensuously: STC first wrote 'sensually'. For the important distinction, see *CL* vi. 729.

64. Things per se: i.e. things in their own right.

332 9. 51^{v} § 2. *CN* ii. 2017. 16–17 April 1804.

333 15. 4 § 1. *CN* ii. 2026. *AP* 70–4 (in part). 19 April 1804.

3. Queen's Metal is an alloy of tin, antimony, bismuth, and lead (*OED*).

4. *Green* : Green *CN*.

5. [?even it] : even it *CN*. The page has faded, especially at the edges: here, *J* does not help much.

8. very obscurely : only obscurely *CN*. A doubtful reading.

8–9. i.e. a memo that pictures showing silver moonlight falling on the sea are untrue to life.

42. Shakespeare is supposed to have planted a mulberry tree in the garden of his Stratford home; it was felled by a subsequent owner, irritated by pilgrims.

51. Bruno (see 221 n.) was tried for heresy by the Inquisition and finally burned at the stake.

54. morti ultro occurrens: i.e. 'going to meet death of his own accord'.

58. 'Lycidas', l. 142: 'Bring the rathe primrose that forsaken dies'. Another legend has the young Shakespeare leaving for London in a hurry after a career as a poacher.

61. uncalled & sudden : uncalled and sudden *CN*.

68. defecated: i.e. 'cleared of impurities'.

81. gratification : gratifications *CN*. (gratification *AP*.)

84–6. Colourful episodes from *Paradise Lost*.

87. Johnson actually wrote of *Paradise Lost*, 'None ever wished it longer than it is. Its perusal is a duty rather than a pleasure': *Lives of the English Poets*, ed. George Birkbeck Hill (3 vols.; Oxford, 1905), i. 183. STC quotes Johnson calling a reading of the poem 'a task' elsewhere (*BL* ii. 188).

334 **15. 10 § 1.** *CN* ii. 2035. 19–20 April 1804.
1. For 'The Soother of Absence' see 242 n.

4. words still : words halt *CN*. A doubtful reading, but there seems sign of an initial 's'. *J* is no help: the photocopy is blurry toward the edge of the page.

335 **15. 10 § 2.** *CN* ii. 2036. 19–20 April 1804.
4–5. Cf. 'Dejection: An Ode', ll. 87–91: 'For not to think of what I needs must feel, | But to be still and patient, all I can; | And haply by abstruse research to steal / From my own nature all the natural man – | This was my sole resource, my only plan' (*CPW* i. 367).

6. *you* : you *CN*.

8–9. [?some Rock] : some Rock *CN*. [?together or] : together or *CN*. *J* is not much help recovering these readings from the bottom of the page.

9–11. Walks in the Lake District, presumably with SH.

336 **15. 23v § 1.** *CN* ii. 2057. 30 April 1804.
1. from a Sea : from Sea *CN*.

20. *CN* considers this part of the same entry as the preceding passage; but it is over the page and strikes off in a different direction. The 'Recluse' is WW (see 243 n.). The connection between the 'I' (the Ego) and the principle of Co-adunation (that is, the act of joining things into one) would become central to STC's philosophy of mind: the principle in question is what STC will discuss in *BL* as Primary Imagination (*BL* i. 304).

337 **15. 27v § 1.** *CN* ii. 2062. 1 May 1804.

338 **15. 40.** *CN* ii. 2086 (excerpt). 11 May 1804.
CN prints this as part of a longer entry.

1. [?out] : [?about] *CN*. There is some sign of a word after 'dealing'; *CN*'s suggestion would fit.

7. —[?] good night —— : – [?and so] good night – *CN*. There is some attempt at a word or phrase, but it is impenetrable.

339 **15. 42 § 1.** *CN* ii. 2088. 13 May 1804.
Cockermouth was WW's birthplace. STC was currently reading (or trying to read: see 341) WW's verse autobiography, which includes an evocation of his infancy in Cockermouth, the boy sung to by his nurse while listening to the River Derwent flowing past the bottom of the garden.

340 15. 42 § 3. *CN* ii. 2090. 13 May 1804.
The resonance which the incident has with 'The Ancient Mariner' is difficult to miss: see 326.

2. gyre: i.e. a revolution or circuit.

341 15. 44 § 1. *CN* ii. 2092. 14 May 1804.
1. Mrs I. was one of STC's fellow passengers.

2–3. [?mainsail] : mainsail *CN*. [?almost] : almost *CN*. The bottom of the page has become very dim.

4. An early version of what would be posthumously published as *The Prelude* (1850) copied out for him to take on his journey. It was known in the Wordsworth circle as the 'Poem to Coleridge'.

6. The Babe was the Wordsworths' son John, born in June 1803.

342 15. 44v § 1. *CN* ii. 2093. 14 May 1804.
Another aspect of the struggle with associationism: against Erasmus Darwin's associationist account of sublime feelings (we experience the sublime because a sight or sound arouses previous feelings of fear or terror, as of lightning and thunder), STC argues that some things are *intrinsically* sublime, independent of their associations in a particular mind.

6. *CN* identifies the passage from Darwin as a chapter 'Of Instinct' in *Zoönomia*. entire dependence : dependence entire *MS*, with a line indicating the transposition.

14–15. [?on our notion] : on our notion *CN*. [?of Lightning] : of Lightning *CN*. [?with its] : with its *CN*. Words lost at the bottom of the page.

343 16. 75 § 4. *CN* ii. 2112. May–June 1804?
An important entry, anticipating later distinctions between the way heterogeneous elements are differently gathered into unities by the imagination and by the fancy.

4–5. 'The Breeze I see is in the tree: | It comes to cool my babe and me', from WW, 'The Mad Mother' (later retitled 'Her Eyes are Wild'), ll. 39–40 (*WPW* ii. 108). In *BL* STC superbly praises the lines: 'so expressive of that deranged state, in which from the increased sensibility the sufferer's attention is abruptly drawn off by every trifle, and in the same instant plucked back again by the one despotic thought, and bringing home with it, by the blending, *fusing* power of Imagination and Passion, the alien object to which it had been so abruptly diverted, no longer an alien but an ally and an inmate' (*BL* ii. 150).

7–8. 'And like a *Lobster* boyl'd, the *Morn* | From *black* to *red* began to turn', from Samuel Butler, *Hudibras* (1663–78), II, ll. 37–8. STC alludes to the same passage in *TT* (i. 489–90) to exemplify fancy, which 'brings together images which have no connection natural or moral, but are yoked together by the poet by some accidental coincidence . . . The imagination modifies images and gives unity to variety; it sees all things in one.' Pope is said to write 'a *conjunction disjunctive* . . . of epigrams' (*BL* i. 19).

10–12. An obscure line or two, but the point is presumably that stated to Sotheby in 1802: 'a great Poet must be, implicitè if not explicitè, a profound Metaphysician' (*CL* i. 810).

344 **16. 75ᵛ § 1.** *CN* ii. 2113. June 1804?
For STC and Catholicism, see 363.

3–4. *there-are-good-&-bad-in-all-religions* : there-are-good-&-bad-in-all-religions *CN*.

6. Magog! : Magog *CN*. Gog and Magog are apocalyptic figures in Ezekiel and Revelation.

345 **21. 101ᵛ § 1.** *CN* ii. 2137. 4 July 1804.
STC arrived on Malta on 18 May and presented himself at Stoddart's house. He gained an introduction to Sir Alexander Ball (1757–1809), Governor of the island, who soon appointed him under-secretary, in the place of one Chapman (*CMI* 142–3; 165; 166).

7. One 'A' is presumably a mistake for 'B'. The ages do not fit SH: perhaps an entirely notional scenario?

346 **21. 103 § 1.** *CN* ii. 2151. *AP* 77. 12 July–3 August 1804.
A visionary account of the simultaneity of Oneness and manyness: see 248, 280.

347 **21. 104 § 1.** *CN* ii. 2192. *AP* 78. 27 September 1804.
On 10 August, STC left Malta for Sicily (*CMI* 193). He climbed Etna (or claimed to, twice): the mountain disappointed him (*CL* ii. 1157). He returned to Syracuse in time for the new opera season. He seems to have struck up a relationship with the singer Cecilia Bertozzoli ('the too fascinating Siren': *CN* iii. 3404).

1. 1804. [I]n : 1804. in *MS*.

2. '*meeting* soul' is from Milton's 'L'Allegro': 'And ever against eating cares, | Lap me in soft Lydian airs, | Married to immortal verse | Such as the meeting soul may pierce | In notes' (ll. 135–9); and in Collins's 'Ode to Simplicity' (l. 48). WW also uses it, in 1820 (*WPW* iii. 164). For memory contrasted with recollection, see 355.

348 **21. 2v § 1.** *CN* ii. 2193. *AP* 79. 5 October 1804.

7–8. For Bacon and Harrington, see 407.

8. STC first wrote 'may be', before hardening the claim to 'is'.

13–14. Sint unicuique sua præmia: i.e. 'to each his own deserts'.

15. never never : never *CN*.

16. desecration : desacration [?] *MS*. [?even vanity to talk to] : even vanity to talk to *AP*, *CN*.

17–18. [?talked with Wordswor]th & Sir G.Beau[?mont] : [talk]ed [with Words]worth & Sir G. Beau[mont?] *CN*. ([were talking to] Wordsworth or Sir George Beaumont? *AP*.) The page has become very hard to decipher at the bottom.

349 **21. 104 § 2.** *CN* ii. 2194. *AP* 78–9. 5 October 1804?

5. Lombard Street was the money market. The date is underlined; *CN* interprets it as referring to conversations of that day, rather than the date of the entry.

350 **21. 105 § 1.** *CN* ii. 2208. *AP* 81. 13 October 1804.

An eminently Coleridgean view of the human self as a place of contest between the One and the many (cf. *CL* v. 496–7). Enough of the Godlike inhabits man to inspire in him a taste for oneness and 'the Universal'; but the 'notions' that he seeks to make universal, each strong enough momentarily to displace all others, are merely partial and peculiar ('Society, Habit, Education', etc.)—and experience soon refutes their spurious claims to universality. Only 'the Inspired' may resolve the conflict between such manifold partial truths and the oneness of the abiding Truth—an act of divine unifying caught in the etymology of '*Atonement*' as '*at-one-ment*' (*LS* 55).

3–4. De gustibus non est disputandum: 'there is no accounting for taste'. experience : experiences *CN*. (experience *AP*.)

8. '(Spinoza)' has been added after 'the Jus extrinsecum fortioris' ('the external law of the stronger'). *CN* tracks the phrase down to a book of metaphysics by A. W. Rehberg that STC was reading about this time (*CM* iv. 207–12): a phrase attributed to Spinoza (for whom, see 110 n.).

351 **21. 106 § 1.** *CN* ii. 2211. *AP* 82. 14–17 October 1804.

An important distinction in STC's aesthetics: to complain of the non-realism of the opera is beside the point, for any theatrical representation aims not at *copying* reality, but at its *imitation*. A reporter at one of his lectures in 1811 heard him say, speaking of poetry, that 'the pleasure we receive arose, not from its being a *copy*, but from its being an imitation, &

the word imitation itself means always a combination of a certain degree of dissimilitude with a certain degree of similitude. If it were merely the same – as looking at a glass reflection [–] we should receive no pleasure' (*LL* i. 223–4). See Frederick Burwick, *Illusion and the Drama: Critical Theory of the Enlightenment and Romantic Era* (University Park, Pa., 1991), 210–29.

352 **21. 107ᵛ § 1.** *CN* ii. 2237. 21 October 1804.
9. *month*! : *month. CN*. live! : live *CN*.
11. materials : material *CN*.
14. The next four leaves have been cut out of the book.

353 **15. 66ᵛ § 2.** *CN* ii. 2245. 26 October–6 November 1804.

354 **21. 58 § 3.** *CN* ii. 2266. *AP* 87. 10 November 1804.
STC's ship was held in the Quarantine Harbour on his return from Sicily (*CL* ii. 1153).

355 **21. 58 § 4.** *CN* ii. 2267. 10–22 November 1804.
Aristotle's 'On Memory' calls recollection 'a sort of investigation': it involves an inward *act* of searching for a resemblance, and so evades the associative self-suggestion that STC would habitually attribute to the '*mechanical* memory', close kin to the '*passive* fancy' (*BL* i. 104).

356 **21. 109 § 1.** *CN* ii. 2271. *AP* 83–4. 23 November 1804.
Back in post, STC was working hard for Ball again: in the new year, he would be appointed Public Secretary (*CMI* 263). Ball is clear of any such moral failings in the eulogistic portrait in *F* (i. 532–8). The distinction between a person and a thing was precisely that the former should not be used instrumentally, that is, as a *means*: 'A Slave is a *Person* perverted into a *Thing*' (*EOT* iii. 235).

357 **21. 59 § 2.** *CN* ii. 2274. *AP* 87. November–early December 1804.
See 351. There is a slim possibility of a later date (see *CN*).
6. Proteus the sea god could assume any shape: the idea that Shakespeare had a magical genius for imaginative self-transformation into his dramatis personae was not new to the Romantics, though it reached a climax in the criticism of STC and WH. In *BL* Shakespeare 'darts himself forth, and passes into all the forms of human character and passion, the one Proteus of the fire and the flood . . . becomes all things, yet for ever remaining himself' (ii. 27; 28). The last clause there (analogous to 'yet known & felt not to be the Thing') is a characteristic Coleridgean addition to the standard Protean analogy.

358 **21. 109 § 4.** *CN* ii. 2279. November–early December 1804.
Another idea for the poem.
6. [?] : ⌈Sara⌉ *CN*. The name has been thoroughly scratched out.

359 **21. 111 § 2.** *CN* ii. 2304. 7–12 December 1804.

360 **21. 111 § 5.** *CN* ii. 2307. 7–12 December 1804.
Connected with the entry about Shakespeare's imitative art vividly conjuring up a sense of 'the very thing' being represented, while (of course) not being that thing (357)? In a 'wooden cut' (i.e. a woodcut) an unprinted space on the page can convincingly represent part of a body, etc.

361 **21. 112 § 2.** *CN* ii. 2315. *AP* 87. 7–12 December 1804.
The question of the origin of the universe is a theological, not a scientific, question. *CN* traces the thought to STC's reading in Kant.

362 **21.113v § 2.** *CN* ii. 2322. *AP* 91–2. 12–13 December 1804.

363 **21.114 § 1.** *CN* ii. 2324. *AP* 92. 12–13 December 1804.
STC's attitude toward Roman Catholicism was mistrustful; and his experience of Mediterranean life exacerbated that (*CMI* 149).
1. *Λαδι βαλλ*: i.e. 'Lady Ball', the wife of the Governor, Sir Alexander (in transparent code).
2. the ? is: i.e. 'the question is'. Sugar of Lead :i.e. lead acetate.
3. Oil of Vitriol: i.e. concentrated sulphuric acid.
5. A best-selling patent medicine (*CN* 1982 n.).

364 **21. 115v § 2.** *CN* ii. 2332. *AP* 96. 13–15 December 1804.
Cf. WW's treatment of pre-existence in 'Ode' (*WPW* iv. 279–85; and see 464–5 for STC's knowledge of it whilst on Malta).

365 **21. 116 § 2.** *CN* ii. 2334. 13–15 December 1804.
STC has been reading about strange things in the natural historian Hermann Samuel Reimarus (1694–1768) (*CN* ii. 2321; and see *CM* iv. 215–31). He plans a fanciful thought experiment to test the irrepressibly instinctive nature of animals.

366 **21. 117 § 2.** *CN* ii. 2344. *AP* 100. 17 December 1804.
The One and the many again, here in the visual apprehension of the Mediterranean.

367 **21. 117 § 3.** *CN* ii. 2345. *AP* 100. 17 December 1804.
5. *AP* and *CN* read 'perishing'; but the word is scribbly: 'persisting' may just be possible.

6. in indulging : indulging *CN*.

368 **21. 118ᵛ § 3.** *CN* ii. 2347. *AP* 101. 17 December 1804.

369 **21. 117ᵛ § 5.** *CN* ii. 2352. *AP* 95. 18–22 December 1804
4. Sara! Sara! : the words have been deleted, but the second 'Sara!' especially is still discernible. [children!] : the word has been deleted by a firm spiral; *CN* makes out 'children!' The Sara in question is presumably SC.

370 **21. 118 § 1.** *CN* ii. 2353. *AP* 96. 18–22 December 1804.
An unwritten Coleridgean comedy of opposites reconciled?

371 **21. 118 § 3.** *CN* ii. 2355. *AP* 96. 18–22 December 1804.
The imaginative poet as a Godlike tamer of the chaos of normal experience: a crucial Coleridgean idea. Cf. his remarks on the '*Ego*' and 'the principle of Co-adunation – without *it* every where all things were a waste – nothing, &c' (336); and cf. 'a Poet cannot be a *great* Poet but as being likewise & inclusively an Historian and Naturalist in the Light as well as the Life of Philosophy. All other men's Worlds (κοσμοι) are *his* Chaos' (*CM* iv. 161–2).

3. them: i.e. 'Fancy, Imagination, Superstition'. A harmonious exertion of several faculties in unified concert: cf. 'The poet, described in *ideal* perfection, brings the whole soul of man into activity, with the subordination of its faculties to each other, according to their relative worth and dignity', etc. (*BL* ii. 15–16). Protoplasts: i.e. first or original shapers, Gods. (See 11.)

372 **21. 119ᵛ § 1.** *CN* ii. 2360. *AP* 102. 18–22 December 1804.

373 **21. 120 § 1.** *CN* ii. 2367. 22 December 1804.
Written in a very large, evidently drunken hand. An awareness of weakness ('the injured mind') accompanies a description of powers in many Coleridgean writings, exemplarily 'Dejection: An Ode'.

374 **21. 120 § 2.** *CN* ii. 2368. 23 December 1804.
2–3. The sentence gets waylaid: the sense is 'I wrote it after being convulsed', etc.

7. One relief that lasted: he told Charles Cowden Clarke shortly before his death that 'he never in his life knew the sensation of head-ache; adding, in his own peculiarly vivid manner of illustration, that he had no more internal consciousness of possessing a head than he had of having an eye' (*IR* 209).

7–8. weaker-bowelled : weak-bowelled *CN*.

15. In 'Dejection', 'viper thoughts . . . coil around my mind' (l. 94: *CPW* i. 367). His anxiety about alcohol merged with his self-hatred about opium. STC's addiction to opium has spawned an immense literature of its own: the incomprehension of his age about the psychology of addiction was disastrous, leading to a tragi-comedy in which signs of withdrawal were misinterpreted as symptoms of the self-diagnosed diseases which the opium was intended to alleviate. Molly Lefebure's *Samuel Taylor Coleridge: A Bondage of Opium* (1974) is a full-scale biographical interpretation of the artist as opium addict. The guilt induced by opium-taking is serpentine elsewhere: he adds, 'never was I led to this wicked direful practice of taking Opium or Laudanum by any desire or expectation of exciting *pleasurable* sensations; but purely by *terror*, by cowardice of pain, first of mental pain, & afterwards as my System became weakened, even of bodily Pain' (*CL* iii. 491).

375 **21. 121 § 1.** *CN* ii. 2370. *AP* 102–3. 25 December 1803.
David Hume (1711–76) was repeatedly one of STC's philosophical targets: he had a large part scheduled in the unwritten *History of Metaphysics in England*, where he was to be 'besprinkled copiously from the fountains of Bitterness and Contempt' (*CL* ii. 928). STC's antagonism was inspired partly by the 'impious and pernicious tenets' of Hume's religious scepticism (*BL* i. 291), and partly, as here, by the portrait of the mind in his *Treatise of Human Nature* (1739–40).

1. e.g. 'For the same reason, that the year 1737. cannot concur with the present year 1738. every moment must be distinct from, and posterior or anterior to another. 'Tis certain then, that time, as it exists, must be compos'd of indivisible moments' (*Treatise* I. ii, § 2).

7. unübersehbar: i.e. 'immense, unbounded'.

8. *Light*-point (and 'Licht-punct', i.e. 'Lichtpunkt', below): that part of a scene or a painting to which attention is primarily drawn by its illumination, as the face in a dark Rembrandt self-portrait.

11. Lichtpun[k]t : Lichtpunct *MS*. Literally, 'point of light'.

12. The passage goes on to describe his room in the Treasury.

376 **21. 121ᵛ § 1.** *CN* ii. 2371. *AP* 103. 25 December 1804.

377 **21. 121ᵛ § 1.** *CN* ii. 2372. *AP* 103–4. 25 December 1804.
A fine piece of self-portraiture; but also an important statement of the rival claims made by sameness and difference on the human intelligence. For the place of this rivalry in his thinking about art, see 497.

3. [than] there : than *CN*.

11–12. An aspiration to see all subsumed into the whole, and ultimately into the unity of God, 'At once the Soul of each, and God of all' ('The Eolian Harp', l. 48: *CPW* i. 102), grants everything—in STC's phrase—'a portion as it were of His Omnipresence' (*LambL* i. 53); but this may emphasize the oneness of the world at the expense of something *also* dear to STC, the apprehension of its multiplicity.

12–15. A cod-physiological explanation: his brain makes connections promiscuously with 'all things', seeking out points of similarity and sameness, rather than discriminating differences.

13–14. STC's early interest in animal luminescence, including (as here) luminescent putrefaction, is traced in Ian Wylie, *Young Coleridge and the Philosophers of Nature* (Oxford, 1989), 145–51.

16. likenesses : likenessnesses *MS*. (like~~ness~~nesses *CN*.)

24–6. The opinion, perhaps, of Underwood and Mackenzie, disenchanted assistants in the Maltese Treasury, who reportedly claimed years later that 'there was more humbug in Coleridge than in any man that was ever heard of' (*IR* 101).

378 **21. 122ᵛ § 1.** *CN* ii. 2373. *AP* 104–5. 25–7 December 1804.
More of the case against associationism, this time betrayed by STC's own associative habits into self-reproach.

379 **21. 123 § 2.** *CN* ii. 2375. *AP* 106. 25–7 December 1804.
An important entry for the dating of STC's readings in German philosophy. STC read Johann Nicolaus Tetens (1736?–1807) while on Malta (*CM* v. 824–9): for the possible impact on his thinking about imagination, see Thomas McFarland, *Originality and Imagination* (Baltimore, 1985), 100–19. He had translated a passage from the *Wissenschaftslehre* (1794) of Johann Gottlieb Fichte (1762–1814) in a letter to DW in 1801, at least partly as a joke about its obscurity (*CL* ii. 673–4; and see *CM* ii. 596–646). (For Kant, see 140 n.) Fichte is applauded in *BL* as the first who, writing in the wake of Kant, placed the innate creativity of the 'I' (rather than the reality of the external world) at the starting-point of philosophy, so 'commencing with an *act*, instead of a *thing* or *substance*'—the downside of this same emphasis being an insistence on the 'I' so great that the system 'degenerated into a crude egoismus, a boastful and hyperstoic hostility to NATURE, as lifeless, godless, and altogether unholy' (i. 158; 158–9).

1. Work : works *AP*, *CN*. The 's' is little more than a dot, and a singular 'work' makes as good sense; but the reading is not indisputable. Does STC mean his works in general, or a specific volume?

11. quoted : quoted so [?] *MS*. The upstroke of the 'd' curls round to some purpose.

380 **21. 124 § 2.** *CN* ii. 2378. *AP* 106–7. 25–7 December 1804.
Cf. 'Hast thou ever raised thy mind to the consideration of EXISTENCE, in and by itself, as the mere act of existing? Hast thou ever said to thyself thoughtfully, IT IS! heedless in that moment, whether it were a man before thee, or a flower, or a grain of sand? Without reference, in short, to this or that particular mode or form of existence? If thou hast indeed attained to this, thou wilt have felt the presence of a mystery, which must have fixed thy spirit in awe and wonder' (*F* i. 514).

4–6. The philosophical materialism that STC associated with the mercantile spirit of the United Kingdom (see 407) finds 'yourself' to be a contradiction because (in STC's view) it has no argument for the continuity and integrity of the self at all: the empiricist self dissolves into the elements of its worldly experience, rather as the Unitarian God dissolves into the plurality of his Creation. (See 195 n.)

381 **21. 126ᵛ § 1.** *CN* ii. 2396. *AP* 108–9. 9–11 January 1805.
1. The top of the page is cut off. *CN* makes out 'learnt' before 'not'. *AP* begins, obviously with some reconstructive surgery: '[I] have learnt, sometimes not *at all*, and seldom *harshly* . . .'

6. parts : part *CN*. There seems a firm gesture at an 's'. o o o : i.e. 'the many'. The quotation is 'Thus he that overrul'd I overswayed, | Leading him prisoner in a red rose chain': Shakespeare, *Venus and Adonis*, ll. 109–10. Shakespeare's poem serves to exemplify the imagination's momentary freedom ('off-starts'), yet freedoms combined (like individual movements within a dance) with a sense of the controlling purpose of the overall form: it is a point STC made earlier by the figure of the serpent (see 104). For his important lecture notes on the poem, see 449, 451.

8–9. Alexander Geddes (1737–1802), Catholic author of a translation of the Bible.

9. The Latin means 'Yesterday, I saw the frail break; today the mortal die'—the (untraced) text, presumably, that STC had attempted to defend to Geddes.

382 **21. 127 § 1.** *CN* ii. 2398. 11 January 1805.
Page 127 of the Notebook is currently bound out of sequence, after 134.

6. The 'itch' is scabies: along with ringworm, the subject of STC's first recorded poem (*IR* 4).

7. 'Duns' are importunate creditors: Eric Partridge, *A Dictionary of*

Slang and Unconventional English (5th edn.; 2 vols.; 1963), i. 248. STC fell badly into debt at Cambridge, partly (he maintained) because of the expense of having his rooms furnished by unscrupulous tradesmen (*GLC* 41–2).

8–9. Mary Evans was STC's first sweetheart, with whom he evidently remained much in love ('She ws VERY LOVELY, Southey! We formed each other's minds – our ideas were blended') even as RS was pressing him to marry SC (*CL* i. 112–13; 123; 145). There was a sad later meeting, her marriage having proved as unhappy as his (*CL* iii. 91).

14. The Pantisocratic scheme finally collapsed in acrimony when RS came into an annuity and rethought his position on private property: 'O Selfish, money-loving Man! what Principle have you not given up?' (*CL* i. 171).

30–2. A simple code (1=a, 2=b, 3=c, etc.: see *CN* ii. 2383). The passage here works out as: '[eunuchs] – in all degrees even to the full [ensheath]-ment and the [both] at once.' I take it he resorts to code when making reference to the sensitive subject of bilateral castration (which produces castrati singers).

383 **21. 131 § 1.** *CN* ii. 2407. *AP* 115. 17 January 1805.
Cf. 'Johnson's style has pleased many from the very fault of being perpetually translateable; he creates an impression of cleverness by never saying any thing in a common way' (*LL* ii. 237). *BL* announces as 'the infallible test of a blameless style . . . *untranslatableness*' (ii. 142; cf. i. 23).

384 **21. 132ᵛ § 1.** *CN* ii. 2414. *AP* 116–17. 23–8 January 1805.
9. After resurrecting the archaic 'agnized' (*OED* cites Cowper using it), STC returns to write in as a gloss the German word 'anerkennt' (i.e. 'anerkannt': 'recognized').

11–12. The phrase is muddled by STC's additions, '*pains correlative*' being written in twice; but his intention seems clear.

13. 'often' replaces his first thought, 'once'.

385 **17. 1ᵛ § 3.** *CN* ii. 2431. *AP* 118–20 (in part). 4–7 February 1805.
This is among the earliest entries in Notebook 17, which STC turned to as Notebook 21 (the book Cottle had given him in 1797) was finally filled up—as he thought anyway (but see below: 446, 447). STC has written throughout the book, in the topcorners of the pages, 'Coleridge' and '*ΣΑΡΑ*' (with some variations): see *CN* ii (n.), pp. xxiii–xxiv.

A great swooping meander of an entry, which begins with an immense pile of preambulatory phrases ('That . . . that . . . that'), before finding its main verb in line 29 ('all this I can fully comprehend . . .').

8–9. The facility the German language enjoys to make 'compound epithets . . . approaches to the Greek' (*BL* ii. 89 n.)—'It is hardly possible to conceive language more perfect than Greek', STC says in *TT* (i. 301).

12. falernian strength: i.e. the strength of the famous Falernian wine from Campania in Italy. (For the capacity of wine to bring forth articulate power, see 525.)

19. *tri-unely*: i.e. as three-in-one, like the Trinity—here, meaning, image, and passion at once.

21–9. STC took a robustly low view of all things French, including its language, which intensified with age into something of an act: '"I hate," he would say, "the hollowness of French principles: I hate the republicanism of French politics: I hate the hostility of the French people to revealed religion: I hate the artificiality of French cooking: I hate the acidity of French wines: I hate the flimsiness of the French language: – my very organs of speech are so anti-Gallican that they refuse to pronounce intelligibly their insipid tongue"' (*IR* 268–9). In *TT* French is said to have lost its poetical capacity by over-developing its abstraction (*TT* i. 75).

29. STC's footnote sign leads to a later addition (not included in this selection) some pages further on in the Notebook, concerning the connection of 'manners' and 'morals'.

37–8. WW's poetry had struck STC at once (he later claimed) for its 'union of deep feeling with profound thought' (*BL* i. 80).

39. STC's footnote sign (the circle) leads to the additional note: here, beginning on line 86.

42–3. The 'particularized' description of Burns's that STC most frequently adduced was from 'Tam o'Shanter', ll. 61–2: ' . . . like the snow falls in the river – | A moment white, then melts for ever' (*F* ii. 74; *BL* i. 81)—a simile which, he claimed, he would rather have written than all Scott's poetry (*IR* 143). STC's early praise for WW singled out 'manly sentiment, novel imagery, and vivid colouring' (*CPW* i. 97 n.); and in *BL*, WW is associated with a Burnsian excellence, reawakening a particular attention to 'forms, incidents, and situations, of which, for the common view, custom had bedimmed all the lustre, had dried up the sparkle and the dew drops' (i. 80).

46. STC's square brackets: he closes them in line 64.

48–57. STC attempted to distinguish between fancy and wit elsewhere: Crabb Robinson attended a lecture in 1811 in which STC also tried to establish their difference 'not very clearly' (*IR* 151).

48. be, that : be, [that *MS*. A square bracket inked in heavily, possibly on re-reading, to try and establish some order: it seems more a mark of emphasis than the beginning of yet another parenthesis, and does not appear to have a closing partner.

52. STC's square-brackets-within-square-brackets: this parenthesis is quickly closed, in line 54.

53. res illustrate : i.e. 'thing illustrated'.

64. STC has written 'end' in afterwards. The rest of the entry, down to 'just and true' (line 85), is lightly crossed through.

66. a dozen Lines : a dozen a Lines *MS*.

69. move : moved *CN*.

72. having less : having a less *CN*. The article has been crossed out, I think.

77. STC first wrote '*dramatic poetry*', then crossed out '*tic*'.

78–80. A union of inner and outer worlds which STC had long held an excellence: sonnets, for instance, 'create[d] a sweet and indissoluble union between the intellectual and the material world' (*CPW* ii. 1139).

81–2. Shakespeare, Sonnet 33, ll. 1–2.

84. Shakespeare, Sonnet 86, l. 1. An illustration, that is, of images combined with images, as the former quotation exemplified images combined with the intellectual (or mental), '*flatter*' a projection from the mind onto the material scene. In *BL* the same illustration is quoted as evidence of Shakespeare's power to give 'a dignity and a passion to the objects which he presents' (ii. 23–4).

91–6. From Schiller, 'Die Worte des Glaubens' , as noted in *CHH* (35), where it is translated: 'And there is a God, a Holy Will is living, however the human will wavers. High above time and space the highest Thought lives and acts. While all revolves in eternal change, *one* steady spirit persists in this change.' (The emphasis on 'one' is STC's: the permanent One and the mutable many again.) Friedrich von Schiller (1759–1805), had been an object of admiration since STC thrilled at *The Robbers* in 1794 (*CL* i. 122) and wrote a sonnet to him (*CPW* i. 72–3); he later translated Schiller's plays (*CPW* ii. 598–811). M. J. Kooy writes suggestively about their kinship in 'The End of Poetry: Aesthetic and Ethical Investigations in Coleridge and Schiller', *Wordsworth Circle*, 26 (1995), 23–6.

101–3. Cf. 'The reader should be carried forward, not merely or chiefly by the mechanical impulse of curiosity, or by a restless desire to arrive at the final solution; but by the pleasureable activity of mind excited by the attractions of the journey itself' (*BL* ii. 14).

110–13. The monastery of Chartreuse, founded by St Bruno, is near Grenoble. STC's accents are not exactly done. Trans.: 'Here it is that Death and Truth raise their terrible torches; it is from this house, inaccessible to the world, that one passes to Eternity.'

111. Elevent : Elevant *CN*.

386 17. 10^v § 1. *CN* ii. 2433 (excerpt). *AP* 121–3. 4–7 February 1805.
An example of STC's close reading, mindful here of the poetic propriety of diction—one of the matters that would later feature in his criticism of WW in *BL*. The poem in question is written out a couple of pages earlier in the Notebook: 'To Mary' by William Cowper (1731–1800), a favourite poet with STC from early days (*CL* i. 279). The offending stanzas (ll. 9–20) read:

> Thy needles, once a shining store,
> For my sake restless heretofore,
> Now rust disused, and shine no more;
> My Mary!
>
> For though thou gladly wouldst fulfil
> The same kind office for me still,
> Thy sight now seconds not thy will,
> My Mary!
>
> But well thou play'dst the housewife's part;
> And all thy threads with magic art,
> Have wound themselves about this heart,
> My Mary!

2. Quere: i.e. 'quære', 'question'.

8. [are] : is *MS*.

14. *το καθολου* : *το καθολον* *MS*. The Greek properly means 'the whole' or 'in general': in this context, 'the overall effect'.

26. The dots are STC's.

387 17. 21^v § 1. *CN* ii. 2446. *AP* 121. 11 February 1805.
I not able : I am not able *CN*. (I not able *AP*.)

6–7. The close proximity of virtues and failings is often noted: see 285, 391.

388 17. 21 § 1. *CN* ii. 2448. 12 February 1805.
2. The Revd Samuel Horsley (1733–1806) disputed over Unitarian doctrine with Priestley: STC had been reading the controversy in 1802, by

which time he had already decided that Priestleianism and Christianity were incompatible (*CL* ii. 821).

6. STC's square brackets: he closes them in line 9.

6–9. A path from Priestley and Hartley, through Spinoza, and (through the agency of German idealism) into the clear light of Plato and St John: a spiritual progress which we often find STC describing.

14. The 'great essential' is the Incarnation: the assertion that Christ is God (and hence that God exists in Holy Trinity). STC's efforts to bring himself to a full assent in this position (not merely an 'intellectual or spiritual' awareness of it) were protracted.

16. to him : to *him CN*.

20. their: that is, 'historical' and 'intellectual' Christianity. An abstract faith in the logos (the Word, the second person of the Trinity) is less difficult than a faith in the incarnation of God in Jesus—an embarrassment that theologians call 'the scandal of particularity'.

389 17.25 § 2. *CN* ii. 2453. *AP* 125. 16 February 1805.
A few pages after an intent embracing of Trinitarianism, evidence of the cast of mind that had so attracted STC toward Unitarianism and Spinozism: the sense of divinity adhering to the objects of nature. See *CPT*, *passim*, but particularly 251–3.

11. Sabeism: i.e. Sabaism, the worship of the stars (*OED*).

390 17.30[v] § 1. *CN* ii. 2470. *AP* 121. 4–8 March 1805.

391 17.30[v] § 2. *CN* ii. 2471. *AP* 166–7; 127. 4–8 March 1805.
1. That is, Notebook 21: see 257.

9. Samuel Richardson (1689–1761), author of *Pamela; or Virtue Rewarded* (1740) and *Clarissa* (1748). STC later compared them (*TT* i. 496) unfavourably with 'the charming . . . wholesome' novels of Henry Fielding (1708–54), author of *Joseph Andrews* (1742) and *Tom Jones* (1749), the first beginning as a parody of Richardson, and the second written in a spirit pointedly counter to his novels (and much to Richardson's distaste).

11–12. The sense is: to portray the mixed complexity of Richardson's personality would be a feat of characterization worthy of Richardson himself.

392 17.34[v] § 2. *CN* ii. 2482. 8 March 1805.

393 17.34 § 3. *CN* ii. 2483. 9 March 1805.

394 17.35 § 1. *CN* ii. 2484. *CHH* 149–50. *AP* 128. 16 March 1805.
9. Cowper, *The Task*, I, ll. 169–71: 'While far beyond and, overthwart the

stream | That, as with molten glass, inlays the vale, | The sloping land recedes into the clouds'.

10. Shakespeare's : Shakespere's *CN*. (But the writing is scrawly.) The reference is obscure: *CN* finds a likely compound of tags from *1 Henry IV*, *Antony and Cleopatra*, and elsewhere. It is not quite clear what is being quoted even: in *MS* there is a quotation mark after 'wits' (or before 'applied'), but no visible partnering mark.

395 17. 38 § 1. *CN* ii. 2495. 21 March 1805.

4. The code remains impenetrable—indeed, some of the letters and number '9' are not at all certain. Might '*Mss*' suggest 'Miss'?

5. Their : There *MS*.

11. STC's footnote sign: the passage indicated begins, here, at line 17.

17. Hercules : his first thought (crossed out) was 'Jupiter'.

19. The entry goes on, self-laceratingly, to the subject of SH.

21–2. mean to me : me and to me *CN*. concentered : concentrated *CN*. The writing is crushed into the bottom of page 39 and not very clear, so my readings are tentative; but the 'd' of 'and' is elusive, and the spacing of the letters allows 'mean' (which corresponds to 'great and good' nicely enough).

23. symbolical sense: i.e. the physical sense most important to the person—as, for most normally sighted people, vision. Perceiving becomes 'narcissine' when objects are only significant once associated with our mental appropriation of them: cf. the early sentiment, 'There is one species of egotism which is truly disgusting . . . that which would reduce the feelings of others to an identity with our own' (*CPW* ii. 1136).

396 17. 44[v] § 1. *CN* ii. 2516. *AP* 153–4. 1 April 1805.

5. old –)[. T]wo kinds : old –) two kinds *MS*.

11. reconciled with : reconciled to with *MS*.

12. 'Edwina and Angelina' is a ballad from Oliver Goldsmith's *The Vicar of Wakefield* (1766).

397 17. 45 § 1. *CN* ii. 2517. 1 April 1805.

The page is apparently tear-stained. John Wordsworth (1772–1805) impressed everyone by his undemonstrative intensity: 'Your Br. John is one of you', STC told DW, 'a man who hath solitary usings of his own intellect, deep in feeling, with a subtle Tact, a swift instinct of Truth & Beauty' (*CL* i. 543). The *Earl of Abergavenny*, his ship, was wrecked off Portland Bill on 5 February 1805: John's conduct was exemplary. See Richard Matlock, 'Captain John Wordsworth's Death at Sea', *Words-*

worth Circle, 31 (2000), 127–33. The impact on his siblings was devastating: see Stephen Gill, *William Wordsworth: A Life* (Oxford 1989), 239–41.

2. in his : in in his *MS*. STC writes 'in' at the bottom of one page and the top of the next.

10–11. the Brother : His Brother *CN*.

17. whom I in : whom ~~I~~ in *CN*.

19. like a hollow : like an hollow *CN*.

21. O Christ : the words are deleted but still just discernible.

30. The entry breaks off as the next two pages have been cut out of the Notebook.

398 15. 70 § 1. *CN* ii. 2518. 2 April 1805.
1. leaves of the figures : leaves. Of the figures *CN*.

399 15. 70 § 2. *CN* ii. 2519. 2–4 April 1805.

400 17. 50 § 1. *CN* ii. 2526. *AP* 129–30. 5 April 1805.
16. Manufacturies : Manufactures *CN*. Is there some sign of an 'i' being dotted (by analogy with 'Manufactories', in 385)?

401 17. 51 § 1. *CN* ii. 2527. 6 April 1805.

402 17. 61^{v} § 1. *CN* ii. 2537. *AP* 132–3. 8 April 1805.
9. The previous year, the East India fleet had engaged successfully with a larger French contingent under Linois.

403 17. 67^{v} § 1. *CN* ii. 2543. 10–13 April 1805.
Anxieties over day-dreams about SH perhaps?
18. In fact, 'desecrated' looks like 'desacrated' in *MS*.

23. ὑλή means here something like 'stuff', 'material', 'unformed matter', glossed here as 'disorder, suffering, termination', and opposed to 'Reason, Action, and "forming form"'.

24. The square brackets are STC's: the explanation of his symbols has been added at a later date in a smaller hand. For streamy association and evil, see 293.

404 17. 69 § 1. *CN* ii. 2545. 14 April 1805.

405 17. 69 § 2. *CN* ii. 2546. *GL* 311; *AP* 136–7. 14 April 1805.
An important entry, illustrating (among other things) the importance of the idea of symbol: the objects of nature serve as a symbolical language, not (as the Unitarian STC maintained) because God is somehow immanent within them, but because they seem to represent a something divine within the human percipient. Cf. 'the material universe which splendent, as it is, is yet but the faint resplendence of that intellectual world, that

already is in us essentially, and which we thus behold only as it is in us' (*CN* iii. 3941). For some suggestive introductions to the Coleridgean symbol, see L. C. Knights, *Further Explorations* (1965), 155–68; and Douglas Brownlow Wilson, 'Two Modes of Apprehending Nature: A Gloss on the Coleridgian Symbol', *Publication of the Modern Language Association of America*, 87 (1972), 42–52.

8. λογος: i.e. Logos, the Word, the second person of the Trinity (as John 1: 1–5). The Logos was to become the centre of STC's theological speculations: he announced his (unforthcoming) treatise on the subject in *BL* (i. 136). 'and the Evolver!' has been added subsequently.

10. A new page, and only dubiously the same entry.

11. [?] : [? &/a] *CN*. Undecidable.

17–18. STC's sensitivity to the entanglements of perceived intellectual indebtedness anticipates the long posthumous controversy about this plagiarism (or so-called 'plagiarism', depending on your position). The fiercest recent case against is Norman Fruman, *Coleridge, the Damaged Archangel* (1972), which should be read in conjunction with the first chapter of *CPT*; and see John Beer, 'How Far Can We Trust Coleridge?', *Wordsworth Circle*, 20 (1989), 79–84.

406 17.76 § 1. *CN* ii. 2557. *AP* 143. 17–21 April 1805.

4. After 'healthy!', STC has returned to write, in a smaller hand between the lines: 'And who can long remain body-crazed, & not at times use unworthy means of making his Body the fit instrument of his mind? Pain is easily subdued compared with continual uncomfortableness – and the sense of stifled Powers! – O this is that which made poor Henderson, Collins, Boyce, &c &c &c – *Sots!* – awful Thought – O it is horrid! Die my Soul, die! – Suicide – rather than this the worse state of Degradation! It is less a suicide! S.T.C.'   stifled Powers! : stifled Power! *CN*. Henderson (see 45 n.) and Samuel Boyse (1708–49) were both helped toward premature graves by drink; William Collins (whom STC admired: see 39 n.) was troubled by insanity rather than alcoholism.

6. 'They raised their limbs like lifeless tools – | We were a ghastly crew': 'The Ancient Mariner', ll. 339–40: (*CPW* i. 200).

10. A line and a half have been deleted.

18. Ideas and Impressions feature in the opening pages of Hume's *Treatise of Human Nature*.

407 17.80 § 1. *CN* ii. 2598. *AP* 150–2. May–June 1805.

1. That is, the sub-Shakespearian mannerisms of playwright August von Kotzebue (1761–1819).

11–12. The centrality of Shakespeare, Milton, and WW in STC's literary thought hardly needs noting. His admiration for Philip Sidney (1554–86) is evident in several places (see 512); Edmund Spenser (?1552–99) is praised in *BL* for possessing 'a mind constitutionally tender, delicate, and, in comparison with his three great compeers, I had almost said, *effeminate*' (i. 36; and cf. *CN* iii. 4501). Francis Bacon (1561–1626) was a great hero on the idiosyncratic grounds of his Platonism (*F* i. 483–93), he was celebrated by the opposition as a founder of the empirical method: even STC had to admit 'no man was ever more inconsistent' (*TT* i. 212). The inclusion of Jonathan Swift (1667–1745), intimate of Pope, is interesting: like Sidney, he was a second thought, his name added to the original list; unlike Sidney (or Spenser or Milton) he is not an obvious participant in any Platonic tradition (nor is he English). *Gulliver's Travels* and *Tale of a Tub* are preferred to the poetry in *BL* (i. 62–3); he appears to be the origin of STC's definitions of prose ('words in the best order') and poetry ('the best words in the best order') in *TT* (i. 90). STC held the political writings of James Harrington (1611–77) in high regard (*LS* 17; *BL* i. 54).

15–17. 'Mercy on the Age, & the People, for whom Lock [*sic*] is profound, and Hume subtle' (*CM* iv. 75). Most of the villains we have met before (including Hume, who was not English). STC's hostility to Alexander Pope (1688–1744) and his influence on the language and manner of eighteenth-century verse is a recurrent feature of the criticism (cf. *BL* i. 18–19). William Hayley (1745–1820) was a minor poet and man of letters; Henry Viscount Dundas (1742–1811) was sometime Pitt's Secretary of State for War.

19–20. Gottfried Wilhelm von Leibniz (1646–1716), philosopher and mathematician: Leibniz qualified the Lockean position, 'nihil est in intellectu, quod non prius in sensu' ('there is nothing in the mind that was not previously in the senses') with the addition 'præter ipsum intellectum' ('except the mind itself') (*BL* i. 141). His importance to STC is lucidly set out in *CPT* 137–47. Johann Heinrich Voss (1751–1826), made translations of Homer and Virgil which much impressed STC (*CL* iv. 655). For Lessing, see 82 n.

21–2. For STC's Dantesque enthusiasms, see 44 n. Lodovico Ariosto (1474–1553), author of *Orlando Furioso*, is warmly praised in passing in *F* i. 219. Giordano Bruno (*c*.1548–1600) earns a place in STC's pantheon in *BL* (i. 145–6): see Hilary Gatti, 'Coleridge's Reading of Giordano Bruno', *Wordsworth Circle*, 27 (1996), 136–45. In his lectures on European Literature, STC casts Miguel de Cervantes (1547–1616) as contemporary and counterpart to Shakespeare, and interprets the Don's relationship with

Sancho in *Don Quixote* as an allegory of the Reason's properly mutual relationship with common sense (*LL* ii. 159–66; and cf. *TT* i. 322–3).

23–4. Blaise Pascal (1623–62), Christian thinker and controversialist, and mathematician, whose *Provincial Letters* STC read in 1803 'O how eagerly!' and took with him to Malta (*CL* ii. 994; *CM* iv. 32). The playwright Molière (1622–73) escaped STC's general censure (along with Descartes, Pascal, and Malebranche) because his mind apparently enjoyed a predominance of Gothic elements over Celtic (*CM* iv. 78). STC placed Jeanne Marie Bouvier de Guyon (1648–1717), poet and mystic, alongside St Teresa as divinely 'inspired' (*Blake, Coleridge, Wordsworth, Lamb, etc.: Being Selections from the Remains of Henry Crabb Robinson*, ed. Edith J. Morley (Manchester, 1922), 33). STC's opposition to Voltaire, embodiment of French Enlightenment atheism, was implacable: 'scarcely any one has a larger share of my aversion' (*F* i. 131).

408 **17. 40 § 1.** *CN* ii. 2601. *AP* 156. May–June 1805.

1. The ψυεδο-poets: i.e. the false-poets. Thomas Campbell (1777–1844), author of *The Pleasures of Hope* (1799), which STC once tactlessly included in a list of regrettably popular 'poems – or things called poems', during a lecture at which Campbell was present. Samuel Rogers (1763–1855) was author of *The Pleasures of Memory* (1792), a poem devoted to the charm of associative recall, which was also (by implication anyway) on the list: Rogers was in the audience too (*IR* 155). STC had met Rogers just before setting off on the Scottish tour in 1803—'the envy, the jealousy, & the other miserable Passions, that have made their Pandaemonium in the crazy Hovel of that poor Man's Heart', his uncharmed response (*CL* ii. 964). 'Cottle' has been written over, but is still discernible.

5. Cf. Psalm 39: 3.

409 **16. 77v § 4.** *CN* ii. 2593. 24 May–3 July 1805

At once everywhere and nowhere, like God or Shakespeare (285, 338).

410 **16. 80 § 2.** *CN* ii. 2661. *AP* 150. 12 July–6 September 1805.

An exercise in analogy: as a particular watch is to time (as manifested in the movement of the sun and stars), so is an individual conscience to God.

2. a *Watch* : a Watch *CN*.

3. reason & goodness : reason and goodness *CN*.

411 **16. 91v § 2.** *CN* ii. 2703. 20 October 1805.

On 6 September, Chapman returned to his duties in Malta, and STC was free at last. He returned to Syracuse; thence to Naples; and reached Rome at the end of the year (*CMI* 360; 371; 376; 383–4).

1. [of] : of *CN*. The page has been damaged and repaired, but the reading seems obvious.

412 **16. 96 § 2.** *CN* ii. 2711. *AP* 149. 20 October–20 November 1805.
The point was addressed as early as the 1795 lectures: part of his Priestleian account of the corruptions of Christian doctrine described the way 'Metaphors [become] consolidated into realities' (*LPR* 202). One of STC's ambitions in the *Lay Sermons* would be to establish a much-needed 'medium between *Literal* and *Metaphorical*' in Biblical interpretation (*LS* 30).

413 **16. 96v § 1.** *CN* ii. 2712. *AP* 163. 20 October–20 November 1805.
'W.' is, presumably, WW (as assumed by *AP*). Simonides of Ceos (*c.*556–*c.*468 BC) was one of the most versatile and successful poets of ancient Greece; Empedocles (*c.*490–430 BC), philosopher and poet, committed suicide by throwing himself into the crater of Mount Etna. Simonides seems a precursor of WW. Thoughts of suicide were on STC's mind during this period: see 421.

414 **16. 100v § 2.** *CN* ii. 2726. *AP* 158–9. 20 November–15 December 1805.
5. An average would balance the friend's faults against his virtues and iron them out. Cf. STC's opposition to antithetical criticism (501).

415 **16. 102 § 1.** *CN* ii. 2728. *AP* 165. 20 November–15 December 1805.
2. Claudius Claudianus (*c.*370–*c.*408), the last great classical poet. STC spoke more appreciatively of him in *TT* i. 424.

4. Everything in a Chinese painting craves the attention due to the foreground.

416 **16. 105 § 3.** *CN* ii. 2784. 1 January 1806.
A fantastical, punning entry, but a meaningful one. 'Reor' is the Latin verb 'to think': STC's speculative etymology derives 'res' ('thing') from 'reor'—and, cognately, 'thing' from 'think'—so symbolizing in the history of the language the precedence of mind and active consciousness (over passive external things) that he admired in German and ancient idealist philosophies. That language itself might contain important philosophical clues is a habitual Coleridgean belief.

1. The Greek means: 'Body soul-shaped. Soul body-shaping' (*CN*).

3–5. The single word is an epic in miniature, memorializing the philosophies of Kant, Fichte, and Schelling, who themselves are reviving the ancient systems of Plato, Plotinus, and Proclus. Spinoza is keeping interesting company here: more normally, he represents the philosophical tradition against which German idealism reacted.

7. Pure whimsy—the English word 'tank' has nothing to do with the verb 'to think'; and remembering the German for 'tank' would have necessitated some nimble footwork to keep the thesis going. For another version of the idealist position that 'To think (Ding, denken; res, reor) is to *thing*ify', see STC's 1818 letter to DC, which also appeals to etymology—this time to 'thing' as 'The *Ing* . . . a somewhat set apart—thus *Ingle* = the Hearth' (*CL* iv. 885).

10. A cousin-german is a first cousin, with the additional joke here that the words so related are German: they are little Miss Thetas because they all start with 'th', in Greek, the letter theta—*Θ*.

13–14. The distinction between primary and secondary levels of consciousness is interesting: the dot in the middle of the Greek letter stands for the innate, pre-conscious consciousness, and the circle around it our self-aware mental activity: the combined exercise of both creates our experience—'Thought, Things, necessary Possibilities, contingent Realities'.

17. The Greek means 'Being, the Word, Wisdom', a Platonized Coleridgean version of the Trinity. After that crescendo, STC now begins a new theme, imagining the central dot of the theta as an inward breath and the ring as an outward: their combination in the whole letter enacts an entire breath, a synthesis of inner and outer.

21–2. A final spin: an infinite number of radii stretch from the central point of the theta to the outer circle. *Ακτινες* means 'rays' (in the sense of 'beams'), which also puns on 'res'. Delta and tau are other Greek letters; '*Αγω* (acta) *εν θητα*' presumably means 'to act in theta'; but as the letters begin to proliferate, even STC seems to have run out of energy.

22–7. The square brackets are STC's. The joke is that 'crotchet' is the name of a such a square bracket, besides meaning 'whimsical fancy' (*OED*): what the world at large takes to be the truth is what STC holds to be his position in unrecognizable disguise, what the world holds his fancies are his most profound beliefs. (The 'domino' costume, worn at masquerades, consisted of a mask and a long, dark cloak—from head to toe, that is 'cap-a-pie'.)

30–1. gesunder Menschenverstand: i.e. 'sound common sense'.

417 15. 85 § 1. *CN* ii. 2785. 1 January 1806.

Bonaparte's forces were moving closer, and the situation was becoming increasingly dangerous for any Britons left in Italy.

418 **16. 106v § 1.** *CN* ii. 2794. 15 February 1806.
STC befriended the American painter Washington Allston [*sic*] (1779–1843) while staying in Rome, and they remained friends through to Highgate days (see *IR* 102–4). STC's impact on Allston was immense; and Allston influenced him in return, prompting an interest in visual art (as in the next entry). STC's 'Essays on the Principles of Genial Criticism' (1814) were written (partly) to accompany an exhibition of Allston's paintings.

419 **16. 109v § 1.** *CN* ii. 2797. 15 February–8 March 1806.

420 **15. 97v § 1.** *CN* ii. 2832. 4 April–18 May 1806.
The fountains of St Peter's in Rome: the same unity of change and sameness that he had enjoyed in the waterfalls of Cumberland.
5. change. [T]he past : change. the past *MS*.

421 **16. 114 § 1.** *CN* ii. 2860. 7 June 1806.
STC finally left Rome on 18 May and travelled to Florence, hoping to cross into Germany: this proved impossible. By 7 June, he had reached Leghorn, a principal port for American ships (*CMI* 394–5; 396): STC was hoping he might find an American ship bound for England; which he did—the *Gosport* (*CL* ii. 1173; 1184–5). JC embellishes the story characteristically (*IR* 104–7).
13. if remembered : of remembered *CN*.
14. su[?ffocated wi]th : suffocated with *CN*. The words are covered with a stain.

422 **11. 3 § 1.** *CN* ii. 2873. 25 September–5 October 1806.
STC arrived back in England on 17 August, after a terrible voyage: 'I will come as soon as I can come', he wrote to RS (*CL* ii. 1176); but in the event he stayed down south. He finally wrote to SC (at Mary Lamb's insistence) on 16 September (*CL* ii. 1180–2). STC is reviving an earlier plan. Mary Lamb (1764–1847) lived with her brother CL, with whom she wrote *Tales from Shakespeare* (1807).
3. [of] : of *CN*.

423 **11. 48 § 1.** *CN* ii. 2890. *AP* 167. 5–16 October 1806.
Recalling Maltese days. John Stoddart (1773–1856), a friend of CL, was King's and Admiralty Advocate in Malta, and a man of literary interests (*CMI* 52, 33). It was Stoddart who seems first to have put the idea of Malta into STC's mind by inviting him out (*CL* ii. 977).
3. For a different, praiseworthy, kind of minute criticism, see 503.

424 11. 48ᵛ § 1. *AP* 167–8. *CN* ii. 2892. 5–16 October 1806.
Richard Price (1723–91), radical and Nonconformist, whose *Discourse on the Love of our Country* (1789) had provoked Burke's *Reflections on the Revolution in France* (1790). For Unitarianism as light without warmth, see 194.

425 11. 13 § 4. *CN* ii. 2905. 30 October 1806.
More than two months after arriving back in England from Malta, STC turned up at Greta Hall again. By late November, STC was writing to the Wordsworths saying that he and SC 'have *determined* to part absolutely and finally', adducing '[h]er temper, and selfishness, her manifest dislike of me (so far as her nature is capable of a *positive* feeling) and her self-encouraged admiration of Southey as a vindictive feeling in which she delights herself as satirizing me' (*CL* ii. 1200). The date in the entry has been underlined as though (*CN* remarks) recording some kind of epoch.

426 16. 116ᵛ § 1. *CN* ii. 2915. October–November 1806 (*CN*).
A strange allegory of obsessional memory: cf. his remarks on WW's mad mother (*BL* ii. 150–1).

8–13. The grammar goes slightly astray as STC forgets the 'as' with which he began.

13. sub-consciousness : subconsciousness *CN*. A coining, one of many in the Notebook. The word comes over a line-ending, so the hyphen may be meant, or merely the sign of a single word continuing. STC does not always (perhaps does not usually) bother with continuation-hyphens.

427 15. 114ᵛ § 1. *CN* ii. 2933. November 1806?
The relationship of good and evil again: now the optimism of his earlier position (e.g. 3) is subject to some mockery.

428 15. 114ᵛ § 2. *CN* ii. 2936. November 1806?

429 15. 114ᵛ § 3. *CN* ii. 2937. November 1806?
A return to an early image: the Eolian Harp was a wind-harp, to be placed in a sash-window, whose strings were coaxed into making a noise by the stirring of the breeze. STC uses it in 'The Eolian Harp' and 'Dejection: An Ode' (*CPW* i. 100–2; 362–8) as a symbol of the self. It is not STC's private property: Grigson calls it 'the prime romantic image' (*The Romantics*, ed. Geoffrey Grigson (1942), 342–3).

430 15. 114 § 4. *CN* ii. 2938. 28 November 1806.
1. Another name for SH: as *CN* glosses, 'the hoped-for'.

431 **11. 23^{v} § 1.** *CN* ii. 2987. February 1807.

432 **11. 23^{v} § 2.** *CN* ii. 2988. February 1807.
4. winds : wind~~s~~ *CN*.
7. by the meeting : by by the meeting *MS*.
12. one could conceive : one would could conceive *MS*.

433 **11. 29 § 1.** *CN* ii. 2999. February 1807.
Another exploration of levels of consciousness, including an implicit, divine life within, hidden beneath the mind of waking consciousness: cf. the 'primary Perception' in 453.

1. A Coleridgean pile-up of clauses complicates the main line of the sentence: 'that perpetual feeling, to which Imagination [*etc.*] has given a place . . .'

4. Shechinah: i.e. the visible manifestation of God, 'a glory or refulgent light symbolizing the Divine Presence' (*OED*).

8. th[at] : the *MS*.

434 **11. 33^{v} § 2.** *CN* ii. 3024. May 1807.
STC left London for the West Country in May, staying with TP in Nether Stowey (*CL* iii. 18–19).

435 **12. 5^{v} § 1.** *CN* ii. 3064. *AP* 175. May 1807?

436 **12. 40^{v} § 2.** *CN* ii. 3146. Autumn 1807?
STC had gone to stay with the Wordsworths (who were residing in Coleorton, on Sir George Beaumont's estate) in December 1806, and remained with them until the following spring, during which time WW's anxieties about him, and especially misgivings about the relationship with SH, were evidently growing and being voiced.

4. did I not : did I did not *MS*.

437 **12. 41^{v} § 2.** *CN* ii. 3148. 13 September 1807.
3. STC's brief career in the cavalry had been disastrous: see *IR* 18–25.

7. Cf. a letter of 1801: 'O me, my dear fellow! the notion of a Soul is a comfortable one to a poor fellow, who is beginning to be ashamed of his Body' (*CL* ii. 661), an emotion which gradually intensified.

22. The phrase in brackets has been written in between the lines: its position in the complete sentence is not obvious.

32–3. On the morning of 27 December 1806, STC believed he caught a glimpse of SH and WW engaged in some sort of intimate behaviour. He wrote 'The Epoch' in a large hand in the Notebook; but three leaves from the Notebook were later cut out, so if he was more explicit about what he saw, the information is lost: we know the sighting involved a bed. He would later frequently recur to it, retrospectively rationalizing it as phantasmal (*CN* ii. 2975 and n.). See Richard Holmes, *Coleridge: Darker Reflections* (1998), 83–5.

41, 47. Sara's name has been written over with other letters, evidently by STC himself (as *CN* says); but the words are still visible, especially in *J*.

41–3. The startling conviction that WW—whom STC considered '*all* man' (ambiguous praise)—had no disposition to love properly crops up several times (*TT* ii. 391; and cf. i. 206).

438 **12. 47ᵛ § 1.** *CN* ii. 3149. September 1807.

439 **12. 48 § 1.** *CN* ii. 3151. *AP* 184. September 1807.

440 **12. 48ᵛ § 2.** *CN* ii. 3153. September 1807.
For the eye altered similarly altering all, see 251.

441 **12. 30ᵛ § 1.** *CN* ii. 3175. *AP* 178. Autumn 1807?

442 **12. 32ᵛ § 2.** *CN* ii. 3182. *AP* 178. Autumn 1807?

443 **12. 33 § 1.** *CN* ii. 3184. *AP* 178. Autumn 1807?

444 **22. 84 § 3.** *CN* iii. 3232. 1807–10?
CN dates this winter 1807–spring 1808, though I suppose it might have emerged almost any time between the difficult return to the Wordsworth circle after Malta and the rupture with WW in 1810. The mood seems similar to entries in Notebook 12 (above) which appear to date from Autumn 1807.

445 **17. 82 § 1.** *CN* iii. 3238. *AP* 190. Early 1808?
Quere : Quære *CN*.

3. Words for 'man' in the non-gendered sense of 'human'.

9. STC has left out a word like 'opinion' or 'view'. etymon: i.e. the original or primary sense of a word.

446 **21. 59ᵛ § 4.** *CN* iii. 3267. *AP* 88. February 1808?
STC had arrived back in London on 23 November 1807; his first literary lectures, at the Royal Institution, began in January 1808: the second of them (5 February) offered a history of the stage, drawing on Malone's 'Historical Account of the Rise and Progress of the English Stage' (see *LL* i. 48–9 nn.). This entry looks like a sketch for a Pope-like satire on the duncery of editors, especially Edmond Malone (1741–1812), whose (genuinely important) edition first appeared in 1790. This entry appears

in *AP* in the chapter for 1804, and the page opposite has two entries dated 1805, one STC's record of leaving Malta (*CN* ii. 2675, 2676); but *CN* (iii. 3624 n.) argues plausibly that this entry is probably much later, February 1808 (the date given at the top of the next page)—STC is economically returning to fill in empty space. The third lecture turned to *Venus and Adonis* (*LL* i. 66–70; and see 449).

17. *Bur*glossa : *Bur* glossa *CN*. (The *CN* note reads 'Written almost as two words'.) The joke involves a nonce verb meaning something like 'to cling on like a bur', with (perhaps, as *CN* suggests) a swipe at Malone's Irish 'burr' (although *OED* restricts the application of the word to the Northumbrian dialect until later in the century). Maybe WW's idiot boy is there too ('Burr, burr – now Johnny's lips they burr', l. 97: *WPW* ii. 70). A 'gloss' is what Malone's heavily annotated edition supplied in abundance; *OED* also has 'Glossa', from Greek glòssa, as rarely meaning a foreign or obscure word requiring a definition.

19. The meaning of the word does not help much: the point seems to be merely the editors' rote repetition of 'Malone, Malone, Malone' (like reciting the genitive plural of a Greek adjective, the same for all the genders).

447 21. 60 § 3. *CN* iii. 3270. February 1808?

1. Robert Boyle (1627–91), chemist and natural philosopher. In *F* he appears in an eclectic list of 'the first-rate philosophers . . . Kepler, Milton, Boyle, Newton, Leibnitz, and Berkley' (i. 416).

448 25. 2^v § 1. *CN* iii. 3242. *LL* i. 65–6. 1808.

This and the following three entries are most probably associated with the first lecture series given by STC, in the Royal Institution, in the spring of 1808 (see *CN* iii (n), p. xxvii; *LL* i. 60–1). *CN* finds a source for the fourfold comparison of readers in John Donne's *Biathanatos*, a dissertation upon suicide.

5. dozing : dozeing *CN*. STC has changed 'dozes' into 'dozing'.

10–11. an ear-grievance : a near-grievance *CN*. The phrase is split over a line-ending, with little room for ambiguity.

17. The word 'trace' looks firmly like 'trase', which would be just possible, though archaic.

449 25. 6 § 1. *CN* iii. 3247. March 1808.

The first of two entries (STC's lecture notes) about Shakespeare's *Venus and Adonis*, examining it as evidence of his later poetic and dramatic genius: they should be read together, as the second (451) returns to expand revealingly upon the first. STC is noting within the poem the various evidence of later dramatic genius. An important entry, anticipating chapter xv of *BL*.

1–2. Cf. 'the first and most obvious excellence is the perfect sweetness of the versification . . . "The man that hath not music in his soul" can indeed never be a genuine poet' (*BL* ii. 20): and see *TT*, 'The characteristic merit of my verses is their musicalness' (i. 306). WW remembered STC as 'quite an epicure in sound': quoted in Christopher Wordsworth, *Memoirs of William Wordsworth* (2 vols.; 1851), ii. 306. Cf. with this entry, his complaint about modern poetry's anxiety to be *striking* (415).

5. Cf. 'A second promise of genius is the choice of subjects very remote from the private interests and circumstances of the writer himself' (*BL* ii. 20). That poetic genius (of a Shakespearian kind) is characterized by a kind of selflessness is a recurring thought: 'Genius may co-exist with wildness, idleness, folly – even crime – but not long with selfishness' (*TT* i. 91). (Milton's equal but opposite genius, however, was marked by 'intense egotism': *TT* i. 420.)

7. ll. 679–708: a passage which begins:

> And when thou hast on foot the purblind hare,
> Mark the poor wretch to overshut his troubles,
> How he outruns the wind, and with what care,
> He cranks and crosses with a thousand doubles,
>   The many musits through the which he goes,
>   Are like a labyrinth to amaze his foes.

The passage too lengthy to quote seems to have been the sprightly horses (ll. 259–318), which he did read in his 1811–12 lecture series (*LL* i. 243).

9. 13$^{th.p.}$: 13$^{th.sp.}$ *CN*. (13$^{th.p.}$ *LL*.) That is, page 13 of his copy (an example he used elsewhere):

> Full gently now she takes him by the hand,
> A lily prison'd in a jail of snow,
> Or ivory in an alablaster band,
> So white a friend engirts so white a foe:
>   This beauteous combat wilful, and unwilling,
>   Showed like two silver doves that sit a-billing. (ll. 361–6)

11. Fancy 'distinguished' from wit, perhaps.

14–15. WW, 'I wandered lonely', ll. 21–2 (*WPW* ii. 217). STC has omitted a phrase like 'described in the lines'.

20. often afterwards : often after afterwards *MS*.

23–5. The Principle and Fountain is God, whom Imagination emulates: cf. 371. Another favourite illustration (e.g. *LL* i. 243, *BL* ii. 25): 'Look how a bright star shooteth from the sky, | So glides he in the night from Venus' eye' (ll. 815–16). STC had distinguished between 'Fancy, or the aggregating Faculty of the mind' and '*Imagination*, or the *modifying*, and *co-adunating* Faculty' since 1802 (*CL* ii. 865; 866): for a doughty attempt to explain the fancy of the former passage, and the imagination of this, see I. A. Richards, *Coleridge on Imagination* (1934), 76–84; and for STC's own account, see 451.

26–8. The seventh point has been inserted subsequently. The passage alluded to is:

> Lo here the gentle lark, weary of rest,
> From his moist cabinet mounts up on high,
> And wakes the morning, from whose silver breast
> The sun ariseth in his majesty,
> Who doth the world so gloriously behold
> That cedar tops and hills seem burnish'd gold. (ll. 853–8)

31. *CN* cites chapter 4 of John Dennis's 'The Grounds of Criticism in Poetry' (1704) (*The Critical Works of John Dennis*, ed. Edward Niles Hooker (2 vols; Baltimore, 1939–43), i. 338–40) which distinguishes between the 'Passion' excited within ordinary life, and the elevated 'Enthusiasm' aroused by uncommon meditation, both of which are properly to be included in poetry: the former predominantly in dramatic works, the latter in odes and the invocations of epic.

34. 'Chapman's' is an obscure reference: does he mean to contrast Shakespeare's commitment to the drama with the less single-minded career of George Chapman (1559–1634), translator of Homer as well as playwright?

35. That is, a point to be made in the lecture before the rest. An unpleasing subject because about the goddess's unseemly desire.

40. In the 1800 note to 'The Thorn' WW had cited Judges 5: 12 ('Awake, awake, Deborah'), and verses 27–8, to illustrate the power of 'repetition and apparent tautology' (*WPW* ii. 513). STC approvingly adduces WW's appeal to the passage in *BL* (ii. 57).

41. Shakespeare 'darts himself forth, and passes into all the forms of human character and passion, the one Proteus of the fire and the flood . . . SHAKSPEARE becomes all things, yet for ever remaining himself' (*BL* ii. 27; 28).

450 **25. 9 § 1.** *CN* iii. 3287. March 1808.

2. The phrase is 'incidental' in its original appearance: having discussed

the place of rhetoric in the syllabus, Milton says that 'Poetry would be made subsequent, or indeed rather precedent, as being the lesse suttle and fine, but more simple, sensuous and passionate': 'Of Education', ed. Donald C. Dorian; in *Complete Prose Works of John Milton* (8 vols. in 10; New Haven, 1953–82), ii. 403.

16. Poetry is distinguished from works of science (in the sense of 'a branch of learning or study') in *BL* ii. 13.

19–20. Cf. 'The reader should be carried forward, not merely or chiefly by the mechanical impulse of curiosity, or by a restless desire to arrive at the final solution; but by the pleasurable activity of mind excited by the attractions of the journey itself' (*BL* ii. 14).

451 25. 13 § 1. *CN* iii. 3290. March 1808.
10. [as] : as *CN*. The word is beneath a blot.

15. STC's square brackets. Spenser is praised elsewhere for 'The indescribable sweetness of his verse distinguished from Shakspeare and Milton', and for the 'great character of his mind, Fancy under the conditions of Imagination, with a feminine tenderness & almost maidenly purity' (*LL* ii. 409; 411).

28–30. A passage singled out as distinctively representing the Imagination (as opposed to the Fancy) in *BL* (i. 85): 'Nor rain, wind, thunder, fire are my daughters. | I tax not you, you elements, with unkindness; | I never gave you kingdom, call'd you children; | You owe me no subscription' (III. ii., ll. 15–18).

32. operations : operation *CN*.

38–40. *Venus and Adonis*, ll. 815–16: see 449.

45. upon : over *CN*. The word is badly formed, but an initial 'u' is not unlikely.

45–6. STC's own lines, cited in *BL* (ii. 23) as 'a semblance of poetry', improving upon verse merely descriptive: 'Yon row of bleak and visionary pines, | By twilight-glimpse discerned, mark! how they flee | From the fierce sea-blast, all their tresses wild | Streaming before them.'

48. *Venus and Adonis*, ll. 853–8: see 449.

51–4. Cf. the praise for Milton's '*creation* rather than *painting*, or if painting, yet such, and with such co-presence of the whole picture flash'd at once upon the eye, as the sun paints in a camera obscura' (*BL* ii. 128). Cf. Darwin taking studies in 33.

452 14. 45^{v} 3255. *CN* iii. 3255. Spring 1808? (*CN*).
For STC's interest in bulls, see 261 n.

453 25. 19[v] § 1. *CN* iii. 3295. 1808?
The dating is very difficult: its juxtaposition with the next entry is not inappropriate. The 'unific Consciousness' is what he will call in *BL* the 'primary IMAGINATION . . . the living Power and prime Agent of all human Perception' (i. 304): it is that intrinsic activity of the mind that gathers the incoherence of sense data into the unity of individual experience. (The general debt is to Kant.)

2. extreme difficulty: i.e. the great obscurity of the subject.

8. notions : motives *CN*.

9. Epictetus (*c*.50–*c*.130), Stoic philosopher: STC quotes him obscurely in *BL*, advising that the study of words is the beginning of education (ii. 31).

10. *the effects* : the *effects CN*.

454 15. 120[v] § 1. *CN* iii. 3281. 24 March 1808.
Another attack against the materialists who, denying the reality of the spirit or the soul (and hence the conscience, as STC describes it), are less philosophers than they are apothecaries (and worse).

8–9. In fact, it was RS who said '*Metapothecaries*' sportively: 'your own most excellent word (for the invention of which you deserve a pension far more than Johnson for his Dictionary)' (*CL* ii. 767–8).

9. The prefix 'cata-' implies a derogatory diminution: here, 'sub-physicians'.

10–11. They are really '*passive*' because they emulate the kind of human being expounded in their philosophy, existing in a state of passive impressibility to outward impressions.

11–12. The prefix 'hypo-' has the sense, 'under, beneath', etc. Zoophyte was the term given to primitive creatures considered to occupy an indeterminate place between plant and animal: STC's jocular point is that only materialist man really occupies a contradictory place since he insists on the passivity of his being which (like all human beings) must really be innately and essentially creative.

455 15. 123[v] § 1. *CN* iii. 3285. Spring 1808?
1–4. Claudius's observation, from *Hamlet* IV. vii, ll. 114–15.

7–8. The monk (Naucratius, eulogizing St Theodorus Studita) is cited again in *BL* (ii. 19 n.) and again in the 1818 *Friend* (*F* i. 453).

456 20. 2 § 2. *CN* iii. 3314. *AP* 193. 16 May 1808.
STC had taken lodgings above the offices of the *Courier* in the Strand (*CL* iii. 36–7). Samuel Carter Hall recalled him telling a story about living

in a newspaper office in the Strand (he remembered it as the *Morning Post*) and leaving to 'the song of a caged lark . . . Thirty years had passed, but that unforgotten melody – that dear bird's song – gave him then as much true pleasure as when, to his wearied head and heart, it was the matin hymn of nature' (*IR* 282).

9. A return to an early metaphor. 'And what if all of animated nature / Be but organic Harps diversely fram'd . . .': 'The Eolian Harp', ll. 44–5 (*CPW* i. 102). See 429.

457 20. 2ᵛ § 1. *CN* iii. 3359. *AP* 194. 1808?
CN suggests this is not (as it seems in *MS*, and as *AP* presumes) a continuation of the previous entry, but a later thought.

458 21½. 8 § 2. *CN* iii. 3320. May(?) 1808.
A return to the mysterious interrelations of body and soul, here symbolized by a weight and a spring.

2. The Platonic opinion in question being, presumably, the hostility to the body found (for instance) in the *Phaedo*: 'So long as we keep to the body and our soul is contaminated with this imperfection, there is no chance of our ever attaining satisfactorily to our object, which we assert to be truth' (66b).

6–10. An old Coleridgean image—the body as an instrument (as in 'The Eolian Harp')—but now played upon, not by the movements of an external breeze, but by the inward musicianship of the soul. It is not unlike the position of which he had been so scornful in his youth, where the '"Soul" [is] a being inhabiting our body, & playing upon it, like a Musician inclosed in an Organ whose keys were placed inwards' (*CL* i. 278). Opium sharpens the tuning of the body-instrument, enabling the soul to articulate itself (to achieve its 'Epiphany') more perfectly.

12. STC has in mind 1 Corinthians 15: 39–58, where Paul, talking about human resurrection, distinguishes between 'a natural body' and 'a spiritual body'.

15. Arbitrement: i.e. the free will. (See 262 n.)

20. He uses the German elsewhere, mindful of the English word's possible ambiguity: see 539.

22. toward the increase : toward to the increase *MS*.

459 21½. 9 § 1. *CN* iii. 3321. May(?) 1808.
The Notebook's campaign against Johnson continues.

8. *CN* points to a passage in Boswell, where Johnson calls Leibniz 'as

paltry a fellow as I know': *Boswell's Journal of a Tour to the Hebrides . . .*, ed. Frederick Pottle and Charles H. Bennett (1936), 256.

9. Boswell felt obliged to defend Johnson against the charge of 'absurd credulity' regarding the existence of ghosts (*Life of Samuel Johnson, LLD* (Everyman edition; 2 vols.; 1906, repr. 1949), i. 251–2): his biography includes several instances of Johnson's evident fascination. For STC on ghosts see *F* i. 144–6.

460 **21½. 10 § 1.** *CN* iii. 3322. *AP* 195–7. 18 May 1808.
Another hand—identified by *CN* as Anne Gillman's—has written at the end of the entry, 'alas! alas!'

1. Daniel Stuart (1766–1846) was STC's editor, first at the *Morning Post* and then at the *Courier*.

15–17. The 'Night-mair' can affect equally, with or without recourse to imagery—as the self-destructive impulse will exert itself with or without the mediation of a recognizable motive.

30–5. The verse is based on a speech from STC's play *Remorse*, IV, ll. 68–73 (*CPW* ii. 861), not published (or performed) until 1813.

33. *stifled* with *fear* : *stifled with fear CN*.

461 **21½. 11 § 1.** *CN* iii. 3323. 18–20 May 1808.
A nice example of the Notebook's sometimes startling shifts in mood. The book in question had recently begun to appear: George Chalmers, *Caledonia: Or, an Account Historical and Topographic, of North Britain . . .* (1807–24).

462 **21½. 11 § 2.** *CN* iii. 3324. *AP* 197. 18–20 May 1808.
Anne Gillman (identified by *CN*) writes after this entry: 'ah me!' For STC's ghostliness, see 233 n.

8. analogon: i.e. 'analogy'.

9. STC's feelings of superior alienation from Mackintosh were well established (see 104): he once proposed that Mackintosh have written on his forehead, '"Warehouse to let"' (*TT* i. 42). The other people named are Richard 'Conversation' Sharp (1759–1835), critic and MP; Robert Percy ('Bobus') Smith (1770–1845), politician and wit—the undergraduate STC called him 'a man of immense genius' (*CL* i. 34); his brother Sydney Smith (1771–1845), co-founder of the *Edinburgh Review*, and the drollest man of his day; and Sir James Scarlett (1769–1844), later first Baron Abinger, whose courtroom eloquence STC praised in *TT* (i. 397).

11. For the other-worldly perspective of genius, cf. Shakespeare in *Venus and Adonis*: see 449.

463 21½. 12 § 1. *CN* iii. 3325. 18–20 May 1808.
An immense Coleridgean sentence loses its way in a list of the 'meaner passions' of egotism (from line 14), finally picking itself up for its main business at line 36 ('I say . . .'). The entry shows beautifully a wholly characteristic involvement of personal feeling, psychological speculation, and abstract thinking.

4. only once profaned: only once read by another? (SH?)

5. this last minute : the last minute *CN*.

9. The Greek is from πoθos: 'longing or yearning' (i.e. '*desiderium*').

11. For Berkeley's use of 'outness', see (for example) *Principles of Human Knowledge*, § 43: Berkeley's idealist argument is that the external placement of objects at various distances from us is not really a feature of the outward world, but rather a quality of our subjective perception. (STC retains the word within the much more nuanced idealism learnt from Kant and others.)

18. A rout was 'a fashionable gathering or assembly, a large evening party or reception, much in vogue in the eighteenth and early nineteenth centuries' (*OED*). Townshend was a celebrated Bow Street runner: no doubt a priceless guest at such an event.

32. 'himselves' is odd, but looks certain.

34. whose : whatose *CN*. STC wrote 'what', crossed through the last two letters, and wrote 'ose' above.

36. STC writes the words supplied here in square brackets in a cipher: see *CN*. (It is not clear to which incident STC is referring.)

40–1. And a phrase with Platonic credentials: in the *Symposium* Aristophanes explains how Zeus cut the original human beings (wondrous globular creatures with four arms and four legs) in two, leaving 'each half with a desperate yearning for the other', and so creating love, which 'is always trying to reintegrate our former nature, to make two into one' (189c–192d).

45. STC originally wrote 'sole unkind'—which might have interested so keen a theorist of the mind's subterranean purposes.

464 21½. 14 § 1. *CN* iii. 3326. 20 May 1808.
A reported anecdote, presumably.

465 21½. 17v § 4. *CN* iii. 3335. *AP* 280–1. May 1808?
2–3. STC recalls comparing Darwin's poetry to 'the Russian palace of ice, glittering, cold and transitory' in *BL* (i. 20).

5. [It] : It *CN*. The word is blotted.

7. Alluding to the proverb that STC uses again in *BL* (i. 159 and n.):

'All my eye and Betty Martin', or 'That's my eye, Betty Martin' (meaning, 'That's a lot of nonsense'). The strain-rhyme on 'sartain' sounds like it is making fun of an accent.

11–12. 'fructiferous' is in the *OED* ('fruit-bearing'); 'ramescent' (cf. 'ramifying') seems STC's invention.

13. typical of: i.e. 'a symbol of'.

17. scorbutic: i.e. 'scurvy'.

466 **21½. 18 § 1.** *AP* 199–200. *CN* iii. 3336.

5. Neighbour : Neighbor *CN*.

467 **21½. 18v § 2.** *CN* iii. 3339. *AP* 203–4. May 1808?

A nice example of STC's growing antipathy to nature: see 209 n.

468 **20. 7 § 1.** *CN* iii. 3342. *AP* 189. 1808?

469 **13. 52 § 2.** *CN* iii. 3352. Summer 1808?

3. *ωΠΜ.*: i.e. opium.

470 **13. 52 § 3.** *CN* iii. 3353. Summer 1808?

4–5. Mark 9: 23–4: 'Jesus said unto him, If thou canst believe, all things *are* possible to him that believeth. And straightway the father of the child cried out, and said with tears, Lord, I believe; help thou my unbelief.' STC's opium habit had become a burden like a possessing spirit.

471 **13. 49 § 1.** *CN* iii. 3356. August 1808.

472 **13. 49 § 2.** *CN* iii. 3357. 1 September 1808.

The new house was Allan Bank, which the Wordsworths had taken to accommodate their growing family, Dove Cottage having finally proved impracticable.

473 **13. 48v § 1.** *CN* iii. 3358. September 1808.

Presumably an idea for a piece in STC's new journal, *The Friend*, which began to appear the following June. (Was WW to write the essay, or was some work of his to exemplify the thesis? 'Michael'?)

474 **13. 31§ 1.** *CN* iii. 3383. September 1808.

A private address to SH? The return to the Wordsworth circle did not prove easy.

475 **13. 27v § 1.** *CN* iii. 3400. September–October 1808.

Another plan for the periodical (later renamed *The Friend*).

2. & thence : ~~&~~ thence *CN*.

476 **13. 17 § 1.** *CN* iii. 3420. November 1808–January 1809.
1. the thousandfold : one thousandfold *CN*.

477 **14. 45ᵛ § 1.** *CN* iii. 3449. 1809?
For STC's hostility to Gothic writing see his review of *The Monk* (*SWF* i. 57–65). He once protested in a letter: 'My head turns giddy, my heart sickens, at the very thought of seeing such books in the hands of a child of mine' (*CL* ii. 905). WW attacks 'frantic novels, sickly and stupid German Tragedies, and deluges of idle and extravagant stories in verse' in the 'Preface' to *Lyrical Ballads* (*WPrW* i. 128).

1. Ann Radcliffe (1764–1823), author of *The Mysteries of Udolpho* (1794) and other Gothic novels, including *The Italian* (1798), which STC reviewed rather kindly (*SWF* i. 79–82); and Matthew 'Monk' Lewis (1775–1818), author of *The Monk* (1796) and *The Bravo of Venice: A Romance Translated from the German of Johann Heinrich Zschokke*.

4. STC is objecting to the way Radcliffian Gothic couples the frisson of supernatural phenomena with the reassuring under-presence of a rational explanation for everything that occurs.

478 **24. 19 § 1.** *CN* iii. 3615. 1809 (*CN*).
A definition STC reworks in the second of his 1811–12 lectures (*LL* i. 205–7); and cf. *BL* ii. 13. The emphasis on representations 'in relation to human affections' is important: what he calls elsewhere 'Humanizing Imagery and Circumstance' (*CN* iii. 3246). *BL* says: 'images however beautiful, though faithfully copied from nature, and as accurately represented in words . . . become proofs of original genius only as far as they are modified by a predominant passion; or by associated thoughts or images awakened by that passion; or when they have the effect of reducing multitude to unity, or succession to an instant; or, lastly, when a human and intellectual life is transferred to them from the poet's own spirit' (ii. 23). See 451.

7. A phrase taken from Milton's *On Education*, which STC used several times as a short definition (see 450): 'It truly comprizes the whole, that can be said on the subject,' he told RS in 1802 (*CL* ii. 830).

479 **24. 21 § 2.** *CN* iii. 3626. 1809 (*CN*).
Addressed to WW? Or to SH?

480 **24. 22ᵛ § 1.** *CN* iii. 3628. 1809 (*CN*).
The difference between ancient realists (for STC, the Platonic tradition), who hold that abstract concepts and universals (like 'man') refer to some essence or idea, and nominalists (including modern materialists—'*true*

realists', I suppose, in that their philosophy is circumscribed by material 'reality'), who hold that such concepts are merely names with no corresponding objective referents. The Platonic tradition grants its adherents a 'System', investing nature with religious significance; the nominalist tradition abandons its non-thinking followers to a wilderness of unrooted verbalism.

12. whereas : where as *MS*.

481 **24. 24 § 1.** *CN* iii. 3659. *AP* 232. 1809–10 (*CN*).

482 **14. 16ᵛ § 1.** *CN* iii. 3636. 18 November 1809.
1. forms : forming *CN*. Very doubtful: the pencil is extremely faint, though a little clearer in *J*. The first letter of 'Mountains' is possibly an 'f'; but the matter is practically imponderable.

483 **14. 11 § 2.** *CN* iii. 3646. December 1809–Winter 1810?
1. tune : time *CN*. Not a well-formed word: either is possible.
3–4. The dislike of Johnson is frequently expressed. 'Junius' is the anonymous author of *Letters of Junius* (1769, *etc.*). The 'Scotch Translators' doubtless include Sir James Mackintosh and Jeffrey.

484 **18. 6 § 1.** *CN* iii. 3649. *AP* 150. Late 1809/early 1810 (*CN*).
The first of this selection to come from Notebook 18, which, like 16 and 17, has names inscribed in its pages' corners: '*ΣΑΡΑ*' and 'Coleridge' in the top corners of the inside front cover, 'William' and 'Dorothy' in the bottom corners, and, on the facing page, 'W+M+D = W' and 'Coleridge' at the top, and 'William' and 'Mary' at the bottom. (The inscriptions change through the Notebook; they are sometimes very elaborate, including his children's names, Latin epithets, and anagrams: see *CN* ii (n.), pp. xxv–xxvii.)
Cf. this entry with Margaret's 'shaping' eye in 'The Ruined Cottage', ll. 454–7: Jonathan Wordsworth, *The Music of Humanity* (1969), 46–7.

485 **18. 6 § 2.** *CN* iii. 3650. Late 1809/early 1810 (*CN*).

486 **17. 86ᵛ § 4.** *CN* iii. 3696. *AP* 223. January–June 1810?
In *BL*, STC offers qualified praise for Pope's translation of the *Iliad*, while deploring the artificiality and wit of his school, its '*conjunction disjunctive* . . . of epigrams' (i. 19; and cf. entry 343).

487 **17. 86ᵛ § 6.** *CN* iii. 3698. January–June 1810?

488 **17. 98ᵛ § 1.** *CN* iii. 3767. *AP* 255. January–June 1810?
4. prosilience: i.e. from 'prosilio', to jump up, spring forward.

489 14. 21ᵛ § 4. *CN* iii. 3692. 4 February 1810.
That dreams are a kind of visual language: 'exponent' here in the sense of that which symbolizes (as in *AR* 321, cited *OED*)—'the representative or *expression* (= the *exponent*)' (*AR* 233 n.).

7. 'Bœhmen' or 'Behmen' is the English version of Böhme: see 45 n.

9. infinity of : infinitely of *MS*.

490 18. 14 § 1. *CN* iii. 3718. Spring 1810.
A sentiment he found in Fulke Greville, *Alaham*, 1. i. 72 (*CN*): he quotes the line again in *LS* 144, though there as an exception to a general rule.

491 18. 14 § 3. *CN* iii. 3720. *AP* 223. Spring 1810.
STC frequently recited 'Christabel' (to the Beaumonts, for instance: *IR* 93–4), and evidently gave much thought to finishing it; but the poem eventually appeared, in its fragmentary state, in 1816.

492 18. 16ᵛ § 2. *CN* iii. 3731. Spring 1810.
STC had mentioned to RS in November 1809 the prospect of a new volume of poems (*CL* iii. 261): this looks like a memo for it.

493 18. 17 § 4. *CN* iii. 3737. *AP* 148. Spring 1810.
It was a favourite Coleridgean observation that appeals to self-evident 'fact' were often wholly untrustworthy (cf. *CN* ii. 2122).

The Fracastorius book he refers to has a long passage in a chapter 'De sympathia et antipathia rerum', listing bizarre 'facts' of different kinds (that even mild bulls become maddened when tied to a fig tree, and the like: *CN* translates a page); the 'Alchemy' book would presumably have contained similarly weird material.

494 18. 20 § 1. *CN* iii. 3743. Spring 1810.
A scarcely concealed apologia for his own Unitarian past, and a statement of his later view, that belief in the Trinity was an inward act ('turning the mind in upon itself'), rather than the product of analytical reasoning.

4–8. Common logic, which governs our knowledge of the material world, allows things to be either singular or multiple, and comprehends them within the forms of time and space: the mistake is to apply such habits of thought to God and Soul, which evade them. Cf. 'A thing cannot be one and three – *at the same time.* True! – but Time does not apply to God' (*CN* iii. 3973).

9. Deity : Duty *CN*.

18–19. His early relationship with RS?

24–5. The apparently clear truths of Unitarianism are merely the spurious translation into concepts of material images. An important shift in STC's opinions: 'A whole Essay might be written on the Danger of *thinking* without Images,' he told his philosophical patron Josiah Wedgwood in 1800 (*CL* i. 646); but, as he aged he grew more attracted to Pythagoras and Plato, whose systems were expounded in non-visual terms of arithmetic and musical harmony (cf. *CN* iii. 4436).

24. metathesis: transposition.

31. catechumens: i.e. those preparing for confirmation in the Church.

33–4. Cf. his later advice: 'There must be Reflection – a turning in of the Mind on itself' (*CL* v. 517).

35. in *posse*: i.e. 'in potential' (as opposed to *in esse*).

38–9. The Greek means 'to behold one's face in a glass', and 'to look into the perfect law of Liberty', phrases adapted from the Epistle of James (1: 23, 25).

40–1. The delayed last item on the list of causes for Socinianism: that the Bible itself is sufficient basis for religious doctrine (a position STC associated with the theologian William Chillingworth [*sic*], whose works he was annotating in 1809: *CM* ii. 24–31). The Bible makes no unambiguous case for the Trinity.

495 **18. 108v § 2.** *CN* iii. 3820. Spring 1810.

4. For *belles esprits*, see 134 n.

5. For STC's enthusiasm for Platonic and neoplatonic writers, see 500.

6. *abile*: i.e. 'skillful'.

496 **18. 115 § 1.** *CN* iii. 3826. *AP* 218. Spring 1810.

Spring cleaning. Observers often noted the immense quantities of snuff STC took (e.g. *IR* 172, 255, 287). In this entry, he spells SC's Christian name in its pre-Coleridgean form (as *CL* i. 105; 115).

497 **18. 114v § 1.** *CN* iii. 3827. Spring 1810.

1. For Brunonian, see 141 n.

3–12. Cf. the definition of a poem given in *BL* ii. 13.

16–18. Cf. 'The poet, described in *ideal* perfection, brings the whole soul of man into activity, with the subordination of its faculties to each other, according to their relative worth and dignity' (*BL* ii. 15–16); and, for this as the source of a scale of relative merit, see 205. (By 'genus' I take it STC means 'genre': different kinds of writing will have different preponderances of the faculties.)

18. proportion : proportions *CN*. A nicety, as the word is up against the page's edge.

20–1. Reason is glossed as 'unified through Ideas, the Mother of Law'. After this, STC has added, at some later stage, 'Arbitrement, Legibilitatis mater,'—meaning something like 'Judgement, Mother of Readability' (?). Reason's activity is a unifying one, with which the Imagination's '*fusive*' power obviously has some relation; Judgement and Fancy, meanwhile, seem involved more in establishing or maintaining discrimination and difference: a tension between oneness and manyness that characterizes much of STC's thought.

28–32. An attempt to establish objective criteria in taste on the categories of his faculty psychology.

31. The 'Sources' being the different faculties: cf. 'According to the faculty or source, from which the pleasure given by any poem or passage was derived, I estimated the merit of such poem or passage' (*BL* i. 22–3).

498 18. 41 § 1. *CN* iii. 3881. June 1810.

3. That is, 'thoughts that are thinkable, rather than *my* thoughts'.

5–6. 'Prove all things; hold fast that which is good' (1 Thessalonians 5: 21).

499 18. 55 § 1. *CN* iii. 3906. 17–25 June 1810.

Another repudiation of Unitarianism: the empty shell was a metaphor he used for Unitarianism several times. (James Gillman saw a performance: *IR* 174.) H. E. G Paulus (1761–1851) was an editor of Spinoza, and author of a life of Jesus which STC later annotated with great scorn (*CM* iv. 40–68).

500 18. 69^{v} § 1. *CN* iii. 3935. 26 June–6 July 1810.

The inward turn of idealism versus the 'Lazy looker-on' mind (*CL* ii. 709) of the empiricists, once again.

1. Doctrines : Doctrine *CN*. A faint 's', if there be one: a plural to go with 'Elements' a little later.

9. Even 'passive' attention involves some mental activity, when compared to the *wholly* passive business of mere sense experience.

13. The translations of Thomas Taylor (1758–1835), 'Taylor the English Pagan' (*CL* i. 260), were a long fascination: Taylor translated, among others, the Orphic hymns, ancient mysteries, and the works of the neoplatonists, among them Plotinus, Porphyry, and Proclus. CL remembered STC as a schoolboy spouting neoplatonic authors like Iamblichus and Plotinus (*IR* 3). For Taylor's Coleridgean importance, see *CV* 58.

18. ahndung: STC translates the German, 'inward omening'.

22. awakening : waking *CN*. The words are not scrupulously formed

here; but there seems an attempt at an 'a'. *psilo*sophy: i.e. 'a nominal Ph[ilosophy] without Imagination . . . a *Coiner*' (*CN* ii. 3158).

23–7. Cf. *The Statesman's Manual*: 'At the annunciation of *principles*, of *ideas*, the soul of man awakes, and starts up, as an exile in a far distant land at the unexpected sounds of his native language, when after long years of absence, and almost of oblivion, he is suddenly addressed in his own mother-tongue' (*LS* 24).

26. Judgment, : Judgments *CN*.

501 18. 71v § 1. *CN* iii. 3952 (excerpt). 7 July 1810.

A difficult but important entry: STC's use of the Platonic myth of the Demiurge at the end is one of the most impressive metaphors he uses to describe the 'shaping spirit of Imagination' ('Dejection: An Ode', l. 86: *CPW* i. 366). It is well discussed (in a Kantian context) by G. F. Parker, *Johnson's Shakespeare* (Oxford, 1989), 65–7.

2. conditio sine qua non: i.e. 'a condition necessary to be fulfilled'—here, I take it, the 'endurance' (etc.) in line 3. offence : oftener *CN*. A doubtful reading, but I think there is sign of a double 'f'. STC is talking about (and defending) the aspects of Shakespeare that frustrate neoclassical taste: like his expansive plays' 'offence' against Aristotelian unities of time and place, taking sometimes startling leaps in chronology.

4–5. The sense appears to be 'the wild seeming-comedy of Shakespeare in his *Lear* & other Tragedies', the point being the marked generic mixing of tragic and comic in Shakespeare—noted by, among others, Johnson (and in truth not unsympathetically).

6. *stationes* fluvii torrentis: STC goes on to provide his own translation.

10. το καθαλου : το καθαλον *CN*. i.e. 'the universal': a point about Shakespearian characterization that STC makes again in *BL*: 'Say not that I am recommending abstractions, for these class-characteristics which constitute the instructiveness of a character, are so modified and particularized in each person of the Shaksperian Drama, that life itself does not excite more distinctly that sense of individuality which belongs to real existence' (ii. 45–6 n.).

11–12. for that: i.e. for the opposite-reconciling quality of imagination just described.

15. [?hence] : hence *CN*. The word is not at all clear, but the sense seems right.

19. imprimis : i.e. 'in the first place' (*OED*).

24. 2ndo: that is, second, after the first thing illustrated (in line 18).

27. *Δημιουργος*: 'Demiurge'; he appears in Plato's *Timaeus*, shaping the cosmos in accordance with the divine Ideas: 'finding the whole visible sphere not at rest, but moving in an irregular and disorderly fashion, out of disorder he brought order, considering this was in every way better than the other' (30a). *ὑλή*: i.e. the stuff or raw material getting shaped.

29. [?hinder] : hinder *CN*. The word is practically an indecipherable scribble.

28–31. That the informing 'idea' is greater than the raw material required to express it is part of a growing emphasis upon the superiority of mind over its worldly circumstances that characterizes STC's thinking: cf. his description of '*Poetry* in its most comprehensive sense', in which 'there is a necessary predominance of the Ideas (i.e. of that which originates in the artist himself), and a comparative indifference of the materials' (*F* i. 464). Yet the artist also *depends* upon that raw material to express his shaping 'idea'. The sense that the material of art might resist or impede the artist's shaping spirit is presumably what lies beneath the mention of 'struggle' in *BL*: the imagination 'dissolves, diffuses, dissipates, in order to re-create; or where this process is rendered impossible, yet still at all events it struggles to idealize and to unify' (i. 304).

31. The entry continues over the page with thoughts about RS's *Curse of Kehama*.

502 **18. 80 § 1.** *CN* iii. 3965. 7 July–September 1810.
Not a brilliant joke, but one he liked evidently (*CL* ii. 1191): Anna Letitia Barbauld (1743–1825), whose review of WW's *Poems, in Two Volumes* (1807) had not done.

2. forcing them in : forcing in them in *MS*.

4. *Horror Vacui*: i.e. fear of emptiness.

503 **18. 132 § 1.** *CN* iii. 3970. September 1810.
STC the practitioner of 'practical criticism' (*BL* ii. 19). The poem in question is *The Lady of the Lake* (1810), by Walter Scott (1771–1832): STC was rude about the poem in conversation (*IR* 142–3), and wrote WW a funny letter about it (*CL* iii. 290–6), in which he made passing reference to its 'peccadillos against the 8th Commandment' (against stealing). The metre, and some of the wording, of Scott's earlier *Lay of the Last Minstrel* (1805) had drawn on STC's still-unpublished (but often recited) 'Christabel', so much so that some of the Coleridge circle thought the likeness improperly close: the Wordsworths particularly thought the prospects of STC's poem badly damaged (*WEY* 632–3). See Eric Anderson, 'Two Extraordinary Men: Scott and Coleridge', in Donald

Sultana (ed.), *New Approaches to Coleridge: Biographical and Critical Essays* (1981), 48–60. This entry is evidently notes for his projected review (*CN* iii. 3952): is this the review that he abandoned after DW burst into tears at its barbs (*IR* 46–7)?

8. 'Harp of the North! that mouldering long hast hung | On the witch-elm that shades Saint Fillan's spring, | And down the fitful breeze thy numbers flung, | Till envious ivy did around thee cling' (ll. 1–4).

12. the Harp : this Harp *CN*.

13. Eolian Lute: i.e. a wind-harp, as in STC's 'The Eolian Harp' (*CPW* i. 100–2).

21. The reference to 'My Father's Comedy' is, presumably, to the story STC told of performing in a school play written and produced by his headmaster-father: finding him unable to laugh convincingly in character, his father bounded upon the stage and demonstrated how properly to laugh, which the boy tried unsuccessfully a few times before dissolving in tears, much to the audience's amusement (*IR* 2).

24. At each according pause was heard aloud
Thine ardent symphony sublime and high!
Fair dames and crested chiefs attention bowed;
For still the burden of thy minstrelsy
Was Knighthood's dauntless deed, and Beauty's matchless eye.
(ll. 14–18)

25. a *real* harp : a real harp *CN*.

29. [?intense] : intense *CN*. The word is obscurely written.

50. the cavern, where, 'tis told,
A giant made his den of old;
For ere that steep ascent was won,
High in his pathway hung the sun,
And many a gallant, stayed perforce,
Was fain to breathe his faltering horse,
And of the trackers of the deer,
Scarce half the lessening pack was near;
So shrewdly on the mountain side
Had the bold burst their mettle tried. (ll. 76–85).

52–3. That is, a confusion of past tense and participle.

63. for the purpose : for purpose *CN*.

66–7. metathesis: i.e. the transposition of words, a rhetorical term.

68–9. In the ancient languages, which are inflected, different placings of the words of a sentence are possible to maintain metre without any implication for their significance: in English, largely uninflected, the order of words in the sentence is inevitably much more suggestive and an unusual order demands the sense of a motivation justifying it.

69–70. a *passion* : *a passion CN*.

73. Iago, insinuating Desdemona's infidelity: 'I see this hath a little dash'd your spirits.' Othello replies, 'Not a jot, not a jot' (*Othello*, III. iii., ll. 214–15)—a response STC marked in his copy (*CM* iv. 868). Cf. 'Sh[akespeare] never avails himself of the supposed Licence of transposition merely for the metre. There is always some Logic either of Thought or Passion to justify it' (*CM* iv. 734).

75. is true : is Wise *CN*. The word is indistinctly formed. Capitals for adjectives are rare.

80. The *Edinburgh Review*, criticized in *BL* for proceeding 'without a single leading principle established or even announced, and without any one attempt at argumentative deduction' (ii. 115–16).

504 **14. 35v § 1.** *CN* iii. 3991. 28 October 1810.
STC travelled down to London in the company of Basil Montagu (1770–1851), who chose the occasion tactlessly to pass on WW's (alleged) judgement upon their common friend: that (line 9) he had 'no hope' of him. STC was devastated: their relationship never fully recovered.

505 **14. 36v § 1.** *CN* iii. 3992. 28 October 1810.
It is not clear what particular passage in Hume (if any) STC has in mind: perhaps it is more the tenor of remarks like 'the figure a man makes in the world, the reception he meets with in company, the esteem paid him by his acquaintance; all these advantages depend almost as much upon his good sense and judgment, as upon any other part of his character' (*Treatise of Human Nature*, III. iv, § 4).

506 **14. 40v § 1.** *CN* iii. 3997. 28 October 1810.
STC later recalled the words in a letter: 'I, who "for years past had been an Absolute Nuisance in the Family"' (*CL* iii. 376)—the point of exasperation must have been largely STC's behaviour toward SH. *CN* discerns (and prints as part of this entry), 'God's mercy is it a Dream!', written up the side of the page. The page has worn badly.

507 **14. 41 § 1.** *CN* iii. 3998. 29 October 1810.

508 **14. 41 § 2.** *CN* iii. 3999. 29 October 1810?

509 **24. 27 § 1.** *CN* iii. 4016. *AP* 233. 1810 (*CN*).
Cf. his praise for Burns: 'Who has not a thousand times seen snow fall on

water? Who has not watched it with a new feeling, from the time he has read Burns' comparison . . .' (*BL* i. 81).

4. Pope's *Essay on Criticism*, ll. 297–8: '*True Wit* is *Nature* to Advantage drest, | What oft was *Thought*, but ne'er so well *Exprest*'.

Cf. *BL*, where the poet is said to 'add the gleam, | The light that never was on sea or land' (ii. 151). He is quoting WW's 'Elegiac Stanzas', ll. 14–15 (*WPW* iv. 259).

510 24. 27[v] § 1. *CN* iii. 4017.

The difficult place of duty in STC's ethical thought is best discussed by Laurence S. Lockridge, *Coleridge the Moralist* (Ithaca, NY, 1977), 102–45.

1, 5. knowle[d]ge : knowledge *CN*. Knowle[d]ge : Knowledge *CN*.

12. a priori: before the evidence of experience.

21. saltus: i.e. 'a "leap" or sudden transition; a breach of continuity' (*OED*). See 519 n.

511 24. 30[v] § 1. *CN* iii. 4022. 1810 (*CN*).

1. is his : is is his *MS*.

6. Habiliments: i.e. attire.

11. roused : raised *CN*.

512 24. 33 § 1. *CN* iii. 4034. 1810 (*CN*).

513 18. 83[v] § 1. *CN* iii. 4040. *AP* 246. 1810–11 (*CN*).

8. *CN* notes that STC draws on *Siebenkäs* by 'Jean Paul' (1736–1825), author of 'poetico-philosophical Arguments' (*CM* iv. 261).

9–10. Cf. 'Chill'd friendship's dark disliking eye': 'Lines written at Shurton Bars', l. 14: *CPW* i. 97.

10. A self-allusive addition to Jean Paul. Cf. 'saints will aid if men will call: | For the blue sky bends over all!', 'Christabel', ll. 330–1: *CPW* i. 226.

14. on the : on the the *MS*.

514 18. 135 § 1. *CN* iii. 4046 (excerpt). *AP* 243–5 (excerpt). 25 January 1811.

2. all-zermalming: i.e. 'all-becrushing', as STC translates 'alleszermalmende' (*BL* ii. 89 n.).

20. Elsewhere, to 'double Touch' is attributed 'the generation of the sense of Reality & Life out of us' (*CN* i. 1827). The best account of single and double touch is in John Beer, *Coleridge's Poetic Intelligence* (Basingstoke/London, 1977), 81–8; 256–7—where 'single touch' is associated with a usually pre-conscious inner sense, and often with dreams.

28. The entry continues to elaborate on the non-dreamlike nature of 'Night-mair'.

515 **18. 144 § 1.** *CN* iii. 4055. *AP* 247. Spring 1811.
4. 'To the Evening Star': *CPW* i. 16–17.

5. The New River was an artifical waterway where the schoolboy STC went swimming (*IR* 4).

516 **18. 144ᵛ § 1.** *CN* iii. 4056. Spring 1811.
Cf. 'All deep Passions a sort of Atheists, that believe no Future – ' (*CM* iv. 834).

517 **18. 144ᵛ § 2.** *CN* iii. 4057. *AP* 245–6. Spring 1811.
Another statement of the case against the 'single moment' of Hume et al., here coupled with an argument for immortality: see 375.

9. of limbs : of dark limbs *CN*. The word is ambiguously crossed out. trunks : trunk *CN*. Another ambiguous terminal 's'.

10–13. That life without immortality would reduce man to 'Blank accident! Nothing's anomaly!' is the theme of 'Human Life. On the Denial of Immortality' (*CPW* i. 425–6, where it is dated '?1815').

518 **21½. 71ᵛ § 1.** *CN* iii. 4059. March–April 1811?
Anticipating the account in *BL* (chapter vi), where Hartley is criticized for portraying the mind 'divided between the despotism of outward impressions, and that of senseless and passive memory' (i. 111). Cf. 'any system built on the passiveness of the mind must be false, as a system' (*CL* ii. 709).

519 **21½. 70 § 1.** *CN* iii. 4061. 2 April 1811.
2–3. Act V of *Cato* (1713) by Joseph Addison (1672–1719) opens with a long speech, in which the hero is discovered reading Plato on the immortality of the soul: ''Tis the Divinity that stirs within us; | 'Tis Heav'n itself, that points out an Hereafter'. favour : favor *CN*.

9. The Latin is proverbial: 'Nature makes no leaps'.

11. menstruum: solvent; that into which things are dissolved.

520 **17. 119 § 1.** *CN* iii. 4066. Spring 1811?
A most important entry: the argument of the closing pages of *BL* vol. i. in summary form. The image re-forming power, 'a mode of Memory', passively recalling 'fixities and definites', is distinguished from the 'living Power' of imagination in its *active* sense (*BL* i. 305; 304). Modern philosophers (he means the native empiricist tradition of Locke and Hume) presume the first faculty to constitute the *entire* mind, and so neglect the imagination's projective vitality: hence, the mind they describe is like a

Gorgon head (the Gorgon's gaze turned all it fell upon to stone). (The point is closely related to the internal vitality lamented in 'Dejection: An Ode'—'I may not hope from outward forms to win | The passion and the life, whose fountains are within', ll. 45–6: *CPW* i. 365.) STC is continuing a long argument against philosophies which casts the mind as merely impressible and passive: 'If the mind be not *passive*, if it be indeed made in God's Image, & that too in the sublimest sense – the Image of the *Creator* – there is ground for suspicion, that any system built on the passiveness of the mind must be false, as a system' (*CL* ii. 709), a point which re-emerges years later in the grander language of *BL* chapter xiii, as 'The primary IMAGINATION I hold to be the living Power and Prime Agent of all human Perception, and as a repetition in the finite mind of the eternal act of creation in the infinite I AM' (*BL* i. 304). For some suggestive discussions of this central concern, see Basil Willey, 'Coleridge on Imagination and Fancy', *Proceedings of the British Academy*, 32 (1946), 173–87; Barbara Hardy, 'Distinction without Difference: Coleridge's Fancy and Imagination', *Essays in Criticism*, 1 (1951), 336–44; R. L. Brett, *Fancy and Imagination* (1969); and James Engell, *The Creative Imagination: Enlightenment to Romanticism* (Cambridge, Mass., 1981), 328–66. John Spencer Hill, *Imagination in Coleridge* (1978) is a useful anthology.

2. a *Φαιν*[*ειν*]: i.e. 'from the Greek, "to show"'. The last letters are masked by a blot. *BL* distinguishes between fancy and imagination (i. 84–5; 304–5); and cf. *TT* i. 489–90.

7–12. An intricate passage: the point seems to be that the 'image re-forming power' presents the mind with the necessary fixity of objective knowledge; and one self (or 'Soul') is most obviously differenced (STC's verb) from another by the dissimilarity of their embodiments, objectively known. But the true 'life' of a Soul is not in this: it may be *deduced* from such objective presence (as mental purpose may be from writing on a page), but cannot be *identified* with it, as materialists (who do not believe in the soul) must assert.

10. forma efformans: i.e. 'forming form' (active and progressive as opposed to fixed and pre-formed).

12. '*the dead* letter': 'not of the letter, but of the spirit: for the letter killeth, but the spirit giveth life' (2 Corinthians 3: 6), which STC combines with an attack on Locke, who likens the impressible mind to a sheet of white paper written upon by outward experience (*Essay on Human Understanding*, 1. i, § 1).

521 17. 122ᵛ § 1. *CN* iii. 4071. April 1811.
1. The names in the top corners of the page are (as usual in this Notebook) '*ΣΑΡΑ*' and 'Coleridge': see 385 n.
5. The reference to SH's 'falsity' must allude to STC's traumatizing vision of December 1806: see 437 n.

522 17. 123 § 1. *CN* iii. 4072. *AP* 251. April 1811?

523 17. 123 § 2. *CN* iii. 4190. *AP* 253. 1811–15?
The entry appears below 522 in *MS*, and *AP* estimates 1811–12 as its date; but *CN* connects it with a letter of 1813 and adduces other evidence for a later date (*CL* iii. 449).
7–8. The first line is Miltonic, rather than Milton's: there are a number of lines in *Paradise Lost* including 'Disobedience' (V, l. 541; VI, l. 396) which STC may be remembering. The second quotation is genuine (V, l. 540).
11–12. That is to say, the narrating voice with the characters' speeches.

524 18. 153ᵛ § 2. *CN* iii. 4082. *AP* 256. Spring–summer 1811.
9. A ballad in Percy's *Reliques of Ancient English Poetry* (1765). WW quoted a stanza from one version of the poem in the 1800 'Preface' to *Lyrical Ballads* (*WPrW* i. 154), which STC acknowledged 'half a child of my own Brain' (*CL* ii. 830).

525 18. 154 § 2. *CN* iii. 4084. Spring–summer 1811.
A thought recycled (by the editor, Henry Nelson Coleridge) in *TT* ii. 275. It is based on an aphorism of Jean Paul's *Geist* (printed in *CN*).

526 18. 154 § 4. *CN* iii. 4086. *AP* 254. Spring–summer 1811.
STC's reconciliation with WW after the Montagu disaster, finally engineered in 1812 by the patient intercessions of HCR, proved slow and difficult. (See *CL* iii. 296–7 n.; and Crabb Robinson i. 70–2; 74–81; 84.) Nothing like their first intimacy was ever restored, although relations were friendly enough for them to undertake a European tour together in 1828 (*IR* 257–70).

527 18. 153ᵛ § 3. *CN* iii. 4087. Spring–summer 1811.
The first sentence was quoted by Henry Nelson Coleridge in *TT* (ii. 276). The gist of the passage is similar to one in Jean Paul's *Geist* (reproduced in *CN*).
1. Descartes's argument (which STC refers to in *PL* i. 388) is a version of the ontological argument: God is an idea, the idea of which involves his necessary existence. Cf. *BL* i. 274, in which the contingent reality of

human self, which may only assert 'sum quia in deo sum' ('I am because I am in God'), becomes transferred in the 'absolute self' into the self-necessitating claim: 'sum quia sum' ('I am because I am', or, as STC prefers, 'I am because I affirm myself to be; I affirm myself to be, because I am'). JC reports STC voicing a wholly disreputable version of something similar: 'He said that Holcroft, and other Atheists, reasoned with so much *fierceness* and *vehemence* against a God, that it plainly showed they were inwardly conscious, that there *was* a God, to reason against; for he remarked, a *nonentity* would never excite passion' (*IR* 160).

5–7. STC argues in *BL*—and elsewhere—that idealism (in which one is acquainted only with ideas) and materialism (in which one is acquainted only with sensations) equally remove the self from any immediacy of perception, and so from any sure philosophical realism.

528 **18. 157 § 3.** *CN* iii. 4093. *CPW* ii. 1005. Spring–summer 1811.

529 **18. 163 § 2.** *CN* iii. 4104. August 1811.
The anecdote referred to, from Boswell's *Life* (1791), may be Johnson's famous response when asked to adjudicate the poetic merits of Derrick and Smart: 'Johnson at once felt himself roused; and answered, "Sir, there is no point settling the point of precedency between a louse and a flea"': James Boswell, *The Life of Samuel Johnson, LL.D.* (Everyman edition; 2 vols.; 1906, repr. 1941), ii. 449.

530 **24. 37 § 1.** *CN* iii. 4176. *AP* 236–7. 1813 (*CN*).
Another statement of the important distinction between Imagination and Fancy (here, 'Fantasy'), anticipating *BL* chapter xiii.

2. Imagunculation: i.e. a *little* imagination. 'Einbildungskraft' is German for 'imagination': STC's etymology builds it out of 'in eins Bildung', 'into-one-shaping', which may be a pun (*CN*; but see *BL* i. 168–9 n.). 'Co-adunation' ('the act of being joined into one': *OED*) was long a Coleridgean favourite for the same thing: '*Imagination,* or the *modifying*, and *co-adunating* Faculty' (*CL* ii. 866).

4. Eisenoplasy, or esenoplastic Power: variants on 'esemplastic', introduced to the world in *BL*, where its origins are located in the Greek '*εἰς ἕν πλάττειν* i.e. to shape into one' (*BL* i. 168). The words in square brackets are brought up from STC's own footnote, where they gloss one of his Notebook symbols.

6. catoptric or metoptric: STC promptly glosses the words.

531 **20. 8 § 3.** *CN* iii. 4220. 20 September 1814.
Since early November 1810, in the bleak aftermath of the Montagu crisis,

STC had been living intermittently with the family of John Morgan, an old school-friend, in Hammersmith. In August 1814, Morgan went bankrupt and fled to Ireland, leaving STC to sort out affairs. He lodged Morgan's wife and sister at Ashley, near Box, in December 1813, and Morgan subsequently joined them there. STC spent much of 1814 between Bristol and Ashley, lecturing and writing, until in September he moved himself to Ashley, hoping to recover his precarious health, full of plans for an immense work on Christianity and philosophy (*CL* iii. 529; 533–4).

532 **22. 32 § 1.** *CN* iii. 4253 (excerpt). 1815 (*CN*).
In the spring of 1815, STC moved with the Morgans from Ashley to Calne, in Wiltshire, where he spent the late spring and summer dictating *BL* to Morgan. One of the book's many subjects was the symbol: 'An Idea, in the *highest* sense of that word, cannot be conveyed but by a *symbol*' (*BL* i. 156). The quotation in this entry is from *The Purple Island, or The Isle of Man* (1633) by Phineas Fletcher (1582–1650), from an eminently Coleridgean passage: a Creation scene, in which the contentious elements are tempered into order, before God turns his mind 'to frame an Isle, the heart and head | Of all his works, compos'd with curious art; | Which like an Index briefly should impart | The summe of all; the whole, yet of the whole a part' (I, ll. 298–301). STC's definition of a symbol (as opposed to the arbitrary tokens of allegory) is reworked in *The Statesman's Manual*: 'It always partakes of the Reality which it renders intelligible; and while it enunciates the whole, abides itself as a living part in that Unity, of which it is the representative' (*LS* 30). The point is made clearer when STC returns in his 1819 lectures to 'the Symbolical, which cannot perhaps be better defined, in distinction from the Allegorical, than that it is always itself *part* of that of the whole of which it is representative – ["]Here comes a *Sail*["] – that is, a Ship, is a symbolical Expression – ["]Behold our Lion["], when we speak of some gallant Soldier, is allegorical' (*LL* ii. 417–18).

533 **22. 32 § 2.** *CN* iii. 4254. *CPW* ii. 1010. 1815 (*CN*).

534 **22. 66v § 2.** *CN* iii. 4260. *TT* ii. 191. 1815 (*CN*).
2. ad populum: i.e. 'addressed to the people at large'.

535 **22. 37 § 1.** *CN* iii. 4276. December 1815–1816.
The right and the wrong kind of admiration (see 148).

2. Poet-urus: i.e. 'poet-to-be'. 'Urus' is also the Latin name for the wild ox, but I don't see what to do with that.

4. Camelo pardalus: i.e. 'camelopard', a name for the giraffe, perhaps implying a weird combination.

536 **22. 62 § 2.** *CN* iii. 4287. 1815–16.
3. Aye? : Aye! *CN*.

537 **22. 62[v] § 1.** *CN* iii. 4289. *AP* 282. 1815–16.
This (like the following five entries) draws on the German aphorist Jean Paul.

538 **22. 62[v] § 2.** *CN* iii. 4290. *AP* 282. 1815–16.

539 **22. 62[v] § 3.** *CN* iii. 4291. 1815–16.
Feder is German for 'feather' and also for 'spring' (a mechanical spring, not the season, which is 'Frühling').

540 **22. 62[v] § 4.** *CN* iii. 4292. *LR* i. 342–3. 1815–16.
The source in Jean Paul suggests that the 'books' in mind in the last line are those of German critical philosophy (see *CN*).

541 **22. 62[v] § 6.** *CN* iii. 4294. *AP* 274. 1815–16.

542 **22. 62[v] § 7.** *CN* iii. 4295. *AP* 274. 1815–16.

543 **22. 39 § 1.** *CN* iii. 4308. *AP* 266. 23 February 1816.
That superstitions were related to genuine religious truths was a thought that had long appealed to STC: in 'The Destiny of Nations', 'Fancy is the power | That first unsensualises the dark mind, | Giving it new delights', first steps on the route toward genuine illumination (ll. 80–2: *CPW* i. 134). For the equivalence of Religion and Reason (in STC's sense), see a later poem: 'Whene'er the mist, that stands 'twixt God and thee, | Defecates to a pure transparency, | That intercepts no light and adds no stain – | There Reason is, and then begins her reign!' ('Reason', ll. 1–4: *CPW* i. 487).

544 **18. 150 § 1.** *CN* iii. 4313. *AP* 269–70. 30 April 1816.
In April 1816, his health ruined by years of heavy opium use, Coleridge was referred to the medical care of Dr James Gillman (1782–1839), who lived, with his wife Anne, in Moreton House on Highgate Hill. On 15 April, STC joined the household as a resident patient, as he thought for a month's stay (*CL* iv. 629); but in fact he would live with them—'my most dear Friends—for I am and ever trust to remain, more than can be expressed' (*CL* iv. 869)—until his death in 1834. He moved with his hosts in November 1823 to 3 The Grove, where he established his famous attic study-bedroom. With his move to the Gillmans STC effectively begins a

new career: he promptly saw *BL*, the long-unpublished 'Christabel', and his collected poems through the press; he composed the *LS*. Gradually established as the Christian Philosopher-Sage of Highgate, he turned his energies increasingly towards theological and philosophical concerns: *AR* was published in 1825 and *On the Constitution of the Church and State* in 1830. He gathered around him a large circle of devoted young followers, many of great gifts, who would carry elements of his thought into the later nineteenth century.

14. both in terms : but in terms *CN*. (both in terms *AP*.)

15. Battles : Bacchus *CN*. The reading is very doubtful, but there seem too many letters with uprights for 'Bacchus'. For Blackmore, see 205 n.

20. A pasticcio is a medley of different elements, 'a hotchpotch, farrago, jumble' (*OED*); and a cento a patchwork composition, often made up of fragments borrowed from many authors. Thomas Arne (1710–78), now best known for 'Rule Britannia!', and William Shield (1748–1829) composed operas and pantomimes which STC evidently judged of such a heterogeneous character.

22. 'The Beggar's Petition' (1769), a dismal poem by Revd Thomas Moss: 'But ah! How changed the scene! On the cold stones, | Where wont at night to blaze the cheerful fire, | Pale famine sits and counts her naked bones, | Still sighs for food, still pines with vain desire', etc.

23–4. Gray's 'Elegy in a Country Churchyard' : 'Grays Elegy in a Country Churchyard *MS*. STC's scepticism about the merits of Thomas Gray (1716–71) is evident in several places: 'He spoke with contempt of Gray', recalled WH (*IR* 66; and cf. 139–40).

545 **17.126[v]; 128**: *CN* iii. 4320. Christmas 1816.
Printed as one entry by *CN*. The words are written at the top of the two pages, beside the names normally in the corners in Notebook 17 (see above, 385 n.).

546 **22. 45[v] § 2.** *CN* iii. 4341. 31 March 1817.

1. *Hen Pen* was the Gillmans' little boy Henry.

7. interjacent: i.e. 'lying or existing between' (*OED*).

9. *Αθεοι*: i.e. 'atheists'.

10–12. The religious thought of the Highgate years is largely occupied in consolidating the move away from the Spinozistic conception of God that had attracted him so strongly as a young man: see 110 n.

14–16. Still the problem of the mechanism of Redemption: see 173 n.

16. give then his own : give him his own *CN*.

18. Luke 15: 11–32.

23. excluded the Light : excluded thought *CN*.

27–9. Spinozism finds its theological solution by identifying God with the universe. The anti-Spinozistic (or anti-Pantheist, or—it amounts to much the same thing for STC—anti-Unitarian) point at the end is an important element in his later religious thinking. As he puts it in some equations in *TT*:

Pantheism of Spinoza

W. — G. = o.	i.e. The World without God is an impossible idea.
G. — W. = o.	i.e. God without the World is ditto.
	Christian Scheme.
W. — G. = o.	i.e. as in Pantheism.
G. — W. = G.	i.e. But God without the World is God self-sufficing. (*TT* i. 72)

Unitarianism, in identifying God and the World, dissolves God into the world's physical behaviour: far from retaining a single God, you soon find no God at all.

547 22. 47v. *CN* iii. 4397 (excerpt). *LR* i. 216–30; *Biographia Literaria . . . with his Aesthetical Essays*, ed. J. Shawcross (2 vols.; Oxford, 1907), ii. 253–63; *Coleridge's Miscellaneous Criticism*, ed. Thomas Middleton Raysor (Cambridge, Mass., 1936), 204–13; *LL* ii. 217–25. 10 March 1818.
A difficult but important entry, obscure partly because it is STC's own notes for the thirteenth lecture of the 1818 series on European Literature, published in *LR* and elswhere under the title 'On Poesy or Art'. It is based on an address by Schelling, 'On the Relation of the Plastic Arts to Nature' (1807), available in English as the appendix to Herbert Read's *The True Voice of Feeling: Studies in English Romantic Poetry* (1953), 323–58. The post-Kantian F. W. J. von Schelling (1775–1854), especially the *System of Transcendental Idealism* (1800), importantly influenced STC (see *BL* i. 160–4); and some of the philosophical chapters of *BL* lean heavily on him. See *CPT* 147–60; and James Engell, *The Creative Imagination: Enlightenment to Romanticism* (Cambridge, Mass., 1981), 301–27, esp. 303–9.

14–15. Work of *Art* : Work of Art *CN*.

20. desynonymizing: i.e. distinguishing between apparent synonyms, as STC does between (for example) 'fancy' and 'imagination', or 'imitation' and 'copy'. For the importance of the principle to his thought, see Paul Hamilton, *Coleridge's Poetics* (Oxford, 1983); and James C. McKusick, *Coleridge's Philosophy of Language* (New Haven, 1986), 91–9.

21–3. That is, to use the word 'Poesy' as a general term for 'Art', and to restrict 'Poetry' for that art which uses speech as its medium.

34–5. For imitation versus copy, see 351.

45. The point being, I suppose, that a tragic *dance* possesses the self-delighting aesthetic autonomy of its choreography, making it a thing *different* from whatever it represents; yet if a *tragic* dance must possess too a recognizable *likeness* to human plight.

46. The page reference is to STC's copy of Schelling (*CM* iv. 403–46). The distinction between 'Natura naturata' (meaning 'nature natured', nature considered as a fixed product) and 'Natura naturans' ('Nature naturing', nature considered as a divinely self-productive and self-creative process) is important in much of STC's shifting attitudes toward the natural world. The 'natura naturans' is the 'essence' of line 51, the creative bond shared between the natural world and the imagination: the act of artistic creativity is not merely a *copy* of some fixed aspect of the world, but more fundamentally imitative of the divine energies of nature at large, as though creating a second nature, with the imagination as a secondary God infusing it: 'the SOUL that is every where, and in each; and forms all into one graceful and intelligent whole' (*BL* ii. 18).

51. Giovanni Battista Cipriani (1727–85), whose paintings evidently struck STC as beautiful in a wholly formulaic and lifeless way.

56. no reflex act: i.e. no act of self-consciousness.

57. Man is the 'Head' of creation, with nature a series of incremental stages, from the simplest life-forms upwards, leading toward his crowning self-consciousness.

68. partake of both: i.e. conscious and unconscious, the human and the natural.

71–3. An important statement of the difference between organic and mechanical form: a recurrent distinction in his aesthetics.

77. *the whole* ad hominen: that is, 'Humanizing Imagery and Circumstance' (*CN* iii. 3246).

548 **22. 54^{v} § 2.** *CN* iii. 4400. March 1818?

6. [? strutting] : strutting *CN*. An uncertain word.

12. A reworking of Ovid, *Metamorphoses* 3. 464: 'Inopem me copia fecit' ('This plenty makes me poor'). Cf. *CN* i. 1383.

549 **25. 28^{v} § 2.** *CN* iii. 4468. 1818?

Perhaps a Christmas thought? (See *CN* for the difficulties of dating.)

550 **24. 6 § 1.** *CN* iv. 4590. *AP* 293. 2 September 1819.

STC regularly holidayed at Ramsgate with the Gillmans. The poem in question is Canzone XVIII of Dante's *Rime*, written in the Notebook years before (*CN* ii. 3014). Most of the poem is indeed written in a hand other than STC's: Josiah Wade, a Bristolian, was one of STC's oldest friends (back to Pantisocratic days: *CL* i. 100).

551 28. 19v § 1. *CN* iv. 4655. Early 1820 (*CN*).
1. *Ad Lectorem*: i.e. 'to the reader'.

552 28. 85v § 1. *CN* iv. 4777. 1820–1 (*CN*).
Cf. 'The Blossoming of the Solitary Date-Tree', ll. 50–1: 'delight in little things, | The buoyant child surviving in the man' (*CPW* i. 396).

Index

Reference is made to page numbers (not entry numbers). Figures in bold denote a passage in the main text; other figures refer to the Commentary.